HIST

OF

THE COMMONWEALTH

AND

PROTECTORATE

VOLUME II.—1651-1653

HISTORY

OF

THE COMMONWEALTH

AND

PROTECTORATE

1649—1656

BY

SAMUEL RAWSON GARDINER

HON. D.C.L. OXFORD ; LITT.D. CAMBRIDGE ; LL.D. EDINBURGH ; PH.D. GÖTTINGEN:
FELLOW OF MERTON COLLEGE ; HONORARY STUDENT OF CHRISTCHURCH ;
FELLOW OF KING'S COLLEGE, LONDON

IN FOUR VOLUMES

VOLUME II.—1651-1653

THE
WINDRUSH
PRESS
GLOUCESTERSHIRE · ENGLAND

History of the Commonwealth and Protectorate
Volume Two
was first published by
Longmans, Green and Co.
in 1903

This edition first published by
The Windrush Press
Windrush House
Main Street, Adlestrop
Gloucestershire GL56 0YN
in 1988

ISBN o 900075 75 9 (cased)
ISBN o 900075 80 5 (paperback)

British Library Cataloguing in Publication Data

Gardiner, Samuel Rawson
    History of the Commonwealth and Protectorate
    Volume II: 1651–53
    1. England, Political Events, 1649–1660
    I. Title
    942.06'3

ISBN o 900075 75 9
ISBN o 900075 80 5

Printed and bound in Great Britain by
Biddles Ltd, Guildford and King's Lynn

CONTENTS

OF

THE SECOND VOLUME

CHAPTER XV

ENGLAND AFTER DUNBAR

CHAPTER XVI

WORCESTER

CHAPTER XVII

ENGLAND AFTER WORCESTER

CHAPTER XVIII

PROJECTS OF REFORM

CHAPTER XIX

THE SUBJUGATION OF IRELAND

CHAPTER XX

THE SUBMISSION OF SCOTLAND AND THE COLONIES

                              CHAPTER XXI

                          AN IMPENDING WAR

CHAPTER XXII

THE FIRST MONTHS OF THE DUTCH WAR

CHAPTER XXV

THE DISSOLUTION OF THE LONG PARLIAMENT

CHAPTER XXVI

A TEMPORARY DICTATORSHIP

CHAPTER XXVII

THE NOMINATED PARLIAMENT

CHAPTER XXVIII

THE INSTRUMENT OF GOVERNMENT

MAPS

THE COMMONWEALTH

AND

PROTECTORATE

CHAPTER XV

ENGLAND AFTER DUNBAR

THE news of Cromwell's victory at Dunbar was received enthusiastically at Westminster. On September 10 Major White unrolled the thrilling story before Parliament, and pointed to no less than 160 stand of colours as the evidence of its truth. Parliament at once ordered that the flags should be hung up along one side of Westminster Hall, and those taken at Preston on the other. At the same time bountiful supplies, including medicine, physicians, and apothecaries, were hurried off to Scotland, a thanksgiving day ordered, and a committee appointed to consider the preparation of medals to be given to all who had taken part in the campaign. The result of this resolution was the 'Dunbar Medal,' bearing Cromwell's likeness in spite of his own protest, and celebrated as the first war-medal granted to an English army.[1]

1650.
Sept. 10.
The news
from
Dunbar.

Enthusiasm
at West-
minster.

Such a victory as that of Dunbar could not fail to leave its impress on legislation. The Independents who occupied the benches in Parliament could

Parliament
and the Pres-
byterians.

[1] *C.J.* vi. 464.

B

not but feel that they had now a freer hand. Though nothing hitherto done by them had been irreconcilable with their own principles, they had hitherto been bent upon conciliating the moderate Presbyterians by enacting laws which would give the utmost possible satisfaction to men whose enmity might be dangerous.[1] The last Act of importance passed whilst the fortunes of war were hanging in the balance was notoriously a step in this direction. Its object was the punishment of atheistical, blasphemous, and execrable opinions.[2] That Act, however, had none of the inquisitorial character which attached to the monstrous blasphemy ordinance of 1648. It meted out six months' imprisonment for the first offence, and banishment with prohibition of return on pain of death for the second, and that in two cases only :—the affirming that any human person was God or a manifestation of God, and the affirming that acts of gross immorality were indifferent, or even positively religious. The first of these provisions was directed against such as from time to time asserted themselves to be the Messiah, usually taking with them a female companion under the Scriptural title of ' The Lamb's Wife.'[3] The second was directed against the Ranters, who carried to an extreme the principle of inward conviction which was the basis of Puritanism, holding that ' swearing, drunkenness, adultery, and theft were not sinful unless the person guilty of them apprehended them to be so.'[4] It is quite possible that many of those who propounded this doctrine may have guarded themselves against evil, but its tendency to the encouragement of immorality was undeniable, and it is no matter for surprise that the pamphleteers of the day represented the meetings of the Ranters as held for the very purpose of sensual indulgence in the name of religion.

That this act of repression was no mere concession to the

Aug. 9.
The Blasphemy Act.

The Ranters.

---

[1] See vol. i. 255.   [2] *Scobell*, ii. 124.

[3] See the case of William Franklin and Mary Gadbury, in *Pseudo-Christus*, E, 602, 12.

[4] This is the teaching of *A Single Eye*, attributed by Thomason to Giles Calvert, E, 14, 1.

Presbyterians is shown by the practice of the army in Scotland. Towards the end of October Captain Covell was cashiered by Cromwell for asserting that 'sin was no sin;'[1] and some months later we hear of the Lord General's vehement detestation of opinions 'destructive of the power of godliness.'[2] Yet though legislation in this direction might be deemed necessary by the Independents, it could never be congenial to them. The good news from Dunbar freed them from the necessity of conciliating the Presbyterians, and enabled them to embark on legislation which was all their own. On September 13 a committee appointed to consider the repeal of Acts enforcing attendance at church was revived, and on the 27th Parliament repealed all clauses of Acts imposing penalties on recusancy. No one was thenceforward to be punished for refusing to attend church, provided that on every Lord's Day or day of public humiliation or thanksgiving, he resorted 'to some public place where the service or worship of God is exercised, or' was 'present at some other place in the practice of some religious duty, either of prayer, preaching, reading, or expounding the Scriptures, or conferring upon the same.'[3] So sweeping a measure of relief would stand those in good stead who continued, in private at least, to use the worship of the Book of Common Prayer. The Catholic laity would hardly be allowed to shelter themselves under it,[4] as the Acts prohibiting the saying of mass were left standing, and it would therefore be difficult for them to show to the satisfaction of a Protestant judicatory that in absenting themselves from church they had been taking part in a religious exercise within the meaning of the Act.

Cromwell and the Ranters.

Sept. 27. Repeal of the Recusancy Acts.

Cromwell on legal abuses.   Nor was it only by measures relating to religion that Parliament sought to merit the confidence of the nation. "Relieve the oppressed," Cromwell had

---

[1] *Merc. Pol.* E, 616, 1.   [2] *Ib.* E, 632, 7.

[3] *Scobell*, ii. 131.

[4] The Catholics, however, were hopeful that they might profit by the Act. Croullé to Mazarin, $\frac{\text{Sept. 23}}{\text{Oct. 3}}$, *Arch. des Aff. Étrangères*, lix. fol. 451.

written from Dunbar, "hear the groans of poor prisoners in England ! Be pleased to reform the abuses of all professions; and if there be any one that makes many poor to make a few rich, that suits not a Commonwealth."[1] Parliament took the hint. On October 22 a Committee was appointed to consider expenses and delays in the courts of justice. On the 23rd the Grand Committee on Elections resumed its weekly sittings.[2] On the 25th Parliament resolved that all law proceedings should be conducted in the English language, and ordered an Act to be brought in to give effect to this decision.[3]

Oct. 22-25. Consequent resolutions of Parliament.

That the statesmen of the Commonwealth had little cruelty in their composition is shown by their treatment of the two younger children of Charles I., the Duke of Gloucester and the Lady Elizabeth, who had for some time been living at Penshurst, under the affectionate guardianship of the Earl and Countess of Leicester. On July 24 Parliament resolved to set them at liberty to go beyond seas, and on the 29th Captain Anthony Mildmay[4] was directed to conduct them to Carisbrooke, there to remain till arrangements had been made for their further journey.[5] On September 5, the Council reported that Henry should be sent to his brother in Scotland, and Elizabeth to her sister, the Princess of Orange, each of them to receive 1,000l. a year as long as they behaved inoffensively.[6] Unhappily, one at least of the pair obtained no benefit from the well-intentioned proposal. The Lady Elizabeth, now in her fifteenth year, had always been a delicate child. The gloomy associations of Carisbrooke preyed upon her spirits, and a sudden shower wetting her to the skin, at a game of bowls with her brother, brought on a strong fever, the ravages of which her enfeebled constitution was unable to withstand. Though

The younger children of Charles I.

July 24. They are to be sent abroad.

---

[1] *Carlyle,* Letter cxl.   [2] *C.J.* vi. 485, 486.   [3] *Ib.* vi. 487.

[4] A brother of Sir Henry. For his own account of his services as a spy on Charles I., see *Clarke Papers,* ii. 267.

[5] C. of St. Order Book, *Interr.* I, 8, p. 26.   [6] *Ib.* 9, p. 73.

Mildmay did all in his power to secure the best medical advice available, this tender flower of the House of Stuart, to whom life had brought little of the joyfulness of childhood, passed on

Sept. 8.
Death of
the Lady
Elizabeth. September 8 from the scene of her sorrows. By the order of Parliament, her body was decently interred in the parish church of Newport. The spot where she lay was long marked by her initials alone, till more than two centuries after her death a fitting monument was erected to her memory by a lady who has worn the Royal crown more worthily than any of the male line of the Stuart family.[1]

The first action of Parliament was to increase the pension offered to 'Henry Stuart' to 1,500*l.*,[2] and to order that he

The Duke
of Glou-
cester kept
at Caris-
brooke. should be sent to Heidelberg for his education. For some time the Council of State took into consideration various proposals for giving effect to this vote, but in the end, as danger thickened, its immediate execution was abandoned, and the boy was detained at Carisbrooke for many a weary month.[3] Before the end of the year, it was known at Westminster that the war in Scotland had by no means been brought to a conclusion at Dunbar, and it was perhaps thought unwise to loose hold on a captive who might still be valuable as a hostage.

Project of
a Royalist
insurrec-
tion. Even in the summer of 1650 information had come in from time to time, leaving no doubt of the existence of a project for a Royalist insurrection in

July 18.
Execution
of Captain
Levinz. England. On July 18 Captain Levinz was hanged in Cornhill, by sentence of a court-martial, for bringing 'commissions from Charles Stuart' into the

---

[1] A full account of the last days of the Princess will be found with references to the authorities in Mrs. Everett Green's *Lives of the Princesses*, vi. 381.

[2] *C.J.* vi. 470.

[3] Various entries on the subject are scattered over the Order Book of the Council of State. On Nov. 30 is an order directing that the boy shall be confined to Carisbrooke, as his going up and down in the island is dangerous to the peace of the nation. C. of St. Order Book, *Interr.* I, 14, p. 18.

country.[1]   The case of Eusebius Andrews was more complicated. He was a lawyer who had served as a colonel under the
King in the first Civil War, and had the misfortune

Case of
Eusebius
Andrews.

to have for a friend a certain John Bernard who had
served under him as a major.   This man was now a
spy of the Council of State, and there is good reason to believe

1649.

that in the latter part of August or the beginning of
September 1649 he suggested to Andrews—after the manner of
such creatures—to take up again an old plan of Andrews's own,
for the seizure of the Isle of Ely in the event of affairs in Ireland
or Scotland going against the Commonwealth.[2] Andrews readily
seized the bait, and placed himself in the hands of Holmes and
Benson, two men introduced to him by Bernard. Of these
Benson suggested that Sir John Gell, whose pay, due for
services as a commander before the New Model was formed,
was still outstanding, was highly discontented. In December,
in consequence of Cromwell's success in Ireland, the plan of
seizing the Isle of Ely was dropped. Andrews, however, had
an interview with Gell, who grumbled at his treatment by the
men in power, and hinted that if ever he took up arms again it
would be on the Royalist side.

1650.
March 18.
He signs
an engage-
ment.

Whether drawn into the movement or not,
Andrews threw himself into it heart and soul. On
March 18 he signed an engagement, binding himself
and others that signed it to 'use all . . . possible

---

[1] *A Brief Relation*, E, 608, 11 ; *Merc. Pol.* E, 608, 11. He was a
D.C.L., who had returned to Oxford after the end of the first Civil War.
See an account of him in the *Dict. of Nat. Biogr.* xxxiii. 161.

[2] There is no full report of Andrews's trial. We have the so-called
report printed in the *State Trials*, v. 1, which gives us Andrews's own
narratives and his legal arguments, but no word of other evidence against
him. *The True State of the Case of Sir John Gell* (E, 612, 17) gives us
Sir John's view of the matter, and Bernard's *A True Confutation* (E,
613, 9) treats it from his point of view. In the latter pamphlet Bernard
prints some important documents, but the extreme weakness of his
defence against the allegations that he had been the first to suggest the
seizure of the Isle of Ely carries conviction that Andrews spoke the truth
in charging him with it.

skill and endeavour . . . to settle and establish Charles the Second, our rightful and lawful Prince, in his throne of England against all rebels, usurpers or opposers whatsoever,' and this engagement was signed also by Benson and a certain Ashley, as well as by Bernard, and one Pitts, who called himself Smith, and was another of the Council's spies. This precious pair entertained Andrews with wild tales of risings in the counties. What they most wanted, however, was to obtain Gell's signature, but Gell was too cautious to comply, and on March 25 both Andrews and Gell were arrested. On August 16, Andrews was tried before the new High Court of Justice on a charge of treason. He was condemned, and was

Sentence on Gell. executed on August 22. Gell was subsequently sentenced to lose his estate and to imprisonment for

Oct. 7. Execution of Benson. life for misprision of treason. Benson and Ashley were both condemned to death. On October 7 Benson alone was executed.

The Government, after the discovery of this plot, was in the uneasy position of being aware that influential

Oct. 8. The Presbyterian ministers will not keep the thanksgiving day. classes were arrayed against it, though it was unable to discover the persons who held the threads of the conspiracy. The Presbyterian ministers, especially, were a sore trouble. On October 17, for instance, there was a report from the Council of State that considerable numbers of them had refused to keep the day of thanksgiving for the victory at Dunbar,[1] but though in individual cases ministers displaying hostility to the Government were ordered to leave the towns in which they

Nov. 27. Ministers refusing engagement to be removed from towns. preached,[2] it was not till November 27 that a sweeping order was given to remove from all garrison and other towns ministers who were obstinate in refusing to subscribe to the engagement. A month later the Council of State reported 'a wilful

---

[1] See for the case of two ministers at Hull, C. of St. Order Book, *Interr.* I, 11, p. 40; of one at Bristol, *ib.* I, 13, p. 52.

[2] *C.J.* vi. 501, 502.

and strict observation of the day commonly called Christmas Day.' Shops had been closed and contemptuous speeches uttered. In some places mass had been sung, ' to the great dishonour of Almighty God, notorious breach of the laws, and scandal of the Government.' Moreover, the arms and pictures of the late King were still to be seen in public places in London.[1]

It was useless to strike at the symptoms of disease when the disease itself was beyond reach. Yet its existence was now manifested by evidence more alarming than the shutting of shops and the keeping up of prohibited pictures. On December 5 Parliament received the news of a Royalist outbreak in Norfolk. Isolated as it was, it was easily suppressed, and its only result was that its leaders were tried by a High Court of Justice specially instituted for the purpose, and lost their lives on the gallows.[2] There was, however, a probability that the Government would be confronted by something more than a local rising if Charles contrived to slip past Cromwell and to throw himself into England with part, at least, of the new and formidable army which he was gathering in the North.

By the middle of January the members of the Council of State were in possession of a great part of the Royalist plans. A certain George Bishop, who had been employed to make discoveries, had in his pay not only members of the council which directed the Royalist movements in England, but also some of the messengers who carried their secret despatches abroad. By this means Bishop learnt that arrangements had been made for a great rising before Christmas. Every district in England had its appointed officers, and its men marked out for the service, whilst Newcastle and Von Karpfen were to land in Kent as soon as Dover Castle had been surprised, with 4,000 Germans

---

[1] *C.J.* v. 516.

[2] *Ib.* vi. 505. The proceedings of the High Court may be traced in the newspapers of the day. See also Middleton to Lenthall, Dec. 2, Rich to ——, Dec. 4, Grey's *Impartial Examination*, iv. 105, 107.

at their heels. Though the unauthorised outbreak in Norfolk
had interfered with the execution of this design, an insurrection on a far larger scale was not likely to be long delayed.[1]
Much as Bishop had already learnt there was more to be
known, and on January 28 he was able to inform Cromwell
that a woman would before long wait on him in Edinburgh
with a ciphered letter which she had been commissioned by
the English Royalists to place in the hands of the King.[2]

In the Council of State there was much perplexity. On
January 13, when Bishop's story had been told, the committee
appointed to examine into plots against the Government suggested that those who gave information of
such designs should be rewarded with part of the
estates of the conspirators, and that public notice should be
given that all disturbers of the peace should lose their lives and
estates without mercy. The Council for some reason, perhaps
as fearing to hasten the outbreak by revealing its knowledge of
the danger, did not think fit to adopt this proposal, contenting
itself with ordering the re-arrest of dangerous persons
who had been formerly imprisoned, but were now at
large on their own recognisances. At the same time
Parliament was to be asked to prohibit all horse-races, hunting
and hawking matches, as well as football playing, where sport
might easily be made the cloak for military gatherings.[3]   On
February 4, to meet the danger of an invasion from Scotland,
the Council recommended that a considerable force of cavalry
should be despatched to the North of England, where, in consequence of its proximity to Scotland, danger was especially
feared.[4]

By this time the official year of the second Council of
State was drawing to an end. In choosing the third Council,
the sittings of which commenced on February 17, Parliament

Jan. 13. Proposed threats of confiscation.

Measures of the Council.

---

[1] Bishop to Cromwell, Jan. 14, 18, 21, with enclosures, *Milton State Papers*, 49, 54, 55.

[2] Bishop to Cromwell, Jan. 28, *Ibid.* 57.

[3] C. of St. Order Book, *Interr.* I, 16, p. 31.

[4] *Ib. Interr.* I, 17, p. 32.

resolved to reserve twenty [1] seats for new members, amongst whom were two officers, Harrison and Fleetwood, the latter of

Feb. 17.
The third
Council of
State.

whom had lately returned from Scotland. As Cromwell, Skippon, and Hazlerigg were re-elected, the military element was more strongly represented than before. Amongst those excluded were Fairfax and Marten. For some unknown reason the powers of the new Council were limited to the last day of November.[2]

Earlier in the year Hazlerigg and Scot had been with Cromwell in Edinburgh,[3] doubtless to concert plans for the

Jan.
Hazlerigg
and Scot
visit
Cromwell.

Attitude of
the new
Council.

suppression of the expected insurrection. For some time the new Council maintained an attitude of prudent reserve, occasionally ordering the arrest of some person of whom suspicions were entertained, or directing the destruction of some fortification which might be dangerous in the hands of an enemy.

The new militia,[4] too, was warned to be in readiness to play its part whenever occasion served. Nor was the High Court

March 4.
Execution
of Sir
Henry
Hyde.

of Justice idle. On March 4 Sir Henry Hyde was executed by its sentence on a charge of having accepted an embassy to Constantinople from the King, and of having used his influence with the Sultan to procure the discharge of Sir Thomas Bendish, the minister acknowledged by the Commonwealth, as well as of having urged the merchants to declare for the King.[5]

The case of another victim demands more careful examination. Brown Bushell was one of five whose trial for life had

---

[1] In her preface to her *Calendar* (1651) Mrs. Everett Green puts the number incorrectly at fifteen.

[2] *C.J.* vi. 530–533; Act constituting a Council of State, *Interr.* I, 89, p. 9.

[3] They made their report, after their return, on Jan. 23, *C.J.* vi. 527.

[4] See vol. i. 267.

[5] *A Perf. Diurnal*, E, 784, 22. He was about to 'seize upon our merchants' goods for the use of the King of Scotland.' This may mean only that he tried to get a contribution from them. We have no report of the trial, and cannot speak positively of the details of the charge.

been ordered in 1649.[1] Having been passed over at that time he had been again selected as one of the six whose trials had been

Case of Brown Bushell.

ordered in consequence of Ascham's murder.[2] The causes which placed him in this unenviable position are not far to seek. He had played fast and loose with both parties. When Cholmley betrayed Scarborough Castle to the King, it was Bushell who got up a mutiny in the garrison and gave it over to Parliament, and who after no long delay again betrayed it to the Royalists. After the end of the first Civil War he expressed his devotion to the victorious cause with such vehemence that he was entrusted with the command of a ship which, when a great part of the fleet revolted in 1648, he gave up to the Prince of Wales. This was his last treachery. He was captured and lodged in prison. The fate long suspended over his head overtook him

Feb. 25.
Bushell at the bar.

March 25.
His trial.

March 29.
and execution.

at last, and on February 25 he was brought to the bar of the High Court of Justice on the charge of the betrayal of Scarborough Castle. His actual trial took place on March 25. He was sentenced to death and executed on the 29th,[3] doubtless as a warning to all who might be tempted to give up fortified posts to the enemy.

This conclusion is rendered the more probable as Parliament was by this time in possession of fresh information

Fresh information.

concerning the dangers by which it was menaced. We have no means of knowing whether the female messenger who carried the correspondence of the Royalists had actually placed in Cromwell's hands [4] the letter entrusted to her by the conspirators. It is, however, probable that Cromwell became acquainted with its contents, as his subsequent actions betray a knowledge of Charles's secrets. It was, for instance, by his orders that Robert Lilburne pounced, in the second week in March, on a knot of Royalists as they

---

[1] See vol. i. 41.   [2] See vol. i. 308.

[3] *Merc. Pol.* 626, 13; *The Speech and Confession of Capt. Brown Bushell*, E, 626, 14. See Bushell's Life in the *Dict. of Nat. Biogr.*, where, however, the date of his execution is incorrectly given.   [4] See p. 9.

were embarking at Greenock for the Isle of Man with the intention of concerting measures with Derby for a rising in Lancashire. Some of them succeeded in putting to sea, but Birkenhead, the former editor of *Mercurius Aulicus*,

Seizure of Birken- head at Greenock. now a captain in Charles's service, was captured, and with him the correspondence he carried. A few days later a letter from Charles to the Levellers was seized on board a vessel taken in the Firth of Forth.[1]

Of the letters taken with Birkenhead the most important was one directed to a Royalist agent, Tom Coke, a younger son of the former Secretary of State of Charles I.[2]

Projected Scottish expedition to Lanca- shire. From this letter it appeared that Argyle had pro- mised the Lancashire Royalists to lend them 2,000 of the best Scottish horse, and the same number of Highlanders, in return for an engagement to rouse the county for the King. Massey and Buckingham were to command the force, and Buckingham had already begun raising a troop of horse amongst Englishmen at that time in Scotland.[3]

March 12-20 Measures of the Council. On March 12 the papers seized on Birkenhead were before the Council of State. No time was lost in calling upon the authorities in every part of the country to be on the alert, especially those of the districts most threatened—Lancashire, Cheshire, and North Wales. In the West, too, vigilance was needed to provide

[1] Letters from Edinburgh, March 11, 15, *Merc. Pol.* E, 626, 13. Lord Hatton, writing to Nicholas on April 2 under the assumed name of Simon Smith, says :—" We hear that Mr. Denzil Holles had lately sent unto him forty or fifty of the King's blank commissions, which he filled up with Presbyterians' names, and sent them into England with so much policy that they miscarried by the way, and so the parties are discovered, which will make the second part of the Earl of Derby's plot discovered," *S.P. Dom.* xv. 49.

[2] In the Index to Mrs. Everett Green's *Calendar of State Papers* he is confused with an earlier Thomas Cook of Drayton. He is correctly described by her in her Calendar of *The Committee for Compounding*.

[3] Buckingham to Coke, Feb. 25, Cary's *Mem. of the Civil War*, ii. 418. The editor has misdated the letter, placing it in 1652, as if Buckingham could possibly have written ' from the Court, Scotland,' more than five months after the battle of Worcester.

against an expected landing of a Royalist force from France; and farther East, Colchester had to be guarded against surprise, and the militia of London and Westminster to be in readiness against possible danger. Harrison himself was to be sent to the North-Western counties at the head of a small force, to be augmented by drafts from the militia; whilst Fleetwood was directed to take charge of London and its neighbourhood in his absence.[1]

The most striking thing about these orders is the reliance placed on the new militia. No doubt every militia-man en-

Import-ance of the new militia. rolled was avowedly a partisan of the Government, but the existence of the force may at least be accepted as evidence that the Government had a con-

siderable number of partisans, and that by the side of Cavalier noblemen and gentlemen and discontented Presbyterians there was a not inconsiderable body of men—freeholders, farmers, townsmen, or whatever else they might be—who regarded the Parliament of the Commonwealth as a protection against anarchy at home and invasion from abroad. It was the first time since the New Model Army was called to arms, that Parliament had entrusted its defence, even in part, to a citizen soldiery.

The Council of State took care to supplement their warlike preparations by a continuance of activity in the detection of conspiracy. The fact that Buckingham's letters found in Birkenhead's possession had been directed to Tom Coke

March 18. Tom Coke eludes arrest. furnished a clue, and on March 18 orders were given for his arrest. He succeeded in slipping away from his pursuers, but so important was his evidence

March 20. He is at-tainted. likely to prove that an Act of Parliament was hurriedly passed on the 20th to declare him an attainted traitor if he did not surrender within four days. It

March 29. His cap-ture. was not till the 29th that he was apprehended by Harrison at an upholsterer's in the Strand.[2]

---

[1] C. of St. Order Book, March 12–19, *Interr.* I, 65, pp. 92 129; *C.J.* vi. 551.

[2] C. of St. Order Book, *Interr.* I, 89, p. 718; *C.J.* vi. 521; *Perf. Diurnal*, E, 784, 30.

Coke's life was thus forfeited to the State. He was, however, told that he might still save it by giving full information of the names and designs of his associates. He was not one of those who prefer death to infamy, and from March 31 onwards for the next eight weeks he rolled out the tale of the inception and progress of the great conspiracy. A list of the leaders in each county was given, their plans set down, and the London merchants on whose financial assistance the execution of the design depended, were pointed out by name. Coke even disclosed the place in which Charles's instructions to himself were concealed, and suggested that he might still make himself useful by continuing to receive the correspondence of the Royalists in Holland, and by revealing the contents of their ciphered letters to the Council of State.[1]

March 31- May 28. His discoveries.

No part of Coke's disclosures told so heavily as his announcement of a design for a rising in London. Every house, he said, concealed arms which the apprentices and servants were prepared to use. When the fitting moment arrived, a crowd was to pour through the streets to Westminster, and put an end to Council and Parliament. This design, added the informer, was principally entrusted to certain noblemen and to a group of Presbyterian ministers. He gave the names of some of the latter, Calamy, Vines, Jenkins, Cranford, Love, Gouge, Case, and Fuller. They, he said, held correspondence with other ministers in different parts of the country. He could not, he said, remember the names of all of these last. Their

The design in London.

A Presbyterian plot.

---

[1] The chief part of Coke's confessions are printed by the *Hist. MSS. Com.* Rep. xiii. App. i. 576-602. One of them is in *Charles II. and Scotland*, 154. See also a letter from Coke to the King in the same volume, p. 132. In pursuance of the offer referred to above, Coke wrote a letter on April 3 under the assumed name of George Edwards (*S.P. Dom.* ix. 102) to Colonel Thornhill at Rotterdam, asking for a complete list of the Royalists in England. Thornhill was too cautious to reply. Clarke to —— (?), April 25, *Milton State Papers*, 65; Thornhill and Heath to Nicholas, $\frac{\text{April } 23}{\text{May } 3}$, *Nicholas Papers*, i. 238.

object, he added, was to restore the members secluded by Pride's Purge, and then to urge the King to grant the concessions demanded of his father at Newport. That they should have imagined that their Cavalier allies would content themselves with this may serve as a gauge of their own political incapacity.

During the month of April the activity of the authorities was strained to the uttermost. Suspicious persons were arrested in all directions. A force of 3,000 horse and of 1,000 foot, selected from the militia of the different counties, was ordered to be in readiness on May 1, and of these 2,500 were entrusted to Harrison to be employed, together with any other troops he might gather in the North-Western counties in pursuance of his former commission,[1] in guarding against an irruption either from Scotland or the Isle of Man.[2] Lord Beauchamp, who was known to have been appointed to the command of the projected Cavalier rising in the West, had been already secured.[3] On May 2 three of the London Presbyterian ministers named by Coke—Love, Jenkins, and Case—were arrested, together with five laymen, amongst whom was a brother of Massey and a servant of Holles.[4] Why the more important Presbyterian ministers denounced by Coke, such as Calamy and Gouge, were untouched there is no evidence to show.

Of the ministers arrested Love was selected for trial by the High Court of Justice. It was at his house that the Presbyterians who had opened communication with Charles in Jersey through Titus[5] had held the greater part of their meetings, and it seemed reasonable to make him responsible as their ringleader. When, however, the trial

April. Activity of the Council of State.

Harrison to guard the North-West.

Love selected for trial.

[1] See p. 13.
[2] *C.J.* vi. 557; C. of St. to Harrison, April 15; Instructions to Harrison, April 19, *Interr.* I, 96, pp. 123–133.
[3] C. of St. Order Book, *Interr.* I, 65, p. 273.
[4] Bishop to Cromwell, May 3. *Milton State Papers*, 66.
[5] See vol. i. 184.

commenced on June 20 an unexpected difficulty arose. The witnesses relied on by the prosecution were accomplices to the plot, and they one and all evinced a disposition to swear to as little as possible. One, indeed—a minister named Jackson—refused to give evidence at all, and was fined 500*l.* The others exhibited a lamentable defect of memory whenever they were required to be certain of Love's presence on critical occasions. Love, besides, was able to argue, with considerable force, that if the witnesses had said more in their previous examinations than they did in open court, it was because they had been threatened with being put on trial for their own lives if they did not appear against him.

June 20–
July 5.
Love's trial.

Taking the evidence as a whole, it is hardly possible to doubt that Love was an assenting party to all the proceedings of the conspirators. It is indeed probable that, as he declared, he had never actually signed any compromising document. The business was not one for which signatures were required. If, however, he had not been in substantial agreement with the other conspirators, he would never have allowed them to continue holding their meetings in his house, and it can hardly be doubted that he had approved of their invitation to Charles to come to terms with the Scots at Jersey and Breda. With respect to his recent conduct all that could be proved was that early in 1651 he and his comrades had received letters from Massey and the Scottish leaders asking that 5,000*l.* might be collected to support a rising in response to Massey's expected invasion. It appeared, however, that nothing had been done to satisfy this demand, though a small sum had been raised in relief of the personal necessities of Massey and Titus. The evidence which is now sufficient for the historical inquirer was then sufficient for the Court. Love was sentenced to death, as was a few days later another man, named Gibbons, who had also joined in the movement.[1]

The
evidence
against
Love.

[1] *The Whole Trial of Mr. Love*, E, 790, 6. This contemporary account is reprinted in *State Trials*, v. 43–294.

Parliament hesitated to authorise the execution of the sentence, and granted to Love a month's reprieve. On the

July 15.
Love's
execution
suspended.

one side might be pleaded the necessity of warning the Presbyterians that if they chose to combine with Cavaliers they must not expect exemption from punishment. On the other hand, it might be argued that it was unwise to alienate the large body of Presbyterians who might at some future time be converted into allies. The clamour

Demand for
his life.

for Love's death was loudest amongst the most sturdy Independents. " To what end," wrote one of them, " serves all the providence of God in bringing these designs to light, if so be such a malefactor as Mr. Love escape ? " [1]

On the same side, it can hardly be doubted, was the most devoted literary champion of the Independent cause. In

March.
Milton's
Defence
of the
People of
England.

February or March, Milton had published in the Latin tongue a *Defence of the People of England*, against the attacks of Salmasius, at that time the autocrat of the world of scholarship. Milton's name, long familiar to Englishmen, was now spread abroad in Europe to be mentioned with admiration for the purity of his Latin style and the vigour of his strokes, with horror for the opinions he entertained. A later generation, caring for none of these things, may pause over the heroism of the man who, with eyesight already failing, knowingly courted blindness rather than spare a line in defence of that Commonwealth which, imperfect as he acknowledged it to be, was to him the only road leading to that ideal government by a sage and noble people which formed the object of his dreams.

So acutely did Milton feel the importance of the crisis, that he was unable to content himself with addressing the learned

Milton as
a political
writer.

alone. It was in the spring of 1651 that the leading articles—if they may be so styled—of *Mercurius Politicus*, hitherto written by Marchamont Needham,[2] for the first time show traces of Milton's pen. During the past

---

[1] *C.J.* vi. 604. Bishop to —— (?), July 20, *Milton State Papers*, 75.
[2] See vol. i. 252–255.

winter, Needham had set forth assiduously indeed, though
with wearisome monotony, the doctrine that obedience was
due to the power of the sword, and later on had no less
monotonously urged that a new government could never with
safety share its power with any persons who were not irrecon-
cilably hostile to the old one.   On April 3 Milton, if evidence
of style be worth anything, snatched the pen from Needham's
hands to insert a fierce attack upon the folly of the Scots and, by
implication, upon the folly of the English Presbyterians in
hoping to use Charles to their ends.

"Now"—surely here we are listening to the voice of
Milton—" when God hath opened the eyes of the Scots so far
as to consider that they have an Ishbosheth among
them, heir of a family of the very same complexion

The 'Ish-
bosheth'
article.

and condition against whom destruction hath been
written in broad characters by the special hand of Providence ;
that no party whatsoever that joins with it doth prosper ; that
by bringing him in they have undone themselves, their armies
defeated, themselves cheated, and their country reduced even
to the utmost extremity.   And further when they consider how
they suffer all these miseries for one that mortally hates them
and detests both their Kirk and Covenant, . . . when they
observe and remember what an attempt he made to run away
to the Royalists in the north of Scotland, how he rejoiced at
the defeat at Dunbar,[1] and took occasion thereby to overtop
all his tutors both of Kirk and State ; the principle whereof
he hath outed [2] from command and either discontented or debarred them from his counsels to make room for Cavaliers and
malignants of all sorts and sizes who now are the only courtiers.
If they please likewise to consider that from such beginnings as
these nothing but revenge will follow in the end ; revenge for his
father, revenge for his darling Montrose that acted by his special
commissions—and truly it must needs be justice on God's part,
if He permit him to revenge the deed upon the Scottish ring-

[1] See p. 331.
[2] A Miltonic word.   One remembers his statement that he had been
' Church-outed ' by the prelates.

leaders, because they were so blindly and basely imparted as to bequeath the servant to a death of highest infamy on the gallows, and yet at the same time take his master that set him on work into their bosoms—I say, once again, if it please God to open the Scots' eyes and hearts to consider all these things . . . they cannot be ignorant which way to make use and application of the former text for the saving of their nation." [1] (2 Samuel iv.)

Holding these strong opinions on the folly and criminality of the Presbyterians who supported Charles, Milton was not

June 19.
Milton
cries for
justice. likely to side with those who stood in the way of the execution of the sentence on Love. In *Mercurius Politicus*, he—for here again the language bears distinctly the impress of Milton's mind—had, even before Love's trial began, cried out for justice on clerical offenders who ' vilify the Government, fill their pulpits with alarms and invectives, preach disobedience and treason with open mouth, keep private fasts for the destruction of the Parliament, damn them and all their friends for heretics and schismatics, and in their licentious way excommunicate the State out of all possi-

---

[1] *Merc. Pol.* April 3, E, 626, 17. Professor Masson, in his *Life of Milton*, iv. 327, was the first to call attention to the probability that Milton took some part in writing these articles. Those in the first numbers with their rather ineffective jocularity, he, of course, assigns to Needham. With Sept. 19, 1650, he notices ' the introduction of a graver and more serious style,' and though he does not come to any positive conclusion he seems inclined to attribute this to Milton's influence. This is possible, but Milton can have done no more than to induce Needham to substitute one of his styles for another. The argument that obedience is due to force, which appears with wearisome iteration up to Feb. 6, and again on Feb. 27, is not only one most unlikely to be put forward by Milton, but it is the very opinion to which Needham had already declared his adherence in *The Case of the Commonwealth of England* (see vol. i. 253). Moreover, a passage about Warwick the Kingmaker in *Merc. Pol.* of Feb. 20, is, as Mr. Firth has pointed out to me, reproduced with slight variations in *The Excellency of a Free State* (p. 20), published anonymously by Needham in 1656. I cannot see anything distinctly Miltonic earlier than the ' Ishbosheth ' article, though from that time Milton's hand can be occasionally traced.

bilities of heaven, [out of] their sovereignty on earth, and out of the very hearts of the people. Nor is this all, but they proceed underhand to confederate with the nation of Scotland and with Charles Stuart their king, by which means they join issue with all the malignants and rebels of the three nations, whose design they now act and have laboured to effect by laying and preparing new insurrections of late so happily prevented. Thus they have preferred their own unrighteous discontents before the peace and liberty of their native country, so that upon their score too we must lay this third war now in being against the people of England.'[1]

It was understood that the decisive word was to be spoken by Cromwell. To him the Presbyterian ministers compromised in Love's conspiracy addressed a petition for mercy.[2] Hammond—always shrinking from deeds of violence —hoped for the powerful intercession of the Lord General on behalf of Love. "If the providence of God," he wrote, "so dispose your lordship's heart that you should become a mediator for the sparing his life—for probably there seems no other way to effect it—according to the frame and temper men who have been exceedingly averse are now in, it may so gain upon them that the victory may be greater than winning a field, for certainly the joining of hearts is the best—the surest victory."[3]

July 20.
A petition
to Crom-
well.

July 22.
Cromwell
asked to
intercede
for Love.

The appeal for mercy reached Scotland at an unseasonable moment. The death struggle between Cromwell and the Scots had already commenced, and the officers of the army before whom the petitions in Love's favour were laid expressed their wish that justice might take its course.[4] Parliament, however, still hesitated, and it was not

The army
refuse to
interfere.

---

[1] *Merc. Pol.* E, 622, 15. This number was published on June 19.

[2] Bishop to —— (?), July 20, *Milton State Papers*, 75.

[3] Hammond to Cromwell, July 22, *ib.* 75.

[4] "The officers of the army have lately entered into consultation about the business of Mr. Love, and after some time spent therein, resolved that they would not intermeddle therein, but that it will be their rejoicing that justice may run in an interrupted channel." The word here should evidently be 'uninterrupted.' Letter from Scotland, undated but evidently

till August 22, when a Scottish army was already in the bowels of the land, that Love and Gibbons were executed on Tower Hill.[1]

Aug. 22. Execution of Love and Gibbons.

For a Government struggling against dangers from within and without it cannot be said that the death penalties inflicted were at all excessive. In one direction, indeed, it was impossible, as matters stood, to disarm antagonism.

Weight of taxation.

Nothing would have strengthened the Commonwealth more than a remission of taxation, and yet in the face of hostile forces abroad and at home such a remission was impracticable. Though no complete balance sheet of revenue and expenditure has been handed down, the expenses of the Government at this time cannot have been far short of 2,750,000*l.*, if indeed they did not exceed that amount.[2] To meet what for those days was an enormous sum—it was more than three times the revenue[3] of Charles I. in 1635—taxation had to be swelled by sales of Crown and ecclesiastical property.

Expenditure of the Commonwealth.

Difficulty of raising money.

written before the end of July. *The Protestation of Divers Well-affected Scots*, E, 640, 6. This together with the following extract from a letter written on Aug. 2 from J. Baynes to A. Baynes (*Letters from Roundhead Officers*): "Colonel Foskur, who came to speak friends in the army from Mr. Love, but got none in return, was taken prisoner by moss troopers," disposes of the story told by Naunton (*Journal of the High Court of Justice*, pref. xxxvii), that Cromwell consented to Love's pardon, but that the post-bag containing his letter was intercepted by some Cavaliers, who destroyed the letter, thinking Love 'not worthy to live who had been such a firebrand in the Treaty at Uxbridge.' [Colonel 'Foskur' means Colonel Fortescue.]

[1] *Mr. Love's Speech*, E, 641, 8.

[2] An estimate of the expense of the army and navy is given in *C.J.* vi. 467, 550, 579.

Army in England, Ireland, and Scotland	£1,953,098
Navy	589,219
	£2,542,317

To this may be added at least 200,000*l.* for the expenses of home government and expenses not provided for by the estimate. In *An Impartial Examination*, iv. 97, Grey puts the expenses of the home government in 1649 at 71,174*l.*, but his list is obviously incomplete.

[3] 818,000*l.*, including an estimate of 200,000*l.* for ship-money.

Even loans on good security were scarcely to be obtained, and loans on no better security than a Parliamentary assurance were not to be raised at all.

In this distress the wish to make some part of the burden fall upon those whose evil deeds—at least in the opinion of the members sitting at Westminster—had caused the mischief was July 16. irresistible. On July 16 a Confiscation Act was passed,[1] by which the estates of no fewer than seventy persons were to be sold for the benefit of the Commonwealth, almost all of them being old Royalists such as Newcastle, Buckingham, and Hopton. At one time there appears to have been an intention of spreading terror by proceeding to the trial and execution of the five remaining hostages selected after Ascham's murder, one of whom, Sir John Stowell, was brought before the High Court of Justice. His plea that he was freed by the Articles of Exeter[2] from all inquiry into his actions during the first Civil War was, however, accepted as valid,[3] and neither he nor any one of his four companions in misfortune was even brought to trial.

July 16.
The first
Confiscation
Act.

It is not unlikely that posterity would have pardoned a few more executions more easily than a series of acts against which no outcry was raised by contemporaries whether Royalists or Parliamentarians. To raise the money grievously needed, the splendid collection of pictures formed by the taste of Charles I. had been rapidly disposed of. Titians and Vandykes which might have formed the nucleus of a national storehouse of art were dispersed over the Continent, and some of them are at this day to be found in Paris and Madrid, though others have wandered back to the land which had sheltered them in more peaceful days.

The sale of
the pictures
of Charles I.

The old Cathedrals of England were within a little of going the same way as the masterpieces of the painter's art. On February 18 a Parliamentary Committee advised ' that all cathedral churches where there are

Feb. 18.
Proposal to
pull down
Cathedrals.

[1] *Scobell,* ii. 173.   [2] *Great Civil War,* iii. 91.
[3] *C.J.* vi. 585.

other churches or chapels sufficient for the people to meet in for the worship of God be surveyed, pulled down and sold, and be employed for a stock for the use of the poor.' [1] On

April 4, Parliament resolved to make a beginning with Lichfield Cathedral, which, since the siege in 1643, had remained in a ruinous condition.[2] In October this order was so far carried out that the lead was stripped off the roof. The great bell was broken up two years later.[3] Here, however, the forces of destruction were stayed. A cathedral in ruins might be sold and given to the poor. A cathedral not in ruins might still serve their spiritual needs. On August 15 it was resolved that 'the minster of Peterborough should be employed for the public worship of God' if the inhabitants would bear the expense of maintaining the services. For a few months no more was heard of the demolition of cathedrals.

Marginal notes:
April 4. Lichfield Cathedral to be first attacked.

Aug. 15. Peterborough to be preserved.

What a light is thrown by these resolutions on the character of the men who now bore sway in England ! For the bodies and souls of men they cared much. They would do anything in their power to preserve them from misery, much, too, to save them from sin and crime. Of the elevating sense of natural or artistic beauty they had no comprehension. After all, let it stand to their credit that it was for the sake of the poor that they proposed to work this desolation. They did not, like Protector Somerset, pull down churches in order that they might make wide their own palaces. For them the temple of God was the temple not made with hands, the human body and soul which He had created.

---

[1] *C.J.* vi. 535.   [2] *Ib.* vi. 556.
[3] Harwood's *Hist. of Lichfield*, 49.

CHAPTER XVI

WORCESTER

NOT by judicial sentences or popular legislation, but by the argument of pike and gun must the English Commonwealth make its title good. During the first weeks of June the new Scottish army gathered round Stirling. Nothing more was heard of those threats of purging which had distracted the army overthrown at Dunbar. The merest semblance of a test was now sufficient to satisfy the exigencies of the clergy. Engagers who would merely promise to leave unassailed the laws relating to religion and to abstain from taking revenge on their former opponents 'in the matter of the sinful engagements,'[1] were received with open arms. Any who felt conscientious qualms at making this acknowledgment of their fault contented themselves with throwing the blame on those who exacted it. "Behold," wrote one of them, "a fearful sin ! The ministers of the Gospel received all our repentances as unfeigned, though they knew well enough they were but counterfeit ; and we on the other hand made no scruple to declare that engagement to be unlawful and sinful, deceitfully speaking against the dictates of our own consciences and judgments. If this was not to mock the all-knowing and all-seeing God to His face, then I declare myself not to know what a fearful sin hypocrisy is."[2]

The spiritual basis of the Scottish resistance to Cromwell

June.
The Scottish army at Stirling.

A mild test.

Sir J. Turner's comment.

---

[1] *Balfour*, iv. 306.   [2] Sir James Turner's *Memoirs*, 94.

having been thus rejected, there was but little to take its place amongst the rank and file of the army. Those who did not Weakness of fight for 'Christ's Crown and Covenant' were sadly the army. wanting in that spirit of discipline and devotion to duty which made the strength of their enemies. Dragged from his home at the bidding of his lord, the Highlander with his claymore and his bow and arrow had little in common with the Lowland musketeer or pikeman from Angus or the Mearns. Many of the new recruits had still to learn the art and usages of war. For their commanders they had little or no respect, and charges of treachery or incompetence were every day hurled against Leslie as having been defeated at Dunbar, or against Holborn as one who having formerly served in an English army was likely to be in imperfect sympathy with his own countrymen. To make matters worse, the plan of sending Buckingham and Massey into Lancashire, whilst the main army continued to face Cromwell in Scotland, had been long ago detected by the enemy. The Englishmen who should have led the projected insurrection which was to have burst out upon the arrival of the Scottish expeditionary force [1] were for the most part in, confinement, whilst Harrison lay in Cumberland keeping strict guard on the Western Borders.

There was therefore nothing for it but to recur to the defensive tactics which had baffled Cromwell in his sallies from June 28. Braid Hill in the preceding year. On June 28 the The Scottish whole of the Scottish forces marched out to Torwood, army at Tor- wood. taking up on the hills south of Stirling an easily defensible position from which the ground sloped away to the banks of the Carron. Leslie—for surely it must have been Leslie who chose the ground—had not long to wait for the approach of his redoubtable antagonist. Cromwell indeed had

---

[1] Almost every letter from Edinburgh in the English newspapers (see, for instance, a letter of Jan. 14 in *Merc. Pol.* E, 622, 8) from January onwards is occupied with this plan, and it is therefore probable that it was carried to Cromwell's head-quarters by his spies at Perth and Stirling, with details additional to those contained in Buckingham's intercepted letter, for which see p. 12.

been assailed by a severe illness in the spring months, and at one time it seemed unlikely that he would be able to endure the labours of a campaign. He was now, however, fully recovered, and on the 25th he and his troops took up their quarters at their old post on Braid Hill.[1] On the 30th, having received intelligence of Leslie's movements, he marched in the direction of the enemy. During the next fortnight he strove in vain to bring on an engagement. The hills beyond the Carron were an insuperable obstacle to a direct attack, and in spite of numerous feints and of a successful attack by the English army upon Callander House close to Falkirk, Leslie had taken too thoroughly to heart the lesson taught him on Doon Hill to descend into the plain.[2]

June 25.
Cromwell on Braid Hill.

June 30- July 14. Cromwell fails to bring on a battle.

If a battle could not be had in any other way, the attempt made in 1650 to cut off the Scottish army from its supplies in Fife must be repeated in 1651. Once more the command of the sea stood Cromwell in good stead, and on July 17 he despatched a small force across the Firth of Forth with instructions to entrench themselves in the peninsula of North Queensferry. On the 19th reinforcements were sent over under Lambert, and by the 20th about 4,500 men were firmly established on the northern side of the Firth under his command.

July 17-20. Forces sent into Fife.

Leslie, perhaps imagining the English force in Fife to be less numerous than it was, contented himself with sending against it 4,000 men under Sir John Brown.[3] On the 20th Lambert, anticipating the blow, fell on the Scots on a hillside to the north of Inverkeithing, and in spite of the disadvantage of the ground put them to the rout. About half the Scottish force was slain outright,

July 20. The fight at Inverkeithing.

---

[1] *Merc. Pol.* E, 633, 5.

[2] Walker to A. Baynes, July 14; John Baynes to A. Baynes, July 19; *Letters from Roundhead Officers*, 33, 34; *Several Proceedings*, E, 786, 26.

[3] See *Great Civil War*, i. 336. Carlyle confuses him with Major-General Richard Brown, formerly Governor of Abingdon.

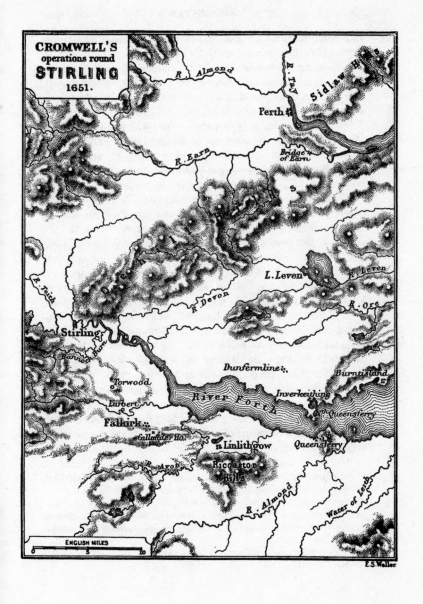

CROMWELL'S
operations round
STIRLING
1651.

R. Almond

R. Tay

Sidlaw Hills

Perth

R. Earn

Bridge of Earn

L. Leven

R. Leven

R. Ore

R. Devon

R. Teith

Stirling

Bannock Burn

Torwood

Carbert

Falkirk

Callander Ho.

R. Avon

Riccarton Hills

Dunfermline

Burntisland

Inverkeithing

N. Queensferry

Queensferry

River Forth

Linlithgow

R. Almond

Water of Leith

ENGLISH MILES

0   5   10   20

E.S.Weller.

and more than fifteen hundred prisoners, amongst whom was Brown himself, fell into Lambert's hands.[1]

Whilst Lambert was virtually annihilating Brown's force at Inverkeithing, Cromwell watched with delight the withdrawal from Torwood of the enemy's main body, which had moved off to give support to Brown. Pressing on across the hills he rode forward with a small number of officers to the historic field of Bannockburn, only to find Leslie too strongly posted in the King's Park to be attacked with advantage. Before night Cromwell drew back to his old position, and Torwood was reoccupied by the Scots.[2]

Cromwell's movements.

Cromwell would hardly have fallen back across the hills unless he had made up his mind to try some fresh method of dislodging the enemy from his fastness. He had in fact resolved to carry his army across the Firth and, by seizing Perth, to cut Leslie off from his supplies in the North. It did not escape his notice that by taking this course he uncovered the road to the South and made it easy for Leslie to carry out that plan of invading England which, as Cromwell well knew, had, in one form or other, been agitated in the Scottish councils for more than half a year. He was, however, too well aware of the danger he incurred by remaining inactive in the north to estimate the risk of a Scottish invasion above its just value. The affair at Inverkeithing had taught him that the materials of which the Scottish army was composed were not really formidable, and, since the English Royalist leaders had been secured, the chance of an English insurrection had been much diminished.

He resolves to carry his army into Fife.

He runs the risk of a Scottish invasion of England.

[1] Cromwell to Lenthall, July 21, *Carlyle*, Letter clxxv., corrected by a subsequent letter of July 22, published by Mr. Firth in the *Eng. Hist. Review*, ii. 151 ; Lambert to Bradshaw (?), July 21 ; *Merc. Pol.* E, 638, 10; J. Baynes to A. Baynes, July 22, *Letters from Roundhead Officers*, 151; *A Great Victory*, E, 638, 2 ; *The Army's Intelligencer*, E, 638, 15 ; *Life of Blair*, 276.

[2] Nicoll's *Diary*, 54 ; Cromwell to Lenthall, July 24, *Carlyle*, Letter clxxvi.

Cromwell did what he could to lessen the danger before setting out on his adventure. Harrison had already advanced with part of the force under his command to Edinburgh, and Cromwell now summoned him to Linlithgow, where the two held a conference on July 23. The result was that Harrison, who would be reinforced by a body of horse advancing from Nottinghamshire under Colonel Rich, was directed to post himself on the Borders and to fight, or at least to keep in check the Scots if they thought proper to march for England.[1]

July 23. His conference with Harrison.

Having made these arrangements, Cromwell lost no time in carrying out his own operations. His base having been secured by the capture of Inchgarvie on the 24th and of Burntisland on the 29th, he pushed rapidly forward through Fife. On August 2 Perth surrendered to his summons. Cromwell had thus interposed his army between Leslie and Middleton who had gone north to hasten the reinforcements which Huntly was collecting.[2] Even if the whole English army remained at Perth it could hardly fall short of supplies. The fertile Carse of Gowrie was at no great distance, and the Firth of Tay would bear shipping to a point not far below Perth itself. Once more the indented character of the east coast of Scotland was in favour of an invader holding the command of the sea.

July 24-29. Capture of Inchgarvie, Burntisland,

Aug. 2. and of Perth.

The capacity of the district round Perth to support the invaders was not, however, put to the test. On August 1, the day before the surrender of Perth, a rumour spread through the army that the Scots

Aug. 1. A rumour that the Scots are marching South.

---

[1] *The Army's Intelligencer*, E, 638, 15. " His Excellency hath reserved a force here of Horse and Foot, which at present lie in and near Edinburgh and himself in Leith ; these—in conjunction with the Horse under Col. Rich in Nottinghamshire and those left by Major-General Harrison in Northumberland and Cumberland, all which Horse my lord hath sent for to be upon the Borders—will be in a capacity, through God's assistance, to engage or at least impede their march if they attempt that way." This, in a letter from Leith of July 26, puts it out of doubt that Cromwell foresaw the possibility of the Scots marching southwards.

[2] *The Weekly Intelligencer*, E, 640, 4.

had taken the step which Cromwell had anticipated. Before
long the rumour developed into sure intelligence. Cromwell,
Cromwell is not in a hurry. however, had already taken every precaution in his
power, and he was not the man to let a present suc-
cess escape from his hands in pursuit of a distant
achievement.[1] He waited at Perth till the capitulation was
signed, and then—leaving five or six thousand men behind
Aug. 2. under Monk's command to reduce Stirling—he started
Cromwell in pursuit. on the 2nd with the remainder of his army in hot
Aug. 4. pursuit. On August 4, after his arrival at Leith,
Cromwell justifies himself, Cromwell justified himself in a letter to Lenthall.
The enemy, he wrote, ' in his desperation and fear
and out of inevitable necessity, is run to try what he can do
this way.'

"I do apprehend," continued Cromwell, "that if he goes
for England, being some few days' march before us, it will
trouble some men's thoughts ; and may occasion some inconveniences ; of which I hope we are as deeply sensible, and have
been, and I trust shall be as diligent to prevent as any. And
indeed this is our comfort that in simplicity of heart as towards
God we have done to the best of our judgments, knowing that
if some issue were not put to this business it would occasion
another winter's war to the ruin of your soldiery, for whom the
Scots are too hard in respect of enduring the winter difficulties
of this country, and [have] been under the endless expense of
the treasure of England in prosecuting this war. It may be
supposed we might have kept the enemy from this by interpos-
ing between him and England ; which truly I believe we might,
but how to remove him out of this place without doing what
we have done, unless we had a commanding army on both
sides of the river of Forth, is not clear to us ; or how to

[1] "To Cromwell at Perth," writes Professor Masson (*Life of Milton*,
iv. 290), "on the 2nd of August, this news was a thunderclap. Never had
he been more taken by surprise : people would soon be saying he had
been outwitted." That this is a mistake is shown by the extract from
The Army's Intelligencer given at p. 29, note 1, if not by Cromwell's
own letter of August 4.

answer the inconveniences above mentioned, we understand not."

Cromwell, in short, held that he had done the best possible thing under the actual circumstances, though if his army had been twice as numerous as it was he could have done better. It remained to bid fainting spirits at Westminster—if any there were—to be of good cheer. " We pray therefore," he went on, " that—seeing there is a possibility for the enemy to put you to some trouble—you would, with the same courage grounded upon a confidence in God, wherein you have been supported to the great things God hath used you in hitherto, improve,[1] the best you can, such forces as you have in readiness as may on the sudden be gathered together to give the enemy some check until we shall be able to reach up to him, which we trust in the Lord we shall do our utmost endeavour in. And indeed we have this comfortable experience from the Lord, that this enemy is heart-smitten by God, and whenever the Lord shall bring us up to them, we believe the Lord will make the desperateness of this counsel of theirs to appear and the folly of it also. When England was much more unsteady than now, and when a much more considerable army of theirs unfoiled invaded you ; and we had but a weak force to make resistance at Preston, upon deliberate advice we chose rather to put ourselves between their army and Scotland, and how God succeeded that, is not well to be forgotten."[2]

Harrison had already sped on his errand without waiting for further orders.[3] Instructions were sent after him to gather

(marginal note: and encourages the Parliament.)

[1] 'You would improve,' as printed in *Several Proceedings*, and in Cary.
[2] Cromwell to Lenthall, Aug. 4, *Several Proceedings*, E, 786, 32 ; Cary, *Mem. of the Civil War*, ii. 291, printed, with slight alterations, in *Carlyle*, Letter clxxx. The original is in *Tanner MSS.* liv. vol. 130.
[3] Harrison and others to Cromwell, Aug. 2, *Milton State Papers*, 71. The date given is, according to a custom beginning to spring up amongst religious enthusiasts (see vol. i. 296, note 4), the second day of the fifth month, which usually means July, where the editor has placed it. Internal evidence shows it to have been written in August, Harrison counting April as the first month instead of March.

what horse and dragoons he could, and to march against the
enemy, doing his best to outflank them, shorten their provisions,
and fall upon them as opportunity arose. Lambert,
with 3,000 horse, was detached to hang upon their
rear. Cromwell himself, with the infantry and a
competent body of horse, started from Leith on the
6th. On the 5th Harrison had reached Newcastle, where he
stayed awhile to collect his scattered forces. On the 7th he
was able to announce that he had 3,000 horse under his orders,
besides some foot which he had mounted for swiftness sake.

*Aug. 5.
Instructions to
Lambert
and
Harrison.*

Like Cromwell, Harrison was full of confidence in
the future. " So," he wrote, " that the Lord hath
now tempted out the enemy from all his trenches,
fastnesses, and advantages, and we doubt not but He will very
speedily discomfit him, and cut this work short in righteousness." In a letter to the Yorkshire Committee his exultant
enthusiasm was even more conspicuous. " Considering," he
wrote, " the battle is the Lord's and not ours, and it is alike to
Him to save by few or many, I hope we may be useful in
this juncture, though we be few, mean, and none more unworthy. The Lord quicken you, me, and all that profess to
fear Him—to give diligence in our stations, to quit ourselves
as the friends of Christ, against the men that will not have Him
to reign, though God hath sworn He will set His Son upon
His holy hill, and they that oppose Him shall be broken in
pieces like a potter's vessel. The enemy's hope is that
Englishmen will be so mad as to join with them—seeing they
have lost their credit with their own countrymen—which we
hope God will prevent in a good measure by your hands, and
also lift up a standard against them." [1]

*Aug 7.
Harrison's
confidence.*

Whether Englishmen would join them was indeed the
only question left for the Scots. But for that hope, their
march from Stirling was one of simple desperation. That
Charles should have urged it indeed requires no explanation.

---

[1] Lambert to Harrison, Aug. 5 ; Harrison to the Yorkshire Committee, Aug. 6; Harrison to Bradshaw, Aug. 7 ; Cary's *Mem. of the
Civil Wars,* ii. 295–303.

MOVEMENTS OF
CROMWELL & CHARLES II.
before the
BATTLE OF WORCESTER

Cromwell's march ——————
Charles II ·······················

English Miles
0 5 10   20   30   40   50

NORTH

SEA

IRISH

SEA

He was weary of Scotland and its sour tyrannies, and the thought of again setting foot on English soil was too exhilarating to be resisted. To his officers, now that Cromwell had cut them off from their supplies, it seemed to offer the only chance of escape from an impracticable situation. On July 31 the whole army, some 20,000 strong, was streaming away in the direction of Carlisle.[1] Leven, with the Earl of Crawford and Lindsay as his Lieutenant General, was left behind to rouse the North, if that proved any longer possible. Argyle with Loudoun and his other supporters refused to take part in the enterprise and returned to their homes. Prudence at least was on the side of Argyle's determination. If the attempt failed, it would bring destruction on himself; if it succeeded, it would but insure the triumph of the English Cavaliers, or of his own bitter enemies, the Hamiltons and the Engagers. Yet the retreat of Argyle, necessary as it was, marks a descent which he would never be able to retrieve. He had disgusted all parties, because, though he was in some respects wiser than any, he had not dared to uphold in the day of peril the standard he had himself raised in more prosperous times.

July 31. The Scottish army leaves Stirling.

Argyle leaves it.

The departure of Argyle and his party was welcome to the Engagers. "All the rogues have left us," wrote Hamilton to an English friend after Penrith had been reached, "I shall not say whether from fear or disloyalty; but all now with his Majesty are such as will not dispute his commands." Of success, indeed, the writer was far from confident. "The last thing I did," declared the Duke, "was to drink your health with Laird Thomas, Daniel O'Neill, and Lauderdale, who are all now laughing at the ridiculousness of

Triumph of the Hamiltonian party.

[1] Blair's *Life*, 279. I take the numbers from Lord Wentworth's letter to Crofts, Cary's *Mem. of the Civil War*, ii. 303. On the other hand, Sir James Turner (*Memoirs*, 94) writes: "The horse and dragoons might be about 4,000; and the foot, as I reckoned them that day we marched from Stirling Park, were upwards of 9,000." The larger estimate seems to agree better with subsequent accounts, and Turner's memory may have been at fault when he wrote his Memoirs.

our condition who have quit Scotland being scarce able to maintain it, and yet we grasp at all,—and nothing but all will satisfy us—or to lose all. I confess I cannot tell whether our hopes or fears are greatest ; but we have one stout argument—despair." [1]

Hamilton's despair.

Hamilton's despair must have deepened as the doomed army pursued its course. From Carlisle onwards scarcely an Englishman joined the ranks. If there was a county in England where help might be expected that county was Lancashire, where Roman Catholics and Presbyterians formed so large a part of the population. Yet even in Lancashire the recruits were deplorably few and the desertions many. Whatever might be said of Charles, the Scots were decidedly unpopular in England, and even if it had been otherwise, the invaders had no arms to supply to those who might be induced to join them.

Few Englishmen join the Scots.

In the meanwhile the Council of State had, in full confidence of success, been making every preparation to counteract the design of the enemy. The militia of the counties threatened was called out.[2] Orders were given to collect an army of 8,000 foot and 2,000 horse in reserve to protect London and Westminster. What was of greater importance was that the militia obeyed the summons. No doubt the men were selected men, but that many thousands of even selected men should have rallied to the defence of the Commonwealth is good evidence that, whether Parliament was unpopular or not, Scottish invaders were still more unpopular.

Action of the Council of State.

At one time there was reason to hope that the invasion might be stayed. Lambert and Harrison effected a junction on

---

[1] Hamilton to Crofts, Aug. 8, Cary's *Mem. of the Civil War*, ii. 305. This letter was intercepted.

[2] C. of St. to the Militia Commissioners of the counties of York and Lancaster, Aug. 7, *Interr.* I, 96, p. 333 ; C. of St. to the Militia Commissioners of the counties of Middlesex and Surrey, *ib.* p. 343. Mrs. Hutchinson's story (*Life of Colonel Hutchinson*, ed. Firth, ii. 182) of the terrors of Bradshaw and the Council of State finds no support in any other contemporary authority.

August 13, and hearing that 3,000 of the militia of Cheshire and Staffordshire were in readiness to guard the exit from Lancashire at Warrington Bridge, they hurried forward to support them with 9,000 horse. On the 16th, however, when the enemy approached the north bank of the Mersey, it was seen that the position at the south end of the bridge was too much cut up by enclosures to be defensible by a force in which cavalry was the preponderating element. The two generals, therefore, fell back. There was a skirmish in which their rearguard was involved, and the Royalists were able to boast that they had driven the enemy before them. The Commonwealth troops fell back in the direction of Congleton, apparently with the intention of guarding the road to London, and of drawing near to the more easterly route by which Cromwell was advancing.[1]

Aug. 13.
Junction
of Lambert
and
Harrison.

Aug. 16.
Skirmish
at War-
rington
Bridge.

It is said that at a council of war Hamilton urged Charles to march straight for London. His counsel was, however, rejected, and a more prudent resolution taken to march nearer the Welsh border, where recruits might with greater probability be expected.[2] Wales was still ever hostile to Puritan ascendency, as had been testified a few weeks before by a local rising in Cardiganshire, which had, however, been summarily suppressed.

Hamilton's
advice.

The army
pursues
a route
near the
Welsh
frontier.

Charles, indeed, had not abandoned the idea of obtaining reinforcements from Lancashire. No man's influence in that county was so great as that of the Earl of Derby, and Derby had been sent for from the Isle of Man to rouse the county on Charles's behalf. As yet, however, he had not appeared, and on the evening of the 16th Charles despatched instructions to him as Captain-General of

A warrant
to the Earl
of Derby.

[1] Brief State of His Majesty's Affairs, *Tanner MSS.* liv. 155. See also evidence on the movements of Lambert and Harrison collected in *Tracts relating to Military Proceedings in Lancashire* (Chetham Soc.), 286-293.

[2] Burnet, *Memoirs of the Dukes of Hamilton*, vii. 26.

the county to levy all the male inhabitants from sixteen to sixty.[1]

On the 17th Charles was gladdened by a sight of the loyal Earl,[2] who had landed in Wyre Water with 250 foot and 60 horse,

Aug. 17. Conference with Derby.

the majority of the latter being gentlemen ready to serve as officers in the army which he hoped to raise.[3] Charles's first thought was to urge a perfect union of Cavaliers and Presbyterians in his favour, and when he despatched Derby back to Warrington he directed Massey,

Massey sent with Derby.

whose influence was great amongst the Presbyterians, to plead with them that no recollection of former disputes should stand in the way of a present com-

A message to Sir T. Middleton.

bination. At the same time he wrote to Sir Thomas Middleton, who was himself a Presbyterian, to rouse North Wales in the Royalist cause.[4]

Once more, as in 1648, the ingrained distrust of the Presbyterian for the Cavalier baffled Charles's hopes. Middleton

Middleton refuses to join him.

arrested his messenger and sent his letter to Parliament.[5] It had done no little damage to Charles's cause that, during his progress through Lancashire, he had lodged in the houses of his Catholic supporters, 'which,' as a London newspaper put it, 'discovers his gross

Distrust of the Presbyterians.

hypocrisy in taking the Covenant, and may let our English as well as Scotch Presbyters see how they were deceived with vain conceits of this man's

---

[1] Warrant, Aug. 16, *Hist. MSS. Com.* Rep. xiii. App. i. 613. This letter was written from Higher Whitley, and therefore in the evening. It shows that Derby was still absent.

[2] A letter from Charles II. to Sir T. Middleton (*S. P. Dom.* xvi. 28), Aug. 17, shows that Charles had then seen Derby. Charles reached Stoke on the 17th, and left it on the 19th. As his delay can only be accounted for by his wish to see the turn taken by his affairs in Lancashire, it appears to show that Derby did not come up with him till the afternoon or evening of the 17th. If Derby had arrived in the morning Charles would have stopped at Higher Whitley instead of pushing on to Stoke.

[3] *Transactions relating to Military Proceedings in Lancashire,* 292.

[4] Charles II. to Sir T. Middleton, Aug. 17, *S. P. Dom.* xvi. 28.

[5] *Merc. Pol.* E, 640, 23.

religion.'[1]   It was the object of Massey's mission to rouse the Lancashire Presbyterians to join Derby's Cavaliers.   Too late Charles discovered that a letter carried by Massey from the Scottish ministers attending the army contained a warning against too close a conjunction with malignants.[2]

Before Charles had time to recall this mischievous letter the poison had done its work.   The Presbyterian gentry and clergy, summoned to Warrington by Derby and Massey, replied to a request for support by calling on the Earl to put away the 'Papists' and to take the Covenant.   In vain Derby, warmly seconded by Massey, urged them to merge all differences in a resolution to defend the Crown.[3]   Derby finding his pleading vain broke off the conference.   "If I perish, I perish," were his parting words, " but, if my master perish, the blood of another

Aug. 18.
A meeting at Warrington.

---

[1] *Merc. Pol.* E, 640, 14.

[2] "I am informed that by some mistake a clause is added to the letter from the Presbytery of the army to the ministers of Lancashire, which may be very dangerous by breeding division amongst those that would own me.   For I hear they do add to the letter a desire that consideration be taken of men's former malignancy.   How dangerous this may be, and how inconsistent with a former expression of the letter of the Kirk of Scotland owning this army, I leave to you to judge.   Therefore I would have you burn the letter, and then I am sure it is lost and can do no hurt. Haste you to the army, where you will be of very great use the way we are to march."   Charles II. to Massey, Aug. 18. *A Letter from the King of Scots*, E, 640, 19.

[3] The account of this interview is given only in Seacombe's *History of the House of Stanley*.   Without pledging myself to the accuracy of the language there assigned to the different speakers, I think the story may be accepted as substantially true.   The letter in the last note shows that Massey was entrusted with an overture to the Lancashire Presbyterians. Moreover, unless this meeting took place, it is difficult to explain why Derby did not issue his warrant for levying troops till the 19th.   If this meeting took place on the 18th, it accounts for the delay, and also for the King's passing the night of the 18th as well as of the 17th at Stoke.   He would naturally be anxious to hear news from the meeting.   There is an undated letter from Derby to the gentlemen of Lancashire in Cary's *Mem. of the Civil War* (ii. 333), which is probably an invitation to this meeting.

Prince and all the ensuing miseries of this nation will be at your doors." [1] On the morning of the 19th, whilst Massey was riding off to rejoin the King, who was at that time breaking up from Stoke on his forward march, Derby held a council of war at Warrington, where it was resolved to raise in the county a force of 1,300 horse and 6,000 foot, by virtue of the obligation under which every able-bodied Englishman had been bound to serve the King in the days when the monarchical system had been in full force. [2]

It would take some time to collect so large a force, and Cromwell had already provided that the necessary time should

Aug. 21–24.
Robert
Lilburne's
move-
ments. not be allowed. On his passage through Yorkshire he had sent orders to Robert Lilburne, who was attached to the force under Lambert and Harrison, to remain in Lancashire, and at Lilburne's request he also sent his own regiment of foot to Manchester. [3] From the 22nd onwards Lilburne was actively engaged in skirmishing with the enemy, but till Cromwell's regiment arrived he had but a handful of infantry with him, and shrank from bringing on a general engagement. On the morning of the 25th he discovered that Derby, by this time at the head of some 1,500 men, was advancing from Preston in the direction of Manchester, where the population was strongly Royalist, and that no less than 500 recruits from that Royalist town were prepared to join the enemy. Lilburne therefore fell back through Wigan, hoping to postpone fighting till he could effect a junction with the infantry regiment by this time advancing from Manchester to his help. Entangled in the lanes to the south of the town, he was compelled to fight in a position as disadvantageous to unprotected cavalry as it was possible to con-

Aug. 25.
Derby
defeated at
Wigan. ceive. In the end, however, superior discipline prevailed, and a complete victory was won. Many of the Royalist gentry were left dead or dying on the field. Four hundred prisoners fell into the hands of the victors.

---

[1] Peck's *Desiderata Curiosa*, 4 ; 1.

[2] ' Resolution of a Council of War,' Aug. 19, *Hist. MSS. Com.* Rep. xiii. App. i. 614.   [3] Hodgson's *Memoirs*, 152.

Derby himself fled, and ultimately rejoined the Royal army.
The danger of a rising in Lancashire was now at an end.[1]

In the meanwhile Charles had been pressing on, uncheered
by those manifestations of English feeling on which he had

Charles summons Shrewsbury. counted. As he passed near Shrewsbury he directed
an invitation to the Governor, Colonel Mackworth,
to surrender the place, telling him that he had
heard that he was ' of very different principles from those with

Mackworth's reply. whom' his employment at present ranked him.
Mackworth not only peremptorily refused to betray
his employers, but scornfully directed his answer to
the Commander-in-Chief of the Scottish army.[2] Mackworth
gained no slight credit by this timely sally. To command a
Scottish army was an insuperable bar to Charles's acknowledgment as an English king.

At last, on August 22, three days before the fight at Wigan,
Charles and his Scottish following marched into Worcester.

Aug. 22. Charles at Worcester. His army, exhausted and vastly dispirited by the
long march, pleaded for rest. Charles was welcomed
by the Corporation, and though a small body of horse
which had been sent by Lambert to occupy the place would
gladly have resisted, it was driven by popular pressure to cross
the Severn and retire to Gloucester.[3] The weary invaders were
in no case to follow.

Charles for one refused to acknowledge that the game was
played and lost. On the 23rd he issued an order that all

Aug. 23. Charles still hopeful. persons between the ages of sixteen and sixty should
meet on the 26th on Pitchcroft, a meadow on the
Severn bank, for the defence of the throne and the

Aug. 26. A political manifesto. liberties of the country. When the 26th arrived he
circulated a manifesto offering to settle religion

---

[1] Lilburne to Cromwell, Aug. 25 ; Lilburne to Lenthall, Aug. 25 ;
Cary's *Mem. of the Civil War*, ii. 338, 341 ; *A Great Victory*, E,
640, 27.

[2] *Merc. Pol.* E, 640, 23 ; *The Weekly Intelligencer*, E, 641, 2.

[3] Milward and others to Bradshaw, Aug. 23, Cary's *Mem. of the Civil
War*, ii. 335 ; *The Weekly Intelligencer*, E. 641, 2.

according to the Covenant, to satisfy the arrears of soldiers deserting from Cromwell's army, to assent to an Act of Oblivion for all who now abandoned the cause of the pretended Commonwealth, with the exception of Cromwell, Ireton, Bradshaw, Cook, and the others who had voted for the murder of his Royal father, or had merely sat in the High Court of Justice. No plundering was to be allowed, and as soon as the enemy had been crushed the Scottish army was to retire to its own country. If, as is not improbable, this manifesto was intended in the first place to be read to the multitude expected to assemble on Pitchcroft,[1] it failed entirely in its object.

English recruits do not come in.   Scarcely a man made his appearance at the rendezvous,[2] and Charles learnt that he must depend for his safety solely on the army which had followed him from Scotland.

The decisive moment could not be long delayed. On August 24, Cromwell effected a junction with Lambert and Harrison at Warwick. There, too, he found Lord Grey of Groby, who was able to assure him of the forwardness of the Midlands, whilst Fleetwood and Desborough were there to inform him of the forwardness of the South. On the 27th he took up his quarters at Evesham at the head of some 28,000 men. That he took so southerly a route is sufficient evidence that he had made up his mind as to his plan of action. The Scots, now numbering 16,000 at the utmost, had been doing their best to repair the half-demolished fortifications of Worcester, and their commanders, after leaving a strong garrison to man the walls, had sent the remainder of the army across the Severn, where they were lodged about a mile and a half from the city under such shelter as they could throw up.[3]

Aug. 24. Cromwell joins Lambert and Harrison.

Aug. 27. Cromwell at Evesham.

---

[1] The two declarations are in the *Historical Review* for 1890, p. 115. Their editor, Miss Constance Everett-Green, thinks that the second was issued after the disappointment on Pitchcroft. The explanation given above seems to me to be more probable.

[2] *The Weekly Intelligencer*, E, 641, 2.

[3] *Merc. Pol.* E, 641, 4.

Cromwell's obvious intention was to hinder them from drawing further westward, lest they should seek for shelter and reinforcements either in the Welsh mountains, or in Gloucester and Bristol, where the Royalist cause was thought likely to find considerable support.

Cromwell's superior numbers allowed him now to carry out in the neighbourhood of Worcester the operation which he would fain have carried out in July in the neighbourhood of Stirling.[1] He could now divide his army into two parts without exposing it to the risk of being crushed in detail. Whilst one division was to remain under his own command guarding the road to London, the other division, under Fleetwood and Lambert, was to cross the Severn and hem in the invaders on the south and west.

He resolves to divide his army.

Accordingly, on the 28th, Lambert with a party of horse and dragoons moved down to Upton, some miles below Worcester, where the bridge over the Severn had been broken by the enemy, who had about 300 men in the town on the other side. While the Scots were still ignorant of their danger eight of Lambert's dragoons clambered over a plank which had been left across the broken piers and threw themselves into the church. Before the enemy, aroused at last, succeeded in expelling them, a party of Lambert's cavalry waded or swam across the river, set fire to the church,[2] and drove the Scots to retreat. The bridge was hastily repaired, and Fleetwood, who was not far behind Lambert, despatched a force of infantry to guard it. Access to the western bank of the Severn was thus secured, and before long 11,000 men passed over the restored bridge.[3] In the struggle at Upton, Massey was severely wounded in the hand.[4]

Aug. 28. Upton Bridge secured.

Massey wounded.

---

[1] See p. 30.

[2] An old picture in possession of Mr. Thomas Collins at Tewkesbury shows the church in flames.

[3] A relation of the taking of the pass at Upton, *Several Proceedings*, E, 787, 12. For the position of Upton, see map at p. 33.

[4] Desborough to —— ? Aug. 31, *ib.*

Having thus secured both sides of the river, Cromwell had gained his first object. Before he could take the offensive further preparations were necessary. Not only must some means of communication between the two parts of the army be found nearer Worcester than Upton Bridge, but, if an attack was to be made against the Scots on the further bank, there must be some means of crossing the river Teme, which runs into the Severn from the west about a mile and a half below Worcester, Powick Bridge, the usual passage, having been destroyed by the Scots. For this purpose Cromwell ordered the construction of boats to support wooden bridges across the two streams.

Bridges of boats to be made.

Whilst this operation was being carried out Cromwell had everything to encourage him. Prisoners taken in occasional skirmishes told him of the growing despondency of the enemy. Massey it was said wished his young master 'safe in some foreign part.' It was believed in Cromwell's camp that on the 31st preparations had been made for the evasion of the cavalry with the King in their midst, but that the infantry had resisted them. To increase the prevailing depression the wounded Earl of Derby reached Worcester before the end of the day, and filled their ears with the tale of the slaughter at Wigan. On the other side everything was going well. Three thousand militia-men from Essex and Suffolk marched in to join Fleetwood, raising the whole English army to some 31,000. A smaller party of Worcestershire men secured the bridge at Bewdley. Other local forces occupied Ludlow and Hereford. Gloucester was securely held, and in Bristol at least the authorities declared for Parliament. In Devon 2,000 foot and 200 horse were ready to start. Two regiments from Norfolk and two more from Suffolk were on their march through Hitchin, and a force of militia from Cheshire was already embodied in the army. In Yorkshire 2,000 men had been raised to clear the country of malignants.[1] In London itself, where the feeling against the Commonwealth was usually very

Discouragement of the Scots.

Activity of the militia.

[1] *Merc. Pol.* E, 641, 4 ; *Several Proceedings*, E, 787, 12.

strong, no less than twelve regiments of the trained bands, numbering it may be presumed at least 12,000 men, were mustered to witness the burning by the hangman of a copy of Charles's manifesto [1] at the head of every regiment, an act of contempt which was received with general applause. [2]

Gratifying as this arousing of popular support must have been to Cromwell, he had force enough in hand to be free from dependence upon it. With an army disciplined and enthusiastic as his own, victory over a dispirited enemy at the highest calculation scarcely half his own numbers [3] was a foregone conclusion. In such a case it needs not, as at Naseby or Dunbar, to dwell on the details of the fight. All through the morning of September 3rd, the anniversary of Dunbar, Cromwell was anxiously waiting for the last touches to be put to his boats. At last, between two and three in the afternoon, the work was done. One bridge of boats was then flung across the Severn just above its junction with the Teme, and another over the Teme itself. Fleetwood's division first crossed the Teme. Cromwell in person came to his assistance, and hurried regiment after regiment across the Severn. The enemy, strongly posted behind hedges, resisted stoutly. Hopeless as their position was, it was not in Scottish nature to give way without a struggle, and it was only after severe fighting that the Scots were driven from their cover, and retreated sullenly across the bridge into Worcester.

Vict·ry assured to Cromwell.

Sept. 3. The bridges laid.

The battle of Worcester.

Scarcely was this advantage gained when the battle was re-kindled on the eastern side of the river. Charles and his advisers, watching the battle from the height of the cathedral tower, took advantage of the central position of the city to pour troops out of the Sidbury Gate against the forces now depleted by the absence of so many of their comrades who had gone to Fleetwood's help. Charles descending from the tower placed himself at the head of the troops, and with conspicuous gallantry

[1] See p. 41.   [2] *The Weekly Intelligencer*, E, 641, 11.
[3] Cromwell speaks of them as 16,000, but other estimates make them fewer. Cromwell to Lenthall, Sept. 4, *Carlyle*, Letter clxxxiii.

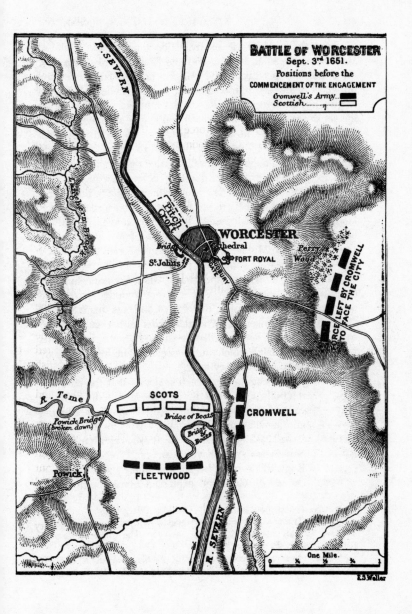

BATTLE OF WORCESTER
Sept. 3rd 1651.
Positions before the
COMMENCEMENT OF THE ENGAGEMENT
Cromwell's Army
Scottish

R. SEVERN

Pitch Croft

WORCESTER

Bridge
St. Johns
Cathedral
FORT ROYAL
SIDBURY

Perry Wood

FORCE LEFT BY CROMWELL TO FACE THE CITY

Long Brook

R. Teme

SCOTS

Bridge of Boats

CROMWELL

Powick Bridge
(broken down)

Bridge of Boats

Powick

FLEETWOOD

R. SEVERN

One Mile

E.S.Weller

fell upon the ranks of the enemy. For a moment the skilful movement proved successful, and the English ranks gave way, till Cromwell, perceiving the danger, hurried back over the bridge of boats with reinforcements, and compelled the Scots to give way in turn. Fort Royal, a strong advanced work at the south-eastern angle of the city walls, was stormed, and its guns turned on the now disorganised masses of the Scottish army pressed hard into the streets of the city. Great was the slaughter, though Cromwell at the risk of his own life rode up to the Scots to offer quarter. Save a few fugitives, all the survivors of the foot laid down their arms. The horse made its way out of the gates to force if possible a road to Scotland,[1] but not a man succeeded in reaching home. Hamilton had been sore wounded, and died after a few days' suffering. David Leslie and Middleton were taken near Rochdale. Derby and Lauderdale were captured by a captain of Lilburne's horse, which was now advancing southwards after accomplishing the subjugation of Lancashire. Massey, sore wounded, gave himself up to Lady Stamford at Broadgates, and was finally carried to London as a prisoner. The remainder either surrendered to the local militia, or were killed or captured by the inhabitants of the places through which they passed.[2] The invading army was annihilated as a military force.

Amongst the conquerors a feeling spread that the haven of internal peace had at last been gained. " When your wives and children," said Hugh Peters to the militia-men who had taken part in the battle, " shall ask you where you have been, and what news : say you have been at Worcester, where England's sorrows began, and where they are happily ended." [3] Cromwell expressed himself with almost

A feeling that peace has been secured.

Saying of Hugh Peters

and of Cromwell.

[1] *Merc. Pol.* E, 641, 2.

[2] Sir J. Turner's *Memoirs*, 95; Hodgson's *Memoirs*, 153; *Another Victory*, E, 641, 14; *Merc. Pol.* E, 641, 20; The Chester Prisoner's Letter, *Clar. St. P.* ii. 560.

[3] That is to say, at Powick Bridge. *A Perfect Diurnal*, E, 641, 15. So it was said that the ' Thirty Years' War ' began and ended at Prague.

equal assurance. "The dimensions of this mercy," he wrote to Lenthall, "are above my thoughts. It is, for aught I know, a crowning mercy. Surely if it be not, such a one we shall have if this provoke those that are concerned in it to thankfulness, and the Parliament to do the will of Him who hath done His will for it and for the nation, whose good pleasure it is to establish the nation and the change of government, by making the people so willing to the defence thereof, and so signally blessing the endeavours of your servants in this great work." [1]

" By making the people so willing to the defence thereof" —in this and in nothing else lay the significance of Worcester.

Part taken by the militia in the battle.   The military critic finds little to say about it ; but it stands out as the first combat since the day on which Waller's levies poured home after the fight at Cropredy Bridge, in which other than professional soldiers took part. It is probable that nearly if not quite a third of the victorious army consisted of local militia regiments. [2] It was the natural result of the system of war which Charles had elected to conduct. As long as the struggle lay between two English parties, it was left to the regular army on either side to carry on the contest. When it came to an invasion by a Scottish army, masses of Englishmen, who otherwise would have held back from exposing their own persons, eagerly threw themselves forward to defend their homes against those who were in that age regarded as foreigners.

Therefore was the victory gained at Worcester in very truth 'a crowning mercy.' Once more, in Cromwell's hand, the

In what sense was Worcester 'a crowning mercy'?   sword had decided not what should be, but what should not be. Two years and a half before it had decided that England should not be ruled by a faithless King who measured his obligations by the rule of his

[1] Cromwell to Lenthall, Sept. 4, *Carlyle*, Letter clxxxiii.

[2] There were about 3,000 from Cheshire and Staffordshire, 3,000 from Essex and Suffolk ; besides which we hear of Lord Grey's regiment from Leicestershire, and another regiment from Warwickshire, making in all about 8,000 men. It is also probable that Fleetwood and Desborough brought with them some numbers of militia-men.

own interests.   Now it decided that she should not be ruled by a King who came in as an invader.   When Charles I. was sent to the block, Cromwell had but the support of the army and of a handful of enthusiasts.   When he shattered the Scottish army at Worcester he had on his side the national spirit of England. Even amongst the Royalists themselves the current of feeling ran so strong that scarce a man of them would rally round the standard of their King as long as it was borne aloft by Scottish hands.   For the first time the founders of the Commonwealth were able to win considerable popular support for their cause.

As far as England was concerned, therefore, Worcester at least opened the prospect of a constitutional settlement other than a Royalist one.   As far as the relations between the three countries were concerned it was absolutely decisive.   England had shown herself strong enough to frustrate the attempts of Ireland and Scotland to dictate the terms on which her internal government was to be carried on.   From this verdict of battle there was not, could not be, any appeal.   So much of Cromwell's work endured without further challenge.

Constitutional prospect.

England, Ireland, and Scotland.

CHAPTER XVII

ENGLAND AFTER WORCESTER

ON the long list of prisoners the name of the man in whose name the invading army had been gathered was not to be found. On September 10, indeed, Parliament issued a proclamation declaring those who gave him shelter amenable to the penalties of treason, and offering a reward of 1,000*l.* for his capture.[1] Yet week after week passed away without tidings of the fugitive. Conjecture laboured in vain to account for the silence of rumour, the most plausible suggestion being that Charles had met with a soldier's death at Worcester, but that his swarthy complexion had rendered his corpse undistinguishable from those of inferior degree.[2] As late as October 13 the Council of State, having received information that Charles and Buckingham had at one time been heard of in Staffordshire, directed search to be made in those parts of England for their apprehension.[3] On the following day a circular letter was despatched to the custom-house officers at the ports, reminding them of the reward offered for the capture of Charles Stuart, and describing him as a tall man above two yards high, with dark-brown hair scarcely to be distinguished from black.[4] It was not till about a week later that it was known at Westminster that these efforts had been happily fruitless, and that the Commonwealth had been saved

Sept. 10.
Proclamation for the arrest of Charles Stuart.

Oct. 13.
Strict search ordered.

Oct. 14.

---

[1] *C.J.* vii. 15. [2] *The Diary*, E, 641, 25.
[3] C. of St. to Ley, Oct. 13; C. of St. to the officers of the Customs, Oct. 14, *Interr.* I, 96, p. 577. [4] *Ib.* p. 578.

from the temptation to deal with the son as it had formerly
dealt with the father.   Even if it had been necessary
that one Royal head should fall on the scaffold as
an example to future kings, that example did not
stand in need of repetition.

Charles's
escape
known.

In effecting his escape Charles had on his side the traditional loyalty to the Crown, strong in every part of England,
especially strong in those western districts in which
the great battle had been fought.   Yet, for all that,
he would hardly have avoided discovery but for his
ready wit and never-failing presence of mind.   It requires some
aptitude of moral and intellectual qualities successfully to play
the part of a hunted hare.   Where Charles I. would have
failed with dignity, Charles II. without any dignity at all was
triumphantly successful.

Causes of
his suc-
cessful
evasion.

Passing out of Worcester with the ruck of mounted fugitives, Charles found himself not long before nightfall on the
road for Scotland.   Knowing better than to trust
himself to a rout of beaten men, he slipped aside in
the dark with about sixty of his immediate followers,
amongst whom were Buckingham, Derby, Lauderdale, and
Wilmot.   Halting not far from Kidderminster to take counsel,
Derby told him how, a few days earlier, on his own flight from
Wigan, he had been sheltered at the old timbered house of
Boscobel, by a certain William Penderel who was employed as
a caretaker by its owner, a Mr. Giffard.   Giffard himself was
amongst the company, and at once offered to conduct Charles
to Whiteladies, a house about half a mile short of Boscobel
owned by another member of his family, and the offer, freely
given, was accepted gladly.

Sept. 3.
Charles's
flight from
Worcester.

In the course which he adopted Charles had consulted well
for his own interests.   As at the time of the Gunpowder Plot,
houses belonging to the Catholic gentry were thickly
strewn over the Western Midlands, each one containing a secret chamber which had often served as a
refuge for fugitive priests, and would serve equally as a refuge
for a fugitive king.   Puritan governments had taken good care

Charles
finds
' priests'
chambers.'

that Charles should be absolutely secure of the devotion of every Catholic in England.

It was by this time the morning of the 4th, and Charles was committed to the care of William and Richard Penderel, two

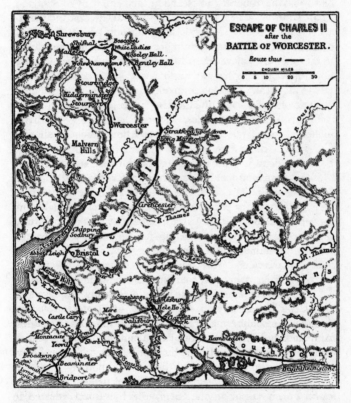

of five brothers who were all of them in a small way tenants or servants of the Giffards, and who could be trusted to the death. By their advice Charles rubbed his face with soot from the chimney, stripped himself of his ornaments and garments and put on in their place a well-

Sept. 4.
Charles at
White-
ladies.

E 2

worn suit belonging to Richard Penderel. Before, however, his disguise was completed, news was brought that about 3,000 of the Scottish horse were on Tong Heath under David Leslie. Charles's suite, with the exception of Wilmot, all rode off to join them, hoping to escape in their company to Scotland. Charles himself had no confidence in runaways, and refused to accompany them. " Men," he afterwards explained, " who had deserted me when they were in good order, would never stand to me when they have been beaten." His own idea was the bold one of finding his way on foot to London. It may be he was in the right. The place in which danger appears to be the greatest often furnishes the most secure concealment.[1]

For the present Charles, warned that a troop of Parliamentary horse was in the neighbourhood, was hidden by Richard Penderel in a coppice. Learning that Penderel had no knowledge of the road to London, he resolved to abandon his original idea and to make for Wales. The ferry over the Severn was, however, found to be guarded, and after passing the better part of the night and the whole of the following day in a barn at Madeley, Charles set out after nightfall on the 5th for Boscobel, his face and hands duly stained with walnut juice. On his arrival on the morning of the 6th Major Carlos, another fugitive from Worcester, told him that the hiding-place in the house was unsafe, as it would certainly be discovered by the soldiers already on the look-out for escaped Royalists, and that a neighbouring wood in which he himself had hitherto lain concealed was likely to be also the object of their search. At Carlos's recommendation, the pair, taking with them some bread and cheese and small beer, ' and nothing else '—as Charles afterwards ruefully explained—climbed into an oak in an open field, which was too isolated to attract attention, and which bore foliage sufficiently thick to prove a shelter against persons viewing it from a

He fails to escape into Wales.

Sept. 5. He hides at Madeley.

Sept. 6. Charles in the oak,

---

[1] See, for instance, the curious account given by Sir James Turner in his *Memoirs* of his own escape and hiding in London.

distance. During the course of the day the pair, ensconced amongst the boughs, could see the soldiers investigating the recesses of the wood, none of whom, however, drew nigh the spot in which the prize was to be found.[1] When evening came Charles, accompanied by Carlos, descended to the *and at* ground, enjoyed a good supper in Boscobel House, *Boscobel.* and slept in the little closet in which the Earl of Derby had been concealed on his way to Worcester. To *Sept. 7.* provide breakfast for the morning, William Penderel stuck his knife into a sheep in a neighbouring fold, and brought it off. Charles, ready to turn his hand to anything, cut slices from the leg, and put them into the frying-pan.

By the evening of the 7th a new refuge was found for Charles. John Penderel, who was rendering the same services to Wilmot that his brothers were rendering to the King, had fallen in with Father Huddleston—a priest who lived to reconcile Charles on his death-bed to the Roman Catholic Church—and through his mediation had obtained a shelter for the fugitive Cavaliers at Moseley Hall, the house of a Catholic gentleman named Whitgreave. Wilmot in the midst of his own trouble did not forget the King's, and telling Whitgreave of an unnamed friend in hiding, obtained permission to invite him to the house.

Accordingly Charles set out on the evening of the 7th under the care of the five Penderels and of a certain Francis Yates. Not far from the house he was met by Huddleston and Whitgreave. The two brought him to Wilmot in his hiding- *Sept. 8.* place, from whom Whitgreave for the first time *Charles* learned the name of the stranger. Charles, worn out *at Moseley* *Hall.* as he was, craved for rest, but no rest was to be had except in a narrow hiding-place, in which sleep was sought in vain.

At Wilmot's suggestion a new plan of escape dawned upon Charles. Colonel Lane of Bentley Hall had a sister, Jane Lane,

---

[1] 'A great oak in a pretty place,' writes Charles. It is certainly untrue that Parliamentary soldiers rode under it. "Whiles we," as Charles told the story, "were in this tree, we see soldiers going up and down in the thicket of the wood searching for persons escaped, we seeing them now and then peeping out of the wood."

who had obtained a pass to visit a friend at Abbotsleigh near Bristol accompanied by a man-servant. It had been arranged that Wilmot should personate her attendant, and it was now determined that Charles should be substituted for Wilmot. For the present, however, so many soldiers were about that it was unsafe to start. One party of them visited Moseley Hall, and Charles had to be thrust into the 'priest's hole.' Another party plundered Boscobel, whilst a third searched Whiteladies, broke down the wainscot, and finding nothing behind it beat the men who had led them there.

Charles in a 'priest's hole.'

It was not till the evening of the 9th that Charles was able to make his way to Bentley Hall. The next morning he started on horseback on his adventurous journey with Jane Lane on the pillion behind him. In the matter of clothing, Will Jackson, as he was now called, was certainly better off than before. The old worn leather doublet and green breeches were discarded for a new suit and cloak of grey cloth, suitable to a farmer's son on a holiday.

Sept. 9. Goes to Bentley Hall.

Sept. 10. Starts with Jane Lane.

The disguise thus obtained, being supported by a ready wit, proved sufficient, the pair even passing through a party of soldiers without suspicion. On the way, however, Charles's horse cast a shoe. Taking it to a forge he asked the blacksmith for news. "There is no news that I know of," replied the man, " since the good news of the beating the rogues the Scots." He had not heard, he added, that 'that rogue Charles Stuart had been taken.' "If that rogue," answered Charles calmly, " were taken, he deserves to be hanged more than the rest for bringing in the Scots." "You speak," said the smith, "like an honest man." Arriving at Long Marston, where they were to pass the night, Charles pushed his way into the kitchen, and was at once asked by the cook to wind up the jack. " What countryman are you," called out the maid as his bungling hands sought in vain to fulfil the task, " that you know not how to wind up a jack?" " I," replied Charles humbly, " am a poor tenant's son of Colonel Lane, in Staffordshire ; we seldom have roast meat, but when we have, we don't make use of a jack."

Fencing with questioners.

After various adventures Abbotsleigh was safely reached. Charles hoped to find shipping at Bristol, but this desire being frustrated, he made his way to Trent, Colonel Francis Windham's house near Sherborne, whence he intended to make his way to the coast, and so escape to France. Jane Lane, leaving him in

Charles at Abbotsleigh and Trent.

trusty hands, turned back to Abbotsleigh. In passing into the South, Charles had exchanged the hospitality of Catholics for the hospitality of Cavaliers. Both were inspired by loyalty equally unswerving. In one respect his chances had improved. At such a distance from Worcester he had no longer to fear any deliberate search for the fugitives from the field of slaughter. Nevertheless he was still at the mercy of accident. It would go hard with him if his face were once recognised by any hostile person. What made in his favour was that he had never been in Dorsetshire, and in days when travelling was a luxury reserved for the well-to-do, the chance of his being met by anyone who had seen him when he kept court in Devon or Cornwall was not very great.

Charles's stay at Trent was not without its amusing incidents. One day a trooper who rode into the village sought to give himself importance by announcing that he had killed Charles Stuart and had taken from him the buff coat now on his own

He witnesses rejoicings for his own death.

back. The villagers at once crowded to the churchyard, lit a bonfire and rang the bells. Charles watched the celebration of his own death, not, as may be imagined, without an adequate sense of the humour of the situation.

After some delay arrangements were made for the escape of himself and Wilmot, who had sometimes followed, sometimes accompanied him in his wanderings. The pair rode into Charmouth, where one Limbry agreed to carry them across the Channel, though they took care only

Sept. 22. He goes to Charmouth.

to inform him that some Royalist fugitives needed his help and were willing to pay him 60*l.* if he would land them safely in France.

Failure of his attempt to escape.

The night of the 22nd was fixed for the voyage. Unluckily Limbry confided the secret—so far as he knew it—to his wife, and she, taking fright lest her

husband should be subjected to the penalties suspended by
Parliament over the heads of those who assisted Charles Stuart
or his abettors to escape, turned the key upon the unfortunate
mariner and threatened to give information to a Parliamentary
officer at Bridport if he attempted to force his way out.

In the meanwhile Charles was in no slight danger of discovery. The ostler of the inn in which he was concealed
formed suspicions of his identity—suspicions confirmed by the
remark of a blacksmith to whom he led Wilmot's horse to be
shod, that the other three shoes had been set in three several
counties, and one of them in Worcestershire. The man gave
information to a neighbouring minister, who at once hurried to
the spot only to find the inn deserted by its guests. " How
now, Margaret," said the minister to the landlady.
" You are a maid of honour now." " Charles Stuart,"
he replied to her surprised inquiry as to his meaning,
" lay last night at your house, and kissed you at his departure ;
so that now you cannot but be a maid of honour." " If I
thought it was the King," answered the landlady, "as you say
it was, I should think the better of my lips all the days of my
life ; and so, Mr. Parson, get you out of my house or else I'll
get those shall kick you out."

Sept. 23.
Charles
leaves Char-
mouth.

Charles soon found the part of the country in which he was
too hot to hold him. Bridport and its neighbourhood were full
of soldiers, and the Royal fugitive had to forsake the coast.
Making his way through Wiltshire, and always finding a welcome
in the houses of Royalist country gentlemen, he reached on
October 14 what was then the fishing village of Brighthelmstone.
A Captain Tattersal, whose vessel, captured by the Royal fleet
in 1648, had been released by Charles's order, gratefully promised to convey his benefactor to a place of safety. Charles
accepted the offer, but prudently kept the honest seaman
smoking and drinking all night long, lest if he were
allowed to visit his home, he too might be locked up
by his wife. Early in the morning of the 15th the
vessel which bore the hope of English Royalists put
to sea. On the following morning Charles, after a

Oct. 15.
Charles
at sea.

Oct. 16.
He lands at
Fécamp,

month and thirteen days of adventurous wandering, set foot
on the hospitable soil of France at Fécamp.[1]   On the
Oct. 19.
and reaches 19th he was welcomed at the Louvre by his mother
the Louvre.
and his brother James.[2]

Charles   Charles was now to exchange a life of dangerous
again in
exile.   but, for one of his temperament, not altogether un-
pleasing excitement, for the dull routine, lightened only by
flickering hopes, of an exile's career.   For a time he found
Charles's   consolation in relating, to all who were ready to listen,
fictitious
account of   a tale of fictitious adventures concocted with the
his escape.   laudable purpose of shielding those who had assisted
in his escape from the vengeance of the ruling powers.   He
therefore asserted that he owed his preservation after the
battle, not to the Penderels or Jane Lane, but to a soldier who,
having been formerly a highwayman, was thoroughly acquainted
with every by-path in the neighbourhood.   He further declared
that after his concealment in the oak, he had made his way to
London, where he had passed through the streets in the disguise of a washerwoman carrying a basket of linen on his head.
Charles in relating this story forgot that the appearance of a
washerwoman more than six feet in height would have been
more likely to attract attention than to elude it.[3]

On one point at least Charles made no attempt to conceal
the truth.   He complained bitterly of the misconduct of the
His lan-   Scots.   To the Duke of Orleans, who mentioned a
guage about   rumour that he meant to return to Scotland, he re-
the Scots.
plied curtly, " I had rather have been hanged." [4]
For the present, Charles's association with Scottish invaders
had alienated not only moderate men in England, but had
even depressed the courage of his own partisans.   Time, however, was on his side.   Light-heartedness combined with ready

[1] The various accounts of Charles's wanderings are collected in
Hughes's *Boscobel Tracts*. [See also *The Flight of the King*, by Allan Fea,
1897.]

[2] Letter from Paris, October $\frac{21}{31}$, *Several Proceedings*, E, 788 6.

[3] Morosini to the Doge, $\frac{Oct. 28}{Nov. 7}$, *Venetian Transcripts*, *R.O.*

[4] N. N. to ——? Nov. $\frac{1}{11}$, *S.P. Dom.* xvi. 84.

wit exercises a power over human hearts, which the serious and earnest-minded often vainly seek to gain.

For the present the tide of national feeling provoked by the Scottish invasion was running on the side of the Common-

National feeling on the side of the Commonwealth.

wealth. In seeking to profit by the situation, the Parliamentary leaders naturally turned to the man by whom the deliverance had been wrought. On Sep-

Sept. 9. Cromwell invited to Westminster.

tember 9, Parliament despatched a deputation consisting of Whitelocke, St. John, and Pickering, to offer its congratulations to Cromwell and to invite him to choose a residence near Westminster in order that he might while reposing from his labours give the members the benefit of his advice on matters of public concern.[1] On

Sept. 12. Cromwell's return.

the 12th the victorious commander, after enjoying a day's hawking at the invitation of the Mayor of Aylesbury, was welcomed back to Westminster with official pomp and with demonstrations of unpremeditated joy.[2]

Sept. 16. Is thanked by Parliament.

On the 16th, when he made his first appearance in the House, he received the formal thanks of Parliament. An Act was already under discussion for settling upon him lands to the value of 4,000l. a year, in addition to those previously bestowed upon him.[3] Some months earlier the reformed University of Oxford had elected him its Chancellor.[4]

With these honours thrust upon him, there were not wanting some who predicted that Cromwell would soon be master of

Cromwell's position.

the State. "This man," thought Peters, "will be King of England yet."[5] A militant scholar, Francis Nelson, burst forth into most un-Horatian sapphics in which he extolled the conqueror by the dubious titles of *Imperator* and *Dominus*.[6] Yet even those who loved him least were driven to

---

[1] *C.J.* vii. 13.

[2] *Another Victory*, E, 641, 14.   [3] *C.J.* vii. 15.

[4] Cromwell to the Vice-Chancellor and Convocation, Feb. 4, *Carlyle*, Letter clxvi.   [5] Ludlow's *Memoirs*, i. 282.

[6] The verses are addressed 'per Franciscum Nelson militem Academicum (*The last News from the King of Scots*, E, 641, 24), honora-

confess that there was nothing imperious in his demeanour. His affability and his eagerness to establish the Commonwealth on a basis of moderation were on everyone's tongue.[1]

The question immediately at issue was the treatment to be accorded to the prisoners of war. The horsemen from whom The Charles had parted so unceremoniously at Kidder-prisoners. minster were no more fortunate than the foot soldiers who had laid down their arms in Worcester itself. Attacked by the inhabitants of the districts through which they passed, they were forced to surrender in large numbers. So cowed were they that a party of noblemen, including the Earls of Derby and Lauderdale, gave themselves up on promise of quarter to a solitary captain.[2]

On September 11, before Cromwell reached London, Par-liament resolved that nine persons, the Duke of Hamilton, Sept. 11. the Earls of Derby, Cleveland and Lauderdale, Nine Massey, the Mayor and Sheriff of Worcester who had prisoners to be tried. proclaimed Charles as King, together with two of

tissimo, invictissimoque Imperatori, Domino Olivero Cromwell.' The last two stanzas may serve as a specimen.

> " Irruunt Urbem rapiuntque prædas,
>   Atque jactantes repulere Scotos,
>   In fugâ tristi cecidere strage
>   Te duce Cromwell.

> " Ista norunt Presbyterique lugent ;
>   Ast ovant Angli celebri triumpho,
>   Imperatoris celebranda dignis
>   Fama trophæis."

[1] The praises of newspaper writers, all party-hacks, are of little moment, but the testimony of Salvetti, no friend to republican institutions, may fairly be accepted. In his despatch of October $\frac{3}{13}$ he writes that Cromwell is both zealous and popular ' et veramente non si scuopre in lui altra ambizione che quella del bene publico, verso del quale impiega tutto il suo spirito et credito, il quale è tale, et è usato da sua Eccelenza con tanto umiltà et respetto verso di ognuno, che viene honorato et stimato (oltre il suo gran valore) per huomo mandato dal cielo per stabilire per servizio celeste questa republica.' *Add. MSS.* 27,962, fol. 251.

[2] *Merc. Pol.* E, 648, 12 ; Hodgson's *Memoirs*, 155.

Derby's officers, Sir Timothy Fetherstonhaugh and Captain Benbow, should be selected for trial.[1] Of these Hamilton had *Hamilton's death.* died of his wounds four days after the battle, Derby and his two followers were lying in prison at Chester, whilst Massey, grievously but not mortally wounded, was in custody at Leicester. On the 13th, in the company *Sept. 13. Arrival of Lauderdale and Cleveland.* of 4,000 prisoners of lower rank, Lauderdale and Cleveland were conducted through the streets to the Tower. " O my Lord," cried a carman to Lauderdale as he passed along Cornhill in his coach, " you are welcome to London. I protest off goes your head as round as a hoop ! " [2] There were Presbyterians enough in London to give assurance at least of sympathy to the Scottish prisoners at the end of their weary tramp. Friendly hands pressed on them offerings of money and of ' good white bread.' [3]

As might have been expected, the feeling in Parliament ran more strongly against the English who had assisted the Scots than against the Scots themselves. In virtue of an Act passed on August 12 directing the trial by a court-martial of persons holding correspondence with Charles Stuart [4] or abetting his *Courts-martial appointed by Cromwell.* cause, Cromwell had issued commissions for the establishment of such courts, and this action had received the approval of the Council of State.[5] Of the English who had supported Charles none were more obnoxious than those who had gathered round Derby in Lancashire, where alone the proposals of the Cavaliers to promote local risings had been even partially carried into execution. On September 5, in the first flush of excitement caused by the good news from Worcester, the Council of State directed that not only the officers but every tenth private soldier captured at Wigan should be brought to trial.[6] It is possible that some

---

[1] *C.J.* vii. 16.   [2] *The Charge against the Earl of Derby*, E, 641, 18.

[3] *Another Victory*, E, 641, 14.

[4] *Act Prohibiting Correspondence with Charles Stuart*, 669, f. 16.

[5] C. of St. Order Book, *Interr.* I, 22, p. 29.

[6] *Ib.* 22, p. 28. Mrs. Everett Green, in her preface to the *Calendar of* 1651, speaking of those taken at or after the battle of Worcester, writes:

persons were tried and even executed by courts-martial in the counties round Worcester, but the silence of Royalist writers is sufficient evidence that the sufferers cannot have been many, whilst as for the private soldiers taken in Lancashire, they were not even tried.

Merciful as, in spite of its first resolution, the Government was inclined to be, it could not pass over the leaders of the Lancashire rising. On October 1, three of the eight survivors amongst the prisoners selected for trial, the Earl of Derby and his two officers, were brought before a court-martial sitting at Chester on the charge of abetting the invasion of Charles Stuart. In vain they pleaded, as Hamilton and Capel had pleaded before, that they had been admitted to quarter by their captors. They were told that quarter was given to enemies, not to traitors.[1] Sentence of death having been passed, Derby appealed to Parliament for pardon and offered to surrender the Isle of Man, still held for himself as King of Man by his Countess, the Lady of Lathom.[2] His petition was strongly supported by Cromwell, either because, as some thought, he was anxious to secure the Isle of Man without bloodshed, or, as is far more probable, because he believed clemency to be the surest means

Oct. 1.
Trial of Derby and his officers.

The sentence.

Oct. 11.
Derby's petition.

" Of the common prisoners, those who were English were decimated, and the tenth man shot." For this statement she gives no authority, and I have not succeeded in finding evidence for it. It is surely conclusive against this barbarous story that neither Heath nor Bate, who may be trusted to report any harsh action of the Commonwealth, says anything about the matter. I have no doubt that Mrs. Everett Green's statement was based on a vague recollection of the passage in the Order Book cited above, which, as it refers to a letter directed to the Militia Commissioners of Lancashire, can only refer to the prisoners taken at Wigan. The court-martial for the trial of Lancashire prisoners sat at Chester, and Heath's statement that only ten were there tried and only five executed is conclusive. *Brief Chronicle*, 563.

[1] *The Perfect Trial . . . of the Earl of Derby ; The Diary*, E, 643, 10, 15.

[2] Derby to Lenthall : *Tracts relating to Military Proceedings in Lancashire* (Chetham Soc.), 368.

of smoothing down the asperities which lay in the way of the victorious Commonwealth.[1]

Cromwell's intervention was unsuccessful, and Parliament refused to interfere with the sentence of the Court. Derby himself was carried to die at Bolton-le-Moors, because when in 1644 he had stormed it in conjunction with Rupert, he had slain with his own hand one of his servants who had joined the

Oct. 15.
His
execution. Parliamentary cause. The 15th was fixed as the day of execution. The Earl's bearing on the scaffold did not belie the high character he bore. "Return it," he said to his son, as he handed him the insignia of the Garter, "to my gracious Sovereign when you shall be so happy as to see him, and say I sent it in all humility and gratitude as I received it spotless and free from any stain according to the example of my loyal ancestors."[2] The headsman's axe ended a life which if it had been prolonged would have been embittered by the spectacle of the triumph of the men whom the Earl and those who thought with him counted as the vilest of traitors.

Benbow
shot. On the same day that the Earl was executed, Benbow was shot to death at Shrewsbury. On the 22nd

Oct. 22.
Fether-
stonhaugh
beheaded. Fetherstonhaugh was beheaded at Chester. Seven other persons were condemned to death by the Chester court-martial, but only two of these were put to death.[3]

Clemency in short was slowly gaining the upper hand. On

Oct. 15.
Pardon
of Love's
accomplices. October 15, the day on which the Earl of Derby was executed, Parliament resolved to pardon nine of Love's accomplices who had acknowledged their guilt

[1] Salvetti, who appears at this time to have had good sources of information, writes that Cromwell 'fa quanto puote per salvarlo,' Salvetti's Despatch, Oct. $\frac{10}{20}$, *Add. MSS.* 27,962 N, fol. 254. Writing again, on Oct. $\frac{17}{27}$, he declares that 'verso di quale,' *i.e.* the Earl, 'il General Cromwell fa buonissimi uffizii per salvarlo la vita, ma con conditione che consegni nelle mani del Parlamento la sua isoletta di Man, della quale se ne intitola Rè.' *Ib.* fol. 258 b.

[2] Particulars of the last days of the Earl and his officers have been collected in *Tracts relating to Military Proceedings in Lancashire* (Chetham Soc.).   [3] See p. 60, note 6.

before the High Court of Justice.[1]　On November 6 it refused to allow a vote to be taken on the question that the Earl of Cleveland, one of the five who still survived out of those other nine who had been selected for trial from amongst the Worcester prisoners,[2] should be brought before the Court.[3]　No further attempt was made to try either the five, or any others who had been subsequently selected, and Parliament contented itself with keeping in the Tower the leaders, Scottish or English, whose lives it had at one time intended to take.　In course of time Massey and Middleton succeeded in effecting an escape.　Others, like Lauderdale and David Leslie, remained in confinement till the Restoration.

The same tendency towards a milder treatment is to be marked in the resolutions taken with respect to the private soldiers and the inferior officers.　On September 16 the Council of State appointed a Committee to send all under the degree of a field officer to the plantations.[4]　Barbados not being at this time available, the first thought of the newly appointed Committee was to sell the prisoners for foreign military service.　As no buyers appeared, a proposal was made to the merchants trading with Guinea, that they should pay for the privilege of carrying off the captives to work as slaves in the gold-mines on that unhealthy coast.[5]　Happily nothing came of this barbarous project.[6]

Sept. 16. A Committee to dispose of the prisoners.

First proposals of the Committee.

Less cruel was the despatch to Bristol of 1,000 prisoners still remaining in the country between Worcester and Chester.　From Bristol they were to

Prisoners to be sent to New England.

---

[1] *C.J.* vii. 28.　　　[2] See p. 59.　　　[3] *C.J.* vii. 36.

[4] C. of St. Order Book, *Interr.* I, 22, p. 52.

[5] Salvetti's Newsletters, Sept. $\frac{18}{28}$, $\frac{\text{Sept. } 26}{\text{Oct. } 6}$, *Add. MSS.* 27,962 N, fol. 244 b, 247 b.　On the mines in Guinea, see *The Golden Coast* (1655), 1298, c. 2.

[6] It is true that under date of Sept. 20, *The Weekly Intelligencer*, E, 614, 21, speaks of 1,500 being in several barges embarked by some merchants, to be employed in the mines at Guinea.　Salvetti, however, writing six days later, speaks of the matter as being still in negotiation, and no more is heard of it.

be carried to New England, where they would have the benefit
of a more salubrious air, and, unless they were less fortunate
than the Dunbar prisoners,[1] would meet with far kinder treatment than they would have received from the planters of Barbados. Their ultimate fate cannot, however, be ascertained.
Though they reached Bristol the merchants who had agreed to
transport them thence broke their contract, and it is possible
that these prisoners never crossed the Atlantic.[2]

The 4,000 Scottish soldiers in London were a source of
embarrassment to the Government. Though it was thought

Prisoners in sufficient to dole out to them a miserable allowance
London.   of biscuit and cheese valued at $2\frac{1}{2}d.$ a day,[3]
even this expense was felt to be a considerable burden.
Efforts of various kinds were therefore made to get rid of
captives who might prove dangerous if restored to their native

Sept. 25.   land. On September 25, members of Parliament
Various   and other well-affected persons were authorised to
projects.   select prisoners—apparently for enforced service—

Sept. 30.   on giving security for their safe custody.[4] On the 30th
there was an order for the discharge of a considerable number
of officers whose rank was not higher than that of a captain, provided that they were willing to give security to leave the country
and never to return either to Scotland or to any territory under

Oct. 1.   the jurisdiction of the Commonwealth.[5] On Octo-
            ber 1, 1,000 were given up to the adventurers for
draining the Fens on condition of an engagement to pay 10l.
for every man who effected his escape to Scotland in excess of
10 per cent., a number which appears to have been expected

---

[1] See vol. i. 296.

[2] The fate of these men can be traced in successive entries in the
Order Books. For the failure of the contractors, see Order in Parl.
Nov. 28, *Interr.* I, 89, p. 80, and the C. of St. to Powell, *ib.* I, 97, p. 1.
After this no more is heard of these prisoners. They may have been sent
back to Scotland under the order of Dec. 17, mentioned in the following
page.   [3] Subsequently raised to 4d. a day.

[4] C. of St. Order Book, *Interr.* I, 22, p. 74.

[5] *Ib.* 23, p. 3.

to cover the desertion certain to occur in spite of all reasonable
precautions.[1]   On the 9th all Scottish prisoners who
had been private soldiers and were confined either at
Tothill Fields or at York were handed over on the same terms,
and on the 14th it was resolved that the prisoners at
Newcastle and Durham, that is to say, the remnants
of the vanquished of Dunbar, should share the same fate.[2]   A
few days later, on October 27, an order was made
for the transportation to Bermuda of some of the
prisoners.   Before the end of the year those who still remained
on hand were either too sickly or too few to be considered
dangerous, and on December 17 the Committee for
Prisoners was empowered to send those about London
back to their own country and to provide them with clothing
and money for the journey.[3]

For some at least of the English prisoners a harder fate
seemed at one time to be reserved.   On October 25, twenty of
them were selected for trial by a court-martial.[4]   On
November 6, however, they were still living,[5] and
there is no evidence that any one of them was put
to death.   On December 16, the Council of State
directed that the whole of the English prisoners then
at St. James's should be sent to Ireland to serve the
Commonwealth, and they were accordingly liberated
on giving security to present themselves at Chester on April 25.[6]
Harsh as was the measure dealt out to the prisoners of both
nations, it was at least somewhat less harsh than that which
had been at first designed for them.

Oct. 9.
Oct. 14.
Oct. 27.
Dec. 17.
Oct. 25.
Twenty English prisoners to be tried.
Dec. 16. English prisoners sent to Ireland.

---

[1] C. of St. Order Book, *Interr.* I, 23, p. 9.

[2] *Ib.* p. 35.

[3] *Ib.* 66, p. 79.   The order of Dec. 4 appointing a committee with
powers to send prisoners to the Plantations is merely a renewal by the
fourth Council of State of the order given on Oct. 16 by the third.

[4] *Interr.* I, 96, p. 591.

[5] *Ib.* 24, p. 10.   Mrs. Everett Green (*Calendar* 1651–2, Preface,
p. vii) says that they were executed, but gives no authority for her statement.

[6] *Ib.* 66, p. 144.

On most, if not on all of these steps Cromwell had been duly consulted.   It is likely enough that the growth of the ex-

Cromwell
consulted.

ternal power of the Commonwealth had somewhat softened the indignation with which he had at first regarded the defeated invaders.   It was known by this time that

Monk in
Scotland.

there was no longer any force in Scotland capable of making head against Monk.   On August 14, the

Aug. 14.
Surrender
of Stirling
Castle.

garrison of Stirling Castle mutinied and compelled the governor to surrender.   Monk then directed his steps against Dundee.   Before the siege was formally opened news arrived that Leven with the Committee of Estates had met at Alyth to consult about raising forces for the relief

Aug. 28.
Capture of
Leven and
the Com-
mittee of
Estates.

of the town.   On the 28th Colonel Alured at the head of a picked force dashed into Alyth and captured Leven himself together with the Earl Marischal, the Earl of Crawford and Lindsay, and more than thirty of the principal nobles and gentlemen remaining in Scotland.   The prisoners having been shipped for England and all semblance of a national authority being thus brought to an end in Scotland, Monk was able to complete his preparations for the siege of Dundee.[1]

To Monk's summons the governor, Robert Lumsden, returned an insulting reply, calling on the English commander

Dundee
summoned,

to submit to the authority of the King.[2]   On September 1, breaches having been effected, the place

Sept. 1,
and
stormed.

was stormed.   Townsmen and soldiers, ignorant that their only hope of succour had been destroyed by the capture of the Committee of Estates at Alyth, had combined in manning the walls and were involved in indiscriminate ruin.   Some four or five hundred were slain on the breaches or in the streets behind them.   The governor, taking refuge in the steeple of the church, was dragged down and slain.   After the slaughter of numbers variously given at 500 and 800, the

---

[1] A narrative . . . of the proceedings of the forces under Lieut.-Gen. Monk, Firth's *Scotland and the Commonwealth*, 1.   Compare Blair's *Life* (Wodrow Soc.), 280, and notices in the English newspapers.

[2] *Perf. Passages*, E, 187, 17.

remainder of the defenders were pushed back into the market-place, and there, when all possibility of further resistance was at an end, quarter was at last given and prisoners made. It is probable enough that before resistance ceased some women and children and some inhabitants not in arms shared the fate of the combatants on the wall. Then followed by Monk's permission twenty-four hours of plunder. For some days afterwards soldiers walked the streets in gay apparel with a store of gold and silver in their pockets, to the value, it was reported, of no less than 200,000*l*., many of the inhabitants of other places having deposited their property in Dundee.[1]

---

[1] That townspeople were killed besides soldiers is clear, but I have little doubt that most of them took part in the defence, though ineffi-ciently. The narrative quoted above gives the following account : "About 11 of the clock the signal was given, and breaches being made into the enemy's forts on the east and west side of the town, our men entered and after about half an hour's hot dispute, divers of the enemy retreated to the church and steeple, and amongst the rest the governor, who was killed with between four and five hundred soldiers and towns-men. When our soldiers got to the market-place they gave quarter and took about 500 prisoners, and among the rest Colonel Coningham, governor of Stirling, who was in the town with many of his soldiers which marched thence. The soldiers had the plunder of the town for all that day and night, and had very large prize, many inhabitants of Edinburgh and other places having sent their ware and gear thither. There was about a 190 sail of ships in the harbour of 10, 6 and 4 guns which were all prize. . . . By the best testimony we could get, the townspeople were most obstinate against a rendition upon terms, being confident of their own works and strength, having formerly beat out Montrose, but they have now suffered for it and paid dearly for their contempt." Monk's own despatch to Cromwell of Sept. 1 (Cary's *Mem. of the Civil War*, ii. 351) says that there were in the town 'about 800 soldiers besides the townsmen,' and that about 500 of the enemy were killed and about 200 taken prisoners. Clarke, writing on the 5th, says, 'There were 1,500 upon the line when we stormed, and now we come to bury the dead . . . we find that there was near 800 killed.' (*Ib.* ii. 366.) The slain and prisoners were therefore more than the number of the soldiers. That the townsmen joined the defence is stated in *The Faithful Scout*, E, 787, 18, where we are told that 'the townsmen and soldiers for two hours manfully defended it.' This is borne out by the

F 2

The massacre at Dundee followed the example of Wexford rather than of Drogheda. No direct order for slaughter is traceable to Monk, but on the other hand he made no effort to restrain the savagery of his soldiers. It is probable that he took the scene of bloodshed as a matter of course, merely following the ordinary military law of the time. He certainly did not expose himself to danger, as Cromwell had done when the defences of Worcester[1] were broken down, in order to plead with the scarcely resisting foeman to bend himself to the acceptance of quarter. No cruelty was needed to terrify other garrisons into submission. Scotland was at Monk's feet, before Dundee was stormed. Such places as still held out in the West were throwing themselves into the hands of his lieutenants. In the North, Montrose and Aberdeen rapidly gave in their submission. Finally, on November 21, Huntly agreed to disband the forces which

Nov. 21.
Huntly's
submission.

Scottish diarists. Lamont says (*Diary*, 34), 'The townspeople were secure, and surprised at unawares.' Balfour (iv. 315) states at greater length that "Monk commanded all of whatsomever sex to be put to the edge of the sword. The townsmen did no duty in their own defence, but were most of them all drunken like so many beasts. There were 800 inhabitants and soldiers killed, and about 200 women and children." Though it may be doubted whether Monk gave orders to kill all 'of whatsomever sex,' Balfour's idea evidently is that the townspeople were appointed to share in defending the wall, but were too drunk to do it efficiently, a statement which is probably an exaggeration. Nicolls (*Diary*, 58) says that Duffus, *i.e.* Lumsden, 'governor of the town and the townsmen, being ignorant what was done to the persons of the foresaid committee, and looking for help from them, stood stoutly to their posture, and defended themselves;—but they being disappointed, they were overcome, the walls of the town slung down, and the enemy coming in furiously upon the people, put all that were found without doors to the sword, both men and women.' On the whole it seems likely that the Scottish authorities exaggerated the slaughter, that there was no intentional killing of the unarmed population, still less of women and children, and that Monk gave no order to put to death even all that were in arms. There was, in short, no parallel between the commanded destruction of life at Drogheda, and the natural result of a storm at Dundee.   [1] See p. 46.

he had been collecting in the North.[1] With the exception of the castles of Dumbarton and Dunottar, Brodick and the Bass Rock, not a post outside the Highlands held out against the army of the Commonwealth.

Equal success attended the efforts of the Commonwealth to overpower the strongholds of Royalist privateers in the immediate neighbourhood of England. On October 31 an

Surrender of the Isle of Man ; of Jersey. expedition headed by Colonel Duckenfield completed the reduction of the Isle of Man.[2] On December 12 Blake and Colonel Heane, who had been landed by Blake in Jersey, received the capitulation of Elizabeth Castle, thereby completing the overthrow of the Royalists in the island.[3] The surrender of Castle Cornet in Guernsey followed on the 17th of the same month.[4]

Whatever may have been Cromwell's part in softening the treatment of the Scottish prisoners, there can be no doubt of

Cromwell demands a new Parliament. his eagerness to use the patriotic fervour called out by the invasion to settle the Commonwealth on a broader basis. His reappearance in Parliament was followed by a renewed attempt to deal with the question of a

Sept. 25. A bill to be brought in to fix the time of dissolution. new representative, and on September 25 it was resolved by 33 to 26—Cromwell and Scott acting as tellers for the majority—that a bill should be brought in to fix a time for the dissolution of the

Oct. 8. A bill brought in. existing Parliament and for the calling of a new one.[5] Such a bill was accordingly brought in on October 8. On the 14th it passed into Committee.[6]

In order to facilitate the appeal to the people which appeared to be impending, Parliament without distinction of parties resolved to disband certain regiments, in the hope that this step would bring with it a decrease of the burden of

---

[1] *A Perfect Account*, E, 651, 3.

[2] *Several Proceedings*, E, 791, 7.

[3] *The Articles of the Rendition of Elizabeth Castle*, E, 651, 9.

[4] *C.J.* vii. 63. *The French Intelligencer*, E, 651, 17.

[5] *C.J.* vii. 20. [6] *Ib.* vii. 26, 27.

taxation. On October 2 a resolution to this effect was adopted
involving, as far as the forces to be kept up in England and

Oct. 2.
The army to
be dimi-
nished. Scotland were concerned, an annual saving of
423,000*l.* out of a previous expenditure upon the
army of 1,410,000*l.*[1] The announcement of a diminution of taxation was, as was believed, to be accompanied by
a general pardon for all except special offenders. The opportunity of gaining public confidence was very similar to that
which had offered itself in the beginning of 1647. Cromwell
at least, with the support of his officers, warmly urged his

A dissolu-
tion be-
lieved to be
impending. colleagues in Parliament not to throw away a chance
which might not offer itself again.[2] When the bill
passed into Committee, there was a general expectation that a dissolution was immediately impending.

Would the Parliamentary Independents show more courage
and knowledge of the world than the Parliamentary Presby-

Difficulties
in the way. terians had shown in 1647 ? The obstacles in their
way were many and great. There was not merely

---

[1] *C.J.* vii. 24, 25.

[2] "Quanto poi alla convocatione del nuovo Parlamento, benche non
sia ancora del tutto risoluto, si crede nondimeno che questi signori ne
verranno ben presto ad una conclusione, non restandoli da fare altro per
venirci, se non le instrutioni da darsi alle provincie di come comportarsi
nel fare l' elezione de' nuovi Parlamentarii ; come ancora nel ventillare un
perdone generale, con riserva però di molte cose che non sono da
perdonarsi, da essere dichiarate nel detto perdone. Trattono ancora di
riformare il loro esercito, et di ridurlo a diciotto mila fanti et cinque
mila cavalli et di alleggerirsi di diversi presidii reputati hora poco
necessarii, affin di potere ridurre le impositioni a segno tale,' da dare al
popolo un poco di sollevatione che, come cosa che l' aggravava molto, et
in conseguenza alienava in buona parte la sua affezione verso del presente
governo ; così hora mediante questo sollievo se gli mosterà altanto
zelante quanto per avanti gli fu contrario.

"Il General Cromuell si mostra molto zelante in portare avanti questo
affare come anche in ogni altro che tende al ben publico, et sopra a tutte
nella amministratione della giustizia senza parzialità, punti tutti due che
lo rendono generalmente amabile et che lo manterranno nella buona fama
et reputatione, che il suo gran valore, prudenza et solertia gli ha acquis-
tato." Salvetti's Newsletter, *Add. MSS.* 27,962 N. fol. 257 b.

uncertainty of what might follow, but with some of the members at least there was fear of results personal to themselves. Cromwell had been talking loudly not only of popular reforms, but also of executing justice without respect of persons. Less

June 25.
Case of Lord
Howard of
Escrick. than four months ago, on June 25, Lord Howard of Escrick had been expelled from Parliament, fined 10,000*l.*, and committed to the Tower for taking bribes from Royalists who hoped to obtain a modification of the fines imposed on them.[1] If there were other members, as was almost certainly the case, who had been guilty of similar malpractices, they were not likely to forget that Howard's accuser had been one of Cromwell's most active supporters, Major-General Harrison. All who had guilty consciences would be certain to vote against a dissolution, and in this they would probably be supported by many others who were merely doubtful of their own re-election.

After all a dissolution might well cause alarm in those who were neither guilty nor more than ordinarily distrustful. Not

A disso-
lution a
doubtful
remedy. only was it, at the best, a leap in the dark, but the democratic view that government ought to conform to the popular will, was by no means likely to secure general acceptance. There were religious men who held that the primary condition of government was to uphold Puritanism, and there were politicians who held that the primary condition of government was to enact reforms. These views obtained recognition in two pamphlets published whilst the issue of the Parliamentary struggle was still undecided.

The first of these, *A Model of a New Representative*,[2]

Oct. 15.
A Model
of a New
Represen-
tative.

Nov. 2.
A Short ·
Supply. recurring to the principles set forth in the manifesto of the Fifth Monarchists in 1649,[3] recommended that the new Parliament should be elected by the Churches of the Saints gathered according to the order of the Gospel. The second, *A Short Supply or Amendment to the Propositions for a New Representative*,[4]

---

[1] *C.J.* vi. 91.   [2] E, 643, 13.   [3] See vol. i. p. 29.

[4] E, 644, 9. This is additional to certain propositions of William Leach, which are not in the Museum Library.

the work of a certain Edmund Leach, asked that the greater
number of sitting members should retain their seats. As for
the vacant seats, the chief officers of the army were to send
to Parliament eight names in every constituency returning
two members ; Parliament was to reduce these eight to four,
from which the constituency was to choose one, retaining the
right of free election only as regarded the second seat. Such
a scheme was too elaborately puerile to be adopted by any
assembly of sane men, but that it should have been seriously
proposed is a sufficient indication of the terror inspired in some
minds by the prospect of an unfettered appeal to the nation.
In Parliament itself it was strongly urged that new members
could not possibly have the indispensable knowledge of affairs
possessed by those whose experience now reached many years
back.[1]

The first divisions on the great question were taken on
November 14. By a majority of no more than four Parliament
decided to vote on the question whether it was a
convenient time to fix a date for the dissolution, and
by a still smaller majority of no more than two, the
question itself was resolved in the affirmative, Cromwell and
St. John acting as tellers for the majority. On the 18th the
date was fixed without a division to be November 3,
1654.[2] No general election therefore would take
place for three years.

*Nov. 14.
A day to be
fixed for
dissolution.*

*Nov. 18.
The day
fixed.*

*The deci-
sion a com-
promise.*

The result was somewhat in the nature of a compromise. The Parliamentarians on the one hand
dropped the design of perpetuating their own position

[1] " Allegando i vecchi che non potendo i nuovi havere conoscenza
di negozii maneggiati da loro, non possino in conseguenza così bene
perfessionarli : et perciò ha molto del verisimile, che i vecchi siano per
insistere sempre la loro continuatione per più tempo et non potendo
ottenerlo, si crede che siano per contentarsi di aggiugnere al loro numero
i dugento in circa, che abbandonorno già il Parlamento quando seguì il
caso della morte dell' ultimo Re." Salvetti's Newsletter, Nov. $\frac{7}{17}$, *Add.
MSS.* 27,962 N, fol. 268. Does this mean that Pride's Purge was to be
undone, or merely that those who had held aloof from the sittings should
be compelled to attend ?   [2] *C.J.* vii. 36, 37.

in the next Parliament.[1] On the other hand Cromwell and the officers had been compelled to abandon their demand for an
The popular feeling. immediate dissolution. That they had failed to secure this caused grave disappointment not only in the army, but generally amongst those who were neither soldiers nor members of Parliament. The hope that the men who had held power so long would at last be made to account for the large sums of money which had passed through their hands appears to have had much to do with the popular cry for a dissolution, and had doubtless much to do with the Parliamentary resistance to it.

The opportunity of appealing to the nation for support at a time when, in consequence of the Scottish invasion, it was
Chances of Parliament. more favourably disposed to the Government than it had been at any time since the establishment of the Commonwealth, passed away for ever. There was, indeed, something to be said for the opinion that the Commonwealth had more to gain by a prolonged course of well-doing—by popular reforms and popular administration—than by relying on the most brilliant victory in the field. Yet, after all, the question must even then have arisen whether such energy was to be expected from an effete and partially corrupt body, out of touch with the nation and dreading to submit its action to the judgment of the people. If not, the army was there to exact the fulfilment of the task undertaken. It was significant of danger that for the first time since Pride's Purge had Parliament and army taken opposite sides, and that there were to be found men who predicted that the army would sooner or later use the sword to enforce its will.[2] If Harrison with his reckless vehemence had

---

[1] See vol. i. p. 243.

[2] " Ai quali," *i.e.* the Parliamentarians, " opponendoseli caldamente la soldatesca, si aspetta con molto desiderio di vedere quale delle due parti sia per prevalere ; benche ognuno sia di parere che havendo questa il Generale, con buon numero delli uffiziali nel Parlamento, sia al certo per prevalere, come prevale in ogni altra cosa. Onde è da credere, che la spada sarà quella che darà la legge a tutto, havendosela con essa acquistata." Salvetti's Newsletter, $\frac{\text{Nov. 21}}{\text{Dec. 1}}$, *Add. MSS.* 27,962 N, fol. 273.

controlled the army, it is likely enough that this catastrophe
would not have been long averted. If, on the other hand,
anything was to be gathered from Cromwell's past life, it was
that he would be very long-suffering and very loth to break with
those in whose hands the symbols of authority were deposited.
It was perhaps the consciousness of this which led Parliament,

Nov. 24.
The choice
of the fourth
Council of
State.

when on November 24 it addressed itself to the
election of the fourth Council of State, to place
Cromwell at the head of the poll whilst Harrison was
excluded. It seemed, therefore, as though the old
Parliament would continue to exist on the tacit understanding
that it should give effect to some at least of the measures
which Cromwell had expected from a new one. If Parliament
fulfilled its part of that compact to which it virtually bound
itself by the honour it conferred on Cromwell, it might, so far
as it was possible to judge by the past, count on his devotion
in time of need, and might reasonably expect to live out its
appointed term. If, on the other hand, it failed to realise
Cromwell's expectations, its members would do well to
remember that his devotion to any cause had never been without limitations, and that, long-suffering as he was, he had more
than once in the course of his life been swept away by strong
emotion to dash to the ground the institutions or the men
whose guardian in all honesty he had professed himself to be.

So great was the secrecy maintained over Parliamentary matters that
Salvetti, writing on the 21st, had not heard of the division of the 15th.
A week later he writes of the feeling aroused by the vote. " Il popolo
in generale non applaudisce molto la lunghezza de' tre anni, come quello
che haverebbe desiderato una pronta annulatione di questo, et una nuova
convocatione d' un altro. La soldatesca medesimamente concorre in
questo particolare col popolo, et di già pare che sussurri di non contentar-
sene, et di volere anche rimediarvi." Salvetti's Newsletter, $\frac{Nov. 28}{Dec. 8}$, *ib.* fol.
276.

CHAPTER XVIII

PROJECTS OF REFORM

THOUGH Cromwell had acquiesced in the decision of Parliament to prolong its own existence, he could not fail to be
1651.
Dec.
Cromwell
dissatisfied
with Parlia-
ment. dissatisfied with the result. He had learnt enough of the cross currents of personal interest in which not a few of its members were involved to render him impatient of the existing system of government, and to rouse in him a hankering after somewhat of the directness of the old monarchy. He accordingly summoned a conference of the leading officers and the more prominent lawyers in Parliament to discuss the future constitution of the Republic at the Speaker's house.[1]

On December 10, Cromwell opened the proceedings by a request for advice upon the settlement of the nation. The
Dec. 10.
A confer-
ence at the
Speaker's
house. lawyers, regarding with suspicion the arbitrary power of a single house, urged that without some admixture of monarchy law and liberty would be endangered. One of their number, Sir Thomas Widdrington, suggested that the young Duke of Gloucester might be placed on the throne. The officers, on the other hand, pleaded for the maintenance of the Commonwealth as the only available guarantee of civil and religious freedom. Cromwell listened patiently till Whitelocke talked of fixing a day on which either

---

[1] *Whitelocke*, 516, where the conference is spoken of as one between officers and members of Parliament. Only lawyers, however, spoke for the latter class, and it is therefore probable that no other members were invited.

the eldest or the second son of the late King might 'come in and accept the government, if it could be done with safety and preservation' of the rights of Englishmen. "That," replied Cromwell, oracularly, "will be a business of more than ordinary difficulty ; but really I think, if it may be done with safety and preservation of our rights both as Englishmen and Christians, that a settlement of somewhat with monarchical power in it would be very effectual."

Cromwell
favours con-
stitutional
monarchy.

Whitelocke had urged the necessity of safeguarding the rights of Englishmen as Englishmen. Cromwell would protect them in their capacity of Christians as well. As Cromwell understood Christianity, therefore, he must have regarded it as hopeless to negotiate with Charles or James. Whether he regarded it as equally hopeless to negotiate with the Duke of Gloucester it is impossible to say; but it is likely enough that his thoughts were beginning to crystallise round the notion of reconciling monarchy and commonwealth by entrusting some undefined measure of executive power to a 'single person' not of Stuart blood. He would have been unlike himself if this idea had at once assumed definite proportions in his mind ; but it can hardly have failed to occur to him that, if such a post were to be created, it could be occupied by himself alone. His admirers and flatterers filled in the blank, and representations were at this time made to influential officers that the title of king might be revived in his favour.[1]

His pro-
bable
motives.

The tendency thus revealed was by no means confined to Cromwell and his supporters. During the last half-century political thought—always in antagonism to existing forms of misgovernment—had been running in the direction of the establishment either of Parliamentary authority or of individual right. The effort to establish Parliamentary authority had bowed England under the power of the sword, and the effort to establish individual right had split the Church into a hundred sects. In most of

Tendency in
favour of
strengthen-
ing the
Government.

---

[1] Lilburne's *Apologetical Narrative*, p. 20, E, 659, 30.

those to whom such a state of affairs was shocking, and who craved for the restitution of peaceful order, there was a revulsion of feeling in favour of the old monarchy. It was reserved for a stern and masculine thinker, Thomas Hobbes, to lead the way towards the same end by another path. In his *Leviathan*, which appeared in the spring of 1651,[1] Hobbes distinctly broke with the past, and no less distinctly opened the gates to discussion on new lines.

April.
Hobbes's
Leviathan.

Discarding the views which would base the State either upon traditional custom re-enforced by Divine right, or upon shifting Parliamentary majorities, he sought to found it on the Roman law of contract, urging that, as some power or other must be supreme, it was alike the duty and the interest of every nation to submit to that authority which they had once contracted to obey. The one evil pre-eminently to be avoided being social combat, obedience was in every case to be preferred to any act which threatened to produce so mischievous a result. It was consequently for the Government to decide without appeal, not only what laws were to be enforced in civil affairs, but what religious worship should be tolerated. One liberty alone remained to the individual, the liberty which no human power can ever take from him, that of thinking his own thoughts, provided that he did not attempt to express them in action contrary to the will of the State.

His political scheme.

The student of political science may point out that, whilst Hobbes did good service in drawing attention to the omnipotence of the State over human action so long as it is able to put to death those who contravene its laws, the conditions which govern the rise and fall of governments are far more subtle than those of which he took account, and that he attached undue importance to the evils accompanying resistance to authority. The historian is mainly interested in the *Leviathan* as a sign of reaction against prevailing beliefs, and will especially note that whilst in theory Hobbes was wedded to no particular form

Scientific and historical importance of the book.

---

[1] Its Dedication is dated April $\frac{15}{25}$.

of government, and admitted that State authority after his
pattern could be wielded with equal justification by monarchy,
aristocracy, or democracy, he himself remained personally
Hobbes's preference for monarchy. attached to monarchy. Of the many reasons given
by him in favour of monarchy, one at least was based
on ideas entertained by some of those who were most
eager to bring the Long Parliament to a speedy end. " Where
the public and private interest are most closely united," he
writes, "there is the public most advanced. Now in monarchy
the private interest is the same with the public. The riches,
power, and honour of a monarch arise only from the riches,
strength and reputation of his subjects ; for no king can be rich,
nor glorious, nor secure, whose subjects are either poor, or
contemptible, or too weak through want or depression to maintain a war against their enemies. Whereas, in a democracy or
aristocracy, the public prosperity confers not so much to the
private fortune of one that is corrupt or ambitious, as doth
many times a perfidious advice, a treacherous action, or a civil
war." Yet the man who used these words found himself more
at home in England than amongst the Royalist exiles on the
Continent. His monarchy, dependent on reason rather than
on sentiment, was not as theirs. Above all, his Erastian Church
was very different from theirs. Branded as an atheist, he
thought it prudent to seek shelter in his own country.

Even the Utopias of the day were making against individual
liberty. In February 1652 Gerard Winstanley, the most
1652. Feb. 20. Winstanley's Law of Freedom. thoughtful of the Diggers who had attempted to
establish community of landed property on St.
George's Hill,[1] dedicated to Cromwell a pamphlet
entitled *The Law of Freedom in a Platform.* Of
Cromwell's power to carry out any scheme upon which he had
set his heart, Winstanley entertained no doubt. "God hath
honoured you," were the opening words of his dedication, " with
the highest honour of any man since Moses' time, to be the
head of a people who have cast off the oppressing Pharaoh."

---

[1] See vol. i. 42.

The scheme which he recommended, however, was nothing less
than a social revolution. Not only kings, but lords of the
manor, lawyers, landlords, and a tithe-supported clergy were to
vanish from the face of the country. In the place of the existing life of competition, was to be established a collectivist
society, in which all worked under the superintendence of
elected overseers for the good of all. No money was to be
tolerated in this strange commonwealth ; and the death penalty
was reserved for two crimes, murder on the one hand and
buying and selling on the other.[1]

Winstanley's socialist effusion was too far removed from
the actual world to move Cromwell either to approval or indignation. It was otherwise with Lilburne and the
political Levellers. For some time, indeed, Cromwell and Lilburne appeared to be on the best of
terms. In 1650, before setting out for Scotland, Cromwell
had intervened on Lilburne's behalf, and had procured a settlement of his claim to compensation for his sufferings in the Star
Chamber. Lilburne, responsive as usual to personal kindness,
accompanied his old antagonist some little way on his progress
towards the North, supped with him at Ware, and embraced
him when they parted on the following morning. Before taking
leave, Lilburne had extracted from Cromwell a promise that
' he would put forth all his power and interest that he had in
the world to make England enjoy the real fruit of all the army's
promises and declarations.' In Lilburne's eyes the real fruit
consisted in the establishment of ' successive parliaments
equally chosen by the people.'[2] That Cromwell upon his
return had done his best to fulfil his promise must have been
known to Lilburne ; and in the course of December
1651 there was again a long and friendly conversation

Marginal notes: 1650. Cromwell and Lilburne.   1651.

---

[1] Winstanley's *Law of Freedom*, E, 655, 8. For a further examination
of Winstanley's book, and for the whole history of the levelling movement, see Bernstein's ' Kommunistische und demokratisch-socialistische
Strömungen der Englischen Revolution,' in *Geschichte des Socialismus*
(Stuttgart, 1895), I. ii. 507.

[2] *Apologetical Narrative*, p. 13, E, 650, 30.

between the two men, in which the Lord-General gave assurance
of having forgotten all former causes of quarrel.[1]

Lilburne would have changed his nature if he had remained
long without giving fresh provocation.   During Cromwell's

Lilburne as a redresser of grievances. absence in Scotland he had employed himself, apparently to relieve the tedium of political quiescence,
in taking up the grievances of various persons who
seemed to him to have reasonable ground of complaint against
the authorities.   Amongst these persons was his uncle, George

The Harraton colliery. Lilburne, who shared in the lease of a colliery at
Harraton, in the county of Durham, from a certain
George Primate.   A counter-claim to the interest of
Primate was, however, put forward on behalf of Thomas Wray,
a recusant and delinquent, whose estate was under sequestration.
Assuming this latter claim to be good, the revenue from the
mine would accrue to the State, and it was in the name of the
State that the county sequestrators seized on the property,
being ultimately backed by the general committee for com-

July. Lilburne's pamphlet. pounding.   In July 1651 Lilburne issued a pamphlet
in which he not only supported his uncle's claim, but
threw the blame of what he regarded as a miscarriage
of justice upon Hazlerigg, whom he charged with having used
his personal influence to extract an unjust sentence from the
committee.   Later on he joined Primate in drawing up a peti-

Dec. 23. Primate's petition. tion, which on December 23 was presented to Parliament in the name of the latter.   On January 15
Parliament, no doubt delighted at the opportunity of

1652. Jan. 15. Sentence on Primate and Lilburne. getting rid of a firebrand, took occasion, from the
intemperance of the language used in the petition, to
treat it as a libel on Hazlerigg, and to impose on
the two a fine which, together with the damages, amounted to
7,000*l*. apiece, and in Lilburne's case added a sentence of
banishment on pain of death if he ventured to return.[2]

---

[1] *Apologetical Narrative*, p. 18.   Lilburne says that this took place
'about three months ago.'   His book is dated April 3, 1652, but it must
have taken some time in passing through the press, and the date I have
given is therefore most probably right.   [2] *C.J.* vii. 71, 72.

There is no need to concern ourselves with the opposing claims to the Harraton colliery.[1] It is enough that it was a

Parliament unfit to act as a judicial tribunal. public scandal that Parliament should, after the fashion of the abolished Star Chamber, not only assume judicial powers for which it was eminently unfit, but should use those powers to vindicate the character of one of its members, and incidentally to promote its own interest in the retention of the colliery for the State. It is, therefore, the more surprising that, if Lilburne is to be credited, Cromwell

Cromwell's part in the sentence. not only threw all his weight into the scale against the prisoner, but even prescribed his sentence. It is possible that Lilburne, as was sometimes the case, swallowed greedily unsupported rumours ; but it is quite as likely that Cromwell, vexed at the recurrence of turbulence on Lilburne's part, gave vent to passion at the expense of consistency.[2]

More satisfactory was the Act of Oblivion[3] passed at Cromwell's instigation on February 24, and declaring a pardon for

Feb. 24. The Act of Oblivion. all treasons and felonies committed before September 3, 1651, the day of the Battle of Worcester. Unfortunately, the exceptions appended to this generous offer took away much of the largeness of the concession. As far as the period between the King's execution and the Battle of Worcester was concerned, only such treasons as were committed by words alone were pardoned, treasonable acts being left to the operations of the law. What was perhaps worse, the financial necessities of the Government demanded a fresh crop of sequestrations and confiscations ; and though Cromwell attempted, without success, to procure some modification of the conditions meted out to delinquents, he could not

---

[1] The story of the quarrel is told from opposite points of view in *A Just Reproof to Haberdashers' Hall*, E, 638, 12, and in *Lieut.-Col. Lilburne Tried and Cast*, E, 720, 2.

[2] Lilburne represents Cromwell's assurances of friendship as hypocritical. It is, however, difficult to understand why Cromwell should conceal his ill-feeling at the time. It is much more likely that Lilburne's pamphlet was subsequently brought to his notice.　　　[3] *Scobell*, ii. 179.

venture, even if he had been so inclined, to propose any thorough change in their position. Payment was still required of rents or fines which yet remained to be levied in consequence of delinquency incurred even before the King's death. Nevertheless, after all allowances are made, the Act of Oblivion liberated a considerable number of persons from danger of prosecution, and contributed to the widening of the basis of the Commonwealth.

By its efforts to reform the law Parliament at first appeared likely to win popular support. On January 17 it completed

Parliament and law reform.

Jan. 17. Commissioners appointed.

the nomination of twenty-one commissioners—none of them members of the House—to inquire into ' the mischiefs which grow by delays, the chargeableness and irregularities of the proceedings of the law.' That the widespread dissatisfaction felt by laymen might find a voice amongst the commissioners, soldiers like Desborough and headlong reformers like Hugh Peters were to cooperate with masters of legal knowledge like Matthew Hale and practised advocates like John Fountain. Last on the list came the name of Sir Anthony Ashley Cooper, who thus, for the first time since his displacement from military command on the formation of the New Model, took part in public business.[1]

The new commissioners took their appointment seriously. From time to time they recommended Parliament to pass bills

Recommendations of the commissioners neglected by Parliament.

with the object of sparing the pockets of litigants by rendering legal procedure less dilatory.[2] Unfortunately for its credit, Parliament turned a deaf ear to these proposals, and month after month passed away without a single one of them being converted into law. The

Jan. 23. Judges to be paid by salary.

only piece of legal reform achieved during the first half of 1652 was the substitution of fixed salaries for fees and perquisites in the payment of judges. The

---

[1] *C.J.* vii. 71-74.

[2] Mr. Inderwick's comments (*The Interregnum*, 205–210) should be read as conveying the approval of a modern lawyer. It appears that of eight draft Acts proposed on March 23, 1652, one became law in 1833, one in 1846, and a third in 1885. So far were these men in advance of their time.

Act embodying this salutary change was, however, passed on January 23, before the Commission had settled down to its work.[1]

The inertia against which legal reformers strove in vain within the walls of Parliament was manifested with far better excuse in the jury-box. It is true that old iniquities warranted by custom roused no indignation. A woman who in a fit of passion killed an unfaithful husband was burnt alive in Smithfield,[2] and alleged witches were hanged without mercy. The line was drawn at the new death-penalty for adultery. During the ten years which followed the passing of the Adultery Act in 1650,[3] only one person was sentenced to death at the Middlesex Sessions on this charge, and it is almost certain that the sentence was not carried out. Here and there in other parts of England death sentences on this score were followed by execution, but, so far as can be judged from the imperfect evidence accessible, these cases were exceedingly rare.[4] How little repressive measures affected public morality is evident from the weekly appearance of an unlicensed newspaper, *Mercurius Democritus,* the sole object of which was to retail coarse stories seasoned with the dull jocularity which in those days passed as wit.[5]

Verdicts of juries.

The Adultery Act not carried out.

Zealous as were the leaders of the Commonwealth in the suppression of vice, they displayed but little of that sour austerity with which they have frequently been credited. On his way to Dunbar Cromwell laughed heartily at the sight of one soldier overturning a full cream-tub and slamming it down on the head of another, whilst on his return from Worcester he spent a day hawking in the fields near Aylesbury. "Oliver," we hear, "loved an innocent jest."[6] Music and song were cultivated in his family. If the graver

The amusements of Puritans.

---

[1] *C.J.* vii. 76.

[2] *The Witch of Wapping*, E, 659, 18.   [3] See vol. i. 256.

[4] See *Middlesex County Records*, by J. C. Jeaffreson, iii. 188–301, and *The Interregnum*, by F. A. Inderwick, 38.

[5] The first number (E, 659, 13) issued on April 8, 1652, is cautious. The true character of the publication appears in the second number, E, 659, 25.   [6] Hodgson's *Memoirs*, 129.

Puritans did not admit what has been called 'promiscuous dancing' into their households, they made no attempt to prohibit it elsewhere. In the spring of 1651 appeared *The English Dancing-Master*,[1] containing rules for country-dances, and the tunes by which they were to be accompanied. In the following November a masque was given in the Middle Temple. The proceedings were opened with the Hundredth Psalm, sung by the Benchers in the Hall, after which these reverend seniors, having drunk a cup of hypocras, retired to their chambers. In their absence the younger members of the society 'began to recreate themselves with civil dancing and had melodious music.' Ladies and persons of quality were present as spectators, though they do not appear to have shared in the display.[2]

The truth is that with the Independents interference with individual liberty was regarded as exceptional, and it was in part

Confusion in the Church.

owing to the same feeling that no attempt had been made to provide a remedy for the chaos which prevailed in ecclesiastical appointments. The rights

Presentations to benefices.

of patrons to present to benefices were still recognised, though where the patrons had been delinquent the

right of presentation fell into the hands of the County Committees, which usually made it a condition of their choice that the consent of the parishioners should be obtained, whilst benefices originally conferred by the Crown were left directly to the parishioners.[3] The result was that the clergy were by no means of one way of thinking. Independents, and occasionally Baptists as well as Presbyterians, became rectors or vicars, and impressed their individual views upon the congregations committed to their charge.

---

[1] Published on March 19, 1651 (M. K. i. a, 8). It has an attractive frontispiece. A gentleman and lady are preparing to dance, and Cupid is playing a stringed instrument behind them. The gentleman is gaily dressed in the height of fashion, the lady more demurely.

[2] *Perfect Passages*, E, 791, 20.

[3] See, for instance, the case of St. Bartholomew Exchange in Freshfield's *Vestry Minute Books* of the parish, pp. viii., xxiv.; and the *Dorset Committee Books* in the possession of Mr. Bankes.

Devotion to the worship imposed by Laud and Charles on every parish in the land was, however, hardly to be reckoned as a factor in the popular religious life of the time. Laud's teaching had been addressed to scholars, not to the multitude, and his disciples were now to be found either amongst students expelled from the Universities by the Puritan visitors, or amongst the Royalist country gentlemen who traced their defeat and impoverishment to the Puritan Government. Here and there a sturdy disciple of Laud, whose existence had been overlooked in some obscure parish, repeated from memory portions of the Prayer Book in the public service. Here and there, and more especially in Oxford and London, persons to whom the worship of the old type was dear met to celebrate in secret the rites of the Church, but there is no trace whatever of any popular demand for the restoration of the Prayer Book, such as that which in the reign of Edward VI. roused whole districts to clamour for the restoration of the Mass.[1]

No popular zeal for the revival of the Prayer Book.

Yet, complete as had been the wreck of Laudian episcopacy, there was little chance that the Presbyterian discipline established by the ordinance of 1648 would occupy its vacant place. The new out-

The Presbyterian system only partially in force.

---

[1] Fox, in his journal, describes at full length the opposition against which he had to contend in every part of England. He was constantly assailed by rude and cruel mobs, but, so far as these were under the influence of any sort of religion, they supported the existing clergy, Presbyterians, Independents, or Baptists. In a conversation held with Dr. Cradock in 1663 Fox complained of being excommunicated for not coming to church. "'Why,' said I, 'ye left us above twenty years ago, when we were but young lads and lasses, to the Presbyterians, Independents, and Baptists, many of whom made spoil of our goods and persecuted us, because we would not follow them. Now we, being but young, knew little then of your principles, and if ye had intended to keep the old men that did know them to you, and your principles alive that we might have known them, ye should either not have fled from us as ye did, or ye should have sent us your epistles, collects, homilies and even-songs ; for Paul wrote epistles to the saints though he was in prison. But they and we might have turned Turks or Jews for any collects, homilies, or epistles we had from you all the while.'"

burst of unrestrained sectarianism combined with the old dislike of clerical interference to strike the weapons out of the hands of any clergyman who imagined himself capable of treading in the footsteps of Knox and Melville. Even in Lancashire, where the system obtained the greatest acceptance, it was hampered by the reluctance of parishioners to elect elders and deacons ; and after the defeat of Charles at Worcester it was still more hampered by the knowledge of the leading ministers that they had become obnoxious to the Government as supporters of the royal claims.[1] The weakness of the London Presbytery was no less manifest. In an appeal made by the Provincial Assembly early in 1652, fears were expressed of 'the utter dissolution of Presbyterial Government.'[2] The Minutes of the Classes of Manchester, Bury, and Wirksworth tell the same tale. Ordinations and the examinations of candidates for the ministry are frequently mentioned, but it was difficult and often impossible to fill up the elderships, the mainstay of ecclesiastical discipline. Presbyterianism as a clerical system, with its jealous safeguards of learning and character in its ministers, met with no serious opposition. Its jurisdiction over the morals of the laity was an exotic which took no root on English soil.

The failure of Presbyterianism drove many thoughtful men into the Independent and Baptist churches, in which discipline was exercised not by ecclesiastical officials recognised by law, but by the spontaneous action of the congregations. Under the Commonwealth this action was supplemented by the burning words of religious enthusiasts, whose utterances, too often based

Effect on the Independent and Baptist churches.

Religious enthusiasts.

[1] Several of these ministers were imprisoned for a time.—Shaw's *Minutes of the Manchester Classes* (Chetham Soc.), 168, note 1.

[2] Their letter, dated January 22, 1652, is amongst the Minutes of the London Provincial Assembly in Sion College, copies of which, as well as of the Minutes of the Bury Classes, have been lent me by Mr. W. A. Shaw. Compare on the situation generally, Stoughton's *Religion in England*, vol. ii. ch. 6. The Minutes of the Wirksworth Classes are in the Derbyshire Archæological and Historical Society's Publications, ii. 135. [See Dr. W. A. Shaw's *History of the English Church during the Civil Wars and under the Commonwealth*, 1900, ii. 97–174.]

on distorted conceptions of life and fact, nevertheless availed
to stir up spiritual emotions and to awaken moral energy in the
ignorant and profane.

Prominent among these enthusiasts was John Bunyan, the
tinker of Elstow. The son of poor parents, he was taught to
read and write, accomplishments which he lost for
a time as soon as he left school. In his boyhood he
followed what was probably the general example of his comrades, giving vent to oaths and curses, and mocking at
religion in his speech. Yet even then his conscience made
itself felt in the vivid imagination of the lot which would
befall him when he should be given up to the torments of
hell. In November 1644 he completed his sixteenth year, and being, according to custom, en-
rolled in the Bedfordshire militia, was sent to serve,
under Sir Samuel Luke, in the Parliamentary garrison of Newport Pagnell. Here he remained for more than two years and
a half, quitting the service on the dissolution of the garrison
in June 1647. There is no reason to believe that he was
ever under fire.[1]

Bunyan's youth. (margin note)

1644-7. In garrison at Newport Pagnell. (margin note)

[1] The source of our knowledge of Bunyan's early life is his own
Grace Abounding. That he was in the Newport Pagnell garrison is a
discovery of Mr. E. G. Atkinson, of the Public Record Office, and
published by him in *The Presbyterian* for May 21 and August 13, 1896.
That Bunyan found his way into it through the militia is an inference
from the age at which he entered (see *Tracts relating to Military Proceedings in Lancashire,* Chetham Soc. p. 31, where it is said that Lord
Strange, in virtue of the Commission of Array, summoned 'all persons
of able body, betwixt sixteen and sixty years of age,' and the *Life of Adam
Martindale* published by the same society, p. 34, where the writer says
that he was but fourteen at the time, 'whereas sixteen would have
brought me in '). What was true of the King's Commissions of Array
would also be true of the Parliament's militia. The last payment to the
garrison was in June 1647, and there is every reason to believe that it was
then broken up, as it had latterly been only kept on foot by Parliament
as a protection against the army, a reason which ceased to be valid
when the army got the upper hand. If Bunyan had been employed in
active service we should expect some reference to the fact in his works.
Dr. Brown, indeed (*John Bunyan,* 50), suggests that when he 'fell into

When Bunyan returned to his native village his character was unchanged by contact with his Puritan officers. That life of unbounded wickedness to which in later years he looked back with horror was never indeed stained with sins of the flesh. He was but a jovial village lad, taking delight in a game of tipcat on Elstow Green, or in ringing bells in the tower of Elstow Church, and seasoning his talk with full-flavoured oaths. It is probable that he owed the first stirrings of conscience to his early marriage,[1] which took place soon after his return, perhaps towards the end of 1647, or in the beginning of the following year.[2] He seems to have met his future wife while wandering in the exercise of his trade.[3] Of the world's goods the young pair had but little. "This woman and I," wrote Bunyan in later life, "came together as poor as poor might be, not having so much household stuff as a dish or a spoon betwixt us both."[4] Poor as she was, her influence was soon felt. She taught her youthful husband to read pious books brought from her father's house, and it was surely through her persuasion that he began to attend church, and to reverence the ministerial dignity of the preacher.[5]

Bunyan back at Elstow.

His marriage.

a creek of the sea,' he was sent on a military expedition. There was, however, no fighting in the eastern counties at this late period of the war, and it seems more reasonable to connect this misadventure with some journey connected with Bunyan's trade. Dr. Brown's excellent biography of Bunyan is too well known to need any commendation of mine.

[1] "So that," he says, "until I came to the state of marriage, I was the very ringleader in all manner of vice and ungodliness."

[2] After narrating the well-known story of his having been saved by a comrade taking his place at a siege to which a party of the garrison had been sent, Bunyan goes on: "Presently, after this, I changed my condition into a married state."

[3] Dr. Brown (p. 53) shows that there was no entry of the marriage at Elstow. His suggestion that the marriage may have taken place before a justice of the peace is inadmissible, as it was prior to the legislation of 1653.

[4] Was there not some exaggeration in this? A tinker ought to have been able to procure a dish or a spoon.

[5] "So overcome was I with the spirit of superstition that I adored, and that with great devotion, even all things (both the high-place, priest,

Bunyan was now interested in religion; he was far from
Spiritual conflict. being possessed by it. A sermon on the duty of re-
fraining from sports as well as from labour on the
Sabbath [1] roused his antagonism. In the afternoon, as he was
in the full swing of a game of tip-cat, the imaginative power
of giving reality to his thoughts awoke within him. A voice
struck upon his ear: "Wilt thou leave thy sins and go to
heaven, or have thy sins and go to hell?" Dropping his cat,
he saw with the inner vision the Saviour looking down upon
him in hot displeasure. For a moment he thought of stealing
away, but the perplexed theology of the time drew him back.
Arguing that as he was certain to be damned he might as well
be damned for many sins as for few, he returned to the
interrupted game.

The desperate tenacity with which Bunyan resisted the
heavenly vision foreboded a long internal conflict. For months
A terrified soul. he lived encompassed by terrors. They pursued
him when he longed once more to join the bell-
ringers and yet drew back lest an amusement so vain might
bring down the beams upon his head. They pursued him
when profane oaths issued from his lips. Fear of hell-fire
might lead him to think and talk about religion ; it could not
make him religious. The impulse heavenwards lighted on him
in more gentle fashion. One day, in the streets of Bedford,
he listened to ' three or four poor women, sitting at a door in
the sun, talking about the things of God.' "Their talk," he
discovered, "was about a new birth, the work of God on their
hearts, also how they were convinced of their miserable state
by nature. They talked how God had visited their souls with
His love in the Lord Jesus, and with what words and promises
they had been refreshed, comforted, and supported against the

clerk, vestments, service, and what else) belonging to the Church."
Dr. Brown sees in the vicar a sort of belated Laudian. Such a solution
of the difficulty is most improbable. A far easier one is to suppose that
Bunyan's memory played him false, and that he misdated his recollection
of scenes witnessed in his earlier childhood.

[1] Hardly likely to have been preached by a Laudian.

temptations of the devil." From that moment the love of
God replaced the fear of judgment in Bunyan's soul. No
longer occupied with his flight from the City of Destruction,
he fixed his longing eyes on the Delectable Mountains.

The new life drew Bunyan to new friends. In 1650 a
little body of twelve persons, some of them of high local
repute in Bedford, formed themselves into a Baptist
church or congregation under the ministry of John
Giffard, formerly a Royalist major, who, having been
taken prisoner at Maidstone fight, succeeded in escaping from
his captors.[1] Since that time he had practised as a physician in
Bedford, where he was notorious for hard drinking and hard
swearing. He had, however, been brought to a better mind, and
became as notable for the purity of his life as he had formerly
been for his vices. Bunyan was naturally attracted by a converted sinner, and though he did not formally throw in his lot
with Giffard's followers till 1653, he was already on terms of
close intimacy with them. It was not till after Giffard's death
in 1655 that he accepted office in this church, and it was only
in 1657 that he was recognised by it as a preacher.

1650-7.
Giffard's
congrega-
tion.

As sinner or as Christian, Bunyan was the least controversial
of men. George Fox, for all his denunciation of carnal weapons,
was amongst the most pugnacious. Demure in childhood, he shrank early from the very appearance of
evil. As a lad, he was distinguished for his obstinate truthful-
ness. 'If George says Verily' (was a common observation
amongst his neighbours), 'there is no altering him.' At a later
time a change came over him, very unlike Bunyan's prolonged
struggle against temptation. "Thou seest," was the voice
sounding in his ears, "how young people go together into
vanity, and old people into the earth ; thou must forsake all
and be a stranger unto all." Fox's mind was agitated by a
craving for truth and spiritual perfection rather than by a

George
Fox.

---

[1] The Bedford Record (Brown's *Life of Bunyan*, 82) says that he
and eleven others were condemned to death. As we know nothing of
any person having been put to death after the battle at Maidstone, it is
probable that the twelve were only terrified with threats of execution.

conflict with indwelling and overmastering sin. He wandered away from home in search of light, getting but scant aid from the ministers—'priests' was the name by which he knew them—to whom he applied for the solution of his difficulties. One jovial clergyman bade him 'take tobacco and sing psalms.' Another, apparently less worldly, at last flew into a rage with him for treading on his flower-bed. A third listened to his conversation, picked his brains, and retailed the youth's spiritual experiences in the pulpit. Gradually Fox's mind cleared. The doctrine of an inner light, of Christ dwelling in the heart of the believer as a teacher and a purifier even to the entire extinction of sin, solved all difficulties. Such a doctrine or something not far removed from it, had led the Ranters into a belief that sin was no sin to those who, being spiritual, willed to do evil.[1] There was a sanity in Fox's mind which restrained him from such abominations. Though he refused to give to the Scriptures the title of The Word of God, he nevertheless held them to be the words of God guiding and instructing in the paths of blessedness, if only they were interpreted by God's light shining in the heart of the spiritual man.

1645. His youthful difficulties.

His doctrine of the inner light.

Fox's doctrine of the inner light was but the quintessence of Puritan protest against external formality, though he carried his opinions into practice with greater consistency than other Puritans.[2] Amongst his followers—styled by himself the Society of Friends, and by the world

1647. The Society of Friends.

---

[1] See p. 3.

[2] Dr. Hodgkin, in completing his biography of Fox, thus sums up the impression left by the character of the man upon him: "He was a man of lion-like courage and adamantine strength of will, absolutely truthful, devoted to the fulfilment of what he believed to be his God-appointed mission and without any of those side-long looks at worldly promotion and aggrandisement which many sincere leaders of Church parties have cast at intervals of their journey. The chief defect in Fox's character will perhaps be best described in the words of Carlyle : ' Cromwell found George Fox's enormous sacred self-confidence none of the least of his attainments.' It is to be remembered that Fox preached the doctrine of Christian perfection as a thing of possible attainment in this

in general Quakers '—Baptism and the Lord's Supper, though not positively denounced, were virtually abandoned. Yet, wide as was the gulf which parted Fox from Laud, these leaders of thought struck a common note in their recoil from the intellectual rigidities of Calvinism. From this point of view, therefore, the new society may be regarded as making as distinct an opposition to Puritanism in one direction as it was its continuator in another, and it was doubtless in consequence of their appeal to the hearts of Christians by a teaching untrammelled by doctrinal formulas, that Fox and his disciples won so large a following among those who yearned for the development of a religious life regardless of the logic of the schools.

That teaching so regardless of established doctrine would meet with resistance was only too probable, and, unfortunately, A war against social formalities. Fox increased the irritation caused by his doctrines, by waging war against accepted social formalities. In bearing testimony against Paganism, by calling Sunday the first day of the week and March the first month of the year, he did but follow the example of other extreme Puritans, such as Harrison and Hanserd Knollys ; but, having no sense of proportion in his mind, he gave unnecessary offence to his countrymen by addressing them as 'Thou' on the plea that

life ; nor is he any the less welcome as a teacher because he does not indulge in that cant of exaggerated self-condemnation which was one of the signs of degenerating Puritanism. Still, it is difficult for a reader of the *Journal* not to feel that Fox is far too confident of the absolute rightness of his own conduct and the utter wickedness of all who oppose him."—*George Fox*, p. 278.

¹ Fox says that Justice Bennet first called him by this name, because he told him to tremble before the Lord. The name, however, fixed itself on the popular mind by the physical excitement which attended the reception of Fox's doctrines. In a Westmoreland petition the enemies of the Friends complain that their 'practices do exceedingly savour of sorcery, the quakings, swellings, roarings, foamings, and such as we never heard of but in such as were possessed of the devil, of persons at their meetings and especially of young children.' The Friends, in reply, without denying the fact, remind their critics that Moses and other Scriptural personages quaked or trembled. *Several Petitions Answered*, E, 703, 4. This pamphlet was published on June 29, 1653.

it was untruthful to use the plural 'You,' in speaking to
a single person; whilst by his refusal to uncover his head
in the presence of exalted personages, on the ground that this
honour was due to God alone, he drew down upon him the
scornful ill-will of that class from which judges and magistrates
were taken. To the clergy of every shade of opinion he gave
special offence. He refused to give to their churches any other
name than that of steeple-houses, on the ground that the term
'Church' was inapplicable to any material building. Far more

Fox's ha-
rangues in
churches.

He makes
enemies of
the clergy,

offensive to the ministers, and, in many cases, to their
congregations as well, was Fox's habit of entering
a church and rising after the conclusion of the sermon, not only to denounce the doctrine of the
preacher, but to hold him up to derision as a hireling
and creature of the State, because he was maintained by tithes.
It is true that the custom of the day permitted laymen to rise
and to add some word of edification after the minister had been
heard,[1] but it can hardly be argued that abuse of the minister's
character and position was included in that right; and it is,
at all events, certain that such words as Fox was accustomed to
pour out in deliverance of his soul must have stung the aggrieved
minister into fury. Nor was it only the clergy whom Fox converted into enemies. If there was a body of men in England

and of the
soldiers.

more powerful than the clergy, it was the army. By
his declaration that war, even in self-defence, was
unlawful, Fox irritated the soldiers as much as he irritated
other bodies of men. With the influential classes thus turned
against him, there was little to restrain the crowd of those who
hugged their rude animal life with its drunkenness and vice, and
who bore malice against the man who branded them as sinners,
much as their descendants a century later bore malice against
Wesley.

When, therefore, Fox set forth as a missionary through
England, as if it were a heathen land, an excuse for persecution

[1] See Barclay's *Inner Life of the Religious Societies of the Commonwealth*, 274.

in legal form was eagerly sought, and, as is usually the case, was easily found. No candid person would now admit that any of his doctrines were really touched by the Blasphemy Act of 1650, but it was easy for ignorant and heated partisans to persuade themselves that his doctrine of the inner light, combined with his teaching that Christian perfection was attainable in this world of sin, was tantamount to the assertion of a claim 'that the true God, or the Eternal Majesty, dwells in the creature, and nowhere else.'[1] An excuse was all that was wanted. Fox

1650-52.
Fox as a missionary.

Fox and the Blasphemy Act.

---

[1] Fox's first imprisonment at Nottingham in 1649 was in consequence of his interrupting the preacher in the midst of his sermon, for which he had no legal excuse. The second imprisonment at Derby, 'from October 30, 1650, to the beginning of winter, 1651,' was purely on the ground of the doctrine he avowed. Unquestionably the ordinance passed by the two Houses of Parliament in May 1648 had ceased to be obligatory since the passing of the Blasphemy Act in August 1650 (see p. 2). The view that Fox was committed under the new Blasphemy Act is fully borne out by a report of the indictment of Nayler at Appleby in January 1653, and by the accompanying documents printed with it in *Saul's Errand*, E, 689, 17. A petition to the Council of State from 'several gentlemen, justices of the peace,' states of the early Friends that ' some of them affirmed themselves to be equal with God, contrary to the late Act, as hath been attested at a late quarter sessions holden at Lancaster in October last past.' Below are given divers blasphemous opinions ascribed to Fox and his companions. Then follow their answers explaining their real meaning. Altogether this pamphlet is invaluable as throwing a clear light on the legal routine of the persecutors. The exact charge is nowhere stated in Fox's *Journal*, legal definitions being little to his taste ; but the Mittimus which is printed as *An Answer to a Book which Samuel Eaton put up to the Parliament*, p. 55 (E, 735, 9), leaves no doubt that Fox was committed, together with John Fretwel, on October 30, 1650, under the Blasphemy Act of 1650. They were 'charged with the avowed uttering and broaching of divers blasphemous opinions, contrary to a late Act of Parliament, which upon their examination before us they have confessed.' This merely means that they confessed having used words which the justices construed as blasphemous. An account of the examination is given on the same page. Probably the following was regarded as proving the charge : "They asked us Had we no sin ? I said, No ! and in Christ was no sin. They said Where is

was in prison oft in days when prisons were sickening recep-
tacles of indescribable filth. His teaching, directed as it was
against the intellectual formalities of Puritanism, was as effective
as had been the Puritan attack upon the ceremonial formalities
of Laud. Moreover, Fox's uncomplaining acceptance of every
evil that befell him, and, above all, the sincerity exhibited by
his refusal to strive with the ruffians who struck him gained
him many a disciple who would not have been won over by the
most attractive preaching. His sobriety of judgment—within
certain limits—was as remarkable as his spiritual exaltation,
and after thousands of excitable converts had swelled the
numbers of the society it was George Fox who was the restraining influence in their midst.

Others there were whose fanaticism was under less restraint.
Reeves and Muggleton announced themselves as the two
Reeves and   Heavenly Witnesses foretold in the Revelation, and
Muggleton.   sentenced all who displeased them to irrevocable
damnation.[1]   At Whitehall, as Sterry was discoursing on the
              Resurrection, a lady 'stripped herself of all her
July 25.
A strange   apparel, and, as she came into the world from top
scene.   to toe, she ran into the middle of the congregation,
over against the pulpit, and cried, "Welcome the Resurrection ! " '[2]

If this spiritual chaos was to be reduced to some orderly
system it was unlikely that the advocates of unlimited toleration,
              and still less those of the voluntary system, would
Is toleration
to be un-   be entirely satisfied. In such a re-establishment of
limited?   order no one was likely to play a more prominent

Christ ? and we said, In us ; and He hath taken away our sin ; so saith
John, One abiding in Him sinneth not."

[1] *Works of Reeves and Muggleton*, i. 1.

[2] *Memoirs of the Verney Family*, iii. 47. The words are given
" Resurrection I am ready for thee " in the *Perfect Account*, E, 672, 3.
See *The Naked Woman* (E, 681, 20), with Sterry's explanation that he
only saw the upper part of the woman's back as she was surrounded by a
crowd, and did not know what had happened till he came down from his
pulpit.

part than John Owen, an Independent minister deep in Crom

John Owen. well's confidence. The son of a Welsh gentleman, he had been educated at Queen's College, Oxford,

where he was noted for his devotion to study and athletic

His early life. exercises. Startled into Puritanism by the Laudian reaction, he was glad to leave Oxford, and to settle

down into a country living. As the intolerance of Laud made Owen a Puritan, the intolerance of Presbyterianism made him an Independent. As minister of Coggeshall, he attracted the notice of Fairfax on his way to the siege of Colchester, and by Fairfax he was carried to London,[1] where he was selected for the arduous duty of preaching before Parliament on the day after the execution of the King.

Though Owen did not utter a word directly bearing on the bloody scene at Whitehall, he distinctly gave a general approval

1649. Jan. 31. A sermon to Parliament. to the course of events which had placed Parliament in its position of sovereignty, whilst the title under which he published his sermon—*Righteous Zeal Encouraged by Divine Protection* [2]—leaves no room for

Owen on toleration. doubting that his approbation extended even further. To this sermon he appended a discourse on Toleration. As an intellectual performance it can never rank with *Areopagitica*, or even with *The Bloody Tenent*. Owen was neither a breaker of new paths nor a master of literary style. His most forcible arguments fall confusedly from his pen, and need

Owen's opinion on heresy and error. close attention to unravel their significance. Owen's position towards heresy and erroneous opinion was that the magistrate was the most unfit person in the world

to interfere in religious disputes. His proper function with regard to such matters was to inflict punishment on those who, in the name of religion, disturbed the public peace, spoke contemptuously of Divine things, or wandered without settled abode from place to place. Certain beliefs, again, like that of the 'Papists,' being direct assaults on the majesty and

[1] Fairfax's patronage of Owen is a nut which those who regard him as exclusively Presbyterian will find hard to crack.

[2] Owen's *Works* (ed. Goold), viii. 133.

honour of God, were so far to be taken account of by the magistrate that he might interfere with the right of those who held them to meet for purposes of worship. On the other hand, it was the duty of the magistrate to maintain places of public worship and to grant support to the ministers officiating in them.

In this and in other respects, Owen's deliverance had points of resemblance to the *Agreement of the People* recently presented by the officers to Parliament, too close to be altogether fortuitous. Both contemplated an Established Church supported by the State, surrounded by self-supporting Nonconformist Churches tolerated by the State. Both contemplated the refusal of toleration to certain classes of persons, whilst, however, the *Agreement of the People* pronounced distinctly only against those who abused their liberty ' to the civil injury of others, or to actual disturbance of the public peace,' and more hesitatingly declared that liberty was not ' necessarily ' to ' extend to Popery or Prelacy.' Owen, as became a theologian approaching the subject from a theoretical point of view, threw his net somewhat more widely to include attacks upon the majesty and honour of God.

It nearly coincides with the Agreement of the People.

With the general purport of Owen's argument Cromwell was in full agreement. "Sir," said he, tapping the preacher on the shoulder when he next met him at Fairfax's house, "you are the person I must be acquainted with." "That," replied Owen, "will be much more to my advantage than yours." Taking him aside, Cromwell insisted on carrying him as his chaplain to Ireland.[1] In 1651, Parliament, doubtless at Cromwell's instigation, named Owen Dean of Christchurch, in succession to Reynolds, who had refused to take the engagement.[2] Unlike Fox, Cromwell believed that the highest culture of the time was a sure support for the religion of the heart, and he

Cromwell and Owen.

1651. March 14. Owen, Dean of Christchurch,

---

[1] Asty's Preface to Owen's *Sermons*, ed. 1721.
[2] *C.J.* vi. 549.

had learnt that Owen was not merely a rational theologian, but a man of rare force of character. Some little time afterwards he appointed him to the Vice-Chancellorship, thus committing the Puritan reorganisation of the University of Oxford into his hands.

and Vice-Chancellor.

Owen's influence soon made itself felt on the ecclesiastical questions of the day. Some time before Cromwell's return from Scotland, a proposed Act for the Propagation of the Gospel had been read a second time, but, as it was referred to the Committee for Plundered Ministers, it is reasonable to suppose that it aimed merely at increasing the maintenance of the clergy.[1]

1651. May 23. Proposed legislation for the Propagation of the Gospel.

It was, however, impossible long to avoid the larger question. For some years John Biddle had asserted the truth of the doctrines of Socinus, and suffered frequent imprisonments as a heretic.[2] In February 1652 an edition of *The Racovian Catechism*, containing the approved doctrines of the Socinian Churches in Poland, was published in London.[3] On this Owen, together with fourteen other ministers, complained to Parliament, with the result that, on April 10, the House ordered the burning of the whole edition.[4] The fifteen ministers accompanied their protest against Socinianism with a scheme for the settlement of outstanding ecclesiastical questions. To this the House responded by appointing, on February 18, a Committee for the Propagation of the Gospel. Before long the number of the signatories of the scheme rose to twenty-seven, including Whalley, Okey, and Goffe.[5]

John Biddle.

1652. The Racovian Catechism.

Feb. 10. A complaint.

April 2. The catechism to be burnt.

Feb. 10. A plan for an ecclesiastical settlement.

The proposals themselves indubitably bear the stamp of

---

[1] *C.J.* vi. 578. Trustees were to be named ; a fact which points in the same direction.

[2] *The Apostolical . . . . Opinion concerning the Holy Trinity*, E, 1479, I.

[3] This edition is not among the Thomasson Tracts, though an English translation issued later is E, 1320.

[4] *C.J.* vii. 114.   [5] *Ib.* vii. 259.

Owen's mind, and may, with strong probability, be assigned to his authorship. There was to continue an Established Church,

Feb. 18.
The Committee for the Propagation of the Gospel.

An established and endowed Church.

Triers and Ejectors.

controlled by two sets of commissioners, partly lay and partly clerical, corresponding to those afterwards known as Triers and Ejectors. The first set, acting as triers, was divided into local bodies, each of which was to exercise its office in a single county or group of counties, and to admit to the office of preaching such persons, whether ordained or not, as could produce a testimonial ' of their piety and soundness in the faith,' under the hands of six godly Christians, two at least being ministers. The other set was to be a national body of ejectors, moving about from one part of the country to the other, and removing unfit ministers and schoolmasters. Ministers appointed by the triers were not to be compelled to administer the sacraments to such as they judged unfit, nor was anyone to be compelled to receive the sacraments at their hands. Outside this loosely compacted Established

Toleration for Dissenters.

Church, persons dissenting were to ' be required to meet—if they have constant meetings—in places publicly known, and to give notice to some magistrate of such their places of ordinary meetings.' Finally, it

Unitarians not to be tolerated.

was asked that the opponents of ' those principles of Christian religion, without the acknowledgment whereof the Scriptures plainly affirm that salvation is not to be obtained—as those formerly complained of by the ministers—may not be suffered to preach or promulgate anything in opposition unto such principles.' [1] Unlike the *Agreement of the People*, Owen's scheme did not mention the proscription of either ' Popery or Prelacy.'

It is unlikely that this scheme would have been proposed

---

[1] *Proposals for the . . . Propagation of the Gospel*, E, 683, 12. There was a last article asking for the suppression of judicial astrology. The terms Triers and Ejectors are not formally applied to the two sets of commissioners, but they are spoken of as trying and ejecting. I have inserted the terms in order to exhibit the parallelism and contrast with Cromwell's subsequent ordinances.

by Owen without at least the general approbation of Cromwell.[1]
As a member of the Committee appointed to discuss it, Crom-

Probable approbation of Cromwell.

well had to fight hard against those who sought to
narrow its comprehensive charity. " I shall need
no revelation," he said, " to discover unto me that

Cromwell defends religious liberty.

man who endeavours to impose[2] upon his brethren."
To another member, who declared that he had
rather be a persecuting Saul than an indifferent
Gallio, he replied with strong decision : " I had rather that
Mahometanism were permitted amongst us than that one of
God's children should be persecuted." [3]

If there were some members of the Committee for whom
Owen's scheme was too liberal, there were others, outside the

Major Butler attacks the scheme as not liberal enough.

Committee, for whom it was not liberal enough.
Major Butler, with five followers, assailed it not
merely on account of its restriction of toleration to
Christians, but on the ground of its support to a

Church established and endowed.[4] Did not Christ Jesus,
asked these men in effect, send forth labourers into His vine-
yard ' without the testimony and reward of men ? ' Was it not
the will of God that the condemnation of false teachers should
be left to Himself ? Was it ' not against the liberties given by
Christ Jesus to His people ' for ' the civil power to assume a
judgment in spirituals ? ' Finally, stirring a question which was
now exercising the minds of Christians for the first time since
the reign of Edward I., was it ' not the duty of magistrates to

[1] The limitation of toleration to Christians appears in the *Instrument
of Government*, Art. 37.

[2] *I.e.* to impose his own opinions.

[3] Preface to *The Fourth Paper by Major Butler*, E, 658. Professor
Masson ascribes this Preface, which is signed R. W., to Roger Williams.
An additional argument in favour of this view is the resemblance of the
quotations from Cromwell's speeches here to the quotations from Vane's
speeches in the Preface to *The Bloody Tenent*. The language of the
second speech leaves no doubt that Cromwell opposed not those who
wanted to enlarge the proposals, but those who thought them too
liberal.

[4] *Ib.* This paper was published on March 30.

permit the Jews, whose conversion we look for, to live freely and peaceably amongst us?'[1]

There was matter enough here for prolonged discussion. Challenged to explain what they regarded as the principles of Christianity, any assault on which was to disqualify from toleration, Owen and his supporters produced no less than **Fifteen fundamentals of Christianity.** fifteen fundamentals, asserting, amongst other things, that none who sought to discover the mind of God except by the Holy Scriptures, who denied the ordinary doctrine of the Trinity, the incarnation, justification by grace, the necessity of forsaking sin, the resurrection, or even forsook and despised the duties of God's worship, were to be allowed to promulgate their opinions.[2]

Question of an Established Church. The question of the toleration of Unitarians or other adversaries of recognised Christianity interested a few advanced thinkers. The question of the

[1] On January 5, 1649, a petition was presented to Fairfax and the Army Council by two inhabitants of Amsterdam for the repeal of the banishment of the Jews (*Clarke Papers*, ii. 172, note *a*). There is evidence that a friendly feeling towards the Jews was spreading in 1652. In a paper drawn up about the beginning of that year on the subject of the importance of acquiring Dunkirk, we are told that 'if there may be a toleration of a synagogue of the Jews' there 'they will give 60,000 or 80,000 pound for that freedom, it will bring all the Portugal merchants from Amsterdam' (*Hist. Review*, July 1896, p. 485). In *Proposals for Propagation of the Gospel* (E, 656, 21), published on March 20, Captain Norwood asks for the readmission of the Jews. In a newspaper published on May 6 we have a sympathetic account by a sailor of a visit to a synagogue in Leghorn. "Shall they," asks the writer, "be tolerated by the Pope, and by the Duke of Florence, by the Turks, and by the Barbarians and others, and shall England still have laws in force against them? When shall they be recalled?" (*Several Proceedings*, E, 794, 33). That Jews were already secretly established in London has been shown by Mr. L. Wolf's *Crypto-Jews under the Commonwealth*. I do not think he has noticed a passage in *Merc. Democritus* of May 12, 1652 (E, 664, 3). "The Jews in Charterhouse Lane have this week such devouring stomachs that they eat up whole families' clothes, gowns, rings, smocks, petticoats; nothing comes amiss under the sun."

[2] These propositions are appended to *Proposals for the Furtherance and Propagation of the Gospel*, published December 2, E, 683, 12.

enforcement of tithes interested the bulk of the community. The opinion that the clergy ought to live on voluntary contributions was welcome not merely to men like George Fox and his disciples, but also to the mobs by which Fox had been persecuted, on the simple ground that if there were no compulsion to support the clergy they would themselves be able to escape payment altogether. Another class of persons were those who, like the framers of the *Agreement of the People* as amended by the Army, were willing to afford a public maintenance to the clergy, but objected to tithe as unequal in its incidence, and entailing evils inseparable from any sort of payment in kind.

On April 29 Parliament resolved to satisfy the last class of critics so far as to throw upon the over-burdened Committee

April 29. A substitute for tithes proposed.

for the Propagation of the Gospel the task of providing a substitute for tithe, whilst it resolved, by a majority of twenty-seven to seventeen, that the payment of tithe should be enforced till some other more fitting provision for the ministry had been discovered.[1] How Crom-

Probable attitude of Cromwell.

well voted we have no means of knowing, but it can hardly be doubted that he voted with the majority, though favourable to the substitution of some more acceptable mode of payment,[2] or that, if we had before us a report of the discussions in Committee, Cromwell would be found in stern opposition to the sweeping conclusions of the

---

[1] *C.J.* vii. 128.

[2] Dr. Hodgkin (*George Fox*, p. 168) quotes a hitherto unpublished statement in Fox's *Journal* : "Though O. C. at Dunbar fight had promised to the Lord that if He gave him the victory over his enemies he would take away tithes, &c., or else let him be rolled into his grave with infamy ; but when the Lord had given him the victory, and he came to be chief, he confirmed the former laws." Dr. Hodgkin notes that the phrase about being 'rolled into the grave with infamy' occurs in Cromwell's speech to his first Parliament on September 12, 1654, and infers that Fox was probably mistaken in connecting it in any way with the abolition of tithes. Mr. Firth suggests that Fox's statement is based upon an imperfect recollection of Cromwell's language in his letter to Lenthall after the battle, of which, however, the theme is action against lawyers, whilst tithes are not mentioned. (See p. 4.)

Fifteen Fundamentals of Christianity. Words of his, now lost to us, must have inspired Milton with that noble sonnet in which he urges Cromwell to save freedom of conscience from hirelings :

May.
Milton's
sonnet to
Cromwell.

> Cromwell, our chief of men, who, through a cloud
> Not of war only, but detractions rude,
> Guided by faith and matchless fortitude,
> To peace and truth thy glorious way hast ploughed,
> And on the neck of crownèd Fortune proud
> Hast reared God's trophies, and His work pursued,
> While Darwen stream, with blood of Scots imbrued,
> And Dunbar field, resounds thy praises loud,
> And Worcester's laureate wreath : yet much remains
> To conquer still ; Peace hath her victories
> No less renowned than War : new foes arise,
> Threatening to bind our souls with secular chains.
> Help us to save free conscience from the paw
> Of hireling wolves, whose Gospel is their maw.[1]

---

[1] The sonnet is headed 'To the Lord General Cromwell, May 1652, on the proposals of certain ministers at the Committee for Propagation of the Gospel.' Professor Masson holds that this refers to the proposals of Owen's party (*Life of Milton*, iv. 441). If by this he means, as I suspect he does, the original proposals presented to Parliament on February 10, and printed on March 30 in *The Fourth Paper presented by Major Butler* (E, 658, 9), I think he is mistaken. In the first place it is unlikely that Milton would have postponed the expression of his indignation for three months. In the second place it is unlikely that he could have hoped to secure Cromwell's support in an attack on those proposals, simply on the ground that they advocated a continuance of maintenance for the clergy. My belief is that the proposal referred to by Milton was, at least in the main, the fifteen fundamentals, though it is true that these were only a development of a clause in the earlier fifteen proposals. In a marginal note to p. 23 of Major Butler's pamphlet we find : " Upon occasion of which motion the Ministers were desired to instance : who therefore presented 15 fundamentals, the copy whereof is not yet come to my hand." At the bottom of the page—apparently as a postscript—we find : " Upon this new project of these fifteen Proposals and fifteen Fundamentals, I do humbly beg of the Father of spirits that He will either graciously please to stir up the hearts of these worthy men to put in some Christian retractation ; or else the hearts of some of His faithful witnesses (against such

Milton's language is that of admiration and expectancy,[1] not of unqualified concurrence. For the close, sympathetic appreciation of an idealist by an idealist we must turn to the sonnet to Vane,[2] written about two months later :—

July.
Milton's
sonnet to
Vane.

> Vane, young in years, but in sage counsel old,
>   Than whom a better senator ne'er held
>   The helm of Rome, when gowns, not arms, repelled
>   The fierce Epirot and the African bold,
> Whether to settle peace, or to unfold
>   The drift of hollow states hard to be spelled ;
>   Then to advise how War may best, upheld,
>   Move by her two main nerves, iron and gold,
> In all her equipage ; besides, to know
>   Both spiritual power and civil, what each means,
>   What severs each, thou hast learned, which few have done.
> The bounds of either sword to thee we owe ;
>   Therefore on thy firm hand Religion leans
>   In peace, and reckons thee her eldest son.

Yet even here a jarring note is revealed. Vane is not only to introduce the reign of perfected religious liberty, but also to

graven images) to present some faithful and truly Christian observations." There was therefore a sharp controversy impending, and it was likely that the attention of the Committee was occupied with it during a great part, if not during the whole, of the month of April. How strong the attack was may be gathered from the fact that the ministers did not publish the fifteen Fundamentals, though they did publish their Proposals. The Fundamentals were not printed till December 2. It would be quite in accordance with Cromwell's character to suppose that he supported the proposals, though he opposed the later attempt to define Christianity with a view to silence those who strayed beyond the definition. Even if Cromwell voted on April 29, as I think he did, for a continuance of public support to the ministers, Milton would feel secure in May of being backed by him in his horror of the fundamentals.

[1] Compare the last lines of the sonnet to Cromwell, with the words in the sonnet to Fairfax: "O yet a nobler task awaits thy hand." There is a greater admiration for Cromwell, but the same expression of hope in what will be done, rather than a certainty that all will be done that the writer wishes to see accomplished.

[2] It reached Vane on July 3. Masson's *Life of Milton*, iv. 441.

hold the threads of diplomacy and direct the courses of war. Even Religion's eldest son could hardly be sufficient for these things.   If there had been a possibility of establishing religious liberty, for which the mind of the community was, as yet, but little prepared, the task could only be accomplished by a statesman unvexed by distracting influences and able to concentrate his efforts on this sole problem.   If Parliamentary effort slackened and the cry for ecclesiastical, like that for legal reform died away at Westminster, it was because Parliament was encumbered with schemes of a more material and therefore of a more immediately attractive nature.   The statesmen of the Commonwealth had to provide for war as well as for peace. They had to complete the predominance of England in the British Isles, and, as if this were a light task, they had already involved the nation in a maritime struggle with the first naval power in the world.   Their energies were necessarily absorbed in business other than the proposals of the Law Committee and of the Committee for the Propagation of the Gospel.

CHAPTER XIX

THE SUBJUGATION OF IRELAND

FOR the future stability of the Commonwealth it was of pre-eminent importance that its relations with Scotland and Ireland

1650.
Relations
with Scot-
land and
Ireland.

should be wisely ordered. Unfortunately, England's claim to attach either of these countries to herself rested on conquest, and it is in the nature of conquest to be a source of weakness. What was true of both was especially true of Ireland, where differences of blood and religion combined with memories of by-past deeds of cruelty to evoke a spirit of opposition far more bitter than even the mastery of the sword could arouse, and to justify in the eyes of Irishmen a prolongation of what was in reality a hopeless struggle.

When Cromwell returned to England after the surrender of Clonmel, there was but one army which could be supposed

May.
Ireland
after Crom-
well's
departure.

capable of holding the field against the English— the Ulster force once led by Owen O'Neill, but now under the strange command of Emer McMahon, Bishop of Clogher.[1] Enticed by information that Coote and Venables were at a distance from one another, he dashed forwards into county Londonderry, stormed Dungevin Fort, and even reduced Ballycastle, on the distant coast of Antrim.[2] Then followed the inevitable retreat. Pursued by

June 21.
The battle
of Scarriff-
hollis.

Coote with less than half his numbers, the episcopal commander insisted on standing at bay at Scarriff-hollis, about two miles from Letterkenny. In vain

---

[1] For the circumstances of his election see vol. i. 153.

[2] The Bishop of Clogher to Ormond, June 1 ; Coote to Ireton, July 2 ; Gilbert's *Contemporary Hist. of Affairs in Ireland*, ii. 422, iii. 147.

were the warnings of Henry O'Neill, Owen's son, and of other
officers who had stood high in Owen's favour, and who now
told his incompetent successor that the worst way of dealing
with an English enemy was to meet him in a pitched battle.
Their caution was justified by the result. Of 6,000 Irishmen
some 2,000 were slaughtered on the field. What was more
disastrous still was that the greater number of the trained officers,
versed in the wiles of war under their beloved chief, either met
their deaths foot to foot with the enemy or were captured and
mercilessly executed. Henry O'Neill and the Bishop himself
were amongst the latter number.[1]

Without an army in the field submission was only a
question of time ; and though fresh troops were subsequently
collected to oppose the invaders, they had neither
the numbers nor the organisation which might have
enabled them to hold head against their well-
disciplined antagonists. Under Ireton, therefore, who remained
as Lord Deputy after the departure of his father-in-
law, the military operations dwindled into a succession of sieges diversified by efforts to repress the
rapine of the natives, who carried off their spoil to the fastnesses of bog or hill. It was of little moment whether these
predatory bands dignified themselves with the name
of soldiers, or were mere outlaws, commonly known
as Tories : in either case they were well pleased to carry off
the goods of an Englishman, and still better pleased to ruin
such of their own countrymen as had demeaned themselves by
seeking the protection of the invaders.

The Irish left without an army.

Nature of the Irish resistance.

The Tories.

The first three months after Ireton had been named Lord
Deputy were occupied by five sieges. Tecroghan submitted
to Reynolds on June 25 ; Carlow to Sir Hardress
Waller on July 24 ; Waterford to the Lord Deputy
himself on August 6 ; Charlemount to Coote on the 14th ;
and Duncannon Fort to Cooke on the 17th of the same

Five sieges.

---

[1] Aphorismical Discovery, Gilbert's *Contemporary Hist. of Affairs in
Ireland*, ii. 82; Letters in *Several Proceedings*, E, 777, 22 ; Advices of
James Haws, July 1, *Carte MSS*. xxviii. fol. 105.

month.[1]   In none of these cases was any cruelty used or any
penalty inflicted upon the garrisons or inhabitants. At Waterford

A threat of
expulsion
suspended
over the in-
habitants
of Water-
ford.

alone was there any indication that a penalty might
possibly follow at a future time.   The inhabitants
who elected to remain within the walls were told
that, if a warning were given them to depart, they
would be allowed three months for the removal
of their property.[2] The clause bears evidence of a conviction rising in Ireton's mind that, if the country was to be
firmly held, it would be necessary to re-people the fortified
towns with settlers of English birth, as Cromwell had suggested
after the massacre at Wexford.

Of fortified towns in Ireland but three—Limerick, Galway,
and Athlone—still held out against the invaders.   The

Ireton
deceived
by Dillon.

importance of Athlone lay in its guarding the first
bridge crossing the Shannon, and thus affording a
practicable route by which an army could advance into
Connaught across a river fringed with bogs.   It is probable that
if Cromwell had been in command he would have turned his
attention primarily to the capture of Athlone ; and it is certain
that, had he done so, he would have thrown himself as
energetically into the task before him as though everything
depended on his own exertions.   Ireton was unwearied in his
attention to duty, and self-willed in the maintenance of
his own opinion ; but he had none of the qualifications of a
great commander.   He fancied that he could win Athlone by
treachery, and opened up a negotiation with Lord Dillon for
the betrayal of the town—a negotiation which Dillon accepted
with the object of spinning out time in order to render a serious
attack on Limerick impossible before the close of the season.[3]

---

[1] Hewson to Lenthall, June 29: *Several Proceedings*, E, 777, 22 ;
Coote to Lenthall, August 22, *ib.* E, 780, 17 ; Preston to Ormond, June 18,
Carte MSS. xxvii. fol. 695 ; *A Perf. Diurnal*, E, 780, 1 ; Diary of a
Parliamentary Officer, *Gilbert*, iii. 219.

[2] Articles of Waterford, *Several Proceedings*, E, 778, 17.

[3] The author of the Aphorismical Discovery (*Gilbert*, ii. 107–113),
with his fine nose for treason to the Irish cause, tells the story in full

Having thus founded his plans for the remainder of the campaign on the supposed treachery of an enemy rather than

Aug.
Ireton advances leisurely.

on his own efforts, Ireton marched leisurely northwards along the western foot of the Wicklow highlands, wasting time in the glens in burning the cottages and destroying the crops of the tribesmen whom he was unable to follow into the recesses of the hills.[1]

Before long news arrived which seems to have convinced Ireton that the resistance of the Irish would break down

News from the West.

without much trouble on his own part. The divisions between Ormond and the Celtic population of the West had been long notorious. In June, Limerick had re-

June.
Limerick resists Ormond.

fused admission to a garrison selected for its defence by the Lord Lieutenant; and it was not till July 15

July 15.
Hugh O'Neill governor of Limerick.

that he yielded so far as to appoint Hugh O'Neill, the gallant defender of Clonmel, to the governorship of the city, at the same time permitting him to choose the regiments to be employed in the garrison.[2]

---

belief that Dillon was in reality a traitor. Dillon, however, had written to Ormond, on August 6 (*ib.* iii. 171): "The enemy desires much to speak with me, but it shall be your Excellency's commands that will guide me in that particular, as it doth in all other things. If your Excellency conceives it not proper for me to give them a meeting by reason of the trust reposed in me by his Majesty, I believe no other prejudice can happen thereout, which I humbly offer to your Lordship's consideration, if you esteem it one. I am confident that it would subject my person to the scandal of those that are not acquainted with my intentions, but that I value not in respect of doing his Majesty the least service that is; certainly it's the time I have taken to consider of this business that has stayed the enemy's advance to this place ere now, and doubt not of their being here very soon. If our forces be here before them, according [to] your Excellency's orders, the enemy will have a hard tax of it." Writing on August 16 (*ib.* iii. 172) Dillon laments the insufficiency of his numbers, and adds that he had written to Clanricarde to bring all his forces to Athlone, a message which he would never have sent if he had intended to betray the place.

[1] Basil to Lenthall, September 13, *Several Proceedings*, E, 780, 17; Diary of a Parliamentary Officer, *Gilbert*, iii. 220.

[2] Commission to O'Neill, July 15, *Carte MSS.* clxii. p. 247. The previous correspondence is scattered over vol. xxviii. of the same collection.

Worse was still to come. The majority of the Roman Catholic prelates, like the Limerick citizens, suspected the Protestant Lord-Lieutenant of complicity with the enemy. Accepting as undoubted truth every calumny raised against him, they met at Jamestown to consider the situation of the country, and on August 12 deposed him from the authority he had received from the King, at the same time launching an excommunication against all who presumed to contravene their decree. As for their country, they had no other remedy to propose but to commend it to the Divine protection. "We well understand," they said, "the present condition of this nation is more inclining to ruin and despair than recovery. . . . Though this nobleman hath left us nothing but weakness and want and desolation, and that the enemy is rich, strong, and powerful, God is stronger and can help us, and for His own name's sake will deliver us."[1]

Aug. 12.
The pre-
lates
depose
Ormond.

It might seem as if the prelates were bent on reviving the days of Hildebrand. In reality they were the mouthpiece of a nation borne down by a flood of disaster. Their hearts were with their own people. It was not so much Ormond in person whom they defied as Ormond representing an alien sovereign who regarded the loyalty of Irishmen as no more than a counter in his game, and who, at that very moment, had suffered himself to become a tool in the hands of the Presbyterian Scots.

The prelates
and the
nation.

Well might Ireton think that the Lord had delivered his enemies into his hands. On August 30 he was so confident of success that he ventured to divide his army, sending Sir Hardress Waller to close round Limerick on the east, whilst he himself was to make for Athlone. There, if, as he fully expected, he gained possession of the town by treachery, he would be in a position, after effecting a junction with Coote, to march down the farther bank of the Shannon and to straiten Limerick on the western side of the river.[2]

Aug. 30.
Ireton sends
Waller
against
Limerick.

[1] Cox, *Hib. Anglicana*, ii. App. xlviii.

[2] That he had formed the latter plan is not shown by any evidence, but it arises out of the situation, and in 1651 Ireton established himself on

Waller indeed did not linger over his portion of the task. On September 9 he was before Limerick, and sent an unavail-

Sept. 9. Waller summons L'merick. ing summons into the city. Ireton was in no such haste. It is possible that he was delayed by the difficulty of provisioning his army. However this may have been, it was not till September 16 that he reached Athlone, only to find the bridge guarded against him, and to renounce all idea of forcing a passage across it. All that he could now do was to leave Coote to establish himself in the English town on the eastern bank of the Shannon, after which, moving through King's County and Tipperary, he occupied the last fortnight of September in securing the fortified towns and houses of the district. Then, far too late to effect anything, he turned towards Limerick, where he rejoined Waller on the

Oct. 6. Ireton summons Limerick. eastern bank.[1] On October 6 he summoned the city, and, finding the citizens indisposed to yield to mere threats, he requested a Council of War to give

Oct. 16. A council of war. him the advice which he had hitherto omitted to require.[2] The Council, being composed of men of sense, told him that it was useless to persist in the siege at so advanced a season. On the 19th, leaving a few

Oct. 19. Ireton marches away. garrisons behind to keep the citizens in check during the winter, he marched off to the succour of his newly-planted strongholds in King's County, now threatened by the incursion of a considerable Irish force. Already, before he had appeared on the scene, Axtel and other

the western bank. The scheme of marching against Athlone was finally decided on at a council of war on September 1, at which Coote was present. Diary of a Parl. Officer, *Gilbert*, iii. 220. That the plan had been discussed before appears from Dillon's letter of May 6. (See p. 108, note 3.)

[1] Diary of a Parl. Officer, *Gilbert*, iii. 219-222.

[2] That Ireton mismanaged the campaign without taking advice is shown by a remark of Ludlow : " The Deputy," he writes with respect to a council of war about twelve months later, " who was now entirely freed from his former manner of adhering to his own opinion which had been observed to be his greatest infirmity, referred it again to the consideration of the Court." *Ludlow*, i. 288.

officers had gathered together their scattered forces, had fallen on their assailants in Meelick Island in the Shannon, and had slaughtered some 4,000 of them in and after the fight.[1]

The addition of King's County and of a portion of Tipperary to the territory of the Commonwealth was the only

Ireton's failure as a general.

result of the campaign undertaken by Ireton after the surrender of Waterford. His incompetency as a commander is displayed alike in his readiness to undertake more than he was able to accomplish and in his failure to proportion his means to the objects which he had in view.

With little effort of their own, the Irish had thus gained a breathing-space to prepare for the renewal of the struggle in the

The Irish opportunity.

Aug. 31. Ormond resolves to leave Ireland.

Oct. 13. He receives leave to go.

Oct.-Nov. An assembly at Loughrea.

ensuing summer. Ormond, at least, refused any longer to stand in the way of united effort. On August 31 he announced that he only waited for the King's permission to leave the country.[2] On October 13 he received from Charles the authority he desired, learning at the same time that his master, acting under Scottish compulsion, had denounced the Irish treaty of 1648.[3] In vain Ormond attempted to induce the prelates now assembled at Loughrea to reverse their sentence of excommunication. They replied that they were the King's obedient servants, but that a Catholic people ought not to be subjected to a Protestant governor.[4] Having appointed Clanricarde Lord Deputy, Ormond sailed for France before the end of the year. If nobility of character combined with almost infinite patience could have availed him, Ormond might have saved Ireland from impending ruin. As it was, not only were the conditions

[1] Diary of a Parl. Officer, *Gilbert*, iii. 223–225 ; Basil to Lenthall, November 4, *ib*. iii. 184.

[2] Ormond's answer to the Prelates, August 31, *Carte MSS*. xxviii. fol. 408.

[3] Charles to Ormond, August 19 ; Ormond to Charles, October. *Ib*. xxix. fol. 645; xxviii. fol. 567.

[4] Proposals of the Commissioners of Trust. *Ib*. October 29. Answer of the Clergy, November 7. *Ib*. xxviii. fol. 623.

of action persistently adverse to him, but his inbred Royalism
made it impossible for him to inspire confidence in his Celtic
countrymen, who were sufficiently keen-sighted to perceive that
they must exist without Charles, or that they could not exist at all.

It was therefore to little purpose that Ormond left behind
him, in the person of Clanricarde, a Lord Deputy who was at
Clanricarde   least a Catholic.   Whatever lip-service Irish priests
Lord   and patriots might render to the idea of Royalty, they
Deputy.   had made up their minds to fight their own battles
without reference to a King who in Presbyterian hands was a
hindrance rather than a strength.   How great this hindrance
might be had been shown by the course of a negotiation
which had been carried on for some months before Ormond's
May.   departure.   In May a certain Colonel Oliver Synott
A message   landed at Galway, having, as he explained, been
from the   commissioned by Charles to treat with the Duke of
Duke of   Lorraine in conjunction with the Royalist Minister
Lorraine.
at Brussels, Sir Henry de Vic.   Unfortunately, according to
his own account, he had been chased by two English frigates,
and compelled to throw his dispatches overboard, but he gave
verbal assurances that the Duke was ready to advance 10,000*l.*
for carrying on the war if some Irish port were made over to
him as a security for the loan; Duncannon, which at that
time had not yet surrendered to the English, being finally
selected.[1]   Ormond, however, shrank from striking a bargain
June.   without better credentials, and contented himself
Ormond's   with sending Lord Taaffe to receive instructions
reply.   from Charles, whose departure for Scotland was at
that time unknown in Connaught.[2]

Months passed away before anything more was heard of
the matter.   Taaffe visited Paris, where, finding that Charles
Taaffe's   was no longer on the Continent, he placed himself
mission.   in communication with the Queen.   By her advice

[1] Synott to Ormond, May 22, *Gilbert*, ii. 420.   Compare a second
letter, undated but received by Ormond on June 13.   *Ib.* ii. 423.

[2] Ormond to Clanricarde, June 5 ; Instructions to Taaffe, *Carte MSS.*
xxvii. fols. 625, 627.

he forwarded Ormond's letters to Charles, and after waiting in vain for a reply betook himself to Brussels to open negotiations with the Duke.[1]   The Duke was favourably inclined, and on

D c. 21.
The·mission
of the Abbot
of St. Catha-
rine.

December 21 commissioned Stephen de Henin, Abbot of St. Catharine, to convey to the Catholic States of Ireland the assurance of his desire to help them.[2]

Expelled from his own territory by the overshadowing power of France, but enriched by the plunder of the Thirty Years' War, the Duke, having at his disposal a considerable armed force, was ready for any adventure which seemed likely to serve his interest.   Moreover, he had special reasons for

Motives of
the Duke of
Lorraine.

placing the Pope under obligations.   Like Henry VIII., he had married a wife in the lifetime of her predecessor, and he was at this time striving to induce Innocent X. to regularise this later union.   He may, therefore, have thought that the deliverance of a Catholic people from the yoke of the oppressor would weigh more heavily in the balance at Rome than any legal arguments which it was in his power to adduce.

At all events, the Duke had no intention of stirring unless he was invested with something like royal authority.   When in

The Duke's
proposals.

February 1651 the Abbot, accompanied by Taaffe's uncle, George Dillon, arrived in Ireland, he declared

1651.
Feb.
The Abbot
delivers his
message.

that if the Duke was to render assistance he must be accepted as Protector of the kingdom, though in due subordination to the King.   As a token of good-will he brought with him 6,000*l.*, and an assurance that his master was ready to employ his men, treasure, shipping, and person in the reconquest of Ireland.[3]   It was easy to conjecture

[1]   Henrietta Maria to the Duke of Lorraine, $\frac{\text{Sept. 24}}{\text{Oct. 4}}$, November $\frac{8}{18}$, Clanricarde's *Memoirs*, 71, 73.

[2]   Commission to the Abbot of St. Catharine, December $\frac{21}{31}$; Answer of the Duke of Lorraine, $\frac{\text{Dec. 22}}{\text{Jan. 1}}$; Taaffe to Ormond, $\frac{\text{Dec. 24}}{\text{Jan. 3}}$, $\frac{\text{Dec. 26}}{\text{Jan. 5}}$, *ib.* 5-22.

[3]   Taaffe to Ormond, Clanricarde's *Memoirs*, 25.   The money is there said to have been 5,000*l.*, but 1,000*l.* more had been added before the Abbot started.

that such a protectorate would leave little room for the King's authority. Moreover, the Duke's letter was addressed, not to the King's representative, but to the Lords appointed to administer the government of Ireland.[1] Whether Clanricarde knew it or not, before the end of the year Father Anthony Geoghegan was despatched from Rome to the Irish prelates with instructions to urge the institution of a Catholic Protector.[2]

To such a consummation the Catholic Clanricarde was no less averse than the Protestant Ormond. Yet, that he might

March.
Its reception
in Ireland. not place the burden of rejection on his own shoulders, he laid the Duke's proposal before the Commissioners of Trust, reinforced by such other prelates and noblemen as were within call. Finding that they were not only unanimously in favour of an acceptance of the offer, but that they were even negotiating directly with the Abbot without his consent, he indignantly told them that to accept the Duke's proposal was tantamount to a dethronement of their Sovereign. Unable or unwilling to avow their action, the members of the assembly drew back, and it was finally resolved that the Abbot should be dismissed, and that two fresh

April 23.
Agents sent
to treat at
Brussels. agents—Sir Nicholas Plunket and Geoffrey Browne —should be sent to the Duke—no longer to treat with him on the Protectorate of Ireland, but merely to solicit a loan on the security of certain towns.[3]

The negotiation with the Duke of Lorraine—a man notoriously ready to promise more than he was able to perform—

The nego-
tiation as a
test of
opinion. unimportant in itself, acquires an importance for the student of Irish history as a touch-stone of the divergent aims of those on whose shoulders lay the burden of Irish defence. In word Irish Royalists and Irish

---

[1] Excellentissimis . . . Dominis in Hibernici regni administratione constitutis, Clanricarde's *Memoirs*, 7.

[2] Aphorismical Discovery, *Gilbert*, ii. 144.

[3] Clanricarde's *Memoirs*, 22–99. Part of this correspondence was known to the English and was published in London on April 24, *Several Proceedings*, F., 785, 12.

patriots might combine ; in reality a thick cloud of suspicion parted them asunder.

The situation was the more desperate as it was unlikely that the military blunders of the last campaign would be repeated in 1651. Even during the winter the English had gained ground. Waller, supported by Henry Cromwell, the second surviving son of the Lord General, had pushed back Muskerry to the mountains in the western part of the counties of Cork and Kerry,[1] whilst Reynolds and Hewson cleared Westmeath, Longford, and Cavan. By the end of March, save for the Tories and other small parties lurking in spots of hard ground in the midst of bogs, or in the higher stretches of the Wicklow Hills, the Irish held nothing outside Connaught, except the mountains of Donegal, Clare, and the western extremity of the counties of Kerry and Cork.

Ground gained by the English.

The mere pressure of a hungry army on a hostile population must, in any case, have been disastrous. Whole districts lay waste without inhabitant, and cruel deeds often tracked the steps of the regiments.[2] Ireton, at least, did his best to put a stop to irregularities condemned by the existing laws of war. He had no better officer than Axtel ; but when Axtel was charged with putting to the sword prisoners who had surrendered to mercy, Ireton brought him before a council of war, and, though it was proved that Axtel had not personally offered quarter, suspended him from his command and sent him back to England on the ground that his soldiers had thrown out some expressions tending that way.[3]

Desolation in Ireland.

Dismissal of Axtel.

---

[1] Ireton to Bradshaw, February 8, *The Faithful Scout*, E, 784, 12 ; Hewson to Lenthall, February, March 14, 18 ; *Several Proceedings*, E, 784, 31 ; E, 785, 4.

[2] There is a collection of such cases in the edition of Clarendon published in 1849, viii. 223-245. It was made after the Restoration, and considerable allowance must therefore be made for the imagination of the informants, as in the case of the Ulster massacres of 1641.

[3] *Ludlow*, i. 263.

In his work of restraining offences, Ireton had the full support of Ludlow and the three other Parliamentary Commissioners,[1] who landed in Ireland in January 1651. In taking up the civil government of the country, they aimed at promoting the welfare of its inhabitants so far as this was compatible with submission to the English Government, and with the payment of the assessments levied for the maintenance of the army;[2] tillage was to be encouraged, and the exportation of cattle and the killing of lambs forbidden.[3]

Jan. Arrival of the Parliamentary Commissioners.

Neither Ireton nor the Commissioners, however, could hide from themselves the unpleasant truth that they held Ireland by force alone. A proclamation, issued in February,[4] embodied the warning suspended over the heads of the inhabitants of Waterford,[5] bidding them to quit the city within three months, with the intention of supplying their places by a regiment of military settlers to be raised in England.[6] Ireton's justification for this harsh step goes far beyond the necessity of securing a fortified post of the importance of Waterford. "I desire," he said, "those that question it but to look upon the late actions of many of those that upon their fair professions to us, and our trust in them for faithfulness, or, at least, for innocent and peaceable demeanours towards us, have received protection from us; who notwithstanding do most of them make

Feb. The inhabitants of Waterford receive warning to quit.

Ireton justifies his resolution.

[1] Vol. i. 265.

[2] Commissioners to Bradshaw, March 24, *Ludlow*, i. 486.

[3] Proclamations by the Commissioners, in *Several Proceedings*, E, 785, 20; E, 786, 22. There are also copies from the originals in the *Egerton MSS.* 1779, fols. 1–14.

[4] The Proclamation printed by *Borlase*, 341–345, is there dated as given at Waterford, March, 1650. Ireton had, however, removed to Kilkenny before February 27, *Egerton MSS.* 1779, fol. 9, and in the proclamation itself gives 'the tenth day of February instant' as the date from which the warning was to take effect.

[5] See p. 108.

[6] Lawrence's Propositions for guarding Waterford, Ross, and Carrick, accepted by Ireton Dec. 12, 1650, *Several Proceedings*, E, 684, 15.

it their daily business to do us all the mischief they can where-
ever they see an opportunity, and for that purpose do harbour,
entertain, and encourage those many Tories in every corner
that otherwise durst not come into our quarters, nor could subsist in them undiscovered, or do that mischief that they do and
escape yet from all our forces and garrisons in every corner
ready to pursue them, but that as they are assured, and find the
protected people are friends to them and, in their hearts,
enemies and false to us, notwithstanding all their professions
to the contrary ; nay, many of the protected people themselves,
upon every slight occasion or ground of hope of doing mischief
to us, do frequently run from their habitations, join with the
enemy in arms, and deliver up their castles to them." The
only wonder is that Ireton should have been surprised at such
a result of the English conquest.

The more Ireton realised that his hold on Ireland was one
of force alone, the more anxious was he to keep his soldiers
aloof from any close connection with the natives.
He was therefore horrified to learn that there were
some amongst them who, invincible in battle against
Irish men, had capitulated to the bright eyes and
seductive grace of Irish girls. He at once denounced
the marriages which were the not infrequent result as destructive of military order. The newly-married wives, it seems, had
allowed it to be understood that they had been converted to
the Protestant faith. In a strongly worded proclamation
Ireton asserted that their alleged conversion was but pretended
'for some corrupt and carnal ends.' Neither officers nor
soldiers were hereafter to marry 'any of the women of this
nation that are papists, or have lately been such, and whose
change of religion is not, or cannot be judged by fit persons
such as shall be appointed to that end, to flow from a real
work of God upon their hearts.' Officers contravening this
order were to be reduced to the ranks, private soldiers to be
degraded to lower positions than those they held, or even
cashiered. If Ireton had had any sense of humour, he would
hardly have erected a court of conscience, before which any

May 1.
Marriages
between
English
soldiers and
Irish women
denounced
by Ireton.

quick-witted Irish woman might succeed in baffling the investigations of God-fearing veterans.[1]

Early in May Ireton was prepared to take the field with better prospect of success than in the preceding summer.

Ireton prepares to take the field.

Not only was his army in a high state of efficiency, but he himself—unlike most other mediocre commanders—having learnt to distrust his own powers,

May 10. A council of war at Clonmel.

had summoned a council of war to meet at Clonmel and decide on the plan of the next campaign.[2] When that council met on the 10th, its members found as much difficulty in coming to a conclusion as the Lord Deputy himself. If Limerick was to be surrounded, part of the English army must establish itself on the western bank of the Shannon. Yet it seemed impossible to force a passage over the broad stream in the neighbourhood of Limerick, and no less impossible to feed an army attempting to evade the difficulty by passing round the Shannon at its source far away in the north. In the end the rumour of a plot to betray Limerick into their hands reached the English commanders, and orders to march were given, in the hope that something unexpected might relieve them from their hesitations.[3]

Arrived before Limerick, Ireton found that he must depend on his own exertions for the reduction of the city. On June 1,

June 1. Ireton forces a passage over the Shannon.

making a feint to cross the Shannon at Killaloe, he carried over about 500 men at Brian's Bridge,[4] lower down the stream, a force which, being supported by cannon planted on the shore it had left, sufficed to put to flight 2,000 Irishmen under Castlehaven's command. Ireton was thus enabled to establish himself on both sides of the river. The shipping of the Commonwealth rode at anchor below Limerick, and secured the landing of

[1] Proclamation, May 1, *Several Proceedings*, E, 786, 22.

[2] Commissioners to Lenthall, April 19, *Ludlow*, i. 488; *Several Proceedings*, E, 786, 4.

[3] Diary of a Parl. Officer, *Gilbert*, iii. 226.

[4] There was no bridge there.

supplies.   Unless succour arrived, the surrender of the city
was a mere question of time.[1] Before the end of

May 31.
Coote in
Connaught.

June.

June the arrival of succour had been rendered well-
nigh impracticable, as Coote, having slipped past
Clanricarde's scanty forces, had broken into Connaught.[2] Athlone, Loughrea, and Ballinasloe fell easily into

July.
Broghill's
victory.

his hands.[3] Moving parties kept the Tories in
check.[4] In July Broghill defeated Muskerry, and
drove him back yet further into the hills.[5]

Meanwhile Ireton had done his best to carry Limerick by
storm.   On June 14 he opened an attack on two forts, the

June 14.
The attack
on Limerick
opened.

one on a weir about two miles above the city walls,
and the other on the western end of the Thomond
Bridge which led from the city itself across the
Shannon.   The first of these was carried on the 16th and the

June 23.
The attack
repulsed.

second on the 21st.   On the 23rd an attempt made
to gain possession of King's Island, on part of which
the English town was built, was repulsed with heavy
loss.   Ireton abandoned the attempt to carry the place by
force, and fell back upon a blockade.[6] It is possible that in
deciding not to renew the assault Ireton was to some extent

June 30.
Proposals
for surrender
rejected.

actuated by his knowledge that two parties were
contending for the mastery within.   On June 30,
however, a week after his repulse on King's Island,
the citizens rejected proposals made by him for a surrender.
The more determined party had got the upper hand.

There was an irresolution in Ireton which showed itself
not only in his conduct of a campaign, but in his want of grip

[1] Diary of a Parl. Officer, *Gilbert*, iii. 230 ; Castlehaven's *Memoirs*
(ed. 1680), 129. Ludlow (i. 268) gives an excellent account of the
passage of the Shannon.

[2] Hewson to Lenthall, June 5, *Several Proceedings*, E, 786, 4.

[3] Ludlow's *Memoirs*, i. 270 ; Hewson to Lenthall, June 19, *Several
Proceedings*, E, 786, 12.

[4] Commissioners to Lenthall, June 5, *ib.* E, 786, 4.

[5] Diary of a Parl. Officer, *Gilbert*, iii. 247.

[6] *Ib.* iii. 238-241.

over his subordinates. Against one military offence, indeed—

A colonel cashiered. the offence of killing prisoners admitted to quarter— he sternly set his face, and he cashiered a Colonel Tothill who, after the capture of the fort on the weir, had been The inhabitants attempt to escape. guilty of this crime.[1] At other times he was more indulgent to his own officers. Having ordered that four wretches out of a crowd attempting to pass his lines should be knocked on the head, he learnt that those to whom the execution of the sentence was entrusted had killed the whole party. We are told that Ireton was disgusted with this ' mistake of orders,' but we do not hear that he punished the offenders.[2]

Every week the situation of those within grew more desperate. The plague was raging in the city, and the more The plague in Limerick. helpless of the inhabitants continued, in spite of the rough warning they had received, to make efforts to escape. Most of them were whipped back within Those who try to escape are whipped back or hanged. the walls, but a few were hanged as an example to others, amongst them a girl whose father begged in vain to redeem her life by the sacrifice of his own.[3] Ireton, however, had no pleasure in cruelty, and his next step was to erect a gibbet in sight of the walls on which he hanged some criminals already sentenced to death, ' that those within might suppose that execution to be for coming out.'[4]

When October came the surrender of Limerick, in spite of frequent messages from Ireton, appeared no nearer than before. Oct. Limerick still holds out. The provisions within were not exhausted, and the war party counted on the inclemency of the approaching winter. "You," called out a sentry from the

---

[1] Diary of a Parl. Officer, *Gilbert*, iii. 238–241 ; *Ludlow*, i. 274 ; Ireton to Lenthall, July 15, *Several Proceedings*, E, 786, 29.

[2] Diary of a Parl. Officer, *Gilbert*, iii. 440.

[3] It may have been thought necessary to execute a woman in order that women might be deterred from breaking out. It may be remembered how women had been thrust back on starving Colchester, *The Great Civil War*, iv. 200.

[4] *Ludlow*, i. 284.

walls, "labour to beat us out with bombshells,[1] but we will beat you away with snowballs." Ireton, in fact, had discovered that the blockade was likely to be prolonged beyond his calculations, and, piously attributing to God his discovery that a battery might usefully be placed in a position which he 'had little observed before,' had opened fire on the city. This attack, which, as far as appears might have been adopted some weeks earlier,[2] proved immediately successful. On October 25, after a three days' struggle between the parties within the walls, during which Colonel Fennell, backed by the majority of the citizens, defied the authority of the Governor, seized one of the gates, and turned his guns upon his brother officers, the war party was compelled to yield. On the following day negotiations were opened for a surrender, and on the 27th articles were signed.[3]

Ireton opens fire.

Oct. 23-25.
Struggle of parties.

Oct. 27.
Surrender of Limerick.

For the most part the terms on which the surrender was accepted were modelled on those granted to Waterford. There was the same liberty of removal given to citizens and soldiers, the same announcement that those civilians who elected to remain might be forcibly expelled on three months' notice, Limerick, like Waterford, being destined in Ireton's mind to receive an English colony. In some respects the articles of Limerick differed from those of Waterford. In the preceding April the Commissioners had announced their intention of bringing to justice all Irishmen guilty of murders committed in or since the massacres of 1641,[4] and a special clause was now inserted to make known that nothing in the

Terms granted.

---

[1] "So," adds the diarist, "they called our mortar-shot." *Gilbert*, iii. 253. The first instance of the word 'bomb' in this sense is given by Dr. Murray as in 1687.

[2] He had however been fortified in his resolve to continue the blockade by the council of war, Ireton to Lenthall, Nov. 3, *Gilbert*, iii. 266.

[3] Diary of a Parl. Officer, *Gilbert*, iii. 253. Account of the surrender of Limerick, *ib.* 263; Ireton to Lenthall, Nov. 3, *ib.* iii. 265.

[4] Proclamation of the Commissioners, Ap. 23, *Egerton MSS.* 1761, fol. 13.

capitulation would be held to free those who benefited by it
from proceedings taken against them in a civil court. As a
special penalty for what was deemed by the victors a useless

Twenty-
two ex-
cepted
from pardon. prolongation of the defence, twenty-two persons, including one Welsh deserter, were excepted from
pardon in the same way as the superior officers had
been excepted after the surrender of Colchester.[1]

It did not, however, follow that all the twenty-two would
suffer death. Many of them succeeded in effecting their escape.

Fate of
those ex-
cepted. Of those who fell into the hands of the conquerors,
O'Neill and four others were selected by the
council of war for execution, though their cases were
ultimately reserved for future consideration. Three more,
Major-General Purcell, Alderman Stritch, and the Bishop of
Emly, who, with Alderman Dominic Fanning, had been the

Oct. 30. soul of the defence, were discovered on the 30th, and
promptly hanged. On the following day Fanning,
who had concealed himself in his family monument in the church
of the Franciscan monastery, was driven by hunger to leave his
hiding-place. In the church was a party of soldiers warming
themselves by a fire. Their captain, suspecting his character,
gave him a friendly kick and warned him to be off. Fanning's
life might have been saved if a treacherous servant had not
given his name to the officer, leaving him no choice but to
arrest him.

On November 1, O'Neill and Geoffrey Barron, two of the
five originally condemned, were again brought before the coun-

Nov. 1.
O'Neill
pardoned. cil of war. O'Neill pleaded that he had but done
his duty as a soldier, and that he had raised his voice
for an earlier surrender. Ireton carried with him
the majority of the council to the side of severity, on the strange
ground that the prisoner had caused the deaths of so many
Englishmen in his heroic defence of Clonmel. Ireton, however,
seeing in the faces of the councillors signs of dissatisfaction, put
the question a second time. This time the vote was given in

---

[1] Articles of Surrender, *A Perf. Diurnal*, E, 791, 22. The name of
the Bishop of Limerick is here omitted by an obvious error of the press.

favour of life, and English officers were spared the disgrace of putting to death an honourable opponent, on the excuse that he had been too successful.

As a civilian, Barron met with less favour in the eyes of soldiers. He had contributed to the resistance of Waterford, as well as to that of Limerick. He now exasperated his judges by pleading that his cause was the same as that of the English army—that of his religion and his country's liberty. Ireland, replied Ireton, sternly, was a conquered country, yet Irishmen had been treated with consideration far beyond their merits, having 'barbarously murdered all the English that fell into their hands.' As for religion, there was no comparison between the two peoples. Englishmen had fought to preserve their natural right, without pretending to impose their own religion on others. Irishmen belonged to a Church which would not be contented without power to compel all others to submit themselves to its claims on pain of death. It was the old argument repeated again and again by every Englishman of the day. Irishmen were rebellious murderers. Irishmen were intolerant papists. What more needed to be said?

Barron condemned.

Barron met his death triumphantly, having decked himself in the white garments of a bridegroom. Fanning was hanged by his side. Two others, Sir Geoffrey Galway and Dr. Higgins, were executed subsequently. If, as appears probable, Woulfe, a friar, shared their fate, the number of victims is brought up to eight, though in his case the accounts are too divergent to enable us to speak with certainty.[1]

Execution of Barron, Fanning, and probably three others.

---

[1] Of five—Purcell, the Bishop of Emly, Alderman Stritch, Fanning, and Barron—there can be no doubt. To these a letter from the Irish Commissioners of December 18 (*Several Proceedings*, E, 791, 23) adds Galway and Higgins, and no more. Ludlow places Woulfe's death in connection with that of the Bishop of Emly's, in which he is not borne out by anyone writing at the time except the author of the Account of the Surrender (*Gilbert*, iii. 263), who writes from hearsay and makes several mistakes. On the other hand Woulfe is stated in De Burgo's

It is undeniable that from a purely military point of view the defence of Limerick was hopeless from the first. No army was in the field capable of relieving it, and there was no sober prospect that any such army could be raised. Before the fall of the city, it was made known even to the blindest that the scattered remnants of Irish resistance would find no support from beyond the sea.

The defence of Ireland hopeless.

Oct. 7.
News from the Duke of Lorraine.

On October 7, Synott returned to Galway with an agreement between the Duke of Lorraine and the two Commissioners, Plunket and Browne,[1] in accordance with which the Duke was to be styled the Royal Protector of Ireland, holding powers little short of those of Royalty itself. On the 20th this offer was summarily rejected by Clanricarde as entrenching on his authority derived from the King. Irishmen in their death-agony had long passed the point in which such considerations had weight; and the Mayor and Corporation of Galway even chose an agent of their own to re-open the negotiation which the Lord Deputy fiercely denounced. The Duke was not likely to lead an army into Ireland on the simple invitation of the Corporation of Galway.[2]

Oct. 20.
His offer rejected by Clanricarde.

Ireton did not live to profit by these distractions. On November 7 he died, a victim to the self-abnegation which

---

Hibernia Dominicana, 568, to have been put to death. The list given by the commissioners is derived from Colonel Abbot, who left Limerick as late as November 21, and would be likely to be accurate and complete. Possibly Woulfe died in confinement, and was counted as a victim. What Irishmen could believe is shown by the wild statement of the author of the Aphorismical Discovery (*Gilbert*, iii. 20), who says that when Limerick surrendered the captors ran hither and thither ' killing every mother's child they met. . . . Three days and three nights were they in this bloody execution, no growte '—*i.e.* grotto, ' cellar, prison, church, or tomb—was unsearched, all therein found made piecemeals and hanged and quartered.' The various documents relating to the surrender are printed by Mr. Gilbert, iii. 263–272.

[1] See p. 115.

[2] Clanricarde's *Memoirs*, 139–180.

refused to spare the body in the service of his country. The fever might have relaxed its grasp, if he had not struggled to the last against the slightest abandonment of duty. His country-men, as has been so often the case, admired his disinterest-edness, and suffered his inefficiency as a commander to be covered by success. They could not forget that when others had risen to wealth by their services in camp or council, Ireton had rejected a grant of 2,000*l.* a year, on the ground that it might be better spent in paying the debts of the Commonwealth. His body was brought to England and buried in Westminster Abbey with pomp which disgusted some of the more pronounced re-publicans. Posterity reverences him not only as the pure-spirited patriot that he was, but also as the author of the *Heads of the Proposals*, the advocate of a wide but sober liberty.[1]

On December 2 the Commissioners appointed Ludlow to command the army in Ireland till the pleasure of Parliament was known.[2] What was now needed was not a great general, but an energetic officer, and Ludlow was therefore the very man for the post. Before the end of the year the Commissioners calculated that there were still 30,000 Irishmen in arms scattered over the country, but their commanders were for the most part weary of a hopeless struggle, and prepared to withdraw from it if they and their men might be allowed to seek service under the King of Spain.[3] The conviction that submission could not long be avoided appears to have been shared by the party of the prelates who, by this time, had been forced to

Dec. 2.
Ludlow provisional com-mander.

Dec. 26.
Report of the Com-missioners.

Growing conviction that sub-mission is inevitable.

---

[1] Ireton has been traditionally connected with what is now called Cromwell House at Highgate. It was certainly the property of his brother Alderman John Ireton, but I do not know of any evidence that it was ever owned by the Lord Deputy. The signatures in a book of the proceedings of the governors of Highgate School alleged to be those of Henry Ireton are really John's, and that too written some years after Henry's death.

[2] Order of the Commissioners, Dec. 2, *Mr. Dunlop's Transcripts.*

[3] The Commissioners to the Council of State, Dec. 26, *ib.*

abandon all hopes of support from the Duke of Lorraine.
Early in February 1652 Father Anthony Geoghegan,
who was in their inmost secrets, expressed himself in
favour of an agreement with the English Independents,
and an appeal to their known principles in the matter
of liberty of conscience.[1] This letter was intercepted by
Clanricarde, and Geoghegan was arrested as a traitor. The
time had passed when defiance of Charles II. could
count for treason in Ireland. The prelates claimed
Geoghegan as amenable only to ecclesiastical
proceedings ; and having once got him into their power,
naturally failed to discover any evil intention in his letter.[2]

The immediate result of Geoghegan's letter was a resolution
taken by Clanricarde to make the best terms with the conquerors. On February 14 he wrote to Ludlow,
asking for a meeting of commissioners to treat for a
settlement of the kingdom on equitable terms.
Ludlow contemptuously rejected the proposal.
What he wanted was not negotiation, but submission. "The settlement of this nation," he declared, "doth
of right belong to the Parliament of the Commonwealth of
England, to whom we leave the same, being assured they will
not therein capitulate with those who ought to be in subjec-
tion, yet stand in opposition to their authority."[3] Ludlow
might well take a high tone. He knew that starvation, if not
the sword, would soon make resistance impossible. The
hideous work of burning and destruction went gaily
on. On March 7, Colonel John Fitzpatrick made
his submission in West Meath. All persons under

1652.
Feb. 4.
Geoghe-
gan's pro-
posal.

His conflict
with Clan-
ricarde.

Feb. 14.
Clanri-
carde offers
to treat.

Feb. 20.
Ludlow's
reply.

March 7.
Submission
of Fitz-
patrick.

---

[1] Geoghegan to Haly, February 4, *Gilbert*, iii. 286. This letter
appears to me conclusive of the part taken by Geoghegan, and convinces
me that the glosses placed by the author of the Aphorismical Discovery,
and by himself on his words are quite worthless. Examination of
Geoghegan, Feb. 13 ; *ib.* iii. 53, 54, 289.

[2] Aphorismical Discovery, *Gilbert*, iii. 54, 55.

[3] Clanricarde to Ludlow, Feb. 14 ; Ludlow to Clanricarde, Feb. 20,
Ludlow's *Memoirs*, i. 504.

him having had a hand in the murders or massacres of English or other Protestants in the first year of the war, or in any murders of persons not in arms since that date were excepted from pardon. All the rest of his party might either transport themselves to foreign parts, or live peaceably in Ireland, submitting to the ordinances of Parliament. Priests, Jesuits, or others of the popish clergy were, however, not to be allowed to reside in the parliamentary quarters.[1]

Fitzpatrick's example was quickly followed. On March 23, O'Dwyer, commanding in parts of the counties of Tipperary and Waterford, submitted on somewhat similar con-

March 23. O'Dwyer's submission.

ditions.[2] Roscommon surrendered on April 3,

April 3- May 12. Surrenders of Roscommon, Jamestown, and Galway.

Jamestown on the 7th, Galway on May 12. So many were the local submissions, that on the day on which Galway surrendered, articles were signed at Kilkenny with the forces then standing out in Leinster, to which those in the other provinces were

May 12. The articles of Kilkenny.

invited to accede. In the main these articles resembled those granted to Fitzpatrick, but, as an additional concession, the Irish Catholics were assured that the Act passed at Westminster for the repeal of the recusancy laws should be held valid in Ireland, so that no one would be prosecuted for refusing to be present at a Protestant service.[3]

General submission.

The summer was employed in the suppression—with no tender hand—of the scattered parties which continued to hold out. In one or two isolated positions indeed the struggle was prolonged even beyond the year.

1653. Surrender of Innisboffin and Lough Oughter.

Innisboffin did not surrender till February 14,[4] and a castle on an island on Lough Oughter not till April 27, 1653.[5]

---

[1] Agreement with Fitzpatrick, March 7, Mr. Dunlop's *Transcripts*, No. 140.

[2] Agreement with O'Dwyer, March 23, *Gilbert*, iii. 294.

[3] Articles of Kilkenny, May 2, *ib.* iii. 95; Additional Articles, May 12, *ib.* iii. 315.

[4] Articles, February 14, *ib.* iii. 364.

[5] Articles, April 27, *ib.* iii. 374.

Heavily had the Irish people suffered. A calculation, rough indeed, but proceeding from a competent statistician, reckons the diminution of the native population as 616,000 out of 1,466,000.[1] Those who perished were the victims of plague and famine, as well as of the sword.[2] Since Cromwell's departure, famine had been deliberately employed as a means of overpowering the scattered remnants who took refuge in bogs and mountains.

Diminution of the Irish population.

The hand of the Englishman was everywhere felt, with the result that the spirit of Irish nationality had never risen higher than on the day when its outward manifestation seemed hopelessly beaten to the ground, because it found a home in the breasts of all who, from whatever race they might be descended, were treated as outcasts on account of their devotion to the Roman Catholic religion. Two centuries before the English sovereigns had been confronted by a congeries of Irish tribes. The English Commonwealth was confronted by an Irish nation. The people under its clergy had shed the organs—the Supreme Council, the Lord Lieutenant, the Lord Deputy—which fostered the notion that Ireland was but part of a larger community inhabiting the whole of the British Isles.

Growth of the national spirit.

It was this steady growth of Irish national feeling which constituted the real difficulty of the conquerors. Merely to deal with the murderers of 1641, or even with the leaders of the insurrection which followed, would have been comparatively an easy task. The murders and the insurrection were but an episode in the deplorable history of that long strife of which Englishmen took little heed. It was only in the nature of things that England should set herself against the establishment of a hostile nation in Ireland ; only in the nature of things that her attempt to hinder it by main force should be the fruitful source of unnumbered

Difficulties of the conquerors.

---

[1] Petty's *Political Anatomy of Ireland* (ed. 1891), p. 18.

[2] Petty sets down 87,000 deaths as due to the sword, and 412,000 to plague, leaving the remainder to starvation, but his calculation is very loose, *ib.* p. 20.

miseries.   It was no longer possible to revert to the intelligent
policy of Henry VIII., and to govern Ireland by rulers developed within herself.   Mary, Elizabeth, James, and Strafford
had struck another note, each time with increasing emphasis.
The Commonwealth, in its own conceit so innovating, could
find no other way than to tread in the steps of its immediate
predecessors.

CHAPTER XX

THE SUBMISSION OF SCOTLAND AND THE COLONIES

In Scotland, even more than in Ireland, English conquest had resulted from measures taken in self-defence. In 1648, indeed,

1648-1651. England and Scotland.

Cromwell, after the destruction of Hamilton's army, had generously offered his alliance to the Argyle Government on the understanding that neither country should interfere with the political or ecclesiastical institutions of the other. That understanding had broken down, partly in consequence of the King's execution, partly on account of the abhorrence with which the Scottish clergy viewed the predominance of a sectarian army in England. When the younger Charles had been proclaimed in Edinburgh as the Sovereign of both kingdoms, an armed conflict between the two peoples had become inevitable, and after a second Scottish invading army had been crushed at Worcester, it was for the English Government to pronounce upon the future relations of the two countries. For the present Scotland was incapable of prolonging her resistance. During the last three years at least 40,000 of her hardiest sons had been either slain or swept into captivity.

It was, therefore, a foregone conclusion that Scotland must be disarmed, and the English Government can hardly be

Scotland to be disarmed.

severely blamed if it imagined that it could temper the bitterness of the cup by offering incorporation with England to her neighbours beyond the Tweed and a full share in the privileges of Englishmen—the very offer, in short, which had recently been made to the citizens of the United Provinces. The work would appear the easier as no

racial distinction separated the Lowland Scot from the North-
umbrian, whilst, with the tolerant ideas prevailing at Westminster, it might appear not so very difficult to surmount even
the obstacles caused by the rooted Presbyterianism of the
North. Of the strength of the national spirit—all the more
powerful because Lowland Scotland was a comparatively small
and scantily populated territory—there was probably but little
idea in the English Parliament. Yet this was precisely what it
was most important for Englishmen to take into account. If
Scotland could not be conciliated, she must be coerced, and,
strong as England was, the cost of coercing Scotland might be
great enough to weaken the government even of England
herself.

When once, however, the Parliamentary statesmen had
resolved on their line of action, there was no room for hesitation. In January 1652 the situation was regularised,
so far as the military authorities were concerned, by
the assessment on each county of an enforced contribution in lieu of the free-quarters demanded for
the English soldiers as long as a state of war was understood
to prevail.[1] The political settlement of the country required
more forethought. On January 15 a body of eight
Commissioners, amongst whom were Vane and St.
John, as well as Monk, Deane, and Lambert, took
up their residence at Dalkeith, having been instructed
to obtain from the Scots themselves what might pass as a voluntary assent to a union with England.[2]

Of voluntary assent in any real sense there was but little to
be found. There were, indeed, a few persons calling themselves Presbyterians prepared to make a merit of
necessity and to give in their submission to the
English Commonwealth, but the two great parties in

*1652.
Jan.
An assess-
ment
levied.*

*Jan. 15.
English
Commis-
sioners at
Dalkeith.*

*Presbyte-
rian oppo-
sition.*

[1] *A Perf. Diurnal*, E, 793, 21.

[2] *C.J.* vii. 30 ; *Perf. Diurnal*, E, 793, 18. [See *The Cromwellian
Union: Papers relating to the Negotiations for an Incorporating Union
between England and Scotland*, 1651–1652, by Mr. C. S. Terry, published
by the Scottish History Society in 1902.]

the Kirk, however hostile to one another, were united in their rejection of this course. The Resolutioners had rallied too ostentatiously round the banner of the King to abandon it now, whilst the Remonstrants, or Protesters as they were more frequently called, were the backbone of resistance to an English government for the very reasons which had made them hostile to Charles whilst he was still in Scotland. It was their part to vindicate the independence of the Kirk in the face of sectarian foreigners, as they had already vindicated it in the face of a worldly and hypocritical king. They would never, they boldly declared, acknowledge a system of government which would bring in its train the establishment of toleration and the sub-

Royalist support.

ordination of the Church to the State in the things of Christ.[1] Strange to say, it was mainly to the Royalist gentry that the Commissioners could at present look for support. Dislike of the severe discipline of the Kirk formed a common bond between them. Sir Alexander Irvine of

Case of Irvine of Drum.

Drum, himself a Roman Catholic,[2] not only refused to appear before the Presbytery of Aberdeen, but appealed to Monk on the ground that he was unable to acknowledge the judicature of the Church courts 'as not being established by the Commonwealth of England.'[3]

In the long run it would little profit the English Commonwealth to rely on Scottish Royalism, and the Commissioners

Jan. 21. Provisions for the administration of justice announced.

were therefore well advised in attempting to secure the goodwill of the bulk of the population by the encouragement of material prosperity. On January 21 they issued a proclamation at the Market Cross of Edinburgh, declaring their resolution to provide for the administration of justice, as well as to withstand the exercise of any authority not derived from the Commonwealth of England.[4] To give emphasis to this last announcement the

---

[1] *Perf. Diurnal*, E, 793, 21 ; Johnston of Warriston and others to Lambert, Jan. 20, *ib.* E, 793, 24.

[2] This name occurs a few years later in a list of Roman Catholics amongst the *Roman Transcripts*, *R.O.*

[3] *Perf. Diurnal*, E, 793, 28.   [4] Nicoll's *Diary*, 80.

King's arms and the crowned unicorn on the Cross were
battered down on February 7, the crown being
suspended to the gallows.[1] The ancient kingdom
of Scotland, proud of her glorious traditions, was no
longer to be counted amongst the nations of Europe.
In compensation, she was to share in the liberties
of Englishmen. Then followed an appeal to the
material interests of the people. The estates of
those who had invaded England in 1648 and 1651
were to be confiscated to pay the expenses of the
war, and the lands thus acquired by the Commonwealth were to be leased at easy rates, thereby enabling
the cultivators of the soil 'to live with a more comfortable
subsistence than formerly, and like a free people delivered
through God's assistance from the former slavery, vassalage,
and oppressions.'[2] The offer was precisely the same as that
which Charles I. had vainly attempted to lay before the Scottish people when he faced their army on Dunse Law.[3]

Feb. 7.
Destruction of the symbols of royalty.

Feb. 12.
Scotland to be incorporated with England.

Confiscated lands to be let at easy rates.

The Commissioners were at least able, as Charles I. had
been unable, to secure that such proposals should reach the
ears of those for whom they were intended. A
beginning was made on February 13, when the declaration was read at Dalkeith to a deputation from
the shires and burghs.[4] The deputies were then asked to
signify within a week their acceptance of the 'tender,' as it
was called, of incorporation with England, upon which their
advice would be taken on the best mode of carrying
it into practice. To make their way easier, an
explanation of the 'tender' was added, assuring the
protection of the Government to all ministers following the
order of the Scottish Kirk, as well as to those who preferred
worshipping in another way.[5]

Feb. 13.
The 'tender' of incorporation.

A general toleration offered.

---

[1] Nicoll's *Diary*, 81. [2] *Ib.* 81–82.

[3] *History of England*, 1603–1642, ix. 9.

[4] *Merc. Pol.* E, 654, 1; *The Faithful Secret*, E, 793, 27.

[5] Nicoll's *Diary*, 83. Nicoll speaks of the explanation as having
been given on the 11th, which must be a mistake, as the main declaration

Attractive as this offer may have appeared to the English Commissioners, it was gall and wormwood to the Scottish clergy and to that numerous section of the laity which was under their influence. Their party was so strong in Edinburgh, that it required all the efforts of the Commissioners to exclude it from the magistracy of the town.[1] Though there was scarcely less difficulty and delay in securing the acceptance of the 'tender' by the deputies of the shires and burghs, yet on March 16 Vane, who had by that time returned to England, was able to report that, with few exceptions, the shires and burghs of Scotland had bent under the yoke.[2] On March 18 an Act for the incorporation of Scotland with England was brought in at Westminster, accompanied by a declaration which announced the intended union, and instructed the Scottish constituencies to choose deputies who were in turn to choose a committee with full powers to discuss and assent to proposals for carrying out the scheme. On April 13 [3] the Act received a first and second reading, after which its progress was suspended, presumably to give time for the election of the committee.

Displeasure of the clergy.

March 16. Vane announces that the 'tender' has been accepted.

March 18. Act brought in for a union.

Accompanying declaration.

April 13. The Act read a second time.

On April 21 the declaration for a union and for the election of a committee to approve of the details was read at the Market Cross at Edinburgh in the presence of a vast multitude. The English soldiers shouted their approval 'as complying with Parliament in their free conferring of liberty upon a conquered people.' The Scottish crowd gave no sign of satisfaction. "So senseless," remarked an English reporter of the

April 21. The declaration for a union read at Edinburgh.

Its reception by the people.

---

was not proclaimed till the 12th. The explanation, which was signed on the 12th, was no doubt read to the deputies on the 13th (*Perf. Diurnal*, E, 793, 32).

[1] *Merc. Pol.* E, 655, 6 ; Nicoll's *Diary*, 87.

[2] *Several Proceedings*, E, 793, 37 ; *Perf. Diurnal*, E, 794, 5; *C.J.* vii. 105.   [3] *C.J.* vii. 107, 118.

scene, "are this people of their own goods that scarce a man of them showed any sign of rejoicing, though the most flourishing of their kings would have given the best jewel in their crown to have procured a vote in Parliament for their equal shares in the laws of England." [1]

The writer of these words knew as little of Scottish history as he knew of the temper of the Scottish people. A reversion

Scottish feeling. to the policy of Edward I. was hardly likely to win favour amongst the sons of the victors of Bannockburn. "As for the embodying of Scotland with England," said Robert Blair, a minister by no means of an advanced type, "it will be as when the poor bird is embodied into the hawk that hath eaten it up." [2] The patriotism of a small nation may, indeed, broaden out in time into a larger patriotism freely offered and freely received ; it will never surrender itself to the masters of victorious legions.

If the national independence of Scotland had still a material symbol within the realm, it was to be found in the

The regalia at Dunottar Castle. regalia—the golden crown which had been placed on the head of Charles at Scone, the golden sceptre which had been borne before him, and the sword, the gift of Julius, the warrior Pope, to the fourth James, [3] which the second Charles had falsely grasped as a token of his resolution to defend the Kirk against all her foes. When the enemy poured in like a flood, these precious relics of a glorious past were hurriedly conveyed to Dunottar Castle, the stronghold from the walls of which the Earls Marischal looked proudly down upon the waves of the German Ocean. By the end of April every other fortress in Scotland holding out for

Fall of Dumbarton, Brodick, and the Bass. the King had fallen ; but after the castles of Dumbarton, Brodick, and the Bass had fallen into the hands of the invaders, Dunottar continued to resist their efforts. At last, on May 26, its governor,

May 26. Surrender of Dunottar. George Ogilvy, was compelled by stress of hunger to capitulate to the besieging force under Colonel

[1] *Perf. Diurnal*, E, 794, 32.   [2] *Life of Blair*, 291.

[3] *Papers relative to the Regalia of Scotland*, 23.

Morgan, and to engage himself to deliver up the regalia to the conqueror.[1] When the besiegers marched in, the treasure—in Scottish eyes the most valuable reward of their victory—was nowhere to be found. As a matter of fact, the governor's wife had already sent the regalia out of the castle, concealing them in a bag of flax carried on a woman's back. The bearer delivered them to Mrs. Grainger, the wife of the minister of Kineff, who buried them under the floor of the church to await better times. Both Ogilvy and his wife were imprisoned for seven months, but were finally liberated on bail, upon the asseveration of the lady that the regalia had been carried beyond sea by a son of the Earl Marischal.[2]

Holding as they did every existing fortress in Scotland, the conquerors had but one district to secure to render their position in the Lowlands impregnable. It was necessary to keep an eye on the fanatical Whiggamores of the West, and to ensure their submission orders were given for the construction of a new fort at Ayr.[3] The erection of new fortresses intended to bridle the Scots was accompanied by the demolition of ancient ones no longer necessary for the purpose. On April 3, the old Castle of Blackness was blown up, and it was reported that the devil was visibly seen sitting on the walls at the time of the explosion,[4] holding grimly on, it may be supposed, to the fastness within which so many faithful Presbyterian ministers had expiated their revolt against the royal authority over ecclesiastical causes.

A fort constructed at Ayr.

April 3. Destruction of Blackness.

The times were, however, passed when an invader could content himself with securing the Lowlands. However little of

---

[1] *Perf. Account*, E, 677, 5; *Perf. Diurnal*, E, 795, 19.

[2] Ogilvy's account is printed in *Papers relative to the Regalia of Scotland*, published by the Bannatyne Club. At the Restoration the young man's mother was base enough to obtain honours and a pecuniary reward for her son on the ground that he had really conveyed the regalia abroad. Additional information will be found in *Papers relative to the Preservation of the Honours of Scotland*, published by the Scottish History Society.

[3] *Several Proceedings*, E, 794, 21.   [4] Nicoll's *Diary*, 92.

national spirit was to be traced in the policy or action of the

Danger from the Highlands. Highland clans, Montrose had contrived to rally many of them to his master's cause, and though the commanders of the army of the Commonwealth had no such enemy as Montrose to fear, they were awake to the danger of leaving a long stretch of coast open to Royalist agents.

Though, under these circumstances, it was of the first importance to secure the co-operation of Argyle even in his

Argyle's co-opera-tion needed. present reduced condition, those who represented the Commonwealth in Scotland were resolved not to buy even his co-operation at too high a price. Ever

He aims at a media-tory posi-tion. since the Scottish defeat at Worcester, Argyle had been negotiating with a view to the assumption of a mediatory position by himself, with the support of some Parliamentary or other body which might represent, or appear to represent, Scotland in the face of the English officials. What he wanted, in short, was to revert so far as it was still possible, to his position in 1648, and to place Scotland— naturally under his own influence—in close connection with England, though with some independent action in her domestic government. It was precisely what the English Parliament had resolved never to tolerate either in Argyle or in any Scottish person or assembly whatever. After a succession of interviews and correspondence with the English Commissioners, Argyle was driven to consent to the bare acceptance of the ' tender' by his clansmen, and on April 26 that acceptance was signified by their deputy at Dalkeith.[1]

The course of military events soon required a more direct personal submission. Monk and Lambert had returned to

Deane's command in Scot-land. England early in the year, and Deane, who had been left in command, resolved that himself and Robert Lilburne should advance into the Highlands by a double line from Argyle's country and Inverness. In August,

[1] The details of this negotiation are given in Mr. Firth's introduction to *Scotland and the Commonwealth* (Scottish Hist. Soc.), and in the documents there referred to.

Deane himself appeared at Inverary. On the 12th of that month, Argyle, reserving his 'duty to religion, according to his oath to the Covenant,' agreed, so far as civil government was concerned, to accept for Scotland a republican Constitution in common with England, and to live peaceably until the neces-

Aug. 19.
His agree-
ment with
Argyle.

sary arrangements could be made.[1] On the 19th an agreement was signed, in which the Marquis not only engaged for himself and his clan to submit to the English Government, but promised that either himself or his son, Lord Lorne, would come to England as a hostage on being summoned by Parliament to fulfil the obligation.[2] He further admitted Deane's right to place garrisons in his territory. Five garrisons were accordingly established, but scarcely was Deane's

Failure of
his at-
tempt to
reduce the
Highlands.

back turned, when three of them were overpowered by the Highlanders. The progress of the main expedition was impeded less by active opposition than by scarcity of provisions ; and in the autumn Deane's attempt to subjugate the Highlands was necessarily abandoned for the year. On October 27 a fresh agreement was made, in which Deane limited his right of garrisoning to Dunstafnage and Dunolly, so long at least as the Campbells kept the peace.[3] Argyle—like Scotland at large—was no doubt ready to bow to necessity, but there could be no pretence of his having accepted the situation with pleasure.

It was the business of the English authorities to superinduce,

Discipline
of the
troops.

if they could, a better state of feeling. The payment of customs at Berwick and Carlisle was brought to an end. That the troops were kept in an exemplary state of discipline could not be denied. Courts-martial dealt out justice to the complaints of the· peasantry, and those hardships which are often the lot of a population exposed to the

---

[1] Declaration by Argyle, Aug. 12, *Scotland and the Commonwealth*, 50, note 1.

[2] Articles of Agreement, Aug. 19, *ib.* 48.

[3] Agreement, Oct. 27, *ib.* 55. The details of the invasion of the Highlands are given in the English newspapers, some extracts from which are printed by Mr. Firth in his appendix.

arrogance of an occupying army were seldom heard of, and, on the rare occasions on which they were reported, were ruthlessly punished. It was also the aim of the Government of the Commonwealth to right the wrongs which the poor endured from civilian oppressors. The administration of justice in Scotland had been notoriously under the influence of powerful families, and it was at the destruction of those families that the English Government was aiming. On April 8 the Council of State appointed seven judges, four of whom were English, to form a provisional Court of Judicature.[1] On May 18 this Court established itself in Edinburgh.[2] If fair and open dealing could win the hearts of Scotsmen, the desired end ought now to have been in sight. " Justice," explained an Englishman, " was wont to be open and free formerly for none but great men ; but now it flows equally to all ; which will, in a short time, make them sensible from what bondage they have been delivered." [3] " Now," wrote another, " the people begin to meddle with many great men against whom, heretofore, they durst not complain." [4] " To speak truth," was the half-reluctant admission of a Scot, " the English were more indulgent and merciful to the Scots, nor was the Scots to their own countrymen and neighbours, and their justice exceeded the Scots' in many things, as was reported." [5]

Administration of justice.

April 8. New judges appointed.

May 18. They take their seats.

Equal justice.

Time alone could discover whether the good intentions of the English Government would avail in Scotland to convert a nominal into a real union. In the case of the colonies there were fewer difficulties. In the first place, their commercial interests drew them to the mother country. In the second place, none of them were sufficiently developed to have acquired a sense of nationality. The sympathies of the New England and Newfoundland settlers were enlisted on the side of the dominant party at home, whilst the remainder, Virginia, Maryland, the Bermudas, Bar-

England and the colonies.

---

[1] C. of St. Order Book, *Interr.* I, 66, p. 546.
[2] *Several Proceedings*, E, 795, 12.   [3] *Merc. Pol.* E, 682, 2.
[4] *Perf. Diurnal*, E, 795, 15.   [5] Nicoll's *Diary*, 104.

bados, Antigua, St. Kitts, and the smaller adjacent slands were Royalist rather through the temporary predominance of a particular party, than from any rooted objection of the bulk of the inhabitants to accept the supremacy of the Commonwealth. It was therefore to be hoped that a merely temporary application of force would bring back normal relations between the recalcitrant colonies and the mother country.

Resistance had been strongest at Barbados, where, since the spring of 1650, the Royalist governor, Lord Willoughby,

1650.
Royalism in
Barbados.

1651.
Feb. 18.
Declaration
of commer-
cial inde-
pendence.

had been in possession of authority, at least so far as he was allowed to exercise it by the Cavalier refugees, who in reality held power in the island.[1] On February 18, 1651, the Assembly of the Island supported Willoughby by a declaration in which they refused submission to a Parliament where they were unrepresented; and in answer to the Act by which

Parliament had forbidden all commercial intercourse with the colonies in rebellion,[2] asserted the right of Barbados to trade with the Dutch or with any other nation. For some time it seemed as if the mother country had no intention of taking

Oct. 15.
Arrival of
Ayscue's
fleet.

up the challenge. Ayscue's fleet, appointed to reduce the colony, had been kept back to take part in the operations against the Scilly Isles,[3] and it was not till October 15 that its sails were descried from the island.

Ayscue's first action was to seize fourteen Dutch vessels waiting for a cargo, on the ground that they were infringing

Seizure
of Dutch
shipping.

Ayscue
fails to
reduce Bar-
bados.

the recent Act. He found it less easy to secure a footing on shore. Emboldened by a rumour that Charles had won the day at Worcester, the colonists rallied to the defence of their commercial independence. Six thousand men were soon under arms, and Asycue could make little impression on such a force. The arrival, however, of more accurate intelligence from England convinced the less ardent Royalists that it was better to come to terms with the Commonwealth than to prolong a now hopeless struggle, and this party, headed by Colonel Modyford, was

[1] See vol. i. 316.   [2] *Ib.* 317.   [3] *Ib.* 326.

strong enough to force Willoughby to accept its views.   Ayscue showed himself generous to adversaries whose strength was in-

1652.
Jan. 11.
Articles of
agreement.

disputable; and on January 1652 'articles of agreement' were signed on behalf of the colony on the one side and the representatives of the Commonwealth on the other.

These articles involved a surrender by the islanders of all claim to political autonomy in consideration of the full acknowledgment of their financial and commercial independence. Willoughby and a few of his leading supporters were to quit the colony, but were to be allowed to retain their property. There was to be almost complete liberty of conscience. 'No taxes, customs, loans or excise' were to be levied without the consent of the inhabitants expressed in a General Assembly. Trade was to 'be free with all nations that do trade or are in amity with England.' [1]

The submission of the other West Indian colonies followed as a matter of course. A small force sufficed to bring Virginia to acknowledge the authority of the Commonwealth.

March 12.
Submission
of Virginia,

As in Barbados, there were two parties, one represented by the Governor, Sir William Berkeley, and a Council of strong Royalist tendencies; the other by the elected burgesses—sitting together with the councillors in a single House of Assembly—who, if they did not sympathise warmly with the English Puritans, were not disposed to risk material loss by resisting them. As there were no Royalist refugees in Virginia to embitter the conflict, there was a mere appearance of resistance. The Governor had, indeed, brought together some 1,000 or 1,200 armed men at Jamestown, but the Assembly refused him its support, and on March 12 agreements were signed which brought the colony under the Commonwealth.[2] Governor and Council were alike to have leave to

[1] N. Darnell Davis, *Cavaliers and Roundheads in Barbados*, pp. 208-259.

[2] Doyle's *English in America: Virginia*, 281. The details of the proceedings before the signature of the agreement are given in a letter printed in *Merc. Pol.* E, 665, 3.

depart, and the people of Virginia were to 'have free trade as
the people of England do enjoy to all places and with all nations
according to the laws of that Commonwealth,' as well as to 'be
free from all taxes, customs, and impositions whatever . . .
without consent of the General Assembly.'[1] By a subsequent
arrangement, the whole internal organisation of the colony was
placed in the hands of the burgesses, who might be trusted not
to break the connection established with the English Commonwealth.[2]

Before the end of March Maryland had given way with
equal facility. Here there were peculiar conditions which did
not prevail in any other colony. There was a Roman
March 29, Catholic majority exercising a wise toleration, and
of Mary-
land, a vehement Puritan minority. The English Commissioners, however, contented themselves with enforcing submission to the Commonwealth in matters of government. Questions of domestic policy were left untouched, and not a word
was said of those concessions in matters of taxation and commerce which had marked the agreements with Barbados and
Virginia. The fact was that Maryland was a proprietary colony,
and as the proprietor, Lord Baltimore, was residing in England,
all questions arising out of his rights or his methods of government could be more fitly considered at home.[3]

With the submission of Maryland the whole colonial
dominion of the Stuarts passed into the hands of the Parliament
and of the of the Commonwealth. The Bermudas, without
Bermudas. waiting for a display of force, had already abandoned
their attitude of resistance.[4]

The establishment of friendly relations with the Royalist
colonies necessarily brought with it the obligation of setting free
Necessity the sea for the operations of commerce. Fortunately
of clearing for the Commonwealth, no active measures were
the seas. needed to overthrow the enemy from whom the

[1] Hening, *Laws of Virginia*, i. 363.
[2] *Ib.* 371, 372 ; see *Doyle*, 296.
[3] Bozman's *Hist. of Maryland*, 437-443.
[4] See vol. i. 316.

greatest danger had been feared. For some months in the

summer and autumn of 1651, Rupert had been hanging about the Azores,[1] where the Portuguese authorities were growing shy of supporting an enemy of the powerful Commonwealth. Caught in a terrific storm,

his own ship sprang a leak and was soon in a sinking condition. In vain his crew entreated him to save himself by the help of a boat. He would rather, he said, perish with his comrades; and it was only by sheer force that faithful arms dragged him into the boat and transferred him to his brother Maurice's vessel. He had scarcely gained the deck when his own ship foundered with all hands before his eyes. Another of his consorts perished in the same tempest, and by the end of the year he was driven to carry those yet

remaining to a desolate harbour on the West Coast of Africa, where they could be careened in safety. It was not till the end of May 1652, four months

after the surrender of Barbados, that he made his appearance in the West Indies. Finding every harbour in the English islands closed against him, he threw himself on the hospitality of the French colonists, by whom he was gladly welcomed as an enemy of the English Commonwealth.

In all but name Rupert was embarked on a career of piracy, as far, at least, as English commerce was concerned ; and, as soon as his little squadron was again ready for sea, he put out in search of prizes. He had not counted on the storms

which sweep these tropical seas. A fierce hurricane swooped down upon him, and his own ship barely escaped destruction on the ill-famed rocks of the Anegadas. When the storm had died away Rupert looked round him on a sailless sea. Some of his comrades had sought refuge in dis-

tant harbours. Of Prince Maurice no word ever reached mortal ears. Whether he had been dashed on the rocks which his brother had escaped, or had foundered at sea, was never known. Rupert could but tarry

[1] See vol. i. 315.

to pick up a few prizes, one of which was an English vessel, and with them he recrossed the Atlantic, putting into Croisic

1653. Rupert returns to Europe. Bay early in 1653.[1] English commerce had received singularly little damage from his ill-starred adventure. Even before the days of steam and iron a basis of operations was essential to the success of naval warfare.

Long before Rupert's return, Parliament had adopted a restrictive commercial policy which was no doubt suggested by

1651. Result of the failure of the negotiations with the Dutch. the failure of those exaggerated notions with which Strickland and St. John had undertaken their embassy to the Hague, but which was the more easily accepted as having its roots in the commercial ideas almost universally accepted at the time. In July 1651, the two ambassadors had returned with anger in their hearts, and their personal mortification made them eager to enlist their countrymen in a design for exalting the commerce of England at the expense of that of the neighbouring republic.

Of the United Provinces, Holland and Zealand alone possessed harbours which enabled them to devote themselves

Trade of Holland and Zealand. to maritime traffic. Producing few commodities excepting cheese and butter, these two provinces, and more especially the wealthier Holland, had in their hands not merely the whale-fishery of the Arctic regions, the herring-fishery of the North Sea, and the spice trade of the

The carry-ing trade. East, but the carrying trade of the world. The spectacle which had met Ayscue's eyes at Barbados, where he found Dutch ships employed in the transport of the produce of a soil not their own, was common enough in Europe. Even if an English gentleman wished to send his trunks to France, he was compelled to ship them in a Dutch bottom to Rotterdam, that they might be conveyed also in a Dutch bottom to Calais or Rouen.[2] Cheapness of freight was attained by the aptitude of Dutchmen for trade, by their familiarity with the sea, by the ease with which the use of capital could be

---

[1] Warburton's *Memoirs of Rupert*, iii. 328.

[2] This was done by Sir R. Verney when he emigrated to France in 1643.

obtained in a country in which peasants and small tradesmen were accustomed to invest their savings in commercial ventures, and by the facilities for applying capital to commercial purposes offered by the banks of Amsterdam and Rotterdam. Other causes combined to favour the trading spirit. The Provincial States of Holland and Zealand were filled with persons either themselves engaged in commercial pursuits or

Legislation and diplomacy of the Dutch.

in close touch with those who were. The legislation and diplomacy of these men were directed mainly to the maintenance of the commercial supremacy of their country, and they were by no means scrupulous as to the means by which they attained their ends. Englishmen had not forgotten the refusal of the Dutch to do justice for the massacre of Amboyna,[1] or the mixture of force and fraud by which English traders had been driven from Pularoon, their last foothold in the Eastern Archipelago.[2] A few weeks before the

Feb. 21.
March 3.
A treaty between the United Provinces and Denmark.

arrival of St. John and Strickland at the Hague, the States General had ratified [3] a treaty with the King of Denmark, by which they acquired for thirty-six years the right of commuting the Sound dues payable by their ships for an annual contribution ; and this concession was accompanied by an express declaration from the King that no other nation was to benefit by a similar act of grace.[4]

It was not difficult under these circumstances to rouse the indignation of Englishmen against their trade rivals, and there

Dissatisfaction in England.

is no reason to distrust the tradition that it was St. John who urged Parliament to rid itself for ever of Dutch competition. At all events, a retaliatory measure, subsequently known as the Navigation Act, was re-

Aug. 5.
Introduction of the Navigation Act.

commended to Parliament by the Council of State on August 5, 1651, though no effort was made to push it on till Cromwell's victory at Worcester had

Oct. 9.
It becomes law.

enabled Parliament to speak proudly in the face of foreign Powers. On October 9 it passed into law.[5]

---

[1] *History of England*, 1603–1642, v. 242.   [2] *Ib.* iii. 167, 407.
[3] Aitzema, *Saken van Staet en Oorlogh*, iii. 654.   [4] *Ib.* iii. 335.
[5] *C.J.* vii. 11, 27.

Though, as far as language went, the Navigation Act made no distinction between one nation and another, it was well understood to be aimed at the Dutch alone. It pro-hibited the introduction into any territory of the Commonwealth of produce of any country in Asia, Africa, or America, except in vessels owned by Englishmen, or by the inhabitants of English colonies, and manned by crews of which more than one-half were of English nationality. Imports from any part of Europe might be brought in only in English vessels, or in vessels the owners of which belonged to that nation in which the goods were manufactured or produced. Henceforth the Dutch would be disabled from bringing into England or her colonies anything but the scanty produce of their own soil. It is true, indeed, that the Dutch were not forbidden to exchange their own products for the sugar pro-duced in the English West Indian colonies, so long as the sugar was carried by them to a continental port. For all that the Dutch trade with these colonies was practically annihilated, because Dutch vessels arriving at Barbados or Antigua would henceforward be compelled to cross the Atlantic in ballast, neither butter nor cheese being adapted for consumption within the tropics. The gains of the Dutch fishermen were equally stricken, so far as English consumption was concerned. Salt-fish and fish-oil were to be imported only in English vessels, and salt-fish was to be exported only on the same terms.[1]

Commerce restricted by it.

Though the Navigation Act was passed in a fit of irritation, it was too thoroughly in unison with the economic ideas of the time to be regarded as a mere reprisal. It sought to provide employment for the English mariner and fisherman and business for the English merchant at the expense of raising the price of commodities to the English consumer. In the colonial policy of England it worked a change no less in harmony with the prevailing current of ideas. For a time after the outbreak of the Civil War, there had been a tendency to subordinate all other considerations to spiritual and ideal aims ; to advance the godly and depress the profane

The Act consonant with the ideas of the time.

[1] *Scobell*, ii. 176.

had been the aim of statesmen and soldiers. Now, as ever happens, the neglected body of man, with its material needs and passions, was beginning to assert itself. Though there had been an ideal element in the conquest of Ireland and Scotland, a desire to render the populations of those countries better and happier by forcing upon them in the one case English religion, in the other case English justice and toleration, there had been *Growing influence of material ideas.* a painfully material side as well : a greed for land or power, and, at the best, a determination to impose the English yoke upon peoples firmly purposed to lead their own life in their own fashion. The new commercial policy did not profess to have other than material aims. The intention of its framers, by the very nature of the case, was not to make England better or nobler, but to make her richer.

About ten months after the passing of the Navigation Act, the agreement entered into by Ayscue with Barbados and *1652. Aug. 18. Confirmation of the Barbados agreement* Virginia came up for consideration in Parliament, the articles of Barbados being confirmed on August 18, and those of Virginia on August 31. At first sight it appears that at least in the Barbados *Aug. 31, and of that with Virginia.* case a settlement had been arrived at, which, by precluding the right of the English Parliament to levy taxes, direct or indirect, in the colony, or to put a stop to its freedom of trade with foreign countries in amity with England,[1] would, if only these terms had been granted to other settlements, have gone far to postpone, if not to avert, the rupture which tore the colonies on the mainland of America from the parent stem. Yet, important as the issue was, there is no evidence that there was any serious debate on the subject, and the unanimity with which the treaties were confirmed may perhaps be attributed to the fact that when they were laid before Parliament England was already at war with the Dutch. The confirmation of the article admitting foreign shipping of nations in amity with England to Barbados would therefore have no effect at all for some time to come.[2]

[1] See p. 142.
[2] The Navigation Act of the Commonwealth prohibited imports into

It is noteworthy that the Navigation Act was the one

The Navigation Act indicates a reactionary feeling.

legislative achievement of the Commonwealth which not only found favour in the eyes of the Parliament of the Restoration, but was actually rendered more

English colonies when brought by foreign shipping, unless the cargoes were produced or manufactured in the countries to which the ships belonged. Still this was not actually a stoppage of trade, and Mr. Darnell Davis informs me that the local records of Barbados show no trace of any objection to the restriction of trade after the conclusion of the Dutch war. It was the Navigation Act of Charles II. which forbade exports as well as imports in foreign bottoms. It is to this full-blown system that Mr. J. A. Doyle refers in discussing the results of the Act. "In considering the Navigation Act," he writes, "we are liable to two errors. We should be wrong if we judged it either by the events of the eighteenth century, or by the political theories of the present day. The doctrine that the community is most benefited when its means of production are allowed the fullest and most spontaneous development, had but dawned on the speculative thinkers of the seventeenth century, and assuredly no reasonable man will find fault with practical statesmen for being in the rear of theory. Nor is it fair to blame the originators of the system embodied in this Act for the evil results that flowed from that system a hundred years later, when the social and industrial life of our colonies had undergone great changes. Yet even after these deductions we cannot set down the Navigation Act as a measure of undoubted expediency or unmixed wisdom. In subordinating the welfare of the colonies to the commercial prosperity and naval greatness of the mother country, the Long Parliament was in some degree reverting to the principles of the sixteenth century. To make England the centre of a great naval empire was the idea ever present to the minds of Gilbert and Raleigh and their followers, and the colonisation of America was mainly valued as a step towards that end. Under the Stuarts that ambition had given way before meaner views, and, like the foreign policy of Elizabeth, it revived under the sway of the Protector. But though the principle of the Navigation Act might be ambitious and elevated as it concerned the mother country, it was repressive and blighting in its effect on the colonies. In the middle of the seventeenth century, indeed, its influence was but slightly felt. It did not weigh down the industry of the colonies because that industry scarcely existed, but it hindered the development of it. It condemned the plantations to be, commercially, at least, little better than factories for the benefit of English trade."—*The English in America—Virginia, &c.* 297.

stringent in 1660, nor is the reason far to seek. The framers of the Act, convinced Republicans as they were, had changed the course of the ship of State, and were, all unwittingly, heading towards a restoration. If the leaders of the Commonwealth were to be but as the leaders of other nations, to seek after material wealth and material power, what end was to be served by keeping them in authority? The old monarchical system would serve the purpose just as well. The empire of custom, on which its claims were based, would be more in harmony with the demands of a nation eager to become rich than a government which professed to hold its title from the Lord of Hosts, and justified its claim by giving free scope to religious enthusiasm and projects of social reform.

Nor was the significance of the Navigation Act confined to domestic politics. In the international relations between England and the continental Powers it led the way to new developments. During the century and a quarter which preceded the Treaties of Westphalia, religion had been, if not the exclusive cause, at least the frequent pretext of the wars by which Europe had been desolated. In the wars which raged for nearly a century and a half after the signature of those treaties questions of commerce took the place formerly occupied by questions of religion. Of these wars, the first was that which broke out in 1652 between England and the Dutch Republic, and though that war was not directly brought on by the Navigation Act, the commercial restrictions imposed by the new legislation at least created a tension of feeling between the two nations which could not fail to pass rapidly into open hostility.

International significance of the Act.

Religious and commercial wars.

It might seem that, of all men living, Cromwell was best suited by nature to stand forth as a mediator between the old enthusiasm and the new commercialism. The zeal with which he had thrown himself on the side of religious and social reform won him the high praise of Milton. Yet he also took the warmest and most practical interest in his country's greatness and prosperity. He was as

Cromwell's attitude towards them.

eager in the seventeenth century as Chatham in the eighteenth to foster commerce, and the necessary condition of commerce, maritime power. It is mainly this combination of interests which has raised Cromwell to the position of the national hero

He is the
national
hero of the
nineteenth
century. of the nineteenth century. Like him, modern Britain has waged wars, annexed territory, extended trade, and raised her head amongst the nations. Like him, her sons have been unable to find complete satisfaction in their achievements, unless they could persuade themselves that the general result was beneficial to others besides themselves. It is inevitable that now as then such an attitude should draw upon itself the charge of hypocrisy, inevitable too that in the eyes of foreign nations the benefits accruing to ourselves have been more conspicuous than those we have conferred on the world at large. It is easy to perceive how hard it is to realise the ideal we have set before us.

It was still harder in Cromwell's day, and the obstacles presented by his own character and mind were not the least of

Cromwell's
ignorance
of con-
tinental
feeling. the stumbling-blocks in his path. To him—fresh as he was from the strife which had raised victorious Puritanism to mastery at home—it seemed the most natural thing in the world to regard the armed support of Protestantism on the Continent as equivalent to well-doing of the highest kind. His ignorance of the drift of continental feeling, and especially of the significance of those Treaties of Westphalia which had closed the period of religious wars, blinded his eyes to the limits within which useful interference was possible. His mind still worked on the lines of the Elizabethan period, when the championship of Protestantism was imposed on Englishmen by interest as well as by duty. He failed to perceive that there was no longer a European conspiracy against Protestants, and that where any danger to their liberties still remained, it came from the isolated action of national or state governments, to interfere with which would be openly to defy the public opinion of the Continent. It was not possible for Cromwell to forecast the future, but it is possible for those who in later ages study the lessons of his career to remember that it was by appealing to the desire for national independence rather than to sectional Protestantism, that William III.—the man who is justly regarded as Cromwell's successor in the fruitful guidance of the foreign policy of England—achieved those permanent results which Cromwell's activity failed to produce.

CHAPTER XXI

AN IMPENDING WAR

So little did the authors of the Navigation Act contemplate a war with the United Provinces that for some months after their
measure passed into law they were hesitating between two strongly opposed lines of foreign policy, the adoption of either of which would bind England hand and foot in the presence of the Dutch navy. On the Continent the most noteworthy phenomenon of the time was the temporary effacement of France. In the autumn of 1651 the civil broils of the Fronde had blazed up afresh. The liberation of Condé early in the year[1] had not turned out to the Queen's advantage. Harassed by the insults which the masterful Prince showered upon such of her ministers as were known to be under the influence of Mazarin, she resolved to follow the traditions of the monarchy by announcing her son's majority as soon as he entered his fourteenth year. It is true that for some years to come the boy's personal influence would be but nominal. Yet the King's name, especially in the France of the seventeenth century, in which all the currents of thought and feeling ran towards monarchy, was a strong charm wherewith to conjure.[2] If Condé's

(margin notes)
1651.
The authors of the Navigation Act did not contemplate war.

Renewed troubles in France.

Aug. 27.
Sept. 6.
Majority of Louis XIV.

---

[1] See vol. i. 315.
[2] 'L'heure solennelle a sonné, et Condé ne l'a pas entendue. Plus de régente espagnole, plus de ministre étranger. Qu'importe la fiction légale ! la prétendue minorité de fait succédant à la minorité de droit, qu'importe ! c'est le Roi, le roi de France qui règne.' Le duc d'Aumale, *Hist. des Princes de Condé*, vi. 91.

character had been equal to his assumptions, he would have
Condé's recognised the full meaning of the change, and might
mistake. have secured for himself a high place in the court of
the young sovereign. As it was, he was the last to perceive
the significance of the formal act. His political intelligence
was but slight, and except on the day of battle his strong words
seldom covered strong deeds. His resolutions were moulded
by dependents and flatterers. Resenting the Queen's nomination of ministers who refused to consult his wishes, he hurried
He raises a off to his own Government of Guienne, that he might
standard of raise a standard of rebellion against the boy who, in
rebellion. his tender years, stood forth as the representative of
national unity.

The nobles of the south flocked round Condé as sixty years
before they had flocked round Henry of Navarre. The
Condé in municipal spirit too still moved in the southern
Guienne. towns, and Bordeaux in particular, irritated at the
interruption of its wine trade with England, the result, it
seemed, of Mazarin's refusal to recognise the Commonwealth,
placed itself unreservedly on his side. Condé had now but
Causes of one more fault to commit, the fault of calling in the
his foreigner to redress the balance of domestic faction.
weakness. He did not hesitate for a moment. His first act
He sends to was to despatch one agent, Lenet, to invite help
Spain and from Spain, and another agent, La Rivière, to invite
England. help from England. Lenet was welcomed at Madrid,
Oct. 27. and there, on October 27, a treaty was signed which
Nov. 6. admitted a Spanish garrison into Bourg, a fortress at
A treaty
with Spain. the mouth of the Dordogne.[1] The task of La
Rivière was less easy. He arrived in England early in October,
and at once asked Cromwell for 100,000*l.* and 10,000 men.
Oct. Cromwell derisively replied that he would come in
La Rivière's person with 40,000 foot and 12,000 horse, if he
proposal to
Cromwell. could be assured that at the end of the struggle
France should be as England. A Protestant and Republican

[1] *Hist. des Princes de Condé*, vi. 60–103 ; Chéruel, *Ministère de Mazarin*, i. 10–33.

France was hardly within the limits of political forecast, and Condé's agent had to return to his master a disappointed man.[1]

La Rivière was succeeded by Conan, a native of Rochelle, who brought a proposal from Le Daugnon, the governor of Rochelle, who at this time held the place for Condé. He now offered to admit an English garrison into the towers which at that time formed the only defences of the place, the town-wall having been destroyed after Richelieu's siege. Cromwell listened to Conan, called for a map of France, and, after poring over it for some time, refused to support the scheme.[2]

Oct. 16.
An offer from Rochelle.

Cromwell's interest was nevertheless roused. So far as he had hitherto taken a line in foreign politics he had been hostile to the French Government, on account of its friendliness to the Presbyterian party and the exiled House of Stuart. He now despatched Vane to France to enter into communication with De Retz, the clerical demagogue of the Fronde.[3] The attempt to come to an understanding with him appears to have failed for the time:[4] in any case Cromwell was unlikely to repose much confidence in a mere intriguer. If Cromwell was to take part in the French complications, protection to the French Protestants must be a prominent feature of his policy. It is true that

Cromwell and France.
An overture to De Retz.

[1] Morosini to the Doge, Oct. $\frac{18}{28}$, *Venetian Transcripts R.O.*

[2] Conan to Brun, $\frac{Oct. 31}{Nov. 10}$; Cardenas to Philip IV., Nov. $\frac{8}{18}$; Consulta, Feb. $\frac{8}{18}$. *Simancas MSS.* 2,084. Conan had been for some time absent from Rochelle, and had been sent with Le Daugnon's message by the Spanish ambassador at the Hague.

[3] *Mém. du Card. De Retz* (ed. 1859), ii. 267. The account of De Retz's interview with Vane is placed in these memoirs amongst the events of 1650, Charles's defeat at Worcester being also dated a year too soon. However, as Cromwell was in Ireland and Scotland during almost the whole of 1650, it seems safe to put Vane's mission down to the latter part of 1651, when Conan's message turned the attention of Cromwell to the thought of an intervention in France.

[4] De Retz was not as irreconcilable as he gives out. In 1653 he became one of the regular correspondents of Scot, who was at the head of what would now be called the Intelligence Department of the Commonwealth. 'Scot's Confession,' *Hist. Rev.*, Jan. 1897.

Mazarin had shown himself well disposed towards them, and
Condition of that Royal edicts had from time to time been issued
the French in their favour; but the Government, even if its
Protestants. authority had been greater than it was, would have
found it hard to bear up against the weight of the Catholic
organisation resting upon a large majority of the population.
Bishops and clergy were of one mind in their resolve to
encroach on the privileges secured to Protestants by the Edict
of Nantes, and Catholic lawyers and Catholic nobles seldom
failed to discover legal excuses for injustice. Protestant
temples, as they were styled, were frequently closed, Protestant
ministers harassed, and Protestant children kidnapped to be
educated in the dominant creed.[1]

What Cromwell and the Council of State wanted in their
present mood was information as to the real condition of the
Sexby's south of France, and they therefore resolved to
mission. despatch thither a trustworthy agent, on whose
reports they might ground their policy. Such an agent they
found in Sexby, the Agitator of 1647, who had risen to the
rank of lieutenant-colonel. Sexby, however, had been recently cashiered by the sentence of a court-martial for
having irregularly detained the pay of some of his men,
though the court acknowledged that ' as to his own intentions
he did it for the advancement of the public service.'[2] He
was now sent to Bordeaux together with four other persons,
one of whom, named Arundel, he kept in his own company.
The remaining three were ordered to travel amongst the
Protestants of the south. One of these was arrested and
put to the torture, from the effects of which he died.[3]

---

[1] Benoit, *Hist. de l'Edit de Nantes*, iii. 134–155. For a detailed
account of the treatment of Protestants in one particular locality, see *Les
Protestants à Pamiers*, by G. Doublet, an interesting pamphlet, a knowledge of which I owe to M. Gustave Monod.

[2] *Letters from Roundhead Officers*, 27 ; Letter from Edinburgh,
June 14, *Clarke MSS.* xix. fol. 26.

[3] Statement by Sexby, May 9, 1654, *S. P. Dom.* lxxi. 49. Compare
Dyer's Information, *Thurloe*, vi. 829.

On the proceedings of the other two no information has reached us.

When Sexby arrived at Bordeaux, Condé had left the town to take command of his army, having entrusted the place to his brother Conti, a man of no great abilities. Conti found it hard to control a population in which party spirit ran high, especially as the merchants and lawyers were opposed by the Ormée,[1] a faction advocating advanced democratic principles. Recognising language with which he had been long familiar, Sexby proposed to Conti to issue a manifesto[2] demanding for France a constitution, which he copied with such changes as were necessary from the first twenty-two articles of Lilburne's latest edition of the *Agreement of the People*. To this he attached a declaration stuffed with the commonplaces of the Levellers, and leading up to demands which were probably for the most part suggested by his allies of the Ormée. With few exceptions, such as a perfunctory complaint of the treatment of 'our heroic princes,' these latter demands either seek to encourage Protestantism, or, redolent of the spirit of 1789, call for the protection of the poor against the insolence of the rich and powerful. A demand for the punishment of drunkenness and other vices in accordance with the laws of England bears the imprint of Sexby's brain; whilst a request for the opening of the ports to English trade must have been equally agreeable to an Englishman, and to the vine-growers of the Medoc. The force of ignorance and folly could go no further.

Sexby at Bordeaux.

He proposes the adoption of the Lilburnian Agreement of the People.

Demands of the Ormée.

It would be unfair to hold Cromwell responsible for his agent's absurdity. Yet it is impossible to acquit him of

[1] From their place of meeting under ' les Ormes.'

[2] This marvellous document is printed in Cousin's *Madame de Longueville* (ed. 1859), ii. 464. Lenet, amongst whose papers it was found, notes that it was given to Conti 'par les sieurs Saxebri et Arrondel que je n'approuve pas.' Saxebri is, of course, Sexby. M. Chéruel (*Ministère de Mazarin*, i. 58) quotes it from another copy as *L'accord du Peuple*, but does not recognise its connection with the English *Agreement of the People*.

hankering after a policy which, by assailing the national unity
of France, headed straight for disaster. In the course
of his military career he had grown accustomed to
regard war, not as Elizabeth was wont to regard it,
as a hateful necessity, but as a righteous method of
advancing the holiest of causes; and, if war there was to be
for the benefit of Protestants, there were many reasons to
induce him to advocate alliance with Spain rather
than with France. It is undeniable that by advanced Puritans the policy of agreement with Spain
was at that time held to be the Protestant policy;
probably because Spain, though still remaining the home of
the Inquisition, had no Protestants left to persecute, whilst
Protestants were still numerous in France. No doubt to this
simple consideration were added others drawn from the
political situation of the day. Spain had been the first Power
to recognise the Commonwealth, and had no conceivable
motive for interfering in the domestic affairs of England. On
the other hand, the Stuart Pretender was a cousin of the
young King of France, and had found refuge on French soil,
whilst the rulers of France had persistently refused to recognise the Commonwealth unless the English Government, by
recalling its letters of reprisal, would take the first step in sup-
pressing the maritime disorders from which both nations were
suffering.

Nor was it only the personal protection accorded by France
to the Stuart princes which gave deadly offence in England.
It was there that Charles was weaving his interminable
schemes for the recovery of his throne. Since his
flight from Worcester he had been holding secret
conferences with a Roman Catholic ecclesiastic, and
had given him to understand that he was willing to
change his religion if only the Pope would make it worth his
while. Innocent X., however, refused to accept a convert who
demanded a price, and Charles then fell back on his earlier
position, offering protection to English and Irish Catholics, if
the Pope and the Catholic princes would give him the means

Cromwell hankers after a policy hostile to France.

A Spanish alliance favoured by extreme Puritans.

Oct.-Dec. Charles seeks aid from the Pope.

of recovering his throne.[1] Meanwhile Charles's brother, the

The Duke of York a colonel in the French service.

Duke of York, accepted a colonelcy in the French service and fought vigorously against the Fronde. Was it likely that a government which showed itself so friendly to the Stuarts would ever become a hearty ally of the Commonwealth?

With Cromwell himself the disposition to see England ranged on the side of Spain was hardly more than tentative.

Cromwell's vacillation on questions of foreign policy.

To him as yet foreign alliances were somewhat like constitutional forms at home—no more than the means to rescue Protestantism from oppression; and if that end was to be achieved by a direct agreement with the French Government, he was quite ready to take the alternative into consideration. Scarcely indeed had Sexby been despatched to Bordeaux when an opportunity of securing a better understanding with France opened itself before him.

Spanish successes in Flanders.

On every point of the frontier at which France had pushed forward her territory in the days of her unity, Spain was regaining her lost possessions. In the campaign of 1651 the Spanish army in Flanders had made itself master of Furnes and Bergues in the immediate vicinity

Danger of Dunkirk.

of Dunkirk, and in the course of September had proceeded to blockade Dunkirk itself. Estrades, the French Governor, reported that his provisions were running short, and that he would therefore be unable to hold out beyond January.

Oct.-Nov. Cromwell's overture to Estrades.

Scanty as our information is,[2] we may take it that some time at the end of October or in the beginning of November a certain Colonel Fitzjames, who

---

[1] Cardinal Bagni to ——? Nov. $\frac{7}{17}$; W. Grant (*i.e.* Father Leyburn) to Father Pripa, Nov. $\frac{12}{22}$; Cardinal Pamfili to Bagni, $\frac{\text{Dec. 29}}{\text{Jan. 8}}$; the Duchess of Aiguillon to Innocent X., March $\frac{8}{18}$; Pamfili to Bagni, Apr. $\frac{12}{22}$, *Roman Transcripts R.O.*

[2] An account of the negotiation which followed, supported by documents, will be found in an article of mine published in the *Historical Review* for July 1896, and it is therefore unnecessary to repeat the references to be found there.

had formerly served in the Royal army, was going to Dunkirk
to arrange for the exchange of prisoners captured by privateers
on either side, when Cromwell seized the opportunity to commission him, without the knowledge of the Council of State,
to make some overture of a larger import. There can be little
doubt that Fitzjames was charged with a proposal for a cession
of Dunkirk to England. Subsequently, after his return to England, Fitzjames received two letters from Estrades which he
was not allowed to answer, containing, if we accept a story
afterwards told by Whitelocke, an offer made by Estrades to
bargain in his own name for the surrender of the place to an
English garrison—an offer which Cromwell refused to accept
because he was unwilling to owe anything to treason. On the
whole it is reasonable to suppose that Estrades communicated
Cromwell's proposal to his government, and was instructed to
play a traitor's part in appearance, in order not to compromise
his superiors. In any case Cromwell's refusal to answer
becomes intelligible, not merely on moral or sentimental
grounds, but on the substantial argument that if England
accepted Dunkirk from Estrades' treason she would be exposed
to the enmity of both the contending monarchies, whereas if
she accepted it from the French Government she would gain
an ally at the same time that she made an enemy.

In our own day a proposal to occupy a fortified post on the
opposite side of the Channel, and therefore assailable by continental armies, would be reprobated by all Englishmen without distinction of party as wilfully throwing
away the advantage of the moat placed by nature
round the island-state. No such thought of danger appears to
have crossed Cromwell's mind. To him the long tenure of
Calais was mere glory, and he could hope to make of Dunkirk
not only a place of arms from which he might throw an English
army on the Continent at pleasure, but a great commercial
centre from which waterways stretched eastward, thus enabling
trade to be carried on with central Europe without any obligation to the Dutch.[1]

Alleged advantages of holding Dunkirk.

[1] See *Hist. Rev.* (July 1896), p. 484.

Attractive as the hope of possessing Dunkirk might seem, we may be sure that, at this time as well as later in his life, Cromwell did not confine himself to considerations arising out of the utility of the port itself. An alliance with France would imply on the one hand the carrying out schemes of conquest in Spanish America inherited from the sea-rovers of Elizabeth's day, and on the other hand the obtaining of an engagement, tacit or explicit, from the French Government that the persecutions to which the Huguenots were subjected should definitively come to an end. Cromwell's double object of doing something for religion, as well as of securing an extension of empire for England and with it an increase of trade, would surely be attained in this way far better than by an understanding with Spain and Condé.

Object of the French alliance.

Such an alliance was as yet far distant. Finding that no reply came to Estrades' proposals, the French Government offered Dunkirk to the Dutch.[1] This negotiation however came to nothing, owing to the protestations of the Spanish ambassador at the Hague, whom the Dutch were unwilling to offend. It is likely enough that the failure of this overture led to an order given to Gentillot in the King's name, almost certainly without Mazarin's knowledge,[2] to betake himself to London.

Dunkirk offered to the Dutch.

Gentillot was a Protestant, who had been sent to England in the preceding February to open a negotiation, and had been expelled because he was not authorised to recognise the Commonwealth.[3] Finding on his arrival that no credentials had been sent to him, he left the country hurriedly, no doubt because he feared punishment for reappearing without authority after his expulsion earlier in the year. The failure to send credentials may be attributed to the vacilla-

Dec. 12/22.
His mission to England.

---

[1] In a letter to Estrades of Nov. 16/26, Mazarin approved of what was being done, as far as the Dutch were concerned (*Lettres de Mazarin*, iv. 518).

[2] In a letter to Estrades of Dec. 16/26, Mazarin wrote strongly against the surrender to the English (*ib.* iv. 576).

[3] See vol. i. 314.

tion of his government on the subject of Dunkirk. Yet the chance of gaining English aid against Spain was too alluring to be lightly dismissed.

The actual opening of negotiation came from England. Early in January a third letter, written about a month before by

1652.
Jan.
The Coun-
cil of State
hears of
Estrades'
corre-
spondence. Estrades to Fitzjames, fell into the hands of some members of the Council of State, and Cromwell was thus compelled to share his plans with his colleagues. In the end it was resolved to entrust the management of the affair to Whitelocke and Bond, who would

Jan. 5.
Fitzjames
sent to
Dunkirk. naturally pay considerable attention to the opinion of Cromwell. On January 5 Fitzjames was ordered to return to Dunkirk. According to an account subsequently given by Estrades himself, Fitzjames began by offering him a personal bribe, but was so cowed by the indignation he aroused that he turned his treacherous proposal into an assertion that the English Government wished to come to terms, not with Estrades personally, but with the ruling powers of France, and was prepared to offer that, if Dunkirk were surrendered, the Council of State would not only pay over a considerable sum of money, but would make a strict alliance against Spain, and contribute a contingent of 10,000 infantry and 100 ships. Estrades, however, had so much to conceal, that it is impossible to put confidence in the truth of his narrative, and it is by no means unlikely that the proposal of a public negotiation with the French Government formed the sole object of Fitzjames's mission.

However this may be, the first result of the communication was that Estrades was despatched unavowedly to England either

Visit of
Estrades to
England. by Mazarin or by the ministers who ostensibly acted in the name of the young King. That Mazarin looked on any plan for throwing Dunkirk into English hands with the deepest aversion is beyond doubt, and he had already written as much to Estrades himself; but he was one of those who know how to yield to necessity, and if he were convinced in January that Dunkirk could not hold out many days longer before the attacks of famine, he may very well have preferred to see it in English rather than in Spanish hands. Whatever may have been the nature of the message carried by Estrades, it was such as to raise the hopes entertained in England, and before the end of January the arsenals were busy with the fitting out of a squadron of twenty-five ships to be placed under the command of Blake, the object of which was shrewdly suspected to be Dunkirk.

In the meanwhile efforts were being made to draw Cromwell and with him the Council of State to the other side. Early in

Mission of
Barrière
and
Cugnac. January Barrière arrived as a Minister of Condé, and he was soon joined by Cugnac as a representative of Le Daugnon and the Huguenots ; whilst, in the course of the month, Cardenas suggested that if an English force would assist in the reduction of Dunkirk and Gravelines, Spain would help the English to reduce Calais, a proposal of which no notice seems to have been taken. Nor was Cromwell any better satisfied with Barrière's offers. "They come," said

Feb. 14.
A conver-
sation with
Cromwell. Cromwell [1] on February 14 to Choqueux, an unavowed agent of the French Government, "to treat with us on the Prince's behalf. What ! does he mean to destroy the monarchy, or what is it that he has on his mind ? He must promise liberty to the Huguenots, and give us a considerable seaport as security and other things besides, before he has a single man from us. But we see that M. de Cugnac has come with more meat in his mouth than Barrière." To speak thus to a Frenchman in constant communication with his government was obviously a hint that it would be well to outbid Condé.

Of that government Mazarin was now once more undisguisedly the master. Returning to the Court at Poitiers on

Jan. $\frac{17}{27}$.
Return of
Mazarin. January 17, he had at once taken up the task of defending the monarchy against all opponents. Having to make war with Condé's partisans not merely in the Garonne but also on the banks of the Loire, whilst he had at the same time to parry the assaults of the

---

[1] Choqueux does not give Cromwell's name, but no one else can have spoken in this fashion.

Spanish armies, Mazarin could hardly expect to be able to maintain Dunkirk against a formal siege. For the present, indeed, the place was safe. Provisions had been brought in, and there was no longer a danger of its being starved out in January as had once been feared. Some time too must elapse before the season would allow the Spaniards to open the trenches either before Dunkirk or before the neighbouring fortress of Gravelines. Under such circumstances it was in accordance with Mazarin's character that he should await events, and postpone as long as possible the decision which Cromwell and the English Council of State were pressing upon him.

On Gentillot's return to France he remained for some time at Calais, where he was accosted by Robert Villiers, the adulterine son of Lady Purbeck and Sir Robert Howard, who was on his way to Italy on a secret mission from the Council. Villiers, who was in the confidence of that party in the Council which distrusted Cromwell, pressed on Gentillot the advantage to France of purchasing an English alliance by the cession of Dunkirk, and of making an agreement to divide the Low Countries between the two States.

Jan.
An offer to Gentillot.

With these proposals before him, as well as those which had been communicated through Estrades, Mazarin resolved to send Gentillot back to England to treat for an alliance against Spain. Yet, naturally enough, he could not prevail upon himself absolutely to surrender Dunkirk. Some half-measure, he flattered himself, would suffice to gain the military support of England. He accordingly instructed Gentillot to propose, not indeed the cession of Dunkirk, but an arrangement by which the English would be allowed to use the place as a port of shelter for their ships of war, and for the debarkation of troops, whilst they would also be permitted to land their merchandise on its quays without restrictions. The possession of the place was however to remain with the King of France. As security for the carrying out of the treaty the Swiss soldiers who were to compose the

Feb. 23.
March 4.
Instructions to Gentillot.

entire garrison were to take an oath to the two governments
binding themselves to observe these conditions. A few days'

March $\frac{1}{11}$.
Estrades
receives in-
formation
that Dun-
kirk is to
be kept.

reflection, however, convinced Mazarin that such a
proposal would never be accepted in England, and
before the end of February [1] he sent off a courier
to Estrades telling him that the King had resolved to
keep Dunkirk, and that the negotiation for its surrender must come to an end.

Yet it was difficult for Mazarin to preserve this uncompromising attitude. There were combats on the Loire which
turned out, indeed, to the advantage of the Royalists, but they

Doubts
whether it
will be
possible to
maintain it.

gained no crushing victory which would have set
the government free to face the Spaniards. Bad
news, too, arrived from Dunkirk. The greater part
of the garrison was in a mutinous condition, the
soldiers refusing to mount guard unless they received their pay.
It was thus, to say the least of it, doubtful whether it would be

Renewed
negotiation
of Fitz-
james.

possible to keep the place much longer. Fitzjames
again made his appearance, and on March 14, Louis
himself signed a letter authorising Estrades to treat

March $\frac{14}{24}$.
Estrades
authorised
to treat.

on the proposed alliance. Though the letter contains no mention of Dunkirk, there can be little
doubt that it was accompanied with instructions to

negotiate the cession of the town, perhaps only in case of

March 22
April 1.
The
Spaniards
before
Dunkirk.

absolute necessity. On March 22 the Spaniards
drew closer to Dunkirk, and six days later opened
the siege of Gravelines. Estrades did his best to
obtain English aid without compromising his government, and actually assured Fitzjames that, if the

March 28
April 7.
Gravelines
besieged.

soldiers of the Commonwealth were once inside Dunkirk, they would be strong enough to make themselves masters of the place. Obviously neither Crom-

well nor his colleagues were likely to consent to such terms

Progress of
the negotia-
tions.

as these. They must take Dunkirk at the hands
of the King of France or they would not take it
at all.

[1] The message reached Estrades on March $\frac{1}{11}$.

The exact nature of the negotiation which followed cannot now be traced, but there is strong reason to believe that Cromwell was at last satisfied, and was prepared, together with his two colleagues, to bring the matter to an issue before the Council of State.   At all events, early in April, Cromwell de-

Troops despatched to Dover.

spatched to Dover 4,000 foot and 1,000 horse on the pretext that they were to serve on board the fleet, but in reality that they might be ready to occupy Dunkirk at a moment's notice.[1]   Such was the state of affairs when the committee which had hitherto had charge of the negotiation laid its report before the Council of State.   In the

The project not taken up by the Council of State.

Council the opposition to a French alliance was strong, and the growing complications with the Dutch made it undesirable to provoke fresh enemies. The scheme on which Cromwell had set his heart met therefore with a cool reception.[2]

[1] Since writing the article in the *Hist. Rev.* (p. 505) I have seen a letter from Cardenas, of April $\frac{13}{23}$, *Simancas MSS.* 2,569.   The writer is explicit on the point that Dunkirk was to be surrendered.   Fitzjames, he writes, ' bolvió aqui con un Frances de la confianza del Gov^{or}, y con una plenipotencia que el tenia del Rey Christianisimo para poder entregar a los Ingleses las plazas de Dunquerque, Mardike y Gravelingas, con condicion que le pagaren una soma muy considerable de dinero, y viniese el Parlamento à hazer liga ofensiva y defensiva con la Francia, Suecia y Portugal, en el qual caso se havia de compreender tambien la entrega de Gravelingas ; y trujo diversas cartas de aquel Rey, que encargava al Governador apresurarse la negociacion, sobre que el Strades, no juzgandola breve, pidia que entretanto que se ajustase, lo asistiese el Parlamento con gente, viveres y municiones para asegurar a Dunquerque del sitio que por horas estava esperando de las armas de V. M.   Con que los de la junta poseidos de la desaficion de España, y de la conveniencia que se le representava de hazerse dueños de aquellas plazas y sin reparar en la amistad y obligaciones que esta Republica deve a V. M., hizieron bajar acia Dobert quatro mil infantes y mil cavallos con pretesto de que ivan para guarnecer quaranta navios que estaban listos para salir al mar ; pero con fin (segun me han asegurado) de que si el Parlamento resolviere admitir esta platica, se hallasen las prevenciones avanzadas, y la gente pronta y vecina al embarcadero.'   Cromwell's name is not mentioned, but no one else could have given the orders to the regiments, and he is thus seen to be personally committed to the scheme.   [2] *Ib.*

Whilst the Government in England hesitated Mazarin on his part drew back from the sacrifice of Dunkirk. Learning
Mazarin draws back that the mutinous spirit of the garrison had been repressed, and that a relieving force of shipping was being prepared to carry provisions to the beleaguered fortress—he probably hoped that it would, after all, be unnecessary to call in one foreign army to keep out another.

April 13/23. His instructions to Estrades. Estrades was instructed on April 13 to send some one to England to open a negotiation and to cultivate good relations with Cromwell. Yet so far from wishing this person to treat about the cession of Dunkirk, Mazarin contented himself with directing him to ascertain whether, if a French squadron attempted to relieve Gravelines, it would be exposed to an attack by the English fleet. Estrades, however, did nothing, being probably too fully occupied with

April 21. May 1. Gentillot sent to England. his military duties, and on April 21 Mazarin took the matter into his own hands, sending instructions to Gentillot to repair to London as the bearer of a letter to Cromwell from the King of France. In order to gain the favour of all parties Gentillot was to secure the assistance of Robert Villiers, who, as has been seen, was employed by those members of the Council of State who were

He is to offer Dunkirk. hostile to Cromwell.[1] He was also to make an offer of Dunkirk, if the English would agree to a firm alliance against Spain, pay a considerable sum of money for the place, employ their navy in the defence of the French ports, and give a pledge of the earnestness of their intentions by proceeding immediately to relieve Gravelines.

Yet, even at this point, Mazarin, though growing seriously alarmed, had not fully made up his mind to pay the price required by the English Government for its alliance. Gentillot
Gentillot kept in Paris. was detained in Paris more than three weeks, though the fate of Gravelines, which actually fell on May 8, appeared to cry out for immediate action. The delay was possibly due to hopes in Mazarin's mind that the catastrophe might be averted without having recourse to a remedy

[1] See p. 164.

which he justly regarded as scarcely preferable to the disease.
It is possible also that he contemplated buying English aid by
appealing to the religious sympathies of the Puritan Government at the expense of its material cravings.   On May 11 the

May 1/11.
The declara-
tion at St.
Germains.

young King issued a declaration at St. Germains,
in which he confirmed the Edict of Nantes, and recognised the fidelity of his Huguenot subjects.   No
doubt the promise of continued protection was fully deserved
by the refusal of the bulk of the Protestant clergy and laity to
connect themselves with Condé ; yet the date chosen for the
promulgation of the Royal assurances was none the less well
timed for the purpose of the negotiation with England.   Three

May 4/14.
Gentillot
sent without
orders to
treat about
Dunkirk.

days later, on May 14, Gentillot was at last allowed
to start on his mission, but only on the understanding
that he should keep silence on the contemplated
admission of an English garrison into Dunkirk.

He tries to
get the alli-
ance of Eng-
land without
surrender-
ing
Dunkirk.

Mazarin hoped to secure the friendship of England
at a cheaper rate, and gain the goodwill of Parliament
merely by recognising the Commonwealth, though,
for the honour of France, he demanded a preliminary
engagement from the English Government to recall
the letters of reprisal against French shipping.

Evidently Mazarin—and it is hard to blame him—shrank
from the extreme measure of giving up Dunkirk until he felt
absolutely hopeless of saving the place by his own efforts.
Yet it was a grave mistake to imagine that the stern men who
now controlled the destinies of England, after seeing so mag-
nificent a prize dangled before them, would content themselves

May-July.
Gentillot in
England.

with lower terms.   Gentillot, indeed, was allowed to
appear in England for the third time, and even to remain till July, when he was once more sent away
merely on the ground that he was unable to recognise the
Commonwealth unconditionally.

At the time when Gentillot reached England it was already

Gentillot
sent too
late.

too late for Mazarin to hope for armed assistance on
any terms.   The party which had the upper hand in
Council and Parliament was not only friendly to Spain,

but it was on the brink of a war with the Dutch Republic, which would place a combination with France out of the question for a long time to come.   Cromwell found himself hopelessly overruled.

Before the end of the preceding year the States General, alarmed at the Navigation Act, resolved to despatch an embassy

1651.
Dec. 15.
Arrival of
Dutch am-
bassadors.

to procure, if possible, its repeal, and, at all events, to clear away the clouds which overhung the relations between the two republics.   The three Ambassadors, Cats, Schaef, and Van·de Perre, landed at Gravesend on December 15.   At their first audience they were informed that the Navigation Act was irrevocable, but that the Council of State was ready to take up the negotiation at the point at which it stood when St. John and Strickland left the Hague.[1]

As might have been expected, the ambassadors took more immediate interest in the pressing complaints of their seafaring

1652.
Jan. 1.
Dutch
grievances.

countrymen than in a Utopian scheme of union which was never likely to take practical shape.   These grievances were neither few nor slight.   They had to complain that Dutch ships had been seized under letters of

Letters of
reprisal
against the
Dutch.

reprisal issued to English merchants who had, at one time or another, been wronged by Dutchmen at sea. These cases were, however, comparatively few, and with good will on both sides might easily have been provided for by a pecuniary settlement in favour of one side or the other. A far more dangerous bone of contention lay in the recent

Holders of
letters of
reprisal
against the
French
seize Dutch
ships.

pretension of English privateers holding letters of reprisal against the French, to bring into port for trial Dutch vessels suspected of having French goods on board, a pretension which was being put in force with growing severity.[2]   It seemed as if the English

---

[1] Salvetti's Newsletter, $\frac{\text{Dec. 26}}{\text{Jan. 5}}$, *Add. MSS.* 27,962 N. fol. 291.

[2] By the middle of November only two Dutch ships had been brought in as having French goods on board.   Six weeks later the number had largely increased.   Memorandum for the ambassadors, Nov. $\frac{19}{29}$; complaint of the ambassadors, Jan. $\frac{1}{11}$, *Add. MSS.* 17,677 U. foll. 79, 91. [This memorandum has since been printed in *Letters and Papers relating*

Government, having ruined the Dutch trade with England by
Act of Parliament, had made up its mind to ruin the Dutch trade
with France by the action of its Court of Admiralty.   It is true
that this Court conformed to the doctrine of the old laws of the
sea, and whilst taking possession of French goods, liberated
the Dutch ship which carried them, and even made allowance
to her owners for the expenses caused by the delay; [1] but no
amount of money likely to be paid on this score could compensate for the stoppage of trade sure to ensue when once it became known in France that goods were no longer safe on board
the vessels long known as the carriers of the sea.   Nor was
legal injury all that Dutchmen had to fear.   No better evidence
can be shown of the temper of English sailors than the fact

Feb. 16.
Dutch
sailors not
to be
tortured.
that the Court of Admiralty had found it necessary
to threaten them with punishment if they persisted
in torturing Dutch sailors to compel them to acknowledge goods as French which, in reality, were nothing
of the sort. [2]

Not the Navigation Act, but the enforcement of the old
law of the sea from a belligerent's point of view, and that too

Dispute on
the rights
of neutrals.
by a nation whose claim to appear as a belligerent
was at least questionable, made war between the two
Commonwealths almost inevitable.   To the Dutch
belongs the credit of leading the way in a course which has
at last been adopted by the consent of European nations, [3]
when, in 1650, they embodied in a clause of their treaty with
Spain the new principle that the neutral flag protected the

to the First Dutch War, edited by Mr. Gardiner for the Navy Records
Society, 1899, vol. i. p. 58.]

[1] This can be traced in the *Admiralty Prize Acts* in the Record
Office.

[2] Declaration of the Court of Admiralty, Feb. 16, *Admiralty Prize
Acts R.O.* The story of the Dutch prizes can be gathered from the despatches of the Dutch ambassadors in *Add. MSS.* 17,677 U., and from the
proceedings recorded in the *Acts* quoted above. Compare *Hollandsche
Mercurius*, 1652, p. 2. [See *The First Dutch War*, i. 50, 80.]

[3] By the Declaration of Paris in 1856, and the subsequent adhesions
to it.

enemy's goods, except in case of contraband of war.[1] It is true that the very insertion of this article in the Spanish Treaty, not to speak of the opinion of even Dutch authorities on international law, may be taken as evidence that the English Court did but reduce into practice the accepted doctrine ; but this practice was none the less destructive to Dutch trade, and, unless the commerce of the Republic was to be ruined, the statesmen at the Hague could not allow the English claim to pass unchallenged, if only on the ground that England and France were not openly at war. Being well aware of the state of inefficiency into which their navy had been allowed to fall, they resolved to strengthen their line of maritime defence, and on March 5 the Dutch ambassadors had to inform the English Council of State, that their masters had resolved to fit out 150 ships in addition to the seventy-six which were at that time ready for sea.[2] The Council, far from withdrawing those claims which had made these defensive measures necessary, replied by a string of demands for compensation on account of wrongs done almost since the beginning of the century. The high-handed proceedings of the Dutch East India Company at Pularoon and Puloway and above all at Amboyna, together with the more recent failure of the authorities at the Hague to inflict punishment either for the murder of Dorislaus, or for the outrages on St. John and Strickland, found a marked place in the catalogue of offences.[3] It is unnecessary to discuss these demands in detail. The significant thing was, that they were put forward abruptly at a time when friendly negotiation was still in progress. Early in April the Dutch ambassadors were informed of the conditions under which England was ready to

March 5.
Information that the Dutch navy is to be increased.

March 15.
English demands.

---

[1] Treaty, Dec. $\frac{7}{17}$, 1650, Dumont, *Corps Diplomatique*, VI. i. 570. On the whole subject see Phillimore's *Commentaries upon International Law* (ed. 1885), 300–369.

[2] *Memorandum*, March $\frac{5}{15}$, *Add. MSS.* 17,617 U. fol. 124. [See *The First Dutch War*, i. 85–100.]

[3] Geddes, *Hist. of the Administration of John de Witt*, i. 119.

accept the projected alliance.   The Navigation Act must be

carried out, the North Sea fisheries opened to the Dutch only under such restrictions as the English chose to impose, and a heavy indemnity paid for the misdoings of Dutchmen in the East Indies and elsewhere.[1]

In the course of the next few weeks more moderate counsels prevailed.   It was agreed to negotiate on the basis

of the thirty-six propositions which had been presented by the Dutch to St. John and Strickland a few days before they left the Hague.[2]   The discussion was opened on May 3, and was carried on amicably during the next fortnight.   If the propositions had been accepted, freedom of commercial intercourse would have been established, as far as Europe and America were concerned,[3] and even the Navigation Act would have been set aside.[4]   On the other hand, the English Commissioners refused positively to abandon their claim of sovereignty over the British seas with its consequences, the payment of tribute for permission to fish in them, and the dipping of flag and sail by the ships of any other nation.   Nor were they to be brought to accept the Dutch doctrine that the flag covered the goods.[5]

That the negotiation had proceeded thus far, whilst the demand for a political union which had played so large a part

in the programme of St. John and Strickland had been allowed to fall into the background, was, owing to the formation of a peace-party in Parliament, for the most part identical with that which had supported Cromwell in aiming at an alliance with France against Spain, a war with the Dutch Republic being incompatible with a good understanding with France.[6]   So far as it is possible to

---

[1] Salvetti's Newsletter, April $\frac{9}{19}$, *Add. MSS.* 27,962 N. fol. 341b.

[2] Proposed on June $\frac{14}{24}$, 1651.   See vol. i. 328.

[3] Nothing is said about the East Indies.

[4] *Aitzema*, iii. 695.   [5] *Ib.* iii. 698–710.

[6] That the men who brought about the war with the United Provinces were friendly to the Spanish alliance is distinctly stated in a letter

judge, this party was composed of a combination between the personal supporters of Cromwell and the Presbyterian members who either had voted against the acceptance of the King's offers at Newport, or had slipped back into the House by recording their subsequent dissent from that vote.[1]

The existence of strong party feeling is indicated by the resolution of Parliament to consider on May 7 how it might

May 7. The House discusses the supply of members. 'be supplied with members.' As two years and a half had still to elapse before the date fixed in the preceding November for the dissolution it is certain that unless hostile parties had thought to strengthen themselves by throwing over the compromise then agreed to they would have held firmly to a settlement so agreeable to their personal interests. Nor did they even now propose that the sitting members were to vacate their seats. What they asked was that seats already vacant might be filled. At once a difference

Various schemes. of opinion arose as to the mode in which this was to be done. Some members, it appeared, cherished the design of recalling those who had been ejected by Pride's Purge or had absented themselves from Parliament in consequence of that event, on the condition that they should record their approbation of all parliamentary action taken in their absence. Others asked that partial elections should be held immediately, by which, as a disinterested spectator remarked, it was probable that many soldiers would obtain seats. At all events, it was the army which was most in favour of keeping peace with the Dutch, and it may safely be conjectured that it was Cromwell and his supporters who advocated at least a partial appeal to the country.[2] Neither party, however, was strong enough to

written by Ellis Leighton in March 1654, of which I shall have more to say hereafter.

[1] See vol. i. 2. Cardenas, in his despatch of Oct. $\frac{5}{15}$ (*Simancas MSS.* 2,528), characterises those who were then attempting to make peace with the Dutch as Presbyterians. See also p. 181, note 1, where the advocates of war are spoken of as the Spanish party.

[2] "Sono questi Signori Republicanti di presente in consulta, se devono riempere il Parlamento del gran numero che gli mancano, di quelli che parte furono cacciati di esso dalla soldatesca, et parte si ritirorno

gain the upper hand, and the House contented itself with

Grand
Committee
to be
revived.

directing that 'the Grand Committee upon the Act for setting a certain time for the sitting of this Parliament, and providing for successive Parliaments be revived.' [1]

It is possible—no more can be said—that fresh supple-

volontariamente per non volere acconsentire al cambiamento del governo monarchico a quello di una republica, oppure se devono continuare con quel numero che hanno continuato doppo di detto cambiamento. Sopra di che incontrando indi molte difficoltà, molto poca speranza si ha che ne siano per venire all' effetto ; et la principale siando quella se vi devono richiamare i vecchi che ne furno cacciati, et che se ne absentorno, o farne in lor luogo eleggere di nuovi dalle provincie. I discorsi che sopra di ciò se ne fanno sono varii, alcuni tendendo che siano per richiamarvi i vecchi, mentre questi vorranno accettare di ritornarvi sotto le conditioni che le presenteranno : cioè di approvare quanto sino ad hora è stato fatto a conto del cambiamento del governo passato in questo presente, benche altri credino che basterà d'haverne parlato, et che si contenteranno di continuare a governare nella maniera che hanno fatto della morte del Rè in quà ; et se pure faranno innovatione, sarà solamente di aggiugnere al loro numero, in luogo di quelli che ne furno cacciati et che se ne absentorno, altri da essere eletti dalle provincie ; nella quale eletione è da credere che la soldatesca ci haverà buona parte." Salvetti's Newsletter, May $\frac{13}{23}$, Add. MSS. 27,962 N. fol. 357b.

" Quello che più di essentiale si maneggia qui è il riempimento del Parlamento, parendo che si desideri incorporarvi quelli soggetti che partiali del Rè deffunto vi furono esclusi a viva forza. Le conditioni però che loro si propongono sono si dure che alcuni quando potessero con esse entrarvi, non lo farebbono, mentre vogliono questi Signori una previa aprobatione dell' operatosi dal Parlamento in tutte l' occorenze passate, senza escludervi anzi voler da loro aprobata l'essecutione fattasi contro la Maestà del Rè, a che non tutti deveniranno così prontamente come si desidera." Pauluzzi to Morosini, May $\frac{20}{30}$, *Venetian Transcripts R.O.* Pauluzzi was the secretary of Morosini, the Venetian ambassador at Paris, sent to negotiate about the shipping difficulties of Venice. One welcomes the reappearance of a Venetian commentator on English affairs after so long an interval.

[1] *C.J.* vii. 130. There can be no doubt that parties were divided on the ecclesiastical questions which were now being discussed in the Propagation Committee, as well as upon the Dutch war ; but the division did not run quite in the same line.

mentary elections under the influence of Cromwell and the army

War almost unavoidable.

might have averted war. As matters stood a conflict was almost unavoidable. By the middle of May it was known in England that Mazarin was no longer willing to surrender Dunkirk, and with that knowledge one great restraining influence ceased to exist. The questions of the flag covering the goods, and of the right of England to exact a tribute from the Dutch herring fishers might still be discussed at considerable length; but the assertion in practice of the doctrine of the Plantagenets that the English sovereignty of the seas must receive due acknowledgment from the shipping of other nations was certain, in the present temper of the sailors on both sides, to lead to resistance, and the first shot fired in anger would indubitably give the signal for war.

CHAPTER XXII

THE FIRST MONTHS OF THE DUTCH WAR

THOUGH any moment might bring forth an outbreak of hostilities, the Dutch navy was little prepared for war. Its organisation was deplorable. The suppression of the Stadtholderate had broken up the administrative unity of the navy, and the five boards of admiralty, formerly united by their dependence on the Stadtholder in his capacity of Admiral, were now isolated from one another. The order for adding 150 ships to the fleet had been very imperfectly carried out. Nevertheless, on April 6, a sufficient number were ready to encourage the States General to instruct Tromp to put to sea. In nothing was the weakness of the Dutch Government so clearly displayed as in its hesitation to give their Admiral[1] definite orders on the all-important point of the striking of the flag. Tromp, being asked what had been his former custom, replied that he had only struck his flag when he met an English fleet stronger than his own.[2] The old hero's reply was probably too closely in accordance with the sentiments of his masters to admit of further question. At all events no attempt was made to bind his hands.

Side notes:
1652. Disorganisation of the Dutch navy.

April 6/16 Tromp's instructions. No definite orders about striking the flag.

---

[1] He was officially known as lieutenant-admiral, *i.e.* lieutenant of a non-existent stadtholder.

[2] 'Als de Engelsche de sterckste zijn, dan strijcken wy de Vlagh, anders niet.' *Aitzema,* iii. 730. On one occasion Tromp is said to have reproved one of his captains for striking to the English in these terms : 'Were you not as strong as they, and being so, why were you afraid ?' *The Answer of the Parliament* $\left(\frac{527. \, k \, 15}{36}\right)$, p. 12.

On May 14 Tromp, with forty-two ships, was lying off the Flemish coast, between Nieuport and Dunkirk. A strong

May 14.
Tromp off
Dunkirk.

north-east wind sprang up, and, anxious for the safety of his ships, he resolved to seek shelter under the lee of the Kentish cliffs. On the 18th he rounded the southern edge of the Goodwins, and, perceiving eight ships

May 18.
Tromp in
English
waters.

in the Downs, sent a message to their commander, Rear-Admiral Bourne,[1] to explain his presence in English waters. Then continuing his course, and thus avoiding all question of the flag, he anchored for the night in Dover Roads. There he remained till the following afternoon, firing off muskets, as the English, who watched him from the shore, imagined, for the mere purpose of display.[2]

May 19.
He makes
for Calais.

Later in the day he made sail for Calais. Before he reached the French coast, a small Dutch despatch vessel brought him weighty tidings.

On May 12, Captain Young, being off the Start with his own ship and two frigates, fell in with seven Dutch merchant-

May 12.
Three
Dutch ships
forced to
strike their
flags.

men under convoy of three men-of-war. The Admiral, indeed, struck his flag, but the second in command refused to strike. A fight ensued, with the result that the flag was hauled down, and the third captain thought proper to follow the example. Young wanted to carry the ship he had overpowered into an English harbour, but the Admiral, who had remained a passive spectator of the combat, intimated that though he had refused to support his subordinate in the matter of the flag, he could not allow a Dutch man-of-war under his orders to be carried off as a prize, and Young considered it prudent to push his claims no further.[3]

---

[1] Nehemiah Bourne, formerly major, and frequently termed **Major** Bourne, even now that he held a command at sea.

[2] Very likely he merely wanted to take every opportunity of practising his crews, who must have been hurriedly brought together.

[3] Captain Young's despatch is in Penn's *Mem. of Sir W. Penn.* In *French Occurrences*, E, 665, 6, there is a dramatic account of the action. [See *The First Dutch War*, i. 178, 181.]

If this news had been all that the master of the despatch-boat had brought, it would have been enough to tell on Tromp's nerves, already sufficiently irritable on the subject of the flag. He had, however, further intelligence to communicate.

Dutch merchant-men off Fairlight.
Seven richly laden homeward-bound Dutch merchant-men were off Fairlight, where they were confronted by fourteen or fifteen English men-of-war under the command of Blake himself.[1] On the reception of this news Tromp once more changed his course. It was his plain duty to protect his countrymen from the capture to which they were exposed on the pretext of having French goods on board, and he now made straight for Fairlight. Blake, seeing him coming, put out to meet him, barring his way off Folkestone. It is exceedingly likely that Tromp intended to do no more than to remonstrate with Blake—whose orders Young had pleaded for his conduct demanding the lowering of the flags—and to require assurances that the Dutch merchantmen off Fairlight would be allowed to continue their voyage unharmed. How far he had resolved in his mind whether or not to strike his flag as he swept up to the English fleet lying ahead of him it is impossible to say. They were but fifteen, and his own ships counted forty-two. It would be a special indignity after his words at the Hague [2] to strike to so small a number; and

Tromp keeps his flag flying.
though he may not have definitely resolved to keep his flag flying, his heart must have been hot within him in the presence of those whom he regarded as the tyrants of the sea. At all events, as he bore down upon the English fleet, the word to strike was not given, and when Blake fired first two shotted guns across the bows of Tromp's ship, Tromp, it seems, was about to launch a boat to explain his position; but before he could do so, a third shot from Blake burst through his mainsail and killed a man upon the deck. On this Tromp, angered past endurance, ran up the blood-red signal for battle, and fired a broadside into Blake's

[1] *Aitzema*, iii. 711. Virly, or Verly, is Fairlight, that place being marked as Fierly in F. de Wit's *Pascaert van 't Canaal*.

[2] See p. 176.

ship.[1] The engagement which followed was kept up till nightfall, when Tromp, assailed in the rear by Bourne's squadron
from the Downs, retired toward the French coast
with the loss of two ships.

The fight
begun.

The news was received with a thrill of indignation at Westminster, and commissioners, of whom Cromwell was one, were
sent to inquire on the spot into the circumstances
under which hostilities began. After examining
witnesses, they came to the conclusion that Tromp
had deliberately provoked a conflict. Having no
sense of the indignation roused in Dutch bosoms by
the seizure of ships and goods and by the insult to
the flag, they could hardly come to any other conclusion.

A commis-
sion sent to
examine into
the circum-
stances.

They pro-
nounce
Tromp the
aggressor.

The report of the commissioners was at least in accordance
with the common belief in England. In vain Pauw, the aged
pensionary of Holland, was sent to join the three
ambassadors already at Westminster. He was told
that nothing could be done till his masters agreed to
pay compensation for all injuries inflicted by their subjects.
By this time the hostile feeling of the Dutch population was
becoming uncontrollable. Fresh seizures of shipping were

June 5.
Pauw
sent to
England.

[1] This is no more than a conjectural reconciliation of the conflict of
testimony. Each side declared that the other fired the first broadside,
and the Dutch statements do not entirely agree with one another. It
would be according to custom for Blake to fire two shotted guns across the
bows, and a third one into the ship if these had produced no response.
This third shot, which appears to have killed a sailor, might be magnified
into a broadside by the Dutch. I think it is clear that Tromp had not
positively made up his mind not to strike. Thomas White speaks of each
Dutch ship as ' having a man at the top-mast head, as if they intended to
have struck their sails,' *An Exact . . . Relation of the Terrible and
Bloody Fight*, E, 665, 11. On the Dutch side we have Tromp's letter to
the States General on May $\frac{20}{30}$ in *Hollandsche Mercurius*, 1652, p. 35,
Aitzema, iii. 711, and other documents in De Jonge's *Geschiedenis van
het Nederlandsche Zeewezen* (ed. 1858), i. 413, 756. See also Gibson's
account, which hangs well together, *Add. MSS.* 11,684, fol. 5b. The
whole question is discussed in Geddes' *John de Witt*, i. 204–216. [Gibson's
narrative is printed in *The First Dutch War*, i. 2 ; see also i. 169–298.]

reported, and there was an outburst of anger against the authorities which allowed such injuries to pass unredressed. The ruling oligarchy was quickly convinced that any further cringing before the arrogance of Englishmen would bring on a

June 20.
An ultimatum ordered.

revolution in favour of the House of Orange. Accordingly, on June 20, Pauw was ordered to present

June 30.
The ambassadors take leave.

a final demand for redress, and on the 30th, failing to obtain a satisfactory reply, he and his colleagues bade farewell to the English Parliament, and almost immediately afterwards returned to their own country.[1] Before leaving, one of them expressed his own dismal foreboding.

Forebodings of the Dutch.

"The English," he said, "are about to attack a mountain of gold; we are about to attack a mountain of iron."[2] The Dutch, in fact, had an enormous commerce to protect with a comparatively small navy; the English had to protect a comparatively small trade with a large, well-equipped, and efficient navy. Consciousness of

Prospects on both sides.

strength indeed filled the minds of the little group of men, amongst whom Scot and Hazlerigg appear to have taken a leading part,[3] who drew England into war by

---

[1] Pauw's Propositions, June 14/24, *A Declaration of Parliament*, p. 36, E, 669, 19; *Aitzema*, iii. 719; *C.J.* vii 147; *Merc. Pol.* E, 669, 3; *The Weekly Intelligencer*, E, 669, 10.

[2] *Aitzema*, iii. 721.

[3] No names are mentioned in connection with this party, but the language of Scot and Hazlerigg in 1659 leaves hardly any doubt as to their position in 1652. "I believe," said Scot, "we are rivals for the fairest mistress in all Christendom—trade." Hazlerigg declared that God had blessed the Dutch war. Burton's *Diary*, iii. 394, 458. Writing on Feb. 13/23, 1653, Pauluzzi speaks of the authors of the war as being 'in pochissimo numero.' Somewhat later, Daniel O'Neill (*Hist. Review*, 1893, p. 589) writes: "As for sea affairs the war at first was set on by those that were the procurers of the Act prohibiting trade, which Act was procured by some few men for their interest. When it came to be known that the Dutch took it so ill, it was disputed hard whether it should be revoked; it was found that it would be for the dishonour of Parliament to revoke an Act of that nature for the pleasure of any foreigner, and that, if it should be done, it would be thought it were done out of fear; therefore it was resolved that they would maintain it, upon which both

insisting on terms which, if accepted, would have ruined Dutch commerce almost as completely as war itself against a prevailing enemy. Their own confidence in speedy and complete success was unbounded. It would be as easy, said one of them, to drive the Dutch out of the Channel as to subdue a child.

That Cromwell [1] had no liking for the war is beyond doubt, and, according to one witness, he was only reconciled to it by the assurance that it would be quickly over, and that, in any case, there would be no difficulty in coming to terms with a nation capable of living in amity with Spain after a deadly contest ranging over eighty years. He was not likely to be convinced by such arguments alone. He had opposed the war because the Dutch were Protestants, not because he thought them right in the matter of the prizes and the flag. Charitable as he was, there was a limit beyond which his charity could not go. He could no more enter into the feelings special to a Dutchman or a Frenchman than he could enter into the feelings of an Irishman or a Cavalier.

Cromwell accepts the war.

parties prepared for war, which hath continued." O'Neill lays too exclusive stress on the Navigation Act as the cause of quarrel, but he agrees with Pauluzzi as to the small number of men who brought the war about.

[1] " Cromwell *Maistre par tout* bedroock zijn eyghen confraters, gaf eerst voor men moost Hollandt te vrient houden maer siende datte meeste part goet Spaens wiert, en datter eenighe hun beroemden met het sluyten van 't Canael den Hollander soo licht als een kint te dwingen, soo geviel het datter 4 Parlaments-heeren in desen de voorbatigste Cromwel aen hun snoer kregen met desen regel :— Ingevalle dat onsen Oorlogh onse desseynen teghens Hollant niet wel en willen succederen wij konnen althoos ons met hun appaiseren, dewijle zij sulcks aen haer en alle grootsten vyant den Spaenjaert na 80 jaren oorlogh niet en hebben gheweygert." *Hollandsche Mercurius*, 1652, p. 36. The phrase 'goet Spaens' is curious. In a Dutchman's mouth, it may have been a mere survival from the war-time, when to be a friend of Spain was to be an enemy to the Republic. See, however, το ξειφος (*sic*) των μαρτυρων, a pamphlet published on July 10, 1651 (E, 637, 2), in which the Independent party is described as the Spanish faction ; and as a matter of fact they appear to have been hostile to Cromwell's notion of an alliance with France.

It was no misunderstanding of the conditions of war at sea which led the English mariners to fix upon the destruction of Dutch commerce as the best road to success. It has of late years, indeed, become a maxim of naval warfare that the primary object of a commander at sea is to strike down the enemy's fleets, thus securing such preponderance of fighting power as will enable him to blockade the hostile ports and will leave his own government free to despatch military expeditions without hindrance towards any part of the hostile coast which it desires to attack. It was in this way that the victory of La Hogue enabled William and Marlborough to conduct operations in Flanders, and the victory of Trafalgar enabled Wellington to conduct operations in the Peninsula. No such results would have been obtained if Russell in 1692, or Nelson in 1805, had captured every French merchant vessel in existence, because neither the France of Louis XIV. nor the France of Napoleon depended on her commerce for the bare subsistence of her population.

The objects of naval war.

It was otherwise with the Dutch Republic in 1652. Her population received sustenance almost entirely from her enormous commerce. The destruction of that commerce would entail, as a certainty, the starvation and consequently the submission of her people. Her fleets, conscious of the danger, would be employed in the protection of her own trade, whilst there was comparatively little on the English side to invite attack. An English raid upon the enemy's merchant shipping was therefore the easiest way of searching for his fighting force. It followed that the English Government, after detaching a few vessels to convoy its merchantmen, had the whole of its remaining fleet disposable for service in any quarter which it might deem fittest to employ it, whilst the Dutch commanders being of necessity pinned down to certain trade routes, their movements could be calculated to a nicety.

The danger to the Dutch from their commerce.

Nor was this all. The geographical configuration of land and water was eminently advantageous to the island commonwealth. The shores of England—

Geographical advantages of England.

to adopt the language of a sea-captain of the day—covered the track of Dutch commerce 'like an eagle's wing extended over her body,'[1] with the additional advantage that during three-quarters of the year the prevailing winds were westerly, thus making it difficult even for a superior force to inflict much damage on the harbours on the English side of the North Sea. On the other hand, the Dutch merchantmen, with the exception of those engaged in the Baltic trade, had to run the gauntlet of the Channel, where they would be exposed to an enemy able to sally forth from any one of the ports on the northern shore and retreat to a point of safety at his pleasure. The only alternative was the long and hazardous passage round the north coast of Scotland, and even when this risk had been faced by a homeward-bound fleet, a hostile force might easily cut it off before the shelter of the Texel had been gained.

Even under more favourable circumstances the Dutch fleet could hardly expect to meet the enemy on equal terms. *The Dutch commanders.* It is true that its commanders, and more especially Tromp himself, were not easily to be matched in any navy at any time ; but though the fire of patriotism burnt in their hearts and in those of many of their subordinates, it could hardly compensate for the *Sluggishness of the administration.* sluggishness of the administration which again and again in the course of the war was to allow the fleets to put to sea insufficiently provided with the very necessaries of naval life. On the Dutch side too there had been a long intermission of employment in the face of an enemy, dating from the defeat which Tromp had inflicted on Oquendo in the *The English fleet in better order,* Downs in 1639 ; whilst the English fleet, if never actually engaged in battle, had been employed in arduous protective service during the Civil War, and had more recently been actively employed in the blockade of Lisbon and the pursuit of Rupert. Of another cause, often alleged to have contributed to the English success, it is more

[1] *A Discourse between an English Sea-Captain and a Dutch Skipper,* Add. MSS. 11,684, fol. 30. [See *The First Dutch War,* i. 31.]

difficult to speak with certainty. The strong Puritan zeal which is supposed to have animated the officers is, indeed, and the crews more enthusiastic. except in a few instances,[1] conspicuously absent from their letters, and few of them, and still fewer of the crews, can have been under any sort of impression that they were, as far as the war was concerned, specially under Divine protection. Yet the tide of religious emotion which had swept over the country could not fail to leave behind it a mental and spiritual vigour which prompted men to worthy action on mundane fields.[2]

Great however as their advantages were, it was hardly wise in Englishmen to undervalue the enemy, and to forget that the The English undervalue the enemy. Dutch sailors came of a warlike race, inured to the hardships and exploits of the sea, and led by captains second to none in fertility of resource. It was known in England towards the end of May that Tromp had not succeeded in bringing together more than fifty sail, and his retreat after the combat off Folkestone was taken as a confession of inferiority. The Government, therefore, June 26. Blake sails against the herring fleet. did not hesitate to divide the fleet. On June 26 Blake sailed to disperse or destroy that fruitful source of wealth, the herring fleet in the North Sea, whilst Ayscue, who, since his return from Barbados, had been lying at Plymouth, was brought up to the Downs with a small squadron to intercept the tide of Dutch commerce as it swept through the Straits of Dover. Neither Blake nor Ayscue appear to have considered this disposition in any way faulty.

Ayscue was not long in carrying out his orders. On July 2 July 2. Ayscue destroys a Dutch merchant fleet. he made havoc of a Dutch merchant fleet. Twenty-six ships were driven ashore near Calais, seven taken, and three burnt. Another rich vessel was forced on the sands beyond Gravelines, and of the whole

---

[1] Such as that of John Poortmans, a Fifth-Monarchy man, some of whose letters are amongst the *State Papers*.

[2] Mr. Geddes is, I think, mistaken in throwing all the blame of worldliness on the Dutch.

number only seven got clear away.[1] Blake himself was no
less successful in his inglorious warfare. Followed by about
sixty ships[2] he made his way northward, and on
July 12 eight of his frigates, speeding in advance of
the main body, fell in with the herring fleet not far
short of the Orkneys. After a stubborn fight of
three hours they succeeded in capturing the twelve Dutch
men-of-war serving as its guard. Most of the busses made
their escape, but about thirty were captured. Blake, merciful
as ever, contented himself with taking a toll of a few herrings ;
after which he bade the fishermen return home and
fish no more. He then passed on to the Shetlands
to look out for the Dutch East Indiamen, who were
expected to return that way.[3]

*July 12.
Blake
amongst
the herring
busses.*

*He makes
for Shet-
land.*

Tromp, when he heard what course had been taken by the
enemy, would gladly have followed in his wake. By the time,
however, that his ships had left their harbours a
strong northerly wind was blowing, and as pursuit
was hopeless for the present, he resolved to utilise the time of
inaction by striking a blow at Ayscue, who with barely twenty
ships was lying in the Downs. Reaching the back
of the Goodwins on the 8th, he waited his opportunity, and on the 10th sailed in from the northward,
leaving the remainder of his fleet to block the
southern channel. Ayscue had done what he could with the
scanty force at his command. Mariners had flocked to his
assistance, and two platforms supporting heavy ordnance were
raised on the beach between the castles of Deal and Sandown.
Two troops of horse and some companies of the county militia

*Tromp at
sea.*

*July 8-10.
He
threatens
Ayscue in
the Downs.*

---

[1] Ayscue to Pembroke, July 3, *The Weekly Intelligencer*, E, 670, 7.
[See *The First Dutch War*, i. 343.]

[2] The number is variously given, but sixty were counted from Dunbar
on July 1.

[3] Blake's despatch, July 21, *Several Proceedings*, E, 796, 11 ; Letter
from the ' Resolution,' July 31, *Perf. Diurnal*, E, 796, 14 ; Letter from
Leyden, Aug. $\frac{4}{14}$, *Merc. Pol.* E, 673, 1. [See *The First Dutch War*, i.
385, 400.]

were ready to assist in the defence. The wind, however, was feeble, and the tide turned before Tromp could reach the enemy. Before it turned again a strong south-westerly wind sprang up, and Tromp, having no time to spare, abandoned the attack on Ayscue and made all sail after Blake.[1]

July 10.
Sails to the north

Not till the evening of the 26th did Tromp, after passing through the Sound which divides Orkney from Shetland, catch sight of the English fleet far away to the north. Before he could come up with it a furious north-westerly gale sprang up, making all progress impossible. Blake was indeed able to round the northern extremity of the Shetlands into smooth water ; but Tromp was exposed to the full fury of the storm beating on a lee shore. One man-of-war and three fireships were dashed to pieces on the rocks.

July 26.
The great storm.

On the following morning, the fierceness of the gale having somewhat abated, the Dutch Admiral made for home, followed by less than half his fleet. Ultimately the greater number of the remainder reached the ports of Holland, long after their safety had been despaired of.[2]

July 27.
Tromp makes for home.

The first real battle of the war—the fight off Folkestone can hardly be regarded as such—fell to the lot of Ayscue. Having been reinforced, he made his way down Channel on the look-out for prizes, and on August 16, when he was some distance off Plymouth, he fell in with De Ruyter, who was convoying a fleet of outward-bound merchantmen. De Ruyter, nothing loth, prepared for action, bidding his crews fight like men for their fatherland and the freedom of the seas.[3] After a sharp engagement Ayscue fell back upon Plymouth to repair damages, and

Aug. 16.
Ayscue's action off Plymouth.

[1] Letter from Ayscue's fleet, *The Weekly Intelligencer*, E, 671, 5. Tromp's despatches are in the Archives at the Hague. [See *The First Dutch War*, i. 363–374.]

[2] *Hollandsche Mercurius*, 1652, p. 79. [See *The First Dutch War*, i. 389–406.]

[3] Brandt, *Leven.-van M. de Ruyter* (ed. 1797), i. 61. [See *The First Dutch War*, ii. 5, 105, 116, 120, 142–153.]

De Ruyter so far gained his object as to be able to pursue his course without the loss of a single merchantman. Each side declared itself to have been outnumbered, and it is possible that Ayscue counted some of the merchantmen amongst the available forces of the enemy.[1]

Small as the results of the war had hitherto been, it cost money, and the finances of the Commonwealth were in no flourishing condition. Various expedients were thought on to fill up the deficit. On July 9 a committee was appointed—it is said at the instance of the fanatics of the army[2]—to select cathedrals for demolition and sale.[3] A few weeks later its choice fell on Canterbury.[4] Some relics of piety or good sense however sheltered the noble minster, and the monstrous proposal was never carried into execution. An old familiar expedient was resorted to in preference, and on August 4 Parliament directed that the lands of twenty-six Royalist delinquents should be sold for the benefit of the navy.[5]

In the meanwhile some efforts had been made to stop the flow of blood. Cromwell's dislike of the war was shared on religious grounds by many of his officers, whilst Hugh Peters, who had formerly resided as a preacher at Rotterdam, continued to sympathise with the nation which had hospitably entertained him in the days of persecution. On July 21 he urged the Dutch congregation worshipping at Austin Friars to petition Parliament for a revival of the peace negotiations. The petition was drawn up, and Cromwell offered to support it. "I do not like the war," he said to those who brought it, "and I commend your Christian admonition.

July 9. Cathedrals again threatened.

Aug. Canterbury selected for destruction, but spared.

Aug. 4. Lands of delinquents to be sold.

The war disliked in the army.

July 21. Hugh Peters instigates a petition for peace.

Cromwell supports it.

[1] Brandt, *Leven.-van M. de Ruyter* (ed. 1797), i. 58. *A Great Fight near Plymouth*, E, 674, 7.

[2] News from England, July $\frac{16}{26}$, *Clarendon MSS.* ii. No. 770.

[3] *C.J.* vii. 152. See p. 23 for an earlier proposal of the same kind.

[4] Pauluzzi to Morosini, $\frac{\text{Aug. 26}}{\text{Sept. 5}}$, *Letter Book R.O.*

[5] *Scobell*, ii. 193.

I will do everything in my power to bring about peace." [1]   It was probably a result of Cromwell's efforts that, about the beginning of August, Balthazar Gerbier, a Zealander who had served Buckingham as a painter and Charles as a diplomatist, was despatched as an unavowed agent of the Commonwealth to discuss with the statesmen at the Hague the chances of a renewal of the dropped negotiation.[2]   Gerbier carried with him a letter from Hugh Peters, recommending him to Nieuport, one of the leading personages in Holland, and giving assurance that men like Cromwell, Vane, Whitelocke, and Bond were anxious to put an end to the fratricidal war.[3]

Aug.
Gerbier's mission.

In such an overture Cromwell might fairly take his part. It was reserved for Hugh Peters, with characteristic indiscre tion, to urge Ayscue, some little time after his fight with De Ruyter, to leave the service rather than take any further part in a war waged against a Protestant State.   Ayscue appears to have been personally opposed to the war, but he knew his duty as an officer, and at once transmitted the letter to Parliament.[4]

Peters urges Ayscue to abandon the service.

---

[1] *Aitzema*, iii. 731, 732.

[2] An order was made on July 30, by the Committee of Trade and Foreign Affairs, to request the Council of State to grant a pass to Gerbier and to give him 50*l*.   *Interr*. I, 131, p. 16.

[3] De Witt to Van Beuninghen, Sept. 14, quoted by *Geddes*, 281, note 2.

[4] " Lo stesso Generale 'Arcus ha transmesso al Parlamento una lettera scrittagli dal primo ministro predicante di Londra nella quale con molte artificiose et apparenti raggioni di zelo Christiano e di convenienza lo esortava a non combattere gl' Olandesi, popoli della stessa religione ; ma si tiene per certo che motivo così religioso sia provenuto da quello interessato che tiene questa persona di molto contante del suo ingegno nelle passate guerre per cumulare il quale ha egli arditamente e sotto coperta d' ispirazione divina predicata la morte del defonto Rè, e di presente si dice haver egli publicamente detto che il Regno d' Inghilterra non possi quietamente sussistere senza un regio comando.   Il gran credito che tiene questo ministro da à pensare, ma mal intesesi questi suoi concetti et la rissoluzione sua di scrivere contro il servizio pubblico gl' ha dato causa d' absentarsi per qualche tempo et di rittirarsi sotto la salva guardia del General Cromwell, dal favore di cui protetto spera senza

The question of peace or war with the Dutch could hardly be kept entirely apart from that of peace or war with France.

Relations with France and Spain.

If, as can scarcely be doubted, the dismissal of Gentillot in July was mainly, if not wholly, the work of the party which desired to prolong the existing

Aug. 12. An overture to Cardenas.

war, it may be assumed that this party too was responsible for a request made by the Council of State to Cardenas on August 12 that he should prepare the draft of a commercial treaty between Spain and England. On September 2 he complied with their demand and laid his proposal before them.[1]

Sept. 2. Draft of a Spanish treaty.

Some time must elapse before the Spanish ambassador could expect to receive a definite answer on so intricate a pro-

Cardenas urges the Council to support Spain before Dunkirk.

posal. He had already taken advantage of the renewed favour lately shown to him to press the Council to a step which would be eminently conducive to his master's interests. Since · the fall of

dubbio remissione alle sue colpe et alla libertà del 'suo predicare." Pauluzzi to Morosini, Sept. $\frac{9}{19}$, *Letter Book R.O.* The passage about 'regio comando' probably refers to a renewal of the design for placing the Duke of Gloucester on the throne, which will be mentioned hereafter. It may be thought that Pauluzzi's story is contradicted by a statement in *Several Proceedings*, E, 797, 7, to the effect that Peters returned to Whitehall on Sept. 7, and that false reports had lately been circulated to his discredit. This story, however, is more fully given in *A Perf. Diurnal*, E, 797, 14, where we find, under the date of Sept. 14, that Robert Eels had published the following recantation : " Whereas I did lately disperse some malicious, base, scandalous pamphlets of an *Hue and Cry* and *Peter's Keys*, and in it very filthy and lying scandals which were brought to me by one Acton . . . these are to certify to the world that I acknowledge that I have done Master Peters so much wrong that I am ashamed." The pamphlet here referred to is, *A new hue and cry after General Massey and some others who by help of Peter's Keys escaped from the Tower of London.* This was published on Sept. 6 (E, 674, 26), and charges Peters not with political misconduct but with loose living. On Sept. 17 Peters preached before Cromwell at Whitehall, when, according to the *Weekly Intelligencer* (E, 675, 4), ' there were none that heard him but cried down the libels spoken and printed against him.'

[1] Cardenas to Philip IV., Sept. $\frac{10}{20}$; Cardenas's propositions, *Guizot*, i. App. xxi. 8.

Gravelines in May Dunkirk had been closely besieged, and at last Estrades had been compelled to signify to the Spanish commander his intention of surrendering on September 6, unless supplies reached him before that date. To avert that catastrophe Vendôme, the Admiral of France, had been preparing a flotilla of store-ships which, guarded by eight armed vessels, was despatched from Calais on the 4th. Three days earlier, however, Cardenas obtained from the Council of State an order to Blake to frustrate the undertaking on the pretext that the right of reprisal for damages done to English commerce was valid even against ships in the service of the French King.[1] Blake accordingly, in fulfilment of his orders, fell upon the relieving fleet whilst it was still on its way from Calais, carried seven of the men-of-war into Dover, and captured, destroyed, or dispersed the store-ships, with the result that Dunkirk surrendered on the following day.[2] By French historians Blake's action has been characterised as a scandalous attack on a friendly nation.[3] By the English authorities it was regarded as a mere incident in a war of reprisals legitimated by the fact that the commanders of the French King's fleet in the Mediterranean had been the first aggressors.[4] Though no evidence to that

Dunkirk hard pressed.

Sept. 4. A relieving fleet sent from Calais.

Sept. 1. The Council of State orders Blake to prevent the relief.

Sept. 4. The French fleet destroyed.

Sept. 5. Surrender of Dunkirk.

---

[1] Cardenas to Philip IV., Sept. $\frac{10}{20}$, *Simancas MSS.* 2,528.

[2] Report by M. de Menillet, Jal's *Abraham Duquesne*, i. 203 ; Gentillot to Servien, Sept. $\frac{7}{17}$, $\frac{14}{24}$; Vendôme to Blake, Sept. $\frac{13}{23}$; Vendôme to the Parliament, Sept. $\frac{13}{23}$; *Guizot*, i. App. xx. 1–4 ; *French Occurrences*, E, 675, 3 ; *The Faithful Scout*, E, 797, 8.

[3] " Mais," wrote the Council to Vendôme on Dec. $\frac{2}{12}$, " trouvant que depuis quelques années les personnes, vaisseaux et biens des marchands anglais trafiquant ès mers Méditerranées ont été pillés et pris non-seulement par les sujets de France, mais par les navires propres du roi, et qu'on ne peut obtenir satisfaction de ces dommages sur les navires et biens de la nation française, il a autorisé ledit général pour tâcher d'avoir réparation de ces dommages sur les navires et biens de la nation française." *Guizot*, i. App. xx. 5.

[4] See vol. i. 180.

effect exists, it is probable that the English Government was influenced by its disgust at the long hesitation of Mazarin to comply with its wishes by placing Dunkirk unreservedly in its hands, and by refusing to recognise the Commonwealth unconditionally. What part Cromwell took in the matter we have no means of knowing.

The majority in the Council of State had rightly gauged the unwillingness of Mazarin to add to the declared enemies of France. Parliament, indeed, ordered that the crews of the

Sept. 8. The crews restored, but no explanation vouchsafed. captured vessels should be restored, but the vessels themselves were retained, and a claim for redress made by Vendôme was contemptuously rejected, on the ground that the Council 'did not know the Duke.'[1] Any demand of this nature must be made by an ambassador formally appointed by the King, and that ambassador must begin by recognising the Commonwealth in England. The idea of carrying on a lucrative commerce through Dunkirk gained the upper hand, and it was believed that this result would be easy of attainment now that the place was in Spanish hands.[2]

There was, at least, one quarter in which every prospect of increasing the number of the enemies of England was highly

Jan.–Mar. Charles seeks aid of the Catholic Princes. welcome. In the early part of the year Charles had striven to win the aid of the unstable Duke of Lorraine by proposing a marriage between his daughter and the Duke of York.[3] Then came a scheme for a visit to Germany with the purpose of asking the Emperor and the Princes to assist him, or, if a personal appeal proved impracticable, of sending an ambassador with the same object. A more ambitious scheme was one for mediating peace between France and Spain in the hope that the two

---

[1] *C.J.* vii. 175; Salvetti's Newsletter, Oct. $\frac{1}{11}$, *Add. MSS.* 27,962 N. fol. 438.

[2] *Merc. Pol.* E, 675, 20; compare the project for removing the staple to Flanders in *Thurloe*, i. 231.

[3] Instructions to Norwich, Feb. $\frac{5}{15}$, March $\frac{6}{16}$, *Clarendon MSS.* ii. Nos. 644, 685.

governments would then combine to assist him to recover his rights.[1]

The outbreak of the Dutch war appeared to open a more hopeful prospect before the exile. It would be easy, he appears to have thought, to induce the avowed enemies of England to take up his cause, and to gain for themselves the support of his partisans in the country. Early in September his agents at the Hague implored the Dutch to send an expedition to seize Newcastle in the King's name and to bring the Commonwealth on its knees by cutting off the supply of coals. If William II. had been still alive the proposition would at least have received favourable consideration. As matters stood it was unhesitatingly rejected. The oligarchy which commanded the Provincial States of Holland had no desire to aggrandise the uncle of the young Prince of Orange, and they also shrank from a step committing them irretrievably to the prolongation of a war which they would willingly bring to an end.[2] Possibly the overtures brought by Gerbier had strengthened them in their resolution. They knew that the army desired peace, and that when the army had set its mind on anything, it usually had its way. "Churchmen were, lawyers are, and soldiers shall be" was at this time a popular saying in the streets of London.[3]

For the present, however, the continuance of the war was an absolute necessity, and the heavy losses which had been suffered rendered the Dutch people impatient of the disorganisation of their existing constitution. An outcry was raised for the restoration of the Stadtholderate, that unity of authority might be restored to the loose confederation of states. It was almost

Sept.
He asks the Dutch to seize Newcastle.

This proposal rejected.

Outcry for the restoration of the Stadtholderate.

---

[1] Nicholas to Hyde, $\frac{\text{April 29}}{\text{May 9}}$, *Nicholas Papers*, i. 297 ; Hyde to Nicholas, June $\frac{12}{22}$, $\frac{\text{June 26}}{\text{July 6}}$, July $\frac{1}{11}$, August $\frac{13}{23}$, *Clar. St. P.* iii. 77, 80, 82, 89.

[2] Langdale to Clemson, Sept. 13, *Clarendon MSS.* ii. No. 820. [Printed in *The First Dutch War*, ii. 225-231.]

[3] *Aitzema*, iii. 737.

inevitable that men of action should be favourable to the principle of the Orange party, and, in spite of Tromp's unswerving fidelity to his country, the knowledge that his sympathies lay with that party could not fail to expose him to suspicion. His failure to save the herring-fleet was unjustly thrown in his teeth, and the great seaman was suspended from his command whilst an inquiry was held into the causes of that disaster. With or without Tromp, now that Blake was once more in southern waters, a new fleet must be sent to sea to bring De Ruyter back in safety, after he had seen the convoy under his charge well into the open Atlantic. The commander selected was Vice-Admiral De With.[1]

Tromp suspended.

Under any circumstances the successor of the superseded hero would have had an uphill task. De With's difficulties were aggravated by the defects of his character. Though he was brave to the verge of rashness, and ready to throw himself heart and soul into the requirements of the service,[2] he had no self-control in presence of laxity of discipline, and he terrorised his subordinates by the severity of his punishments. He knew nothing of the art of inspiring great deeds in his comrades by a firm persuasion that they were capable of the greatest. The men who served under him felt their inspiration curbed by the knowledge that their conduct in the event of failure would be visited by a shower of recriminations from their commander. On attempting to hoist his flag on board Tromp's own ship the ' Brederode,' he was driven by the crew to seek quarters elsewhere. When at last he was on board a ship which he could call his own, he addressed himself resolutely to the task of reducing the crews of the fleet to order. According to his own

De With in command.

Defects of his character.

---

[1] Geddes, *Hist. of . . . John de Witt*, i. 231, 235.

[2] In a despatch written by him after the battle of the Kentish Knock he enlarges with the utmost fervour on a plan of employing parchment cartridges, which, as he says, will prevent the guns from missing the enemy. He does not say whether they were of his own invention. *Hague Archives.*

account there was much to be amended. The beer was bad
State of
the Dutch
fleet.
and stinking; the ships, perhaps in consequence,
were full of sick men. Those who were in good
health had no stomach for fighting.[1]

Blake had no such complaints to make. His ships were
well equipped, and his men well cared for and full of spirit.
Blake's
movements.
After his exploit off Calais, he sailed down Channel
to pick up Ayscue, in the hope of intercepting De
Ruyter on his homeward voyage with their combined
forces. De Ruyter's seamanship or good fortune enabled him
Sept. 22
Oct. 2.
De With
joined by De
Ruyter.
to slip past them in the night, and on September 22
he joined De With. On the 22nd the united fleets
anchored off Ostend, numbering about sixty-two
sail.[2]

For some days De With's movements were impeded by high
winds, whilst Blake, whose numbers were slightly superior, was
lying in the Downs. Ayscue was no longer with him, having
Ayscue
throws up
his
command.
thrown up his command nominally on the plea of
ill-health; in reality, as there is little doubt, on
account of his disapprobation of the war.[3] It was
Sept. 28.
Battle off
the
Kentish
Knock.
not till the 28th that De With's fleet was descried to
the northwards, not far from the Kentish Knock.
The zeal of the fighting Dutchman had outrun his
discretion, and with the wind in the south-west he found himself to the leeward of Blake coming out of the Downs to
meet him. Of this mistake Blake was not slow to take advantage. As the greater part of his own fleet was still some
distance astern, he lay to till his whole command was assembled.

[1] *Aitzema*, iii. 747 ; *Geddes*, 252. [See *The First Dutch War*, ii. 220,
235, 237.]

[2] *Geddes*, 254 ; *Aitzema*, iii. 749; Salvetti's Newsletter, Sept. 24/Oct. 4, *Add.
MSS.* 27,962 N. fol. 433b ; *Merc. Pol.* E, 675, 20. [See *The First
Dutch War*, ii. 252.]

[3] This pretext of ill-health is mentioned in *A Perfect Account*, E, 676,
6. Writing on Jan. 22/Feb. 1, Pauluzzi says that Ayscue 'con pretesti legitimi ha
rittrovato il modo d' escusarsi dal servizio, e ne sta conseguito il suo
intento con pubblica e sua particolare soddisfazione.' This implies
intentional avoidance of service. [See *The First Dutch War*, ii. 265.]

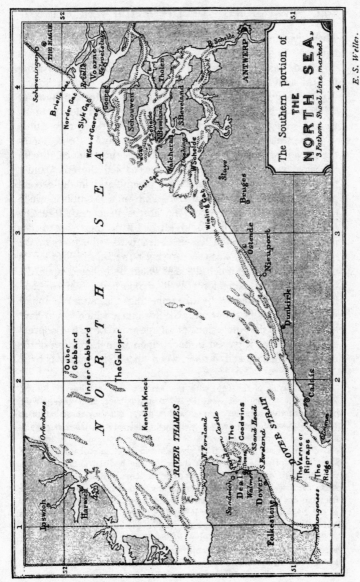

The Southern portion of
THE
NORTH SEA,
3 Fathom Shoal Line marked.

E. S. Weller.

O 2

Then, dashing into the midst of the enemy, he opened the battle.

Blake was no Nelson, and he had none of that innovating tactical skill which had enabled Cromwell to convert a mere Blake as a
tactician. success into a crushing victory. He was however a bold and inspiring commander, and he might be trusted to fight to the last and to do everything compatible with the somewhat primitive tactics of the day.[1] According to the prevailing system, it was of the utmost importance to gain the wind, in the first place because it enabled the commander to launch his fireships against the enemy, and in the second place because it placed his fighting ships in a position in which they could bear down upon the hostile fleet, and, thrusting themselves through it, could attack with their broadsides individual vessels on the less-defended parts—the bows or the quarters.[2] So slight was the carrying power of the cannon of those days, that not much damage would be inflicted upon the bows of the attacking force as it approached. This method had two main defects: by disseminating the attack amongst individual ships, it threw away the advantage which would have been gained if the whole fleet, or a large group of it, had concentrated its fire, as it passed through, upon a single portion of the enemy's defence; and further, when once the attack was over,

---

[1] The tactics of the fight with the Armada are explained by Sir H. Palavicino: "Our fleet had the wind throughout, and gave always occasion to the enemy to open out and to fight; but they chose rather to be followed and to bear away as well from Calais as from Dunkirk than to open out and permit the fight to become general, so as it was not convenient to attack them thus together and in close order, for that our ships being of smaller size would have had much disadvantage; but, in the continued assaults which they gave on them without entering, they made them feel their ordnance, and if any ship was beaten out of their fleet she was surrounded and suddenly separated from the rest." *Defeat of the Spanish Armada* (Navy Records Society), ii. 207. These tactics were out of place with an enemy standing his ground with smaller ships.

[2] On the other hand, if it came to boarding, an attack on the quarter was usually avoided, as the poop was raised so high as to be not easily accessible. See Smith's *Seaman's Grammar* (ed. 1652), p. 57.

the positions of the two fleets with respect to the wind were reversed, and the enemy being now to windward was able in his turn to attack in precisely the same fashion as he had been attacked before.[1] The result was that the advantage would fall to the best equipped ships and the more disciplined crews, but to this result the skill of the commander-in-chief contributed but little. The idea of throwing the whole or a considerable part of a fleet upon one particular spot in the enemy's defence did not occur to any one for some time to come, and Blake was not the man to anticipate it.

De With was, as ever, full of fight. Whilst he was still at Ostend, he had told his despondent subordinates that he Defeat of would bring them into the presence of the enemy, the Dutch. and the devil might bring them off. When Blake fell upon him he was beating to windward on the port tack. Then, probably in the hope of recovering the wind, he tacked to the southward, only to fall into the hands of Penn, who was now serving as Blake's Vice-Admiral. From that time no tactical skill was shown on either side. For three hours, wrote

---

[1] That the ships which had the wind broke through the enemy's fleet individually is, I think, made out by the accounts of the battle of the Kentish Knock. In *A more perfect and exact Relation* (E, 676, 2) we find that Blake 'charged twice through the enemy's fleet with the " Royal Sovereign " and the " Resolution." ' In *A Letter from General Blake's Fleet* (E, 676, 4) it is said that ' Major Bourne with the " Andrew " led on, and charged the Hollanders stoutly, and got off again without much harm '; and, again, that ' the " Sovereign " . . . sailed through and through the Holland fleet and played hard upon them.' [These two accounts are reprinted in *The Second Dutch War*, ii. 282, 288.] *The Dutch Intelligencer* (E, 676, 5) tells us that ' the General . . . charged twice through the enemy's fleet with the " Royal Sovereign " and the " Resolution." ' Of concerted action there is no sign, though ships, seeing a neighbour attacked, naturally came to her help, but this rather in the fleet assailed than in that assailing. That the system of passing through was accepted at the commencement of the war is shown by the fact that it was practised by both Ayscue and De Ruyter in the action off Plymouth. That it was so—De Ruyter boasts that he passed twice through Ayscue's fleet—though Ayscue had the wind at the beginning of the fight, shows that two fleets alternately exercised it upon each other.

De With, in giving an account of the action to the States General, 'I saw nothing but smoke, fire and English.' In the end the larger and more seaworthy vessels, the greater number of guns, and the mistake committed by the Dutch gunners in firing at the masts and sails rather than at the hulls of their opponents,[1] told in Blake's favour.

It was a symptom of the more far-reaching malady which was weakening the Dutch navy, that some twenty captains carried their ships out of the battle and made for home. Of these, as was afterwards noted, the greater number were Zealanders, and the province of Zealand was known to be full of suppressed indignation against the masterful statesmen of Holland. De With, unpopular amongst all under his command, was still more unpopular in Zealand, not only as a Hollander by birth, but as a devoted supporter of Holland against the Orange succession. There were parties enough and to spare in England as well, but there were no parties on board the English fleet.

When night fell the advantage was all on the English side. The next day there was no serious fighting, as De Ruyter and the other commanders compelled De With to abandon what was now a hopeless struggle, so that Blake was unable to do more than inflict some damage on the rearmost ships of the retreating foe. On the 30th the whole of the Dutch fleet was in safety at Goree, and Blake returned in triumph to England.[2] Yet, victorious as Blake had been, he had delivered

Sept. 27.
Retreat of the Dutch.

Sept. 30.
The Dutch at Goree.

---

[1] Only three men were killed in Blake's own ship the 'Resolution,' which was in the heart of the fight. "We," writes Penn, "had two men killed, another past hopes, and about five hurt ; all our masts, except the mizen, very badly shot ; our hull, sails, rigging and gear—as usual in such cases—somewhat shattered." *Mem. of Penn*, i. 447.

[2] *Aitzema*, iii. 750. Most of the English authorities have been quoted in the note on the last page. Penn's own account is in *Memorials of Sir W. Penn*, i. 446. The account given in *Geddes*, 254-258, is specially worth consulting, as he draws much of his information from unpublished sources on the Dutch side. The Dutch believed that Blake was reinforced on the second day by twenty ships. There is no mention of this in any

no crushing blow. Two prizes had been taken by the English fleet, and each side claimed to have sunk some ships of their opponents. A Dutch war proved to be something very different from the child's play which its promoters had anticipated.[1]

In more distant seas the advantage lay more decidedly with the Dutch. An English commander, Appleton, who had

Appleton blockaded at Leghorn. been employed to convoy home the vessels engaged in the Smyrna trade, was blockaded in Leghorn by a superior Dutch fleet, and another commander, Badiley, approaching to relieve him, was on August 27 attacked

Aug. 27. Badiley defeated and driven into Porto Longone. off Elba by the Dutch under Van Galen ; and being defeated with the loss of one ship, the ' Phœnix, took refuge in Porto Longone, at that time in Spanish, and therefore in friendly, hands.[2] Yet more serious was the news that the King of Denmark, whose good understanding with the Dutch was notorious,[3] had detained in the Sound twenty English merchantmen

Ships stopped in the Sound. laden with materials for the construction and repair of shipping.[4] Even before these tidings arrived, the necessity for increased expenditure had been foreseen, and

Sept. 28. Thirty frigates to be built. on September 28, the very day of the battle of the Kentish Knock, an order was given to build no less than thirty new frigates.[5] Parliament was at least resolved to prosecute the war with vigour.

English authority, and it is doubtless an error. [Penn's account is reprinted in *The First Dutch War*, ii. 276, and with it the letters of Blake and Captain Mildmay, and many of the Dutch authorities mentioned above ; see pp. 217-309, *passim*.]

[1] See p. 181, note 1.

[2] Appleton to the Navy Committee, Sept. 3, *S. P. Dom.* xxiv. 120. [See Mr. T. A. Spalding's *Life and Times of Richard Badiley*, 1899, pp. 81-113.]

[3] See p. 146.

[4] *The Weekly Intelligencer*, E, 678, 14 ; Blackborne to Longland, Oct. 22, *S. P. Dom.* xxv. 25. [See *The First Dutch War*, ii. 312, 315, 364, 368, 376.]

[5] *C.J.* vii. 186.

CHAPTER XXIII

THE COMMAND OF THE CHANNEL

FINANCIALLY the Dutch war imposed no slight burden on the Commonwealth. It was calculated that the building of the thirty frigates lately ordered would cost 300,000*l*. Even without this exceptional expenditure the yearly cost of the fleet was estimated at 985,000*l*., whilst the revenue set apart to meet this charge amounted to no more than 415,000*l*., leaving a deficit of 570,000*l*.; or, if the building of the new frigates was taken into calculation, of no less than 870,000*l*.[1]

*1652.
Sept.
Financial
burdens.*

To stop the deficit recourse was once more had to Royalist confiscations, this time on a vastly extended scale. A new Bill was brought in containing a long list of traitors, whose property was to be confiscated for the benefit of the navy. For weeks the House applied itself to the discovery of new names to be inserted, and when, on November 18, the Bill was at last completed, they had risen to the portentous number of 618.[2] For the most part the persons selected for undeserved impoverishment were quite insignificant, and would never have been marked out for punishment but for the pecuniary necessities of the Government.

*Nov. 18.
A new Con-
fiscation
Bill.*

Nor was it by any means certain that this last and most cruel of the Confiscation Acts would attain even the purpose

---

[1] *C.J.* vii. 210. The provision made for the navy is there given as 515,000*l*., but unless 100,000*l*. has been omitted from the items, this must be a misprint.　　　　[2] *Ib.* vii. 218; *Scobell*, ii. 210.

for which it was designed. It was resolved to offer for sale the lands affected, by the now well-established process of doubling,[1] and it was hoped that 200,000*l.* would be almost immediately procured. Unfortunately for those who had made this sanguine calculation, buyers came slowly in. It was said that the extreme injustice of the measure would exasperate the Royalists, and thereby lead to a reaction which would weaken the value of the security.

Doubts raised as to the prospects of sale.

So far, at least, the policy which had brought on the Dutch war had failed to secure popularity for its authors. The Mediterranean and the Baltic trade were alike paralysed, and the preponderance in the number of Dutch prizes captured availed little to redress the balance. When English vessels fell into the hands of the enemy, the losses were borne by individual owners. When Dutch vessels were taken the benefit accrued to the State. The discontent created was the more dangerous to the holders of power because it was shared by the officers of the army,[2] amongst whom there had, from the beginning, existed a strong feeling against a conflict with a Protestant nation. About the middle of November a proposal was made in Parliament, with the full assent of the army, to send ambassadors to Copenhagen and the Hague with the object of ascertaining the views of the two governments on the terms of peace.[3]

Nov. The war not popular.

Feeling of the army against the war.

A proposal to send ambassadors.

Under such circumstances the impending election of a fifth Council of State was regarded with unusual interest. For the first time since the establishment of the Commonwealth, an election of a Council was to be held on the broad grounds of political difference on a matter

Nov. 24–25. Election of a fifth Council of State.

---

[1] See vol. i. 85.

[2] Pauluzzi to Morosini, Nov. $\frac{19}{29}$; *Letter Book R.O.*

[3] The soldiery, writes Pauluzzi, ' non havendo mai assentita la intrapresa della presente rottura con le Provincie Basse, intendono . . . sapere la vera intenzione così degl' Olandesi come delli danesi.' Pauluzzi to Morosini, Nov. $\frac{19}{29}$, *Letter Book R.O.*

of public importance. When on November 24 and 25 the votes were taken, Cromwell was again found at the head of the

Success of the peace party. poll, whilst members in favour of the continuance of the war were for the most part excluded, and members in favour of peace elected in their room. It was no less significant that a considerable number of officers were chosen, and that Blake himself—probably as the incarnation of the war-spirit—was shut out.[1] Yet, greatly as the

Relations between Parliament and Council. balance of power had shifted in the Council, it was far from being answerable to a change of Cabinets in our own times. At present the parliamentary majority which places a government in office can be counted on to support it. In 1652 the majority melted away as soon as formed. Of 179 members qualified to sit in the House,[2] no less than 121 voted at the election. Only 62 remained to take part in a division on the next day, and the day after that there were but 57.[3] The Council of State, though chosen by a majority, might easily find itself with no more than a minority at its back.

Yet, if circumstances had been favourable, the new Council would in all probability have lost no time in proposing the

Dec. 1. Whitelocke in the chair. opening of a public negotiation. On December 1, it showed its leanings by calling Whitelocke to the chair—a parliamentary resolution having, towards the end of 1651, got rid of the permanent ascendency of Bradshaw

---

[1] *C.J.* vii. 220. In his despatch of Dec. $\frac{3}{15}$, Pauluzzi (*Letter Book R.O.*) brings out the situation clearly. Twenty old members of the Council were first re-elected, 'havendosi in essa principalemente mirato a lasciare quelli che ben affetti agl' Olandesi mantengono in conseguenza più spirito di pace che per la continuazione della guerra. Nell' elezione parimente seguita degl' altri . . . si è havuto fine conforme, et a dar grande soddisfazione con essa alla gente di guerra, principalmente con inclusione di 10 colonelli.'

[2] *The names of the knights, citizens, and burgesses . . . as they now sit*, E, 1,246, 2. The date on which the list is taken is May 27, 1652. I have found no mention of any death among the members between that date and Nov. 24 ; and if none took place there would still be 179 at the time of the election.

[3] *C.J.* vii. 221, 222. All these figures include the four tellers.

by declaring the Presidency only tenable for a single month. Next to Cromwell, Whitelocke had received the greatest number of votes when the Council was elected, but it was doubtless in his favour that he was known as an advocate of peace. Before, however, the Council broke up from its first sitting, news arrived which made immediate negotiation impossible. The English fleet had suffered a serious disaster.[1]

For some time after De With's defeat off the Kentish Knock, the Dutch authorities had striven to bring home to the deserting captains[2] the charges made against them by their Admiral. Yet amidst the janglings of rival provinces and rival maritime jurisdictions it proved impossible to secure any adequate punishment.[3] The only practicable remedy for the disease was to reappoint Tromp to the command from which he had been unworthily removed. When, however, he put to sea on November 21, his movements were hampered by the charge of a fleet of 270 merchantmen, most of which were bound for Bordeaux to fetch home the season's wines. Having been joined by Evertsen, he found himself in command of eighty-five ships of war, with which, on the 24th or 25th, he anchored off Dunkirk.[4] Blake, who was lying in the Downs, had no more than forty-two sail under his orders.

It was not altogether Blake's fault that his numbers were so reduced. On October 3, a few days after his victory off the Kentish Knock, he had reminded Parliament of the likelihood that the Dutch, even after their defeat, might send out convoys through the Straits, and had urged it to hasten the work of provisioning the fleet under his own command in order that it might be ready to intercept them.[5] Comparatively little of

Marginal notes:

Sept.-Nov. The Dutch attempt to restore discipline.

Nov. 21. Tromp puts to sea.

Nov. 25. Tromp off Dunkirk.

Oct. Reduction of Blake's fleet.

Oct. 3. He urges Parliament to victual his ships.

---

[1] C. of St. Order Book, *Interr.* I, 68, pp. 1, 2.   [2] See p. 198.

[3] *Geddes*, 158.   [4] *Aitzema*, iii. 762.

[5] Blake to Lenthall, Oct. 3, *Tann. r MSS.* liii. fol. 128. The fleet appears to have been provisioned up to Oct. 1. Navy Commissioners to the C. of St., July 23, *Add. MSS.* 9,306, fol. 81b.

Blake's correspondence during this period has reached us, but
sufficient indications exist to make it clear that he was for some
weeks pressing on the authorities the duty of provisioning and
manning the fleet.[1] A considerable number of his ships were
refitting or victualling in the Thames and elsewhere,[2] and men
and provisions were hard to come by. On Novem-
ber 12 Blake was ordered to detach twenty ships for
service under Captain Peacock in the Mediterranean,
where Badiley and Appleton were hard pressed. It
is true that the Council of State assured him that
these ships, which were ordered to rendezvous in Stokes Bay on
December 1, should be replaced by others;[3] but it was easier
for the Council to promise than to perform. So great were its
financial embarrassments that it had for some time been unable
to pay the wages of the sailors. On November 24
the Navy Commissioners wrote that the crews of three
of the ships in the Thames had mutinied, and, in spite
of the arrest of three of the ringleaders, had deserted in a body.
It was impossible for them, they added, to supply provisions

Nov. 12.
He is
ordered to
detach
twenty ships
for the
Mediterra-
nean.

Nov. 24.
Complaints
of mutiny,

---

[1] Notices will be found scattered over the Order Book of the Council
of State. There was also a letter from Blake on Nov. 2, *C.J.* vii. 210.

[2] Colliber's statement, which has been generally adopted, that twenty
of his ships had gone to convoy colliers, and that twelve more were at
Plymouth (*Columna Rostrata*, 109), rests on no contemporary authority.
As to Plymouth, we have, amongst the State Papers, several letters from
that port in October and November, and though there were ships there,
there is no mention of the arrival of any reinforcement from Blake. As
to the North Sea, the guard there was under the command of Peacock,
from whose letter of Oct. 18 (*S. P. Dom.* xxv. 18) we learn that he had
despatched three of his squadron to convoy colliers. He also mentioned
two other of his ships as being disabled. If he had commanded anything
like twenty ships, I feel sure that we should have heard of it, as we hear
of eighteen ships being sent to the Sound under Ball to bring back the
merchantmen detained by the King of Denmark, and of their return after
they had failed in their object. Neither Ball nor Peacock, however, were
in any way sent out by Blake, and I regard all that has been said in
blame of Blake for scattering his fleet after the battle of the Kentish
Knock as without foundation.

[3] C. of St. Order Book, Nov. 12, 17, 18, *Interr.* I, 35, pp. 67, 90, 94.

unless money were sent. Not a penny had been paid to the victuallers since May, and they declined to continue to furnish

and of want
of victuals.

stores on credit.[1] The Navy Commissioners to whom the details of naval administration were committed were men of zeal and experience,[2] incapable of making such complaints without sufficient justification.

Nor was the want of money the only source of danger. The requirements of the war called for an increase in the number of

Need of an
increased
navy.

ships, which the State was unable to supply, though in the course of 1652 eleven ships of war were built, and thirty-three prizes taken into the service.[3] Even

Merchant
ships
employed.

from the beginning of the war it had been found necessary to revert to the practice of employing hired

Penn's
advice.

merchantmen.[4] Already Penn had pointed out the danger of the system, and had recommended that a captain in the service of the State should be placed in command of each merchantman, the masters being frequently part-owners and therefore apt to prefer the safety of the vessel to the public advantage.[5] Penn's advice, however, was neglected, and it needed a touch of peril to bring its sagacity to light.

On November 24, the very day on which the Navy Commissioners had been complaining of commissariat difficulties,

Nov. 24.
Blake hears
news of the
enemy.

Blake wrote from the Downs to inform the Council of State that the 'Sapphire,' which had probably been sent out to procure intelligence, had captured a Dutch vessel, and had learnt from its crew that Tromp's fleet, though still scattered in the ports of Holland and Zealand, was preparing to put to sea. Later in the day he had to announce

---

[1] Navy Commissioners to the C. of St., Nov. 24, *Tanner MSS.* liii. fol. 150.

[2] See Mr. Oppenheim's *Administration of the Royal Navy,* i. 306, 347.

[3] *Ib.* i. 331, 332.

[4] A list of Blake's fleet at the end of June gives seventy-eight ships of the navy and twenty-six merchantmen, Penn's *Mem. of Sir W. Penn,* i. 429, 430.

[5] *Ib.* i. 427. The behaviour of the crews of the merchantmen at Cadiz in 1625 is a case in point. See *Hist. of Engl.,* 1603–1642, vi. 17.

that he had himself counted eighty sail beating against a south-westerly wind freshening to a gale, and that no less than 200—

the number was, no doubt, somewhat exaggerated—

Tromp's fleet in sight.

had been descried from Margate steeple.[1] What was seen was Tromp's fleet, which either that evening, or more probably the following morning, cast anchor off Dunkirk.

On the 29th, Tromp, audacious as ever, suddenly appeared off the southern entrance to the anchorage of the Downs,

Nov. 29. Tromp comes to meet Blake.

having left the merchantmen behind him in order that his movements might be unhampered. The wind was blowing from the south-west, and Blake, perhaps fearing the fate of Oquendo, hastily summoned a council of war, and by its advice gave orders to put out to sea. Probably he was now better victualled than he had been five days before, but in any case he was well enough supplied to fight a battle in the immediate neighbourhood of the English coast. It is true that he was only followed by forty-five sail—scarcely more than half the numbers of the enemy—yet he had fought at worse odds off Folkestone in May, and he seems to have confided in the superiority of his ships and men.[2]

Blake leaves the Downs.

Soon after Blake left the Downs the wind shifted and, blowing hard from the north-west, compelled

---

[1] Two letters from Blake to the C. of St., Nov. 24, *Tanner MSS.* liii. 152, 154. Was Blake to blame for not having a swift vessel on the coast of Holland to give him notice of the actual sailing of the Dutch fleet ? If the ' Sapphire ' had gone on instead of returning with her prize, she would probably have brought the news. I do not, however, see that on this occasion Blake lost anything by not knowing. Tromp must come through the Straits of Dover, and being encumbered with merchant ships his pace must be so slow that the English Admiral could catch him if he chose to do so. On the 24th Blake was, as far as we are able to judge, not in a condition to put to sea.

[2] Salvetti writes that Blake was confident ' più nella bontà de' suoi vasselli et valore de' suoi offiziali et soldati che nel numero.' Salvetti's Newsletter, Dec. $\frac{10}{20}$, *Add. MSS.* 27,962 N, fol. 482b. This is only valuable as showing the prevalence of a belief in London that Blake's resolution was not altogether unjustifiable.

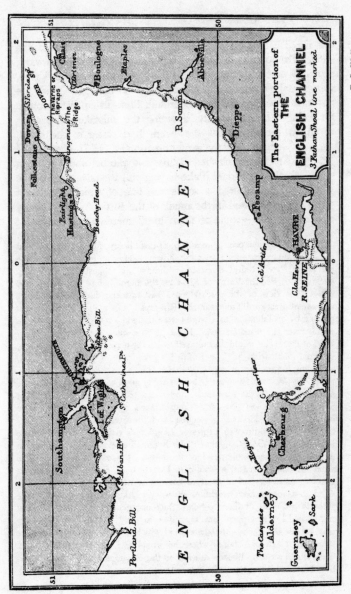

The Eastern portion of
**THE
ENGLISH CHANNEL**
3 Fathom Shoal line marked.

F. S. Weller.

ENGLISH CHANNEL

Calais
Gris Nez
Boulogne
Étaples
R. Somme
Abbeville
Dieppe
Fécamp
C. d'Antifer
Cla. Heve
HAVRE
R. SEINE
C. Barfleu
C. Hogue
Cherbourg
The Casquets
Alderney
Guernsey
Sark

Dover Str. (S. Foreland
DOVER Str.
The Varne or Ripraps
Dungeness
The Ridge
Folkestone
Fairlight
Hastings
Beachy Head
PORTSMOUTH
I. of Wight
St Catherines Pt
Southampton
St Albans Hd
Portland Bill
Nab. Bill
Owers Pt

the English fleet to anchor off Dover, under shelter of the cliffs, Tromp also anchoring at some distance to leeward, probably on the outside of the shoal now known as the Varne, so as to take advantage of what shelter it afforded.[1] With the dawn, the weather having moderated, Tromp shaped his course for Dungeness, and Blake, avoiding the mistake of bearing down on the enemy till they were both clear of the shoal, edged off in the same direction.[2] Off Dungeness the two fleets clashed against one another about three in the afternoon, Blake having still the advantage of the wind. Then followed a scene the like of which has never again been witnessed in the annals of the British navy. Twenty of Blake's ships—some of them hired merchantmen, some of

Nov. 30.
The battle
off Dunge-
ness.

[1] [In the original preface to vol. ii. of this history, Mr. Gardiner added the following explanation : ' I must, however, after an examination of the journal of Vice-Admiral Evertsen, withdraw my suggestion that Tromp anchored outside the Varne or Rip-raps the night before that battle, and revert to a view of the case which I had formerly discarded. Blake's movement westward ' to clear the Rip-raps ' is, I now think, to be explained by his intention to charge before the wind into the midst of the enemy after the usual fashion. If he did so at once from the neighbourhood of Dover, he would find himself, when the manoeuvre was completed, near the shoal, with the danger of drifting on it, or, if that were avoided, of finding it very hard to regain the wind.']

[2] *The Coasting Pilot*, published in 1671, gives to this shoal the name of ' the Vane or the Rip-raps,' and states that there were on it ' but eleven foot at low-water.' It is from Blake's own despatch that I have drawn my conclusion as to his course, and the cause of his keeping near the land, in opposition to Professor Laughton's view in his life of Blake in the *Dict. of Nat. Biog.*, that Blake hesitated to engage, but was driven against the enemy by the trend of the coast. Blake's words are : '' The wind increased at night, we riding in Dover Road, and the enemy about two leagues to leeward of us at anchor. The next morning proving less wind, the enemy first weighing, we weighed, keeping the wind to the Ness to get clear of the Rip-raps before engagement, the enemy sailing fair by us.'' Mr. Oppenheim suggested to me that Tromp's anchorage was outside the Varne—the distance of which from Dover is little more than that given by Blake—where he would find the necessary shelter. This would explain Blake's allusion to the Rip-raps. My own belief is that Blake meant to fight all along.

them men-of-war—held aloof and took no part in the action. The disparity of numbers, great enough before, now became overwhelming. Blake with but twenty-five ships was left to struggle against eighty-five. No heroism could countervail such odds, and after losing two ships, the 'Garland' and the 'Bonaventure,' Blake was well satisfied to return to Dover, whence, on the following day, he made his retreat to the Downs.[1] His honour and the honour of the crews who followed him into the fight remained untarnished.

Blake, deserted by twenty ships, retreats with the loss of two ships.

For a time the mischief was beyond remedy. Tromp picked up prizes at his pleasure, including the 'Hercules,' a man-of-war on her way from Portsmouth to the Thames. It is said that he was only prevented by want of pilots from making a dash at the Thames.[2] A party from his fleet

The Dutch triumph.

[1] *The Moderate Intelligencer*, E, 683, 19. The statement about the desertion was certainly believed in London : The Admiral, writes Bordeaux, had been defeated ' autant par la lacheté de ses capitaines que par la valeur des Hollandois.' Bordeaux to Brienne, Dec. $\frac{12}{22}$, *R.O. Transcripts*. Blake's own despatch is in Penn's *Mem. of Sir W. Penn*, i. 458. Compare a letter from the fleet in *Perf. Passages*, E, 801, 13. ' An account of the sea-action ' in the same newspaper was evidently trumped up in London. Besides other doubtful statements, it says that twenty of the ships were ' Merchant freebooters,' which is untrue. Can the writer have had a sight of Blake's despatch, in which he says that one cause of his defeat was ' the greater number of private men-of-war, especially out of the river of Thames,' meaning that these had taken up so many men as to leave some of his own ships undermanned? Tromp's despatch in *Hollandsche Mercurius* (1652), p. 107, gives a detailed account, mentioning the hours at which various events happened. The first shot was fired at one, but the action did not begin till three.

[2] *Hollandsche Mercurius* (1652), p. 109. Professor Laughton (*Dict. of Nat. Biog.*, art. ' Blake ') expresses his disbelief in the story of Tromp's fastening a broom to his masthead. No Dutch authority mentions it, and no English authority earlier than the *Perfect Account* (E, 689, 14), published on March 9. What is there given is a piece of news written from aboard the ' Nonsuch ' frigate, Portsmouth, Feb. 28, ten days after the first day's fight off Portland. " Their gallant Mr. Tromp," it is there stated, " when he was in France (we understand) wore a flag of broom, and, being demanded what he meant by it, replied that he was going to

landed on the coast of Sussex and carried off cattle. Then, picking up prizes at his leisure, Tromp proceeded on his way, convoying the merchantmen entrusted to him as far as the Isle of Rhé. As he was instructed to remain within easy distance of Bordeaux till the wine fleet had been laden for its homeward voyage, the English Government had some weeks at its disposal in which to take precautions against a repetition of the disaster on his return.

Thus it happened that the new Council of State, chosen to make peace, was confronted with the task of pushing on the war more vigorously than its predecessor. All thought of opening negotiations for peace must be swept aside for a time. The first difficulty of the Government was to soothe the injured feelings of Blake. The Admiral had offered his resignation, perhaps in consequence as much of a resolution of Parliament to give him colleagues in Deane and Monk as of his

[Marginal notes: Tromp proceeds to the Isle of Rhé. / Task of the new Council of State. / Nov. 26. Deane and Monk joined with Blake in command.]

sweep the narrow seas of all Englishmen. And, indeed, at our first encounter, he having the weather-gage, came on so furiously as though he intended to swallow all up." Another pamphlet, *New Brooms Sweep Clean* (E, 689, 13), also published on March 9, tells us that " Van Trump is now pleased to declare against those who have purchased themselves fame . . . as evidently appears by his setting forth a flag or standard of broom, and, being demanded what he meant by it, replied that he was once more going to sweep the narrow sea of all Englishmen." In these two quotations—the other newspapers not mentioning the matter at all—there is nothing about the usual story of a broom hoisted after the battle off Dungeness. The broom is said to have been hoisted in France—that is to say, at a later date, when the Dutch fleet was waiting, off the Isle of Rhé, for the return convoy. It is, in the first place, exceedingly unlikely that a writer on board a frigate at Portsmouth should have been acquainted with anything passing near the mouth of the Garonne ; and even the two publications just quoted know nothing of any broom hoisted during the three days' battle. On the other hand, after the victory had been won, there was every temptation to an English scribbler to invent a story which exposed Tromp as a braggart who had failed to carry out his boast, or even to invent a letter from Portsmouth to conceal his own mendacity. Those who have read Tromp's modest despatches will be the last to credit him with a boastful display.

own defeat.[1] Blake's resignation having been summarily rejected, a request made by him that commissioners should be sent to inquire into the cause of the disaster was at once acceded to.[2]

Dec. 2. Commissioners sent to the fleet.

Whatever improvements might be suggested by the commissioners, there could be no question that the financial difficulties of the Commonwealth had been at the root of the late disaster. On December 10, Parliament, driven at last to face the necessity of increasing taxation, passed an Act raising the assessment from 90,000*l.* to 120,000*l.* a month. Hitherto the whole of the assessment money had been devoted to the army. It was now arranged that a sufficient number of soldiers should be disbanded to enable the army to subsist on 80,000*l.* a month, thus leaving 40,000*l.* for the wants of the navy.[3] To obtain yet further resources an attempt was made to attract fresh purchasers of delinquents' lands, and directions were given for the sale of several of the houses of the late King,[4] whilst even the lapsed project for the sale of cathedrals was subsequently revived,[5] fortunately only to be once more laid aside.

Dec. 10. The assessment increased.

Dec. 17. Delinquents' lands to be sold.

Dec. 31. The late King's houses to be sold.

1653. Jan. 11. Revival of the idea of selling cathedrals.

With this prospect of increased supplies, Parliament was able to give encouragement to the sailors on whose good-will it would have more than ever to rely. On December 21, the pay of able seamen was raised from 19*s.* to 24*s.* a month, and that of other ranks in proportion. At the same time increased advantages were offered in respect of prize-money, and special provision made for the sick and wounded.[6] With this and with the improvement of commissariat arrange-

1652. Dec. 21. The pay of the sailors raised.

Prize-money rates.

---

[1] Blake's commission expired on Dec. 4, which gave Parliament an opportunity of making the change. The appointment was made on Nov. 26, *C.J.* vii. 222.

[2] Blake to the C. of St., Dec. 1 ; Instructions to the Commissioners, Dec. 2, Penn's *Mem. of Sir W. Penn*, i. 458–462.

[3] *C.J.* vii. 228.   [4] *Scobell*, ii. 227.

[5] *C.J.* vii. 245.   [6] *Ib.* vii. 231–233.

ments it became easier to complete the tale of mariners, though
even now men deserted to a considerable extent.   It does not
Desertions
continue. follow that the bulk of the seamen were discontented
with their lot.   It was rather the necessity of adding
new and untried men to make up the large numbers now
required which created discontent, especially amongst those
who were pressed forcibly into the service.[1]   To secure the
obedience of the crews of hired merchantmen, Penn's advice[2]

Dec 17.
Penn's
advice
taken. was at last taken, and directions were given that in
future the captains of these vessels should be chosen,
and even subordinate officers approved by the Government.[3]   With the object of securing discipline in the fleet at

Dec. 25.
Articles of
war. large, articles of war were, on December 25, for the
first time issued.[4]   In order to produce immediate
results some of the delinquent captains who by hang-

Proceed-
ings
against
delinquent
captains. ing back on November 30 had largely contributed
to Blake's defeat were sent to London for trial.   As,
however, proceedings against them were ultimately
dropped, it is probable that they were able to show that their
ships were in truth so undermanned as to necessitate the course
they had taken.[5]

The most formidable difficulty in the way of maintaining   .

[1] The result of pressing, above referred to, will appear hereafter.

[2] See p. 205.

[3] C. of St. Order Book, *Interr.* I, 68, p. 116.

[4] *Laws of War*, E, 684, 9.   'They were,' says Mr. Oppenheim, 'the
first articles of war to which the service has ever been subjected,' though
they ' were grounded on some regulations for the government of Warwick's
fleet passed by the House in March 1648' (*Administration of the Royal
Navy*, p. 311).   Mr. Oppenheim adds very interesting information as to
the subsequent incidence of punishment—mainly, it appears, on delinquent
officers.

[5] Those sent for were Saltonstall, Young, Taylor, and Chapman.
Wadsworth was soon dismissed, and Benjamin Blake, though relieved
from his command, was declared to have been guilty of no crime.   Their
cases can be traced in the C. of St. Order Book.   Of Young we know
that on Nov. 24 his complement of men was short by thirty or forty.
Navy Commissioners to the C. of St., Nov. 24, *Tanner MSS.* lii. fol.
150.

the supremacy of England at sea was, however, the closing of the Sound by the King of Denmark, which had for some

Effect of the closing of the Sound.

weeks been an accomplished fact. The Baltic trade of pitch and tar, of hemp and masts, was thus cut off. At once the good-will of Sweden became valuable in the eyes of the statesmen at Westminster, and on December 30

Dec. 30. Lord Lisle to go as ambassador to Sweden.

Lord Lisle was appointed ambassador to the Court of Queen Christina in the hope that he might induce that eccentric lady to join England in breaking the blockade of the Baltic. For the present, however, sufficient stores were attainable in England, and orders were

1653. Jan. 12. Supplies to be had from Scotland and New England.

given to secure a future supply of masts from Scotland, and to inquire into the capacity of New England to furnish the supplies necessary for the maintenance of shipping. Before the end of January the prospect was, however, darkened by the conclusion

Jan. 29. Treaty between Denmark and the Dutch.

of a treaty between the King of Denmark and the Dutch, in which Frederick III. bound himself to maintain a fleet of twenty ships to exclude England from the Baltic.[1]

In one way or another the fleet, which soon after its retreat to the Downs had taken refuge in the Thames, was manned

The fleet refitted.

and refitted. The sailors, though for the most part manageable enough, grumbled at the appointment of two land-officers to command in conjunction with Blake, especially as one of these—Monk—had never been at sea

Sailors and soldiers.

before. It is possible that this feeling of dissatisfaction gave rise to the only conflict between soldiers and sailors which took place in this war, though in every engagement a large number of the former had been on board the fleet, where they had played the part of seamen to the best of their ability. A party of sailors attacked a post in Kent in which soldiers were on guard, set fire to the magazine, and would have blown themselves up together with their antagonists

---

[1] Order Book of the C. of St., *Interr.* I, 68, p. 140; Order Book of the Com. for Trade and Foreign Affairs, *ib.* 132, p. 24; Sainsbury's *Calendar of Colonial State Papers*, i. 396; *Aitzema*, iii. 790.

but for the intervention of the militia before the flames reached the powder store.[1]

Early in February the fleet, consisting of fifty sail, dropped down the river, and though complaints were still heard that some of the ships were undermanned,[2] there could be no doubt that the force was in far better fighting trim than in November. In imitation of the Dutch practice the fleet was now separated into three divisions, and these were distinguished by the colours of their flags —white, red, and blue. Each division was to have a definite leader, who would command a more manageable number of ships than when, as had happened off Dungeness, the whole fleet had to look for guidance to a single chief. The use of signals, however, was in its infancy. An admiral, when once action was determined on, could only offer to his followers the guidance of an inspiriting example. The services of Penn were retained in the post of Vice-Admiral, and to mark the increased value placed on the services of seamen, Lawson was appointed Rear-Admiral in the place of Bourne.[3]

Feb.
The fleet drops down the river.

Its new organisation.

By the middle of February Tromp was due on his return voyage from Bordeaux with seventy men-of-war and 150 merchantmen. On the 16th the English fleet, now increased to seventy sail, was beating down Channel against a westerly wind. It is impossible to avoid surprise that the seaman whom modern writers vaunt as the equal of Nelson threw out no swift-sailing vessels in advance to bring him tidings of the position of the enemy, but trusted for information entirely to what news he might chance to derive from such shipping as fell in his way. From information thus obtained Blake discovered that Tromp was approaching and was some thirty or forty leagues to the west. It may be

Feb. 16.
News of Tromp's approach.

---

[1] Pauluzzi to Morosini, *Pauluzzi's Letter Book*, Jan. $\frac{14}{24}$, $\frac{Jan. 22}{Feb. 1}$.

[2] Blake and Deane to the Navy Commissioners, Feb. 9, Deane's *Life of Deane*, 530.

[3] Lawson, though he had been in the land-service from 1645 to 1650, had commanded at sea before and after those dates.

that he expected that the Dutch Admiral would choose the French side as less exposed to an English attack ; but as far as the account given in the subsequent despatches of the three admirals goes, there is nothing to show that he was told by which shore the enemy was taking his course, and it can only have been in ignorance of this important matter that on the 17th

Feb. 17.
Blake
stands over
to the
Casquets.

the whole fleet stood over from the English shore to the Casquets, where he learnt from a Spanish vessel that Tromp was now some twenty leagues to the west, and also, it may perhaps be assumed, that he was hugging the English coast.

Whether this was the case or not, the whole fleet made sail to the northward.[1]   In the night the wind shifted to the north-

Feb. 18.
Tromp
descried off
Portland.

west, compelling Blake to tack when he approached the coast.   After daybreak the English fleet, close-hauled on the starboard tack off Portland, caught sight of the Dutch fleet running up Channel on the land-

The
English
fleet
scattered.

ward side.   The sight was the more alarming as, in the night, Blake's fleet had lost all cohesion.   Blake and Deane, who were together in the 'Triumph,' had round them a little knot of ships belonging to the Red

---

[1] The printed despatch in which the three generals give an account of the battle omits the opening paragraphs which are to be found in *Tanner MSS*. liii. fol. 215.   It thus conceals Blake's faulty movements. In the suppressed passage the Generals state that on the 15th and 16th they plied across between the mouth of the Seine and Beachy Head, and heard from ' divers Hamburghers ' and others that Tromp was thirty or forty leagues to the west.   Afterwards the Generals say that ' in sight of the Casquets and Alderney we met a ship of the King of Spain, and learnt that Tromp was some twenty leagues to the west.'   The writers go on to say that in the night they tried to ' lay themselves between Portland and the Casquets, it being not above fifteen leagues from shore to shore.'   It might be gathered from these words that the fleet was ordered to spread itself out in a thin line to intercept Tromp whichever way he came, but this is contradicted by the fact that the whole fleet was off Portland on the morning of the 18th.   Blake is not responsible for the form in which this narrative is found in the joint despatch, as he was severely wounded in the battle.

Squadron, a few more of the same squadron being with Lawson about a mile off on the starboard quarter, whilst Penn in the 'Speaker,' with some portion of the Blue Squadron, was some little distance ahead. Taking them altogether, no more than twenty sail were within striking distance. Monk with the White Squadron was four miles off to leeward, and with him, or further off still, was the mass of the slower sailing vessels, scattered over the sea and incapable of bringing help to their comrades in distress.

For purposes of immediate battle, Tromp, with seventy ships against twenty, had even more odds in his favour than in

Tromp's attack.

the fight off Dungeness. The great Dutch sailor, ranging his convoy behind him, dashed before the wind at the centre of the enemy, where the flag of Blake and Deane waved in the breeze. For a time the battle raged furiously. Blake himself was severely wounded, and the captain of his ship slain. Penn hastily tacking, drove into the thick ranks of the Dutch, who were shortly afterwards assailed by Lawson falling down on them from the eastward. Yet all this did not give equality to the opposing fleets. By degrees the ships to leeward began to come up to the aid of their countrymen. Finally, after a desperate struggle, some English frigates, beating up to windward, assailed the merchantmen under Tromp's protection, and Tromp, terribly weighted by the conditions of his command, was compelled to draw off to their succour.[1] The remainder of the short February day was spent on both sides in repairing damages, and in assisting water-logged

---

[1] The despatch of the Generals should be compared with Gibson's Notes in Penn's *Mem. of Sir W. Penn*, ii. 614, and his account of the battle in *Add. MSS.* 11,684, fol. 9. [See *The First Dutch War*, p. 14.] Gibson was purser on board the 'Assurance' in Penn's squadron. See also the Dutch despatches in *Hollandsche Mercurius*, 1653, pp. 20, 22. Tromp gives the attack of the frigates on the merchantmen as his reason for withdrawing. The account given by Capt. Saunders (*Mem. of Penn*, i. 478) that Lawson 'tacked and stood through the Dutch fleet with the wind on the larboard side' is inexplicable, as in that case he would have headed eastwards away from the battle. Probably 'Lawson' is written by a slip of the pen for 'Penn.'

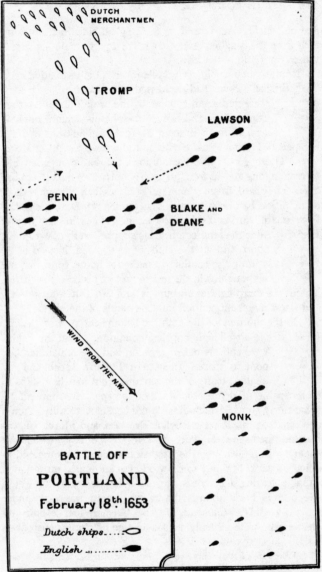

DUTCH
MERCHANTMEN

TROMP

LAWSON

PENN

BLAKE AND
DEANE

WIND FROM THE N.W.

MONK

BATTLE OFF

PORTLAND

February 18th 1653

Dutch ships..... ⚬
English ....

E. S. Weller.

and defenceless ships; and on the English side in transferring men from the smaller vessels to make up the complement of those larger and better armed.

Neither side could as yet claim any definite advantage. The English crews had redressed the balance so heavily weighted against them by the unskilfulness of their commanders. Yet even their heroism might not have availed them, if the geographical conditions had not compelled Tromp to carry with him the dead weight of a convoy. Those geographical conditions, too, had compelled him to remain long absent from his own country. Whilst Blake had taken on board fresh stores since his defeat, Tromp, whose ammunition had been heavily drawn upon at Dungeness, had been unable to supply his powder magazines in the Bay of Biscay. After the long combat his supplies were now running short, and on the 19th he was forced, instead of renewing the conflict, to make for home, spreading out his warships in the rear to protect his precious charge. There was sharp fighting in pursuit, and two Dutch men-of-war and a few merchantmen fell into the hands of the enemy.

Advantages on the English side.

Feb. 19. Tromp retreats.

On the morning of the 20th the Dutch fleet, now off Beachy Head, was in a well-nigh hopeless condition. Half their ships were entirely out of powder, and the remainder had none to spare. In spite of Tromp's threats and entreaties, many of the captains, knowing their ships to be incapable of defence, made their escape. Surrounded by some thirty ships [1] which alone were constant to duty, Tromp and his subordinates, De Ruyter, Evertsen, and Floriszoon, exhausted themselves in efforts to beat off the now triumphant enemy. In the evening the English commanders combined in a fierce attack, but only to draw off after an hour's impassioned struggle, fearing that unless they anchored the ebb tide would sweep them back towards the west. Tromp was now under the chalk cliffs to the south of Cape Grisnez, and Monk and Deane, who were virtually in sole charge of the English fleet,

Feb. 20. Victory of the English.

---

[1] Tromp says from twenty-five to thirty; the English say thirty-five.

were assured by the pilots that Tromp would never weather
that headland. They had not counted on the resourceful seamanship of their opponent. Tromp knew that another half-
hour's fighting would absolutely exhaust his powder and shot,
and, with a skill that was all his own, he performed the feat
which had been pronounced impossible. Before the sun rose
he had doubled Cape Grisnez and not a Dutch sail remained
in sight.[1]

The victory lay with the English, but it was a victory which
they owed to the circumstances under which they fought, and
not to the skill of their commanders. The honours
of that heroic struggle lay with Tromp, whose magni-
ficent seamanship and undaunted courage might have
availed to bind victory to the flag of the Republic if the permanent conditions of the strife had been more equal. Unless
they could change the positions of land and water, Dutch
commerce would always need the protection of a strong fleet
as it passed to the Atlantic, and that fleet would always be exposed to fight at a disadvantage when hampered by a convoy.
At Dungeness Tromp had shown that he understood as well as
any modern commentator that there was everything to gain by
the destruction of the enemy's war fleet, apart from the defence
of commerce. The conditions under which the Dutch Republic existed did not permit a repetition of the experiment.
In the first place, the naval tactics of the day did not readily
lend themselves to the destruction of a fleet, unless when, as in
the case of the Armada in 1588, and of Oquendo in 1639, it was
decidedly inferior in fighting qualities. In the second place, the
Dutch, depending as they did upon commerce for their very
subsistence, were compelled to impose the defence of that
commerce upon their admirals as their first duty—a duty which,

Causes of the defeat of the Dutch.

---

[1] See for references, p. 216, note 1. The despatch of the three
Generals is signed by Blake in a shaky hand, but must have been drawn
up by the other two. For Tromp's statement that he would have been
out of ammunition in half an hour, omitted in his printed despatch, see
De Jonge's *Geschiedenis van het Nederlandsche Zeewesen* (ed. 1858), i.
453, note 1.

as the trade route passed through a narrow channel open to easy attack, it was peculiarly difficult to perform. It was the result of the battle which began off Portland and ended off Cape Grisnez, that the command of that channel had passed into the hands of the English. The end of the war might not be yet, but, whenever it came, the decision could hardly fail to be in favour of the masters of the main line of communication between the Netherlands and the outer world.[1]

[1] " In allen geval als Engelandt aen Hollandt het Canael konde onbruckelijck maeken, soe wast met de Hollandsche Negotie gedaen, ende soude haer equipagie ten Oorlogh meer ende meer verslappen." *Aitzema*, iii. 803.

CHAPTER XXIV

THE ARMY PETITION

THE growing impatience with which the army regarded the proceedings of Parliament was not to be accounted for merely by a difference of opinion on the subject of the Dutch war. One influential officer indeed appears to have been actuated to a great extent by personal motives. After Cromwell, no soldier bore so high a reputation for military ability as Lambert. As long ago as on January 30, 1652, he had been nominated by Parliament as Lord Deputy of Ireland in succession to Ireton.[1] He accordingly returned from Scotland, where he had been serving as major-general, and put himself to some expense in preparing for his new office. About three months later, a question was raised in Parliament whether it would be expedient to renew Cromwell's lord lieutenancy of Ireland,[2] which, having been conferred on him for three

1652.
Ill-feeling between army and Parliament.

Jan. 30.
Lambert appointed Lord Deputy.

---

[1] *C.J.* vii. 79.

[2] " Pare che siano ancora attorno per allegerirsi di molte cariche di spesa et particolarmente di quella del generalato d'Irlanda goduto dal Generale Cromuel con venti mila scudi l' anno di stipendio, et forse anche dell' altra del Vice Rè, da essere per l' avvenire maneggiate da Commissarii Parlamentari. Il che se faranno, sarà segno assai manifesto che il Generale Cromuel comincia a declinare di autorità et del fausto popolare che soleva havere, et se io dicessi che i medesimi del Parlamento sono divisi et predominati da interessi particolari non mi discosterei molto della verità." Salvetti to Gondi, May $\frac{21}{31}$, *Add. MSS.* 27,962 N. fol. 359.

years in 1649, would expire on June 23. The expenses of fitting
out Blake's fleet were at that time weighing on the House, and,
on May 19, in a fit of economy, encouraged perhaps

May 19.
The lord
lieutenant-
ship abo-
lished.

by resentment felt against Cromwell for his opposition
to the war, Parliament abolished the office.[1] Cromwell, however, had sufficient influence to frustrate a
plan for placing the army in Ireland directly under Ludlow
and the other Parliamentary Commissioners,[2] and, on June 15,

June 15.
Cromwell to
appoint a
commander
of the forces
in Ireland.

it was resolved that he was himself to retain his
supervision over the Irish army ;[3] but that, instead
of acting through a lord deputy, he was to appoint a
subordinate commander of the forces, whose pay
and position were to be inferior to Ireton's. Lambert having

July 9.
Fleetwood
appointed.

refused to leave England on such terms, Cromwell
assigned the appointment to Fleetwood,[4] who had
recently become his son-in-law by a marriage with
Ireton's widow.

It was seldom Cromwell's habit to adduce evidence of his
personal integrity. This time, however, he placed on record
the fact that no pecuniary advantage had accrued to him from
an office which had been a sinecure since he left Ireland in

Cromwell
remits his
arrears to
the State.

1650. He informed the Council that he had remitted the whole of the lord lieutenant's salary,
8,000*l.* a year, to Ireton, but that since Ireton's death
he had ceased to draw a penny of it. Of the arrears thus

Aug. 5.
Part of them
paid to
Lambert.

strictly owing to him, 2,000*l.* were at his own request
paid to Lambert to meet the expenses incurred in
preparing for his removal to Ireland, the remainder
being absolutely remitted to the Commonwealth.[5] Lambert
was less magnanimous. His disappointment at his failure to
secure the splendid position in Ireland on which he had set his
heart exasperated him against the parliamentary managers, and

---

[1] *C.J.* vii. 79.   [2] See p. 117.   [3] *C.J.* vii. 142.   [4] *Ib.* vii. 152.
[5] C. of St. to the late Treasurers-at-war, Aug. 5, *S. P. Dom.* xxiv.
93, a. After paying 2,000*l.* to Lambert, and 273*l.* 19*s.* 2*d.* due to Ireton for
a fraction of a month, there remained 2,865*l.* 15*s.* 3*d.*, which was the
amount remitted by Cromwell.

there is good reason to believe that Cromwell, who did not love them, sympathised with his lieutenant. "Not anything,"

He con- Cromwell is reported to have said, "troubles me
doles with
Lambert. more than to see honest John Lambert so ungrate-
fully treated."[1]

The vast majority of the malcontents were, however, moved by no considerations of self-interest. They regretted the

The neglect into which the reforms pushed forward dur-
majority of ing the early part of the year had now fallen, and,
the officers
dissatisfied connecting this with the outbreak of the war, which
on public they attributed to the interested motives of members
grounds.
The army of Parliament, they were eager for a dissolution of
calls for a the House as likely to bring with it both peace and
dissolution.
reform. It is true that in May the House had itself broken through the compromise of the preceding November by appointing certain days on which a Grand Committee should sit to fix a time for a dissolution,[2] but either disinclination or pressure of business had cut short this effort, and after May 26 the Committee ceased to meet. On August 2, the officers,

[1] This was told by Lambert himself in 1659 (*Thurloe*, vii. 660), and is probably true if, as is alleged, the words were spoken in his hearing. The rest of Lambert's story, that Cromwell had already put up Vane and Hazlerigg to refuse to send him to Ireland in order to gain credit with Lambert by compassionating him, is too involved to have been true as it stands. It does not even fit into the situation. Parliament did not refuse to send Lambert to Ireland, except indirectly, by abolishing Cromwell's lord lieutenantship. Still, as Lambert was on good terms in 1659 with Vane and Hazlerigg, he doubtless heard the tale from them ; and it may therefore be concluded that there was some truth at the foundation of it. Can it be that Cromwell assured Vane and Hazlerigg that he willingly consented to the vote of May 19, by which his own office was abolished? He may very well have done so, and yet have regretted that the result of that vote inflicted injury on Lambert. Mrs. Hutchinson's story that Lambert's wife, at the time when her husband still held the appointment of lord deputy, arrogantly claimed precedence over Ireton's widow, and that Fleetwood won her by condoling with her on the occasion, may be true. Fleetwood's marriage took place on June 8, as appears from a newsletter of June 12 in the *Clarke MSS*.

[2] See p. 174.

losing patience, held a meeting which lasted from nine in the
morning till six at night, and resulted in a petition
to which most of those present affixed their signatures.[1]

Aug. 2.
An army
petition
drawn up.

The demands now formulated by the army were tolerably
extensive. They asked that the Gospel might be propagated
and its ministers supported otherwise than by tithe;
that the resolutions of the Committee on law should
be taken into consideration; that profane and
scandalous persons should be expelled from places of authority,
making room for 'men of truth, fearing God and hating
covetousness'; that county-committees should be appointed to
redress grievances arising out of the collection of excise; that
the debts of the Commonwealth should be satisfied before
private persons received anything from the public revenue;
that soldiers should be paid their arrears; that promises made
to Royalists by articles of war should be fulfilled; that the
revenue should be brought into a single treasury, and a
balance-sheet published; that a Committee, on which no
member of Parliament should have a seat, might be appointed
to report on monopolies, pluralities, and exorbitant salaries;
that vagabonds might be suppressed and work found for the
poor, whilst the restrictions placed on employment by corpora-
tions were to be relaxed in favour of deserving soldiers.
Finally, as if distrusting the good will of the existing Parliament
to carry out this extensive programme, the petitioners asked
'that a new representative be forthwith elected.'[2]

Demands
of the
army.

Cromwell's signature was not to be found amongst those
appended to the petition.[3] It is probable that his disapproval

---

[1] Newsletter, Aug. 3, quoted from the *Clarke MSS.* in Mr. Firth's
edition of *Ludlow*, i. 348. Clarke himself was unfortunately absent in
Scotland, so that we have no reports from him of these important meetings.

[2] The petition as finally presented is to be found in *A Perfect Account*,
E, 674, 4. The original form of the last clause as given above is from
A Declaration of the Army, E, 673, 13.

[3] " Il Generale Cromuel non ha voluto sottoscrivere." Pauluzzi to
Morosini, May $\frac{5}{15}$, *Letter Book R.O.*

centred on the demand for an immediate dissolution. At all
events it was this clause which, before the petition was finally

Cromwell stands aloof.

agreed on, was altered to a request that ' for public
satisfaction of the good people of this land, speedy
consideration may be had of such qualification for

Aug. 12. The petition amended.

future and successive Parliaments as ' might secure
' the election only of such as are pious and faithful in
the interests of the Commonwealth to sit and serve as members
in the said Parliament.'[1]

In procuring this alteration Cromwell once more assumed
the position of a mediator between parties. In so doing he

Cromwell as a mediator.

left entirely out of account those few who advocated
a government by the representatives of the nation
freely chosen, regardless whether the result was
favourable to their own political principles or not. He had, on
the one hand, to do with the members of the existing Parliament who, in order to secure the predominance of their
principles and their own continuance in power, had already
declared for partial elections, and were likely to do so again.
On the other hand, he had to deal with those who, like
Harrison, distrusted popular elections altogether, and were
anxious to confine the government to right-thinking persons
selected from ' the godly party.' Cromwell's clause as amended

Nature of the com- promise proposed by him.

provided for a general, as opposed to a partial,
election, and at the same time proposed to fill
Parliament with ' well-affected ' persons, not by
converting it into a merely selected body, but by the
imposition of qualifications such as had been already suggested

---

[1] That Cromwell did not condemn the presentation of a petition by
the army is clear from Whitelocke. " In discoursing with Cromwell,"
he writes, " I advised him to stop this way of their petitioning by the
officers of the army with swords in their hands, lest in time it might come
home to himself; but he seemed to slight, or rather, to have some design
by it, in order to which he put them to prepare a way for him." *Whitelocke,* 541. Ludlow's account, as Mr. Firth observes (*Ludlow,* i. 348,
note 1), 'is very confused,' but it becomes more intelligible if what he
says of Cromwell's opposition is referred to the earlier and not to the
later form of the last clause.

in the *Agreement of the People*, in order to direct the choice of the constituencies into the right channel.

Both by character and position Cromwell was well qualified to act as mediator. "He is a man," wrote an observer who at Cromwell's least echoed the popular conception, "of great fitness for foresight, of a lofty spirit, and capable whatever the office of mediator. happens of parrying blows directed against himself, and of retaining the affection and esteem of both parties, and, in fine, of preserving the independence of the authority which he exercises, disposing at his free will of all military offices, and influencing all by the modesty of his life, in which there is no display or magnificence. At present—it was otherwise formerly—he is applauded, but not loved by all ; his riches, or, to speak more correctly, his treasures, increase daily through his conduct, and he thereby looks to maintain himself in augmented authority and power." [1]

The petition, amended on August 12, was presented to Parliament on the 13th, and at once referred to a select commit-
Aug. 13. tee.[2] On September 14 the Committee reported
The that, in order to the more speedy passing of the Bill
petition presented. on Elections, it would be well to take it out of the
Sept. 14. hands of the Grand Committee to which it had been
Report of a referred in May,[3] and to request the advice of a select
committee on it. committee composed of a small number of members.
The Bill The House at once accepted the proposal, but
for Elec- ordered that the select committee should be iden-
tions re- tical with the Committee which had just reported,
ferred to a select com- and also that a blank should be left for the insertion
mittee. of the date of dissolution.[4] The compromise of November 1651 was thus definitely abandoned by Parliament itself.

It was significant of approaching change, that whilst Cromwell's name appears on the list of this Committee, that of

---

[1] Pauluzzi to Morosini, Aug. $\frac{5}{15}$, *Letter Book R.O.*

[2] *C.J.* vii. 164. It was presented by six officers—Whalley, Hacker, Barkstead, Okey, Goffe, and Worsley—all of whom, except Okey, supported Cromwell during the Protectorate. *Merc. Pol.* E, 674, 6.

[3] See p. 174.   [4] *C.J.* vii. 178.

Vane was omitted. Vane may have objected to legislate under pressure from the army, but a more probable conjecture is,

Cromwell a member of the committee, from which Vane is excluded.

that he was excluded because he had attached himself to the scheme of partial elections in favour of which he had reported in January 1650.[1] The paths of Cromwell and Vane, so long united, were at length beginning to diverge.

On some of the reforms suggested in the petition, there was at least a show of progress. On October 1, ' the distracted

Oct. 1.
A committee for the Treasury.

state of the Treasury ' was taken into consideration, and a committee, formerly appointed to provide a remedy for the evils complained of, was revived.[2] A

Oct. 8.
The propagation of the Gospel.

week later the Committee on the Propagation of the Gospel was recalled to life.[3] On the 12th, an Act

Oct. 12.
The poor to be found work.

for setting the poor to work received a second reading. The passing of an Act disqualifying delin-

Delinquents disqualified from office.

quents from office as well as from taking part in the election of officials,[4] may perhaps be regarded as an indication of a wish to apply qualifications to parliamentary elections as well ; if so, there was no sign of any desire to take up the larger subject. The Committee appointed to consider the Bill for establishing a new Parliament made no report.

Cromwell did his best to bring the parties to an understanding. At his instigation it was agreed that meetings

Oct.
Meetings of officers and members of Parliament.

should take place between the leading members of Parliament and the principal officers. " I believe," he afterwards averred, " we had at least ten or twelve meetings, most humbly begging and beseeching of them that by their own means they would bring forth those good things which had been promised and expected ; that so it might appear they did not do them by any suggestion from the army, but from their own ingenuity : so tender were we to preserve them in the reputation of the people."

---

[1] See vol. i. p. 242.   [2] *C.J.* vii. 188.
[3] *Ib.* vii. 190.   [4] *Ib.* vii. 192.

This tenderness of the army, however, did not involve admiration of the existing parliamentary system. The dissatis-

Cromwell dissatisfied with Parliament.

faction of Cromwell and his brother officers was not solely based on the Parliament's neglect of reforms, nor even on its hesitation to name a day for the dissolution. They did but share the widely spread belief, that important matters of public interest were decided by private cliques. "How hard and difficult a matter was it," Cromwell complained at a later date, "to get anything carried without making parties, without things unworthy of a parliament." [1] It was notorious that many members who had entered the House poor were now rolling in wealth, without having performed any service deserving recognition.

There can be little doubt that Cromwell was still hankering after that 'settlement, of somewhat with monarchical power in it,' which he had favoured ten months before.[2] It

Cromwell in favour of constitutional monarchy.

was natural to him in seeking for a check upon a self-seeking parliamentary majority to hark back upon so much of the old institutions of the country as it was possible to revive. There is therefore no reason

[1] *Carlyle*, Speech I. A pamphleteer, writing in Cromwell's interest after the dissolution, gives the following account of the state of affairs : "Besides that, the House being by the last purge made thin . . . there was an opportunity given them to become so familiar with one another, that what by their ordinary at Whitehall, and what by their conferences at the Speaker's chamber before the sittings of the House, little was determined but out of design and faction : oppositions and conjunctions were laid, private interests intervened—and these commonly by way of exchange—needless things mightily insisted upon, whilst thousands of poor creditors and petitioners starved at their door with their printed papers unheard, unregarded, unless a crafty solicitor had undertaken—for it is a term I hear as common as practice among lawyers—to make some members, and this with such success as commonly taught them what it was to trust " (*A letter written to a gentleman in the Country*, E, 697, 2). Thomason ascribes this to Milton, and Prof. Masson supports him. The real author, however, was, as Mr. Firth pointed out to me, John Hall. See News from London, $\frac{May 27}{June 6}$, 1653, *Clarendon MSS.* ii. No. 1,185. An account of a cheating committee will be found in *A Caution to the Parliament*, E, 712, 6. [2] See p. 76.

to distrust the rumour which credited him with recurring [1]
Sept. in September to the design of raising the young
He proposes to make the Duke of Gloucester king. Duke of Gloucester to the throne,[2] and of making himself Protector under the nominal headship of the lad.

That the suggestion was soon perceived to be impracticable may be readily believed. As week after week passed away without producing a solution of the difficulties of a situation well-nigh intolerable, Cromwell's dissatisfaction rapidly increased.
Nov. Cromwell's conversation with Whitelocke. In November it vented itself in a long conversation with Whitelocke—a fair representative of the well-meaning but somewhat stolid portion of the prosperous classes, whose inertia every statesman in his heart despises. Cromwell now spoke of the distraction in the counsels of the Commonwealth, of the danger of being fooled out of the mercies of God 'by our particular jarrings and animosities one against another.' Whitelocke agreed with him as to the danger, but thought it proceeded rather from the ambition of the officers and the mutinous spirit of the soldiers. To this Cromwell, protesting that he was well able to restrain mutiny, replied by turning the conversation to the misconduct of civilians. "As for members of Parliament," he said, "the
His indictment against Parliament. army begins to have a strange distaste against them, and I wish there were not too much cause for it; and really their pride and ambition and self-seeking, ingrossing all places of honour and profit to themselves and their friends, and their daily breaking forth into new and violent parties and factions; their delay of business and design to perpetuate themselves, and to continue the power in their own hands; their meddling in private matters between party and party, contrary to the institution of Parliament, and their injustice and partiality in those matters, and the scandalous lives of some of the chief of them;[3] these things, my lord, do give much ground for people to open their mouths against them and

[1] *Great Civil War*, iii. 130; iv. 168.
[2] *Nicholas Papers*, i. 310.
[3] Henry Marten, no doubt, was one of those aimed at.

to dislike them, nor can they be kept within the bounds of justice and law or reason, they themselves being the supreme power of the nation, liable to no account to any, nor to be controlled or regulated by any other power; there being none superior or co-ordinate with them."

It was a grave indictment and one reaching far beyond the personal delinquencies of the men at whom it was aimed.

He looks for a remedy.

"Unless," continued Cromwell, "there be some authority and power so full and so high as to restrain and keep things in better order, and that may be a check to these exorbitances, it will be impossible in human reason to prevent our ruin."

Cromwell, it would seem, sympathised with Hobbes' belief in the dangers of an unchecked executive Parliament, though

Cromwell and Hobbes.

A constitutional discussion.

he took no interest in his speculative doctrine on State sovereignty. So anomalous was the position of the existing Parliament that Whitelocke could do little but express a hope that the majority of its members would, when it came to the point, be better advised. Cromwell promptly replied that there was no hope for these men, and that 'some course must be thought of to curb and restrain them, or we shall be ruined by them.' "We ourselves," pleaded Whitelocke, with his eyes fixed on the constitutional difficulty, "have acknowledged them the supreme power and taken our commissions and authority in the highest concernments from them, and how to restrain and curb them after this, it will be hard to find out a way for it." Constitu-

A startling proposal.

tional objections only served to irritate Cromwell. "What," he asked with a sudden outburst,[1] "if a man should take upon him to be King?"

Whitelocke would not have been the imperturbable lawyer

[1] In Lord Bute's MSS., where the story is told in the third person, the sudden flash of the words is noted. In 1648 Major Huntington represented Cromwell as having said: "What a sway Stapleton and Holles had heretofore in the kingdom ; and he knew nothing to the contrary but that he was as well able to govern the kingdom as either of them." Huntington's *Sundry Reasons*, E, 458, 3.

that he was if he had failed to meet this startling question with grave objections. The title, he urged, would be of little advan-

White- tage to Cromwell himself. What was more to the
locke's purpose was that the Civil War had been waged to
objections. establish a free State, and that the oppressions of the
late monarchy were too fresh in men's memories to enable them readily to acknowledge a new one. Besides, if Cromwell became king, the controversy would no more be 'whether our government shall be by a monarch or by a free State, but whether Cromwell or Stuart shall be our king and monarch. The objections were of no slight weight, as Cromwell was one day to know to his cost, but they hardly met the problem of the moment. Pressed for a solution of his own, Whitelocke

He pro- expressed his preference for a restoration of Charles
poses to II. under conditions. No wonder that Cromwell
recall
Charles II. did not find the remedy palatable, and that White-
Cromwell's locke had to complain that for some time the Lord
reception
of the idea. General showed himself 'by his countenance and
carriage displeased' with his plain speaking.[1] Yet there are reasons for thinking that Cromwell perceived the many difficulties lying in the way of that heroic remedy which he had startlingly enunciated, and that Whitelocke's objections drove him to a more patient endeavour to heal the breaches of the Commonwealth by less drastic measures.[2]

[1] *Whitelocke*, 548-551. Without relying upon the accuracy of every word, I accept the report as substantially correct, and probably founded on notes taken at the time. To invent it would require dramatic powers which Whitelocke never showed any sign of possessing. Even the passage about the recall of Charles Stuart, which has been most suspected, contains touches such as : "This prince being now . . . reduced to a very low condition," and " he and all about him cannot but be very inclinable to any terms," which would hardly have been inserted after the Restoration, when we should rather expect some flourish about loyalty. There is, in fact, not a single phrase in any way flattering to Charles. Moreover, the time to which the conversation is assigned is most appropriate, being that when the conferences begun in October showed no sign of producing a satisfactory result.

[2] " Then, says the General," we are told in a newsletter of March 18, 1653, " the Parliament is not the supreme power, but that is the supreme

Whatever may have been Cromwell's intentions, all thought of an immediate solution of the political problem was neces-

Dec.
A lull in
the politi-
cal strife. sarily postponed during the turmoil of warlike preparation consequent upon Blake's defeat off Dungeness. It was perhaps, however, not without reference to the design of crowning the Duke of Gloucester at-

Dec. 7.
The Duke
of Glouces-
ter to be
sent to the
Continent. tributed to Cromwell that, on December 7, Parliament directed that the young Prince should be sent to the Continent, on the shallow pretext that, with Tromp ranging the Channel, it was impossible to

1653.
Feb. 11,
He sails
from
Cowes answer for his safeguarding at Carisbrooke.[1] On February 11 the vessel conveying him sailed from Cowes for Flanders.[2]

Long before this date the Council of Officers had renewed its activity.   Though in presence of imminent danger

Jan.
Prayer-
meetings in
the army the officers had refrained from political action, they had devoted every day in the first week of January to prayer and preaching,[3] an ominous sign of political dis-

and in the
City. content.   At Allhallows the Great in Thames Street, some soldiers openly prayed for a new representative, and though the Government, apparently with Cromwell's support, put them to silence,[4] it was unable to hinder the spread of dis-

power that calls it " (*Clarendon MSS.* ii. No. 1,056).   As Cromwell was then withstanding the persuasions of those who wished him to dissolve Parliament forcibly, this echo of Whitelocke's language is noteworthy.

[1] C. of St. Order Book, *Interr.* I, 68, p. 34 ; *C.J.* vii. 226.   In his despatch of $\frac{Feb. 22}{March 3}$, Bordeaux mentions that Cromwell had opposed a design to make the Duke king, but only to express his disbelief in its correctness.   *Arch. des Aff. Étrangères*, xix. fol. 174.

[2] Sydenham to the C. of State, Feb. 12, *S. P. Dom.* xxxiii. 41.

[3] Bordeaux to Brienne, Jan. $\frac{6}{16}$, *Arch. des Aff. Étrangères*, lxii. fol. 27.

[4] Pauluzzi to Morosini, Jan. $\frac{6}{16}$, *Letter Book R.O.*   Pauluzzi speaks of the ministers as Presbyterians, but Italians cannot always be relied on to distinguish between English sects.   Erbury, in *The Bishop of London* (E, 684, 26), says that 'some army-preaching men joined in a body at Great Allhallows to pray for a new representative, and to preach somewhat against the old, for which they received no countenance, but rather a check from the State and some highest in the army.'

affection. Already, on January 6, Parliament, in alarm at that disaffection, had directed Harrison to take charge of the Act

Jan. 6.
Harrison
to take care
of the Act
of Elec-
tions. 'touching an equal representative,' and to see that the same be brought in with speed.[1] The substitution of Harrison, the most uncompromising opponent of the sitting Parliament, for Vane, the advocate of a mere filling up of vacant seats, was significant of the disinclination of the members to act in defiance of the army.

There can be little doubt that this resolution was supported by Cromwell. Whenever we catch a glimpse of his proceedings

Attitude of
Cromwell. we find him working for a dissolution to be attained by an understanding between Parliament and army,

Jan. 13.
Agreement
that there
shall be a
new repre-
sentative. rather than by revolutionary action. On the 13th a committee, appointed by the officers on the 8th, had an interview with the Council of State resulting in a general agreement that a new Parliament should be chosen.[2] Yet a feeling appears to have prevailed amongst the officers that the parliamentary scheme might not be altogether

Jan. 28.
A circular to
the army. consonant with their desires, and on the 28th, after long consultation, they issued a circular letter to the regiments quartered in the three countries, asking for their support in the work before them. Parliament was to be confronted, not, as at the time of the presentation of the petition of August 13,[3] with the officers of the higher grades, but with the army as a whole.

Revolutionary as was the attitude of the officers, their demands were singularly moderate. After a religious exordium, they begged

Demands
of the
officers. their fellow-soldiers to stand by them in insisting upon four points—the establishment of 'successive Parliaments consisting of men faithful to the interest of the Commonwealth, men of truth, fearing God and hating covetousness;' the reform of the law; liberty of conscience without encouragement 'to such as are popish or profane in the exercise of their superstitious forms and licentious practices;'[4]

---

[1] *C.J.* vii. 244.

[2] Pauluzzi to Morosini, Jan. $\frac{14}{24}$, *Letter Book R.O.*

[3] See p. 224.   [4] Nothing is said about prelacy.

lastly, the assurance of 'due countenance and encouragement to those who faithfully dispensed the Gospel.' These things, the officers declared, had 'been promised by Parliament, and, as we are informed, are under their present consideration.' In these phrases we can hardly fail to recognise the moderating influence of Cromwell.[1]

Some even of those who looked for more drastic reforms were at one with Cromwell in protesting against the use of violence. A petition laid before the officers asked that judges might be replaced by local juries, that tithes might not be enforced or the goods of capital offenders forfeited. The petitioners also asked for the abolition of the penalty of death for theft, for freedom of trade with a leaning to the substitution of direct for indirect taxation, for absolute liberty of religion, and for the prompt election of an annual Parliament without any qualifications. These things they declared, in language redolent of Lilburne, were already established by the fundamental law of the land on which no Parliament was entitled to infringe. Yet, strong as their remedies were, they disclaimed all thought of compulsion. "Nor," they said, "would we for anything in the world that Parliaments should be accustomed to be forced, nothing being of more dangerous consequence to government itself."[2]

A more sweeping petition.

[1] Letter from the officers, Jan. 28, *Merc. Pol.* E, 686, 12. On the 21st 'a paper of advice was endeavoured to be presented to them from several of the churches in London, but it was not received.' Clarke Newsletters, *Hist. Rev.* July 1893, p. 527.

[2] *The only right rule for regulating the laws and liberties of the people of England, presented by way of advice to . . . the L. General Cromwell and the rest of the officers of the army, January* 28, 1652, *by divers affectionate persons to Parliament, army, and Commonwealth, inhabitants of the Cities of London, Westminster, Borough of Southwark, and places adjacent,* E, 684, 33. This, from the title as well as from the contents, is clearly a production of the Levellers. The most curious passage is the one relating to free trade: "All monopolies at home and all restraint of trade abroad to distinct companies of men are all opposite to the ancient rights of the people, and may justly be reduced to a universal freedom to every Englishman, which will make trade in time to

For a few weeks Parliament gave the officers ground to suppose that their counsels would be followed. For two days,

Jan. 20, 21.
Proposed
law reforms.

January 20 and 21, the House listened to the reading of a ‘ system of law ’ as proposed by the Committee on law reform.[1] After that a few legal Bills were brought in and considered, besides one which hopefully faced the ever-recurring difficulty of setting the poor at work. On

Feb. 11.
The proposals of the
Committee
for the Propagation of
the Gospel.

February 11, the proposals which had been some months before the Committee for the Propagation of of the Gospel[2] were at last read in the House. It now appeared that the Committee had been less anxious than Owen and his brother ministers to employ compulsion in matters of religion, and that besides omitting the provision for the suppression of judicial astrology, they had declined to require that persons dissenting from the established forms of worship should give notice to the magistrate of their place of meeting, or to refuse permission to persons opposing the Christian religion to preach or promulgate their

Feb. 23.
The Election Bill to
be taken up.

opinions.[3] On the 23rd, amendments to the Bill for future Parliaments were reported by order of the House, and March 2 was appointed for their con-

flourish, and wealth and plenty of all necessaries to abound, especially if the way of raising money by custom and excise were laid aside, being utterly destructive to trade, and rendering the lives of tradesmen tedious and irksome to them, and hath no consistence with fundamental right ; for, according to that rule, no imposition ought to be laid upon any trade, but what moneys are at any time found needful by Parliament ought to be levied by way of subsidy or an equal proportion on all men's estates, real and personal, in which course the whole within twopence or threepence in the pound is brought into the public treasury, whereas, the other way, vast sums go to the maintenance of officers. So, as you perceive, in this and all other particulars hitherto recited, the most ancient right is not only due, but most for the good and ease of the people."

[1] *C.J.* vii. 250.   [2] See p. 98.

[3] *C.J.* vii. 258. It had been resolved by the Committee that these clauses should not be reported. It does not perhaps follow that the majority of the Committee was opposed to these clauses. They may have thought it inexpedient to mix up points of difference with a proposal for the extension of liberty. However this may have been, the House

sideration.[1] During March the House employed itself from
time to time upon the Bill, but as it only took up the subject
five times in the course of the month,[2] it is evident that the
members were not greatly in earnest. Is it not possible that a
sense of renewed security after the victory in the Channel had
something to do with this remissness in a matter in which the
army was so deeply concerned?

 The Council of Officers moreover was not at unity within
itself. The clause in the circular letter asking for a new repre-
Feb.
Parties in
the army.

Lambert
and
Harrison.sentative composed of men fearing God and hating
covetousness,[3] may be taken as a compromise between
two opposed opinions springing from two tendencies
of the Puritan revolution. Lambert, on the one hand,
represented the demand for parliamentary government, and would probably have been content with the election
of a new Parliament guarded by some guarantees against the
return of Royalist members ; whilst Harrison, now drifting into
the ranks of the Fifth-Monarchy men, represented the demand
for government by moral and religious men, which no less than
the former was inherent in the ideas which had led to the
uprising against Charles. It was the impossibility of reconciling
these two views which ultimately wrecked the revolution and
restored the monarchy. For the present, however, both sections combined in demanding a dissolution, and as Parliament
grew slack in the performance of its promises, both urged
Cromwell to take the lead in a forcible dissolution. From this
Cromwell
objects to a
forcible dis-
solution.Cromwell recoiled with all his soul. " I am pushed
on," he said to one of his officers, " by two parties to
do that, the consideration of the issue whereof makes
my hair to stand on end." [4]

---

insisted on hearing what the rejected clauses were, and they were consequently produced before it.

 [1] *C. J.* vii. 259, 261.

 [2] On March 2, 9, 16, 23, and 30—that is to say, once a week. *Ib.*
vii. 263, 265, 268, 270, 273.   [3] See p. 233.

 [4] *Ludlow*, ed. Firth, i. 346. I incline to date these words about
this time, when the question of a forcible dissolution was reopened.

Opposed by many of his own officers, Cromwell had to seek for allies in Parliament not only amongst those who, like Vane,[1] had supported him against the Dutch war, but amongst those who, like Scot and Hazlerigg, had been its authors.[2] The combination was the easier

Cromwell's supporters in Parliament.

Cromwell's alleged description of the two parties is as follows : " One of these is headed by Major-General Lambert, who, in revenge of that injury the Parliament did him in not permitting him to go into Ireland with a character and conditions suitable to his merit, will be content with nothing less than a dissolution. Of the other Major-General Harrison is the chief, who is an honest man, and aims at good things, yet from the impatience of his spirit will not wait the Lord's leisure, but hurries me on to that which he and all honest men will have cause to repent." It will be seen that this rather describes the men than their aims, so far as these were divergent, and, in fact, Daniel O'Neill, in a report received by Hyde on March 2, and therefore written—as O'Neill was still in England —towards the end of February (*Hist. Rev.* 1893, p. 529) places Harrison and Lambert in one party opposed to Cromwell. It will be seen further on that Lambert and Harrison came to differ in the way described above, and there are indications that, as might reasonably be expected, they differed already. A few weeks later, for instance, we hear that a qualification of 200*l.* for members was accepted by Parliament ' to please the army ' (Newsletter, April $\frac{1}{11}$, *Clarendon MSS.* ii. No. 1,066). As this reappears in the Instrument of Government, in the preparation of which Lambert had had a large part, we may take it that it was granted under his influence, and if so, he must have been working in the direction of an elected Parliament. Again, Daniel O'Neill, in the report just quoted, says that the circular letter to the regiments sent on Jan. 28 asked for ' the settlement of the civil government in the hands of a number of people, in whose hands it should continue but such a certain time as the people agree upon.' As nothing of the kind is to be found in the letter, I conclude that O'Neill had intelligence of Harrison's own scheme, which is very like that which he afterwards advocated. In short, Harrison was the parent of the so-called Barebones' Parliament ; Lambert of the First Protectorate Parliament.

[1] Vane had been one of the supporters of Hugh Peters's correspondence with the Dutch.

[2] O'Neill, in the report just quoted, gives Cromwell's supporters as ' Haslerigg, St. John, Vanes both, Lisle the Lord of Seal ' (*i.e.* the Lord Commissioner of the Great Seal), ' Allen, Scott, Carew, Cawley, Salway, Stricklands both, and many others.' Harrison's party are given as

as many even of the most warlike were now anxious to bring hostilities to a close, if it could be done on honourable terms.

Progress of the secret negotiation.

The victory in the Channel had been dearly bought. No less than seven captains had been slain, and the number of seamen killed was reckoned by thousands. On the Dutch side, too, the loss of trade was bitterly resented. John de Witt, a young statesman, not yet thirty years of age, had appeared in the Provincial States of Holland as a warm advocate of peace. It resulted that the negotiation which had made no way in the hands of Peters and Gerbier, had fallen into those of Sir Robert Stone and Lieutenant-Colonel Dolman, officers in the Dutch service, of whom the former was in Holland, and the latter in England.[1] As early as in January, some time before Tromp's defeat, a secret committee of the States of Holland despatched a letter to England, but there was an informality in its direction, and by Dolman's advice it was not delivered. Conjecturing that another letter would soon follow, Cromwell and Vane, on March 10, carried a motion for adjourning a debate which had been opened on the relations with the Dutch Republic,[2] and on the 22nd, the day to which the debate had been ultimately adjourned, the Speaker was able to acquaint the House that he had received a letter addressed in due form by the States of Holland themselves, proposing to open a negotiation. Such a letter, written in defiance of all constitutional rule without consultation with the other six States, was the strongest possible evidence of the anxiety of the Hollanders to bring the war to an

Jan.
A missive from Holland.

March 10.
A discussion adjourned.

March 22.
A letter received from the States of Holland.

'Colonel Rich, Westrow, Purefoy, Millington, Hutchinson.' If this last name be correctly given, what becomes of Mrs. Hutchinson's account of her husband's attitude? Amongst the officers Cromwell's supporters were 'Whalley, Barkstead, Goffe, &c.;' Harrison's, 'Lambert, Rich, Pride, &c.'

[1] *Nicholas Papers*, ii. 1, 2.

[2] Hazlerigg was one of the tellers for proceeding with the debate, so that he cannot be counted as working with Cromwell on the negotiation with the Dutch. *C.J.* vii. 265, 266.

end. The hand thus held out was accepted, and on April 1
Parliament replied in favourable terms, laying stress on the
common Protestantism of the two peoples, and offering to resume the negotiation at the point at which it
had been dropped by Pauw.[1]

*April 1.
The Par-
liament's
answer.*

The reply of Parliament was a triumph for Cromwell, and
it is not unlikely that his hand is also to be detected in the
course which the negotiation with Spain was taking.
About the end of November,[2] Parliament had placed
in the hands of Cardenas the draft of a commercial
treaty, which it proposed to substitute for the one presented by
him in September.[3] Of the proposed articles one was intended
to enlarge the limited toleration accorded to Protestant Englishmen in the Spanish dominions by the
treaty with Charles I. in 1630. Instead of engaging
that Englishmen should be freed from the interference of the
Inquisition as long as they gave no scandal, Philip was asked
to promise ' that it should be lawful and permitted to that
people either in their own houses, or in those of Englishmen
residing in Spain, or in their shops, to serve God and to comply with all the obligations of religion according to their
conscience, and also to be able to use their Bibles or any other
books without being molested or hindered in any manner,
either by the Inquisition, or its ministers, or by any other
judges; and that neither any person nor the estate of any one
of the said nation could be sequestrated by the ministers of the
said Inquisition.' In another article the King was required to
promise ' that there should be appointed decent places for the

*A proposed
treaty with
Spain.*

*Question of
toleration for
English
Protestants.*

---

[1] *Geddes*, i. 282, 291 ; The States of Holland to Parliament, March $\frac{8}{18}$;
Parliament to the States of Holland, April $\frac{1}{11}$, *Aitzema*, iii. 804 ; *C.J.*
vii. 220 ; De Witt to van Beuninghen, March $\frac{14}{24}$, *Brieven*, v. 97.

[2] Cardenas to Philip IV., Dec. $\frac{21}{31}$, where the ambassador mentions
that he had written on the subject on Dec. $\frac{3}{13}$, *Simancas MSS.* 2,528.

[3] See p. 189. [The draft treaty referred to, which is dated Nov. 12,
1652, is printed from the papers of Sir Richard Fanshaw in *Original
Letters and Negotiations of Sir Richard Fanshaw, the Earl of Sandwich,
etc.*, 2 vols. 1724, i. 487 ; see also i. 465 for the earlier negotiations of
Cardenas.]

burial of citizens of the aforesaid Commonwealth who might
die in any of the dominions of the King of Spain.' [1]

The proposal to insert these clauses may have been due to
Cromwell's inspiration, especially as since the failure of his plan
for the acquisition of Dunkirk he seems to have acquiesced in a policy of friendliness towards Spain.[2]
On the other hand, it is unlikely that either Cromwell
or the parliamentary majority desired to place England unreservedly on the side of that country. By this time
France was more openly vying with Spain for the English alliance,
and it seems to have been thought by all parties in England that
it would be well to make no definite choice, but to allow each of
the contending States to be enticed to larger offers by the attitude of the other.

In September the intervention of Blake and the consequent
loss of Dunkirk [3] seem to have convinced Mazarin of the
necessity of coming to terms with the Commonwealth.
It is true that the growing strength of the French
monarchy might have counselled a more impulsive
minister to seek redress by force. On October 11
the young King entered Paris amidst the acclamations of the citizens. Condé indeed maintained his defiant
attitude ; but by transferring himself and his army to the

Marginal notes:
Probable influence of Cromwell in preparing the draft.

Sept. Effects of the loss of Dunkirk.

Oct. 11. Louis XIV. enters Paris.

---

[1] " Que sea *licito* y permetido al dicho pueblo en sus casas o en las de
los Ingleses que residen en España, o en sus navios, el *servir a Dios* y el
cumpler con todas las obligaciones de la religion conforme a su consciencia
y tambien el poder usar de *sus Biblias o de qualquiera otros libros*, sin
que sea molestado o impedido de ninguna manera, ni por la Inquisicion o
sus ministros ni por otros jueces, *y que ninguna persona, ni la hazienda
de ninguno del dicho pueblo podra ser sequestrada por los ministros de la
dicha Inquisicion. . . . Que si ordenen lugares decentes para enterrar los
de el pueblo de esta republica que murieren en qualquiera de los dominios
del Rey d'España.*" *Simancas MSS.* 2,528. The words in italics are
those to which exception was taken by the Inquisition.

[2] There is no direct evidence of this, but it was certainly the general
belief that the assumption of power by Cromwell when he dissolved
Parliament in April would be to the advantage of Spain.

[3] See p. 190.

northern frontier he showed himself in his true colours, as the instrument of Spain. Mazarin was not the man to be carried off his feet by success, and though in order that his presence might not dim the popularity of his young master, he had retired to Sedan, he still continued to direct the policy of France. To his passionless intelligence the danger of throwing the first maritime power in Europe into the arms of Spain was too obvious to need discussion, and he lost no time in attempting to lay the foundations of a better under-standing between the two countries. On November 22 M. de Bordeaux-Neufville was instructed to betake himself to London, where he was to present a letter containing that recognition of the Commonwealth by the French King which had been so imperiously demanded and so long delayed, and was to ask for an accommodation of existing complaints, the first step being the surrender of the King's ships which had fallen into the hands of Blake.[1] Un-luckily Mazarin—or, as is far more likely, the sub-ordinate employed to draw up the letter—could not prevail on himself to make the submission complete. Not only had Bordeaux received no credentials as a minister, but the letter carried by him was addressed in somewhat contemptuous terms to 'les gens du Parlement de la République d'Angleterre.' As might have been ex-pected, Parliament returned it unopened,[2] with the intimation that even if this difficulty were removed the bearer's want of credentials would preclude his reception by Parliament. He would have to be content with an audience before a com-mittee.

The blunder about the style was easily rectified. On Decem-ber 21 Bordeaux presented the letter acknowledging the Com-monwealth, with an address which satisfied the most punctilious requirements. Yet week after week passed without his negotiation making serious progress.

Marginal notes:
Mazarin at Sedan.

Nov. 22. Dec. 2. Bordeaux ordered to negotiate in England.

His letter insufficiently addressed,

Dec. 14, and rejected by Parlia-ment.

Dec. 21. France ac-knowledges the Com-monwealth.

---

[1] Instructions to Bordeaux, $\frac{\text{Nov. 22}}{\text{Dec. 2}}$; Louis XIV. to the Parliament, $\frac{\text{Nov. 22}}{\text{Dec. 2}}$, *Guizot*, i. App. xxii.   [2] *C.J.* vii. 228.

Nor was Cardenas any better satisfied with the encouragement

1653.
Slow pro-
gress of the
negotiation. given to him or to the agents of Condé and Le Daugnon whom he supported. Parties, according to Barrière, were too equally divided to allow of Parliament taking any definite step on either side.[1] It is possible indeed that many influential members were actuated by a cynical motive. Neither France nor Spain, they may have thought, could afford to come to an open rupture with England, and as long as the existing position endured French prizes were likely to be brought into English harbours in excess of the number of English prizes carried to France. Yet other more avowable motives there were for refusing to close with France. It was but natural that English statesmen, now that the restoration of

Reasons for
distrusting
France. the French monarchy to its old authority was within sight, should ask themselves whether it might not use its powers, as soon as it got its chance, to clear off old scores with England. Nor were the indications favourable to a more trustful view of the situation. The exiled Charles was still the guest of the French King, and his brother James commanded a regiment in his service. It did not escape the notice of the English Government that no attention was paid to its reiterated demands for the surrender of the English prize which had been brought into Nantes by Rupert. When the sympathies of France were so openly declared, it might well be feared that if once the city of Bordeaux were reduced, the monarchical tradition would prevail, and the weight of France would be thrown into the scale of a Stuart restoration.[2]

Yet to break with France by persisting in a refusal even to consider the complaints of her merchants, without security for

Danger of
breaking
with France
without an
under-
standing
with Spain. a good understanding with Spain, was hardly a policy likely to commend itself to any sane politician, and during the first months of 1653 it was becoming doubtful whether any understanding with Spain was in prospect. The Spanish Government had taken

---

[1] Barrière to Condé, $\frac{\text{Feb. 25}}{\text{March 7}}$, *Chantilly Transcripts.*

[2] Bordeaux to Brienne, $\frac{\text{Jan. 27}}{\text{Feb. 6}}$, March $\frac{14}{24}$, *R.O. Transcripts.*

alarm at the English demand for toleration, and had referred it
to the Inquisition for an opinion on the merits of the
scheme. Slow as the Inquisition was to pronounce
its judgment, there could hardly be a doubt what
its character would be, and in fact it did ultimately
visit the clause with a severe condemnation. Meanwhile Cardenas had been directed only to proceed with a more general negotiation for an alliance with England in the case of the Dutch allying themselves with France.[1]

The toleration articles referred to the Inquisition.

It was probably the suspicion that Cardenas was growing slack in his negotiation which, about the end of February, roused Parliament to give a more friendly reception to the overtures of the French ambassador. By that time Bordeaux was able to express an opinion that there was in England a general desire to live at peace with all the world, and that Cromwell shared in this desire.[2] On the other hand he had information that the Council of State was now actively discussing arrangements both with Cardenas and with the Count of Peneguiaõ, a Portuguese ambassador who had arrived in the preceding September to take up the negotiation at the point at which it had been left by Guimaraes.[3] By dropping his demand for the restitution of the King's ships, Bordeaux seized the favourable moment and was soon able to explain to his government that he had handed in the articles of the treaty which had been concluded with Charles I., and had good hopes of its renewal. He had on his side the City merchants, most of whom[4] were ready even to abandon all claims for compensation for their losses, if only trade could again be opened as it had been in old days. In a moment of confidence they explained to Bordeaux their reason for renouncing their

Feb. Turn in favour of France.

---

[1] Points referred to the Inquisition, $\frac{Oct. 25}{Nov. 4}$; Notes of Instructions for Cardenas, $\frac{Nov. 30}{Dec. 10}$, *Simancas MSS.* 2,528, 2,569.

[2] Bordeaux to Brienne, $\frac{Feb. 28}{March 10}$, *R.O. Transcripts.*

[3] Bordeaux to Brienne, March $\frac{7}{17}$, *ib.*

[4] The Levant merchants called for restitution, no doubt because they had suffered most heavily. See vol. i. p. 180.

hope of compensation. If the French King, they said, paid
over the money, Parliament would waylay it, and
but little, if any, would find its way into the pockets
of those to whom it rightfully belonged.[1]

As far as it is possible to discern the truth, Parliament was
at this time desirous of establishing a commercial understanding with both countries, with no intention of embarking on a
warlike alliance with either. The policy which had inspired
Sexby's mission to Bordeaux, and the policy which had inspired
the negotiations for Dunkirk, were alike discarded.

[1] Bordeaux to Brienne, April $\frac{4}{14}$, *R.O Transcripts.*

CHAPTER XXV

THE DISSOLUTION OF THE LONG PARLIAMENT

IT was not on foreign affairs that the parliamentary crisis turned. During the weeks in which Cromwell was guiding the House in the direction of peace with the Dutch, fanatical soldiers were preaching the violent expulsion of the members of the existing Parliament, and on March 11 'the Council of Officers at St. James's had resolved to turn them out had not the General and Colonel Desborough interceded,' asking 'them if they destroyed that Parliament what they should call themselves—a State they could not be. They answered that they would call a new Parliament. Then, says the General, the Parliament is not the supreme power, but that is the supreme power that calls it ;[1] and, besides, the House is now endeavouring a treaty with Holland—which is the only way that we have left for destroying of the combination of our enemies both at home and beyond sea—and if we destroy them,[2] neither Holland nor any other Prince or State will enter into a treaty with us.'[3]

1653.
A crisis approaching.

Cromwell holds back the army from an attack on Parliament.

How long could Cromwell hold his ground between two opposing forces? In Parliament, at least, there were many—probably a majority—who resented his dictation in the matter of the Dutch peace. The leaders, if

Cromwell between two parties.

---

[1] Compare this with Whitelocke's argument, p. 230.
[2] *I.e.* the Parliament.
[3] Newsletter, March 18, *Hist. Rev.* 1893, p. 528.

rumour spoke truly, sent for Fairfax and Lambert to consult
them on the possibility of dismissing the general
from his command.   They wanted a commander
who would be sure to 'obey their orders, and not
give them orders as this one doth.'   It may be taken for
granted that Fairfax rejected the suggestion.   On the
15th, however, Lambert called on Cromwell, who
naturally refused to see him.   A later effort of
Fairfax to visit him, accompanied by Lambert, proved equally
unsuccessful.   "Bottomless Lambert" was the best phrase
that Cromwell had now to bestow on his major-general.[1]   So
angry was Cromwell at the ingratitude with which
his services to Parliament were met, that for a whole
month he absented himself from its sittings.[2]

Fairfax and Lambert consulted.

March 15. Cromwell refuses to see them,

and absents himself from Parliament.

Whatever Parliament might resolve about the Dutch war,
the necessity of increasing the strength of the navy added to
its unpopularity.   The old sailors, inured to service,
and loyal to the Commonwealth which had interested
itself in their welfare,[3] were numerically insufficient
for the service demanded of them, and if the advantage gained
in the Channel was to be maintained it would be
necessary to add new and untried men to their
numbers.   In the middle of March 1,000 men were
pressed, and it was said—no doubt with considerable exaggeration—that not a serviceable man was left behind.   The block
of the Sound, too, began to tell, and on the 25th we hear that
though a hundred ships would under ordinary circumstances
have been ready for sea, so great was the want of
pitch, tar, and cordage that fifteen of them would be
unfit to leave port.   Merchantmen approaching the
coast were boarded, and the greater part of their crews carried
off.   Orders were sent to secure mariners in Jersey, and even

The navy to be increased.

Additional seamen needed.

Want of stores and of men.

---

[1] Newsletter, March $\frac{18}{28}$, $\frac{\text{March } 25}{\text{April } 4}$, *Clarendon MSS.* ii. No. 1,056.

[2] Clarke Newsletters, April 9, 16, *Hist. Rev.*, July 1893, p. 528.

[3] See an instructive note by Mr. Oppenheim, showing the untruth of
the statements that the seamen were Royalist in their inclinations, *The
Administration of the Royal Navy*, i. 310, Note 2.

in Scotland and Ireland. Able-bodied men fled from the sight of one of the State's ships as they would have done from the plague. In London a raid was made on shore, and landsmen, even gentlemen unused to the sea, were dragged out of their beds and hurried on board ship. With the navy in such a state it

April.
Losses at sea.

was impossible adequately to protect commerce. In April a ship laden with silk worth 10,000*l.* was taken by the French, and another worth 80,000*l.* fell into the hands of the Dutch.[1]

Such calamities are amongst the ordinary accidents of maritime war. It was of greater importance that the enemy was triumphant in the Mediterranean. In November,

1652.
Nov.
Cutting out of the 'Phœnix.'

indeed, Captain Cox succeeded in cutting out the 'Phœnix'—an English ship which had been previously captured by the Dutch—from the port of

1653.
March 1.
The English ordered to leave Leghorn.

Leghorn.[2] The Grand Duke, angered by this outrage on his neutrality, ultimately ordered Badiley, who now commanded both his own and Appleton's squadrons, to restore the 'Phœnix' or to withdraw

his ships. The latter alternative was chosen, and, on March

March 14.
Defeat of Appleton.

14, Appleton, without waiting for the approach of Badiley, who lay in the offing, attempted to force a passage with six ships against sixteen of the Dutch,

but was utterly defeated with the loss of all his force except a single ship. Badiley was at too great a distance to render help.[3] For the present, at least, the Levant trade was at the

April.
Distress in London.

mercy of the Dutch. Merchants in London who had embarked their capital in these ventures were breaking daily after the news had been told.[4]

---

[1] Newsletters, March $\frac{18}{28}$, $\frac{March 25}{April 4}$, April $\frac{8}{18}$, $\frac{15}{25}$, *Clarendon MSS.* ii. Nos. 1,056, 1,083, 1,096.

[2] [See Mr. Spalding's *Life of Richard Badiley*, p. 132.]

[3] Appleton to the Navy Committee, Nov. 22; Badiley to the Navy Committee, Dec. 2; Longland to the Navy Committee, March 14, *S.P. Dom.* xxv. 65; xxvi. 2; xxxiv. 32. Compare Professor Laughton's Lives of Appleton and Badiley in the *Dict. of Nat. Biog.* [See also Spalding's *Life of Richard Badiley*, pp. 185–212.]

[4] Newsletter, April $\frac{8}{18}$, *Clarendon MSS.* ii. No. 1,083.

To the majority of the inhabitants of London the interruption of the coal trade was even more serious. The Dutch, beaten out of the Channel, were resuming activity in the North Sea, and hindered the colliers from sailing. It was even rumoured that the greater part of the Newcastle coal ships had been taken by De With. The price of coals, which had been 2*l.* a chaldron, now rose to 6*l.*, and they were only to be procured with difficulty even at that price. Cooks' shops were closed for want of fuel. A wag collected a crowd in the streets by shouting ' coal at 3*d.* a bushel,' and when asked where they were to be sold so cheaply, replied ' At Rotterdam Stairs.' On April 15, a newswriter summed up the position :—" This press hath caused great murmurings among the people, and believe it we do much dread some sudden mischief from them, especially if they once hear that the Dutch have declared for the King. Our dearth of coal exasperates them and, I assure you, if the Dutch keep them from us, we shall shortly cut each other's throats." [1]

Interruption of the coal trade.

This seething mass of popular discontent must have strengthened the hands of those who opposed the Government on political grounds. The military preachers had for some time been able to defy Parliament unchecked. Before the end of March one of them announced at Blackfriars that they intended speedily to destroy ' that accursed Parliament at Westminster.' " Rather," said an officer, " than we will suffer this Parliament to sit any longer, we will bring in the Cavaliers and make a Parliament of them, whom we know have a great deal more of honour and honesty than they." On April 10, a young glazier preaching at Somerset House told his audience that ' they should ere long see greater destruction fall on the Parliament than ever befel the Cavaliers.' At this stage, a woman in the congregation irrelevantly called out : " Why do you wear cuffs? Neither our Lord nor His disciples ever taught in cuffs." The sympathies of the congregation, however, were with the preacher, and as

Military preachers.

April 10. A preaching glazier.

---

[1] Newsletter, April ¹⁵⁄₂₅, *Clarendon MSS.* ii. No. 1,096.

soon as this conscientious questioner had been expelled, he proceeded with his revilings. On the 12th, the day of Thanks-giving for the victory over the Dutch, many churches remained closed, and those open were but thinly attended. Some of the sea-captains, remembering at what a price the victory had been won, left London to avoid offering thanks for a success which had cost the lives of so many of their comrades.[1]

April 12.
Day of thanks-giving for the victory in the Channel.

Signs were, however, not altogether wanting that the excess of fanaticism might lead to a reaction. Early in 1650 an Act had been passed for the propagation of the Gospel in Wales.[2] By this Act power was given to com-missioners—of whom Harrison was one—to deprive all malignant and scandalous clergy, and to establish a preaching ministry in their room, upon the certificate of a certain number of ministers whose names were recited in the Act. The authority thus conferred on the commissioners was to expire on March 25, 1653, and their opponents asked Parliament not to renew it. It can hardly be matter for surprise that the commissioners were highly unpopular in Wales, and that after a considerable number of the clergy had been ejected through their means and the vacant places supplied with vigorous enthusiasts, their nominees were some-times waylaid and soundly beaten, so that they went about in danger of their lives.

The propa-gation of the Gospel in Wales.

The most conspicuous of the instrusive ministers was Vavasor Powell, a perfervid Welshman who was able to speak to his countrymen in their native tongue, and who, by the sincerity of his own life, gained numerous con-verts, even in that unpuritanical land. He had, too, dreams of millennial glory in the near future, which by no means diminished his influence over his imaginative disciples, but which incited the derision of the multitude. Wales teemed with slander against Powell. His morality was called in

Vavasor Powell.

---

[1] Newsletter, April $\frac{1}{11}$, $\frac{15}{25}$, *Clarendon MSS.* ii. Nos. 1,067, 1,096.

[2] On Feb. 22, 1650. The Act is not in *Scobell*, but will be found in E, 1,060, No. 80.

question,[1] and the commissioners were charged with tyrannical conduct. It was now said that Harrison had used 'his preaching people' to enlist 4,000 men in North Wales for his own purposes. So far did the rumour spread that Cromwell thought it worth while to question him, though he readily accepted his denial.[2]

Harrison charged with enlisting men in Wales.

In the streets of London incredulity had the upper hand. On March 27, Powell, who had lately returned from Wales, preached in the Charter House to an overflowing audience, after which he begged his hearers to meet him on the following Monday in the open air at Smithfield, as there was no room for them in a church. On the appointed day Powell failed to keep his word. Learning that Smithfield was occupied by a mob some six thousand strong, he attempted to disarm hostility by sending a cap-maker who was one of his fellow-preachers to take his place. The unfortunate substitute was assailed by shouts of abuse, followed by a shower of stones. He would hardly have escaped with his life but for the intervention of the City Marshal, who pulled him down and carried him off. Even the offence given by Powell and his cap-maker was laid to the discredit of Parliament. The mob 'expressed much hatred against our Government, saying such rogues as he and those who protected him were the cause of all their miseries, but they hoped ere long to be freed from them.'[3]

March 27. Powell preaches in London.

April 3. A riot at Smithfield.

Cromwell was no friend to mob-violence, but he took a warm interest in the propagation of the Gospel in Wales, and he must have regarded with favour the progress of a Bill which had been introduced[4] for continuing the authority of the com-

[1] These charges were printed in 1654 in *Strena Vavasoriensis*, and form the authority for Walker's account of the matter in *The Sufferings of the Clergy*. They were refuted by the testimony of neighbours and other persons qualified to give evidence, afterwards published in *Vavasoris Examen et Purgamen*, E, 732, 14.

[2] Newsletter, $\frac{\text{March 2}}{\text{April 4}}$, *Clarendon MSS*. ii. No. 1,056.

[3] Newsletter, April $\frac{3}{18}$, *ib*. ii. No. 1,083.   [4] *C.J.* vii. 272.

missioners. Hostility to a Bill in which Harrison was concerned was easily excited in Parliament. The commissioners, it was said, had in their hands 60,000*l.* of tithes, and asked for a prolongation of their powers merely to avoid parting with the money. On April 1 the Bill was rejected, and an order made for substituting more moderate ministers for those named in the original Act as the dispensers of certificates to preachers.[1]

March 25.
Bill for
continuing
the authority of the
Welsh
commissioners.

April 1.
It is
rejected.

Whatever may have been Cromwell's feelings in the matter, he was not yet converted to the doctrine that the army was justified in overthrowing Parliament by force. "Our soldiers," says a news-writer, on the day on which the Bill was rejected, "resolve to have speedily a new representative, and the Parliament resolve the contrary. The General sticks close to the House,[2] which causeth him to be daily railed on by the preaching party, who say they must have both a new Parliament and General before the work be done ; and that these are not the people that are appointed for perfecting of that great work of God which they have begun. There came a regiment of horse to town this week full-mouthed against the Parliament, but were not suffered to stay here above two days before they, with three violent regiments more, were despatched out of the way towards Scotland." "We hear," proceeds the same writer a week later, "no talk now of our new representative, the heat of the soldiers being somewhat abated by the

Cromwell
maintains
the authority of Parliament.

April 8.

---

[1] "Friday last the House voted down the preaching propagators of North Wales, and ordered a moderate clergy to be put in their places. They had got into their hands 60,000*l.* per annum of Church livings, which Harrison and others of that party are loth to part with." Newsletter, April $\frac{8}{18}$, *Clarendon MSS.* ii. No. 1,083. Nothing of this appears in the Journals, but at this period they were too irregularly kept to justify distrust on that score. [See Shaw's *English Church during the Civil Wars and the Commonwealth*, ii. 227–229.]

[2] *I.e.* continues to support it ; he had not been present in the House for some time. See *infra*, p. 255.

General's sticking close to the House and sending some of the maddest of them into Scotland." [1]

Cromwell's resolution to stand by Parliament was, however, conditional on its readiness to proceed with the Bill for

Cromwell's
support
condi-
tional.

the new representative which had been hitherto considered once a week. On March 30 the House agreed to establish in the counties a franchise of 200*l.* in pro-

March 30.
The county
franchise
settled.

perty, either real or personal, in lieu of a complicated arrangement, supported by Vane, which took account of landed property only.[2]   On April 6, when

April 6.
The Bill
not called
on.

discussion would in due course have been renewed, the Bill was entirely passed over.   It was no merely ordinary delay based on the pressure of other

business that was contemplated.   " Our Parliament," we hear, " considering the present state of affairs, which are such as require not only unanimity in counsels, but a necessity of reserving the management in those hands that have hitherto governed with such advantage—are resolved to waive for the present a new representative." [3]   It is possible that the par-

Possibility
of dropping
it.

liamentary leaders may at this point have thought of dropping the Bill altogether.   If so, they resolved before many days had passed to transform rather than to destroy it.   Terrified, we may imagine, at the outburst of fanaticism around them, men like Vane and Hazlerigg sought thus to maintain their own grasp on the helm rather than to give way to a Parliament chosen under the auspices of Harrison.

To such a scheme the officers were resolved to offer the most determined resistance.   To them the continuance in any

April 7.
A new
army
petition.

shape of the existing Parliament meant the continuance of a body not merely politically incapable, but governed by corrupt motives and influenced by low intrigue.   On the 7th, the day after that on which the Bill had

[1] Newsletters, April $\frac{1}{11}$, $\frac{8}{18}$, *Hist. Rev.*, July 1893, pp. 528, 529.

[2] *C.J.* vii. 273.   The franchise of 200*l.* was afterwards adopted by the Instrument of Government.

[3] Newsletter, April $\frac{8}{18}$, *Hist. Rev.*, July 1893, p. 529.

been passed over, a fresh army petition was presented, demanding that the House should proceed with the measure, first taking into consideration a definition of the qualifications excluding improper persons from the future Parliament.[1] On the 13th the House so far complied with this request as to

April 13.
Qualifica-
tions
agreed to.

amend the qualifications intended originally to keep out Royalists, by adding a requirement that members should only be allowed to take their seats if they were 'such as are persons of known integrity, fearing God and not scandalous in their conversation.'[2]

The vote of the 13th, although taken in obedience to the army, would in the end render an appeal to force almost

An appeal
to force
almost un-
avoidable.

inevitable. The exclusion of Royalists cannot, under the circumstances, be severely criticised. The imposition of the new test, with its dangerous vagueness, threw supreme power into the hands of any man or body of men charged with its interpretation. That advantage the existing Parliament had no intention of foregoing. Vane's love of finesse as well as the strength of Cromwell's subsequent indignation, point to him as the author of the scheme now adopted, even though no direct evidence to that effect has come down to us.[3] Parliament was to transmute the Bill before it into one for filling up vacancies, leaving the old members not merely to retain their seats but to decide on the qualifications of those newly elected, and there are some reasons for believing that it was intended that this system of recruiting was to be applied to each successive Parliament, so that there would never be a general election again. As soon as the Bill was passed Parliament would adjourn till November, thus rendering it impossible legally to repeal or modify the

[1] " Les officiers ne se voulans plus payer de remise, presenterent il y a quinze jours une nouvelle petition contenant leurs mesmes propositions et les qualitez qu'ilz pretendoient que debvoit avoir ce nouveau representatif." Bordeaux to Brienne, $\frac{\text{April 21}}{\text{May 1}}$, *Arch. des Aff. Étrangères*, lxii. fol. 117.

[2] *C.J.* vii. 277.

[3] Except, at least, that we know the plan of partial elections to have been in favour with Vane.

Act. In the meanwhile the Government would be administered by the Council of State in which, though Cromwell and the officers had a majority as regarded the war, the Parliamentarians had a majority as regarded domestic affairs.[1]

---

[1] Professor Masson (*Life of Milton*, iv. 409, note 1) has set forth the case for holding that Parliament intended to recruit, not to dissolve, itself. He also holds that its Bill provided 'that the elections on new writs for the residue of the seats should be under the supervision of a committee.' If he means of a committee of the whole House, consisting of the old members only, I think he has hit on the most probable explanation of the means by which the new members were to be sifted. A committee in the ordinary sense was not trusted with the trial of election petitions before the Grenville Act in the 18th century, and, in default of positive evidence, it cannot be admitted in the present case. The rest of his contention has received additional strength since his work was published. In the newsletters printed in the *Hist. Rev.*, July 1893, we have the statement, on April 29, that the Act was 'for calling a new Parliament, or rather recruiting the old'; and another—undated—adds, 'on Wednesday morning the House made a delusory adjournment and a new representative on the 3rd of November next.' Hyde, who saw these letters, and probably others as well, writes that 'the members had no mind to quit their benches, and were preparing a Bill to increase their numbers, and then resolved to adjourn till November, and in the meantime to leave the government in the Council of State.' Hyde to Rochester, May $\frac{6}{16}$, *Clarendon MSS.* ii. No. 1,141. That Parliament intended to perpetuate itself is distinctly asserted in the manifesto of Cromwell and his officers, published on April 23 (*Several Proceedings* E, 211, 24), where it is said that the opposition 'to the people of God and His spirit acting in them . . . grew so prevalent that those persons of honour and integrity amongst them who had eminently appeared for God and the public good . . . were rendered of no farther use in Parliament than by meeting with a corrupt party to give them countenance to carry on their ends, and for effecting the desires they had of perpetuating themselves in the supreme government, . . . and when they saw themselves necessitated to take that Bill into consideration, they resolved to make use of it to recruit the House with persons of the same spirit and temper.' The point of the threatened adjournment is not mentioned here, but in a second manifesto issued on May 3 (*Another Declaration*, E, 693, 17) we are told that the House, on the day of the dissolution, intended 'to pass the Act for a new Parliament to be called in November next; and if themselves having passed it had that day then adjourned, as probably they would have done

That Cromwell when he came to know of this scheme should have been deeply dissatisfied was only to be expected.

Cromwell dissatisfied.

Even the qualifications themselves displeased him, now that he knew by whom they were to be interpreted. They would, as he afterwards explained, let in Presbyterians and neutrals who had deserted the cause of God.[1]

April 15. He returns to Parliament.

On the 15th,[2] he reappeared in the House after an absence of at least a month,[3] to plead earnestly for the substitution of a general election in place of a mere scheme for the filling up of vacancies. It is high time,

His resignation demanded.

replied one of the leaders—possibly Vane or Marten —to his demand for a new Parliament, to choose a new General. Angry words were interchanged, and order was only restored by the intervention of the House. Yet, in spite of the line now taken by Cromwell, he had become such an object of suspicion in the eyes of the more violent

---

had they not been dissolved, and by that means their design frustrated, the whole nation would have been in a sad condition.' This is supplemented by a statement in an account of the dissolution in *Several Proceedings*, E, 211, 20, to the effect that 'these present members were to sit and to be made up by others chosen, and by themselves approved of.' Bordeaux' testimony may be accepted as that of an independent witness. Parliament, he says, 'taschoit de s'asseurer de la faveur du peuple de Londres, et ne songeoit qu'aux moyens de continuer son autorité, ordonnant une nouvelle convocation avec telles conditions qu'ilz pourroyent se fermer, et que les officiers d'armée n'y auroient point de part.' Bordeaux to Brienne, $\frac{\text{April 21}}{\text{May 1}}$, *Arch. des Aff. Étrangères*, lxii. fol. 117. My own suggestion that it was intended to recruit each Parliament in perpetuity is founded on Cromwell's statement (*Carlyle*, Speech III.) that the plan was 'that when one Parliament had left its seat another was to sit down immediately in the room thereof, without any caution to avoid what was the real danger, the perpetuating of the same Parliament.' Carlyle suggests that these latter words should be 'the same men in Parliaments.' Unless Cromwell wanted a self-denying Act like that passed in the French Constituent Assembly, which there is no reason to suppose, his objection must have been to a system of recruiting in perpetuity.

[1] *Carlyle*, Speech I.

[2] Clarke Newsletter, April 16 [?], *Hist. Rev.*, July 1893, p. 528.

[3] Clarke Newsletter, April 9, *ib.*

officers, that even Harrison backed the proposal to supersede
him. Cromwell taking his critics at their word offered
his resignation. No officer was found bold enough
to accept the succession, and Cromwell remained at
the head of the force which he alone could wield.[1]

His offer to
resign
rejected.

Cromwell had now to choose between Vane's scheme of
recruiting the existing Parliament, and Harrison's scheme of
erecting an assembly of pious and virtuous men.[2]
Yet he could not bring himself as yet to make a
definite choice. He rather hoped to find a com-

Cromwell
supports a
compro-
mise.

---

[1] " Per pensare a tutto e provedere al possibile seguono applicate e
lunghe riduzzioni del Parlamento, in cui si trovano ben sovente discrepanti
pareri per lo più sopra il progetto della dissoluzione di esso, per il che
ultimamente accadde grande contestazione di parole tra il General
Cromuel et un principale Parlamentario, perche promossasi da quello
alcuna cosa sopra la rinovazione del medesimo Parlamento fu da questo
altamente risposto che non era tempo più proprio alla mutazione di
Generale dell' armi che il presente, onde tra loro furono replicate parole
rigorose et ardite, alle quali fu posto fine dal maggior numero de' radu-
nati; onde resta tuttavia l' apparenza dell' amarezza tra il General
Cromuel et il Parlamentario tenente Maggior Harrison, che sottomano et
anco alla scoperta tende a pregiudiciarli nel comando dell' armi, ma li-
sarà sempre difficile l' avanzar passi contro di lui nell' auttorità che
possiede e nell' accortezza che maneggia, persuaso della quale rissolse egli
ultimamente di presentare la sua commissione e consegnarla nelle mani di
che più havesse aggradito riceverla, e fosse dal Parlamento ordinato; onde
non havendo alcuno osato a tanta intrapresa rimane egli, può dirsi,
maggiormente stabilito, ma il di lui animo intimamente esacerbato."
Pauluzzi to Morosini, April $\frac{17}{27}$, *Letter Book R.O.* [In the original preface
to volume ii. of this history Mr. Gardiner added the following comment
on Pauluzzi's story : ' Since the present volume was printed off I have
noticed that Bernardi, the Duke of Savoy's resident in England, in a
despatch of $\frac{April\ 25}{May\ 5}$, 1653, published by Signor Prayer (*Atti della Società
Ligure di Storia Patria*, xvi.) states that, on the morning of dissolution of
the Long Parliament, Cromwell entered the House, "mentre stavasi per
metter a voto la revocazione della patente di detto Generalissimo e poi di
agiornare il Parlamento sino a S. Michele." The remainder of Bernardi's
story does not agree in details with that told by eye-witnesses, and he
cannot be absolutely depended upon here. Nevertheless, his words are
sufficiently in accordance with what I have stated at pages 255 and 256 to
be worth noting.']   [2] See p. 236.

promise which indeed approached more nearly to the scheme of Harrison than to that of Vane, but which would have the great merit of avoiding a breach in the parliamentary tradition. " If it have but the face of authority," he had said in 1647, " if it be but a hare swimming over the Thames, I will take hold of it rather than let it go." [1]   He was of the same opinion still.   The difficulty lay in the impossibility of forecasting the composition of a Parliament freely chosen.   Why might it not be solved by temporarily suspending the parliamentary system, and by persuading Parliament to appoint a limited body of right-thinking men to take its place, on the understanding that as soon as the country was accustomed to the new order of things parliamentary government should be restored ? [2]   Cromwell appears to have thought that by allowing Parliament to

[1] *Great Civil War*, iv. 4.

[2] The objects of the officers at this time are well put in the Declaration of April 23 : " After much debating it was judged necessary and agreed upon that the supreme authority should be by the Parliament devolved upon known persons, men fearing God and of approved integrity, and the Government of the Commonwealth committed unto them for a time as the most hopeful way to encourage and countenance all God's people, reform the law, and administer justice impartially ; hoping thereby the people might forget monarchy, and understanding their true interest in the election of successive Parliaments, may have the government settled upon a true basis, without hazard to this glorious cause, or necessitating to keep up armies for the defence of the same " (*Several Proceedings*, E, 211, 24). Pauluzzi traces the proposal of this compromise—such as it was—to Cromwell : " Dopo quali avvenimenti "—*i.e.* the scene in Parliament on the 15th — " mi è stato confermato essersi egli trattenuto di portarsi nel Parlamento secondo il suo solito, e che non lasci con li suoi confidenti a parte a parte d' andar consigliendo li proprii interessi e forse quelli ancora dello stato, che continuando questi particolari livori non potrebbe che grandemente rissentirsi dei pregiudizii e dare maggiormente animo a nemici di mostrarsi più che mai rinitenti da un accordo, e grandemente elevati in ogni caso nelle pretensioni. Con la considerazione di che dalli più prudenti et auttorevoli dal Governo si procurerà divertire gl' iminenti sconcerti, riunendo gl' animi, et operando unanimamente alla quiete del Stato, alla riputazione dell' armi, et alla grandezza della Reppublica tanto più prontamente quanto che si scuoprono gl' innimici poderosi al mare, e qui della maggior parte supporti ostinati nella continuazione della guerra." Pauluzzi to Morosini, April $\frac{17}{27}$, *Letter Book R.O.*

select the depositories of power, its objection to the establishment of a government of military fanatics would be amply met.

Having without difficulty obtained the assent of his officers, Cromwell invited the parliamentary leaders to confer with them on the afternoon of the 19th at his lodgings in Whitehall, in accordance with the practice established in October.[1] When the conference opened it became evident that Cromwell's proposal met with no favour with either lawyers or politicians. The reverence for parliamentary institutions was deeply imbedded even in the minds of those who were prepared to manipulate them in their own favour. Widdrington and Whitelocke poured out legal arguments in defence of the parliamentary constitution, and though the names of other speakers have not reached us, we may be sure that Vane and Scot did not hold their peace. The debate reached long into the night. St. John sided with the officers in support of Cromwell's plan. In the midst of heated discussion the personal question overswayed the constitutional. " It is necessary," said a soldier, " the same should be done one way or other, and the members of Parliament not suffered to prolong their own power." [2] Such threats were not to Cromwell's taste. He promptly rebuked the speaker,[3] and the discussion trailed on till the sitting was broken up through sheer weariness. Before leaving, however, the Parliamentarians promised to meet again on the following afternoon, and to do their best to hinder the progress of the Bill at the morning sitting of the House.[4]

A conference summoned.

April 19. Opposition to Cromwell's compromise at the conference.

A threat used.

The speaker rebuked by Cromwell.

[1] See p. 227.

[2] *Whitelocke*, 554. In Lord Bute's MS. this appears in an abbreviated shape: " It is not fit to permit the members of Parliament to sit longer."

[3] "At which expression," says Whitelocke, "Cromwell seemed to reprove some of them " (*ib.*)

[4] "It being consented to by the members present that endeavours should be used that nothing in the meantime should be done in Parliament that might exclude or frustrate the proposals before mentioned" (Declaration of April 22, *Several Proceedings*, E, 211, 24). According

When the morning arrived, a few of those who had been present at the discussion of the preceding night dropped into Cromwell's lodgings to carry on the argument. Before long it was announced that Parliament was sitting, and all who were members, with the exception of Cromwell, went off to attend the House. On their arrival they found the Bill already under discussion. The House, it appears, had no mind to be bound by the stipulations of its leaders. It was not the 'grandees' who had most to fear from the inquiry into peculation which was dreaded from a government under the influence of the army, but the rank and file of the party who had dabbled in corruption. Sweeping aside the promises made by its leaders, the House itself had called for the Bill, and sought to hurry it through before Cromwell could be informed.[1] In vain Harrison warned them of the risk they were incurring.[2] The House had taken the bit between its teeth, and Vane and his companions who had given the promise over night—perhaps excusing their conduct on the ground that they were powerless to resist the current—either joined heartily in the work of the

April 20.
A small gathering at Cromwell's lodgings.

The Bill under discussion in the House.

---

to a newsletter (*Hist. Rev.*, July 1893, p. 532) the members would have, "according to their own promise unto the General, been *felos de se* as on Thursday next." It is not unlikely that something was said to the effect that if an understanding could be arrived at on the 20th the House would dissolve on Thursday, 21st. As a pure hypothesis, it may be conjectured that the parliamentary leaders, whilst rejecting the proposed compromise, expressed willingness to dissolve at once if 'qualifications' satisfactory to both sides could be agreed upon for the election of a new Parliament.

[1] "The members promised to consider and give in their judgment thereof the next day, and in the interim would endeavour to keep the Bill from passing; but this being told to most of the members, the House, in the General's absence, called the next morning for the Bill, and before his Excellency could come had near passed it, contrary to promise, as was then told to them." [It is probable that the opposition of Hazlerigg was one of the causes of the rejection of the compromise. See Burton's *Diary*, iii. 98.]

[2] An account of the dismissing of the Parliament, *Several Proceedings*, E, 211, 20; Clarke Newsletter, April 23, *Hist. Rev.*, July 1893, pp. 531, 532.

majority, or remained silent spectators of the scene.[1] In the eyes of the officers present the danger was not confined to the passage of the Bill. It would be followed first by the threatened adjournment to November, and in the second place by the dismissal of Cromwell and the appointment—already for some weeks under discussion—of Fairfax as his successor. Fairfax in power would bring with him the domination of the hated Presbyterians with their notorious intolerance.[2]

[1] Cromwell stated that ' at parting two or three of the chief of them—one of the chief and two or three more—did tell us that they would endeavour to suspend further proceedings ' (*Carlyle*, Speech I.) Carlyle is probably right in holding that 'one of the chief' was Vane. The account I have given above is founded on the quotation from the Clarke Newsletter of April 23. So far as it is conjectural, it is borne out by its affording the only possible solution of a considerable difficulty. I am loth to believe that Vane and the rest, after promising to endeavour to stop the Bill, should have gone to the house in the morning with the deliberate intention of pushing it on. Vane was capable of finessing, not of a deliberate breach of promise.

[2] This side of the affair is strongly brought out by the Spanish ambassador : " No era el intento del consejo de guerra executar este dia la resolucion que havian tomado, pero vieronse obligados a ello por hacer entendido que el Parlamento trataba de hazer un acto sobre la mudanza del que pedia la militia contrario a lo que los del consejo de guerra havian ajustado el dia antes con veinte miembros de los Principales del Parlamento, sobre el haverles hecho entender que no queria el Ejercito passar mas por las delaciones del Parlamento, sino que holgarian se disolviese con quietud y reputacion suya, porque haviendoles offrezido los veinte Parlamentarios de procurarlo assi en la Casa, no le cumplieron antes trataron y solicitaron que so hiziese luego el dicho acto que era de que el Parlamento se disolvia para el mes de Noviembre con fin de prevenirse entre tanto de la fuerza que tenian de la milicia, con que llegando la noticia dello al consejo de guerra que se hallaba junto, anticipò la noticia de su designio, preveniendo el del Parlamento que dizen miraba a ajustarse con el General Fairfax, y restituirse a su cargo de General que antes tenia para opponerle a Cromuel y dividir por este medio el Ejercito, en que Farfax, como Presbyteriano, tiene a su devocion todos los que lo son " (Cardenas to Philip IV. $\frac{\text{April 22}}{\text{May 2}}$, *Simancas MSS.* 2,528. Cromwell (*Carlyle*, Speech I.) speaks strongly of the Presbyterians. He and his friends had asked whether any of the qualifications reached the Presbyterian party.

Seeing how the tide was running Harrison despatched a messenger to Cromwell. The moment that the news reached

Harrison summons Cromwell. him, Cromwell flamed up in wrath against the promise-breakers, called in an officer and bade him summon a guard of soldiers. Taking the men with him, he stationed them at all the approaches to the House,

Cromwell appears in the House. after which he entered and took his seat. It was noted that he was dressed in plain black clothes, with grey worsted stockings, apparently as if he had not intended to appear in the House on that day.[1] For a while he sat silently watching the proceedings, then beckoning to

"And," he continued, "we were bold to tell them that none of that judgment who had deserted this cause and interest should have any power therein. We did think we should profess it that we had as good deliver up our cause into the hands of any as into the hands of those who had deserted us, or who were as neuters. For it's one thing to love a brother, to bear with and love a person of different judgment in matters of religion, and another thing to have anybody so far set in the saddle on that account, as to have all the rest of his brethren at mercy." Was this fear of a Presbyterian reaction a mere chimera? I am inclined to think that it was not. Every now and then in foreign despatches we come upon statements of the Presbyterian influence in Parliament, similar to that just quoted from Cardenas. The leaders were still, as ever, Independent; but amongst the less conspicuous members there were probably many Presbyterians in religious opinion who had either not voted for continuing the treaty of Newport, or, if they had, had recanted their opinion. Besides, many who had formerly counted themselves Independents might slip back into Presbyterianism through sheer dread of the army. It was, as we learn from the foreign despatches, with 'Presbyterians' that Cromwell allied himself in his opposition to the Dutch war—men, I gather, somewhat lukewarm in religious matters, and friendly to a good understanding with France as well as to peace with the Dutch.

[1] I do not know how he usually dressed himself for the House, but the note taken of the clothes shows that he was more plainly attired than usual. This is another proof—if proof were still necessary—that his action was not premeditated. If he expected nothing of importance to take place till the resumption of the meeting with the Parliamentary 'grandees' in the afternoon, he would not dress himself in the morning for public appearance.

Harrison, he whispered in his ear that he judged the Parliament ripe for a dissolution. Even Harrison was
sobered by the momentousness of the impending
catastrophe. "Sir," he replied, "the work is very great
and dangerous, therefore I desire you seriously to consider of it
before you engage in it." For a quarter of an hour longer
Cromwell kept his seat. At last the Speaker put the final
question 'that this Bill do pass.' "This," said
Cromwell to Harrison, "is the time. I must do it."
Standing up as if to speak to the question, he stirred
the memories which lay within him of the earlier and
better days of that great assembly. He acknowledged its
'pains and care of the public good.' After a while his tone
changed. He told the astonished 'members of their injustice,
delays of justice, self-interest, and other faults,'
'charging them not to have a heart to do anything
for the public good, to have espoused the corrupt
interest of Presbytery and lawyers who were the supporters of
tyranny and oppression,' and finally to have resolved to perpetuate themselves in power.

A conversation with Harrison.

The Speaker puts the question, Cromwell speaks to it.

Attacks the House,

The rush of words betrayed the growing wrathfulness of the
man. "Perhaps," he said, "you think this is not parliamentary
language. I confess it is not, neither are you to expect any such from me." Then, putting on his hat,
he stepped forward and, striding up and down, addressed cutting remarks to individual members. "Some of
you," he said, looking fixedly at Marten and Wentworth as he
spoke, "are whoremasters. Others," he continued, pointing to
one or another with his hand, "are drunkards, and some corrupt and unjust men, and scandalous to the profession of the
Gospel. It is not fit that you should sit as a Parliament any
longer. You have sat long enough unless you had done more
good." At last Sir Peter Wentworth rose to complain of this
unbecoming language, 'the more horrid,' he said, 'in that it
came from their servant whom they had so highly trusted and
obliged.' His words irritated Cromwell past endurance.
"Come, come," he cried, "I will put an end to your prating.

and particular members.

You are no Parliament.   I say you are no Parliament.   I
Orders in the soldiers. will put an end to your sitting." "Call them in ;
call them in," he added, turning to Harrison as he
spoke.

Harrison obeyed orders.   The door was flung open, and
with measured steps some thirty or forty musketeers, led by
Lieutenant-Colonel Worsley, tramped into the House.   "This,"
cried out Vane, indignant at this violation of the sanctities of
the place, "is not honest, yea it is against morality and
Altercation with Vane common honesty."   Surely there was a touch of
sadness in Cromwell's answer to his old friend, who
through eleven troubled years had been to him more than
a brother :—"O Sir Henry Vane !   Sir Henry Vane !   The
Lord deliver me from Sir Henry Vane ! " [1]

From words Cromwell proceeded to acts.   By his direction
Harrison stepped up to the Speaker's chair, and upon Lenthall's refusal to stir, handed him down the floor of the House.
It needed the same show of compulsion to stir Algernon
Sidney from his seat.   Then, as others rose to go, Cromwell
fixed his eye on the mace.   "What shall we do," he asked,
"with this bauble ? " [2]   "Here," he cried to Captain Scott,
The mace removed. who was standing by, "take it away."   Captain Scott
did as he was bidden, and for some months the
highest symbol of parliamentary authority remained in the
house of Worsley, the commander of the detachment by the
help of which Cromwell had achieved his purpose.

The departing members were not allowed to escape with-
out reproof.   "It's you," cried Cromwell, as they trooped past,
Cromwell's reproofs. "that have forced me to this, for I have sought the
Lord night and day, that He would rather slay me

---

[1] Lord Lisle (afterwards Earl of Leicester) says in his journal that
Cromwell had already reproved Vane without naming him, and does not
mention this reproof. [He does, however, say that as the members were
going out, Cromwell addressed Vane by name, telling him ' that he might
have prevented this extraordinary course ; but he was a juggler, and had
not so much as common honesty.']

[2] *I.e.* The jester's staff, surmounted by a cap and bells.

than put me upon the doing of this work." One only amongst
the retreating crowd ventured to reply. Alderman Allen
fatuously told the master of the army that he had not yet gone
too far, and that there was still time to order out the soldiers
and restore the mace. Cromwell's scornful answer was a charge
that Allen was indebted 700,000*l.* to the State, and an order
for his arrest, from which, however, he was liberated on the
following day. When all were gone, Cromwell snatched the
Bill on Elections from the clerk, put it under his cloak, and
as soon as the doors were locked strode away to
Whitehall.[1]

The doors
locked.

Even then Cromwell's work was not entirely done. In the
afternoon he received tidings that the Council of State was in
session as if nothing extraordinary had taken place, and was
proceeding to the election of a new chairman in the place of
Denis Bond whose term of office was to expire on the 23rd.

[1] The main authorities are Ludlow, who, as Mr. Firth points out,
'must have learnt these details from Harrison in 1656' (*Ludlow*, i. 352,
note 1), and Lord Lisle's (Leicester's) Diary (Blencowe's *Sydney Papers*,
139), the latter being an eye-witness. Something also is to be gleaned
from *Whitelocke*, p. 554, and the newsletters in the *Hist. Rev.*, July 1893,
pp. 531–534. There is also a letter from S. Mewce to Lady Hatton,
written on April 21, printed in the *Hatton Correspondence*, i. 7. I rather
suspect that Harrison must have exaggerated his account of his own
language in asking Cromwell to deliberate on the importance of what he
was doing, as it was Harrison's cue to ascribe the origination of the deed
to Cromwell rather than to himself. On his way to execution he said :
" The breaking of Parliament was the act and design of General Cromwell ; for I did know nothing of it. That morning before it was done,
he called me to go along with him to the House." *A Complete Collection
of the Lives, Speeches, &c.,* . . . *of those Persons lately Executed,* p. 9.
This is literally true if only the design of practically carrying out the
measure is intended. I have followed Lord Lisle in placing the removal
of the mace after the expulsion of Algernon Sidney. Lord Lisle was
present, and must have been especially interested in the treatment of his
brother. Other authorities place the scene earlier. Indeed, the arrangement of the various scenes as given in the next can only be taken as a
probable arrangement of discordant authorities. Whitelocke slurs over the
whole affair, being probably unwilling to notice that some of Cromwell's
hard words were directed against himself.

Accompanied by Lambert and Harrison, Cromwell made his way to the Council Chamber. "Gentlemen," he said, "if you are met here as private persons, you shall not be disturbed; but if as a Council of State, this is no place for you; and since you cannot but know what was done at the House in the morning, so take notice that the Parliament is dissolved." In the name of that dissolved Parliament Bradshaw answered him with dignity. "Sir, we have heard what you did at the House in the morning, and before many hours all England will hear it; but, Sir, you are mistaken to think that the Parliament is dissolved; for no power under heaven can dissolve them but themselves; therefore take you notice of that." [1] It was the last defiance of legality to military violence. The only answer which Cromwell could give had been already given in the morning, when he declared the existing House to be 'no Parliament.' It had no claim to represent the people, and for many a long day it had acted in its own name rather than in that of the nation. Yet, forsooth, this mutilated body had resolved to constitute itself the kernel of future assemblies, and to admit or reject to seats in a future Parliament as seemed good in its eyes. Cromwell, in his deed, was a truer representative of the feeling of the nation than the men who posed as its representatives. In him, as in the mass of his countrymen, political distrust was weighted by contempt for the extortions and greediness of the members, and that contempt was best expressed by the words "This House to be let unfurnished" [2] scribbled on its door by some wit of the streets under cover of the shades of evening.

Dissolution of the Council of State.

Bradshaw's defiance.

[1] *Ludlow*, i. 357. Compare other authorities in Mr. Firth's note on this passage. Bradshaw is sometimes incorrectly spoken of as President of the Council.

[2] *Several Proceedings*, E, 211, 24.

CHAPTER XXVI

A TEMPORARY DICTATORSHIP

ONCE more Cromwell, after long hesitation, had stepped forward as the destroyer. As he had broken the power of the
Cromwell
as the
destroyer. King and of the Episcopal clergy, and had subsequently broken the power of the Presbyterian clergy
and the Scottish army on which they relied, so he
now broke the power of the little knot of men who, with parliamentary government on their lips, bitterly distrusted the
nation on which all parliamentary right was based. The
The period
of recon-
struction
arrived. English Constitution was now but a sheet of white
paper. King, Lords and Commons had vanished,
and it was for Cromwell and those by whom he was
supported to substitute for them such institutions as the feeling
of the nation and the conditions of the time would admit.
The work of reconstruction was the task of the day, and, unfortunately, Cromwell had never yet shown that his intellect,
massive as it was, was such as to enable him to rise to the
height of this great argument.

Nor, it must be confessed, were the inherent difficulties of
the work he had undertaken easy to overcome. The whole
Difficulties
in the way. history of the Parliament he had overthrown, even
more by the good it had accomplished than by the
evil it had done, had thrown obstacles in the path of the re-
The first
work of the
Long Parlia-
ment. former. When that Parliament met in 1640, it resolved to carry out certain reforms, political and
ecclesiastical, by the instrument of Parliaments
triennially elected. As always happens, when the passions are

stirred by some great and overwhelming emotion, the end in view was fused in the minds of men with the means by which that end was to be attained. It was not long, however, before the exigencies of conflict with the King taught the Houses that the idea of frequent elections must be temporarily abandoned, and that they must secure their own permanence till they had brought the King upon his knees. The Act prohibiting dissolution of the existing Parliament was their first step in the revolutionary career into which they were forced.

Within Parliament itself, as long as it dealt with political reforms alone, almost complete unanimity prevailed. Then came Its divisions. a time when a majority of the Commons, combining Parliamentary government less thought of than reform. with a minority of the Lords, demanded ecclesiastical reforms which were far from approving themselves to the remaining members of either House. To the majority of the Lords Pym replied that it was for the Commons to save the State without the help of the Lords. It was a second step in the revolutionary direction. The means of parliamentary government were subordinated to the ends desired by the majority of the Commons.

Soon after the conclusion of the first war, the triumph of the Independents over the Presbyterians advanced the reformers The Independents impatient of parliamentary control. to supreme power. Men who longed for religious toleration with a stern conviction were impatient of parliamentary majorities working for uniformity. The intervention of the army in 1647, Pride's Purge in 1648, the dispersal of the remnant of the House of Lords in 1649, were the natural result of the predominance of a party which, without openly renouncing parliamentary traditions, cared less for their maintenance than for securing definite changes in Church and State. Yet, even amongst these, as the cry for reform grew louder, there were some whose hands slackened, whilst there were still left sitting in the House many, probably a majority of the members, bent upon using their position to make money for themselves, with no real interest for the public welfare. It, therefore, needed very little evidence to convince the reformers that the existing House would never respond to their wishes, especially as they were far stronger in the army than they were in Parliament.

The inevitable consequence was that cry for a dissolution to be followed by fresh elections, which had resounded through the country ever since the victory at Worcester. Yet the notion of governing by elected Parliaments, strong in 1640, had become seriously weakened by 1653.

A demand for a dissolution.

Men who had taken part in or had merely witnessed the parliamentary struggle, had become habituated to the belief that to secure what they regarded as right ends, it was not only permissible but even desirable to tamper with the parliamentary representation. Both army and Parliament were of one mind in being ready to exclude Royalists, but when the Parliament proposed to continue their own members not only as sitting by prescriptive title, but as judges of all new elections, the patience of the army, fearing the return of a Presbyterian or a lukewarm majority, took alarm. What was still more ominous was that whilst Cromwell, and probably Lambert, were urging a complete dissolution followed

Views of Harrison and the Fifth Monarchists.

by close restrictions on the choice made by the electors, there had arisen in the army a party, headed by Harrison, which would willingly have dispensed with fresh elections altogether. The Fifth Monarchists and those who, without giving themselves this title, took the same side with them had, at least, the courage of their opinions. The earth they held was to be ruled by the saints, and not by elected Parliaments. Only thus could the nation hope to attain to those reforms on which its heart ought to have been set. A picked body of religious men must be chosen to lead the people in the paths of spiritual and temporal felicity. Such a view, preposterous as it may seem to those who have been nursed in the long tradition of parliamentary government, was, nevertheless, in accordance with that growing distrust of the power of the nation to preserve itself, which had governed events almost from the opening of the Long Parliament.

The benefits offered to the people in exchange for a right of election which had not been exercised for more than twelve years were by no means wholly of a religious nature. The new

Reforms offered.

Government, they were told, would lower taxation by making peace with the Dutch, would pay the debts incurred by the vanished Parliament, and, above all, would reform the law in such a way as to offer justice to the poor.[1]   On the day after the dissolution Vavasor Powell was reported by a Royalist to have announced from the pulpit at Whitehall that, as soon as the new Government was formed, 'law should stream down like a river freely, as for twenty shillings what formerly cost twenty pounds, impartially as the saints please, and it should run as rivers do, close to the doors.'[2]   Such expectations,

Popularity of the new Government.

coupled with the extreme unpopularity of the dissolved Parliament, naturally gained for the officers the goodwill of large sections of the population, and Cromwell himself, for the last time in his life, became the most applauded man in England.[3]   At first, indeed, it had been feared that the City might testify its ill-will, and regiments had been moved forward towards London to keep it in awe.   It

Feeling in the City.

soon appeared, however, that there was no cause for alarm.   On the afternoon of the day on which

April 20. Cromwell and the Lord Mayor.

Parliament was broken up the Lord Mayor was summoned to Whitehall and, upon his proffer of the surrender of his sword of office, was bidden by

April 25. Criminals pardoned by Cromwell.

Cromwell to take it back and fulfil the duties of his place.[4]   On the 25th the General pardoned a batch of prisoners on their way to Tyburn.[5]   "To hang

---

[1] Pauluzzi to Morosini, $\frac{\text{April 29}}{\text{May 9}}$, May $\frac{20}{30}$, *Letter Book R.O.*

[2] Newsletter, *Hist. Rev.*, July 1893, p. 533.

[3] This is attested not only by the newspapers, but by the foreign ambassadors.

[4] Bordeaux to Brienne, $\frac{\text{April 21}}{\text{May 1}}$, *Arch. des Aff. Étrangères.*

[5] "In the morning his Excellency the Lord General sent a pardon for such as were convicted for murder, and an order for staying the execution of all ; which is a gracious jubilee unto them, and if it were so that none hereafter should suffer death for theft, because we read not of any such law in Holy Scriptures, yet there may be found some other way of punishment, which may be as great, if not greater than death itself to

a man for six and eightpence, and I know not what," he declared long afterwards to one of his Parliaments; " to hang for a trifle and acquit murder . . . to see men lose their lives for petty matters, this is a thing God will reckon for." [1] Cromwell, however, save on this one occasion, never achieved that absoluteness which would have enabled him to carry into effect the desire of his heart in this matter.

It was beyond dispute that as long as Cromwell had the support of the army and navy he could deal with the Con-

Cromwell supported by the army.
stitution as he pleased. Of the fidelity of the army there had never been any doubt, and the adhesions which came in from regiments stationed in every part of the country added little to the confidence already existing at head-quarters. As regarded the navy, it was known

Blake's dissatis-faction.
that Blake was highly dissatisfied with the late proceedings; but Blake was at Portsmouth, incapaci-tated by his wound from taking an active part in affairs, and when, before the end of April, he travelled up to London he was still suffering, and in no sense able to throw his influence on the side he favoured. [2] Deane and Monk were, therefore, masters of the situation. Avoiding all suspicion of a wish to draw the navy into the political current, they circulated amongst their captains a declaration signed by themselves, in

such whose minds are held captive with sin and wickedness." *Perf. Account*, E, 693, 9. The first part of this paragraph is in contradiction with the second, and I suspect that the writer intended to say that those ' not convicted for murder' were pardoned. This view of the case is strengthened by a statement by the Nuncio at Brussels that Cromwell pardoned ' tutti condannati a morte eccettuato gl' homicidi volontarii.' *Vatican Archives, Nunz. di Fiandra.* [See also *Clarke Papers*, iii. 2.]

[1] *Carlyle*, Speech V.

[2] "Blake is ousted of his command, and is come to town highly discontented. He is much for the Parliament." Newsletter, $\frac{\text{April 29}}{\text{May 9}}$, *Clarendon MSS.* No. 1,121. A later communication of May $\frac{6}{16}$ states that Blake was to ' go no more to sea' (*ib.* No. 1,135). Another letter of the same date (*ib.* No. 1,144) says that ' Blake is in town, not yet cured nor satisfied, but what power he hath to express his discontents by action, time and opportunity must manifest.'

which they skilfully announced that they had found it set April 22. Declaration of the navy. upon their spirits that they were called and entrusted by the nation ' for defence of the same against the enemies at sea,' and that they were 'resolved in the strength of God unanimously to prosecute the same according to the trust reposed in them.'[1] This declaration received May. Blake serves under the new Government. general support in the fleet, and Blake, mastering his dissatisfaction, accepted the principle of non-political service, and by the second week in May was found taking part in Admiralty business on shore.[2]

It was only natural that the hopes of the Royalists who had suffered such grievous wrongs from the Long Parliament should have been rekindled upon its destruction. "The young man's bargain," wrote one of them, " is two in six better." [3] With the knowledge that the new Government had secured the Royalist hopes die away. support of the army and navy, these expectations died away, and for the remainder of the year nothing is heard of any attempt on the part of the partisans of the monarchy to turn the political situation to their advantage.

If, however, the Royalists were to be kept long at bay, it was necessary that Cromwell and his brother officers should come to a speedy decision as to the form of government to be established. Their first Declaration, drawn up on April 22, April 22. First declaration of the General and officers. simply recited the events of the late struggle, stating that the demand made by the officers had been that ' the supreme authority should be by the Parliament devolved upon known persons, men fearing God, and of approved integrity, and the government of the Commonwealth committed unto them for a time.'[4] When, however, the Army Council set itself to discuss the form which the new governing body should take, wide differences of opinion

---

[1] Declaration of the Generals at Sea, April 22, *Merc. Pol.*, E, 693, 12.

[2] Blake to Cromwell, May 12, *S. P. Dom.* xxxvi. 53.

[3] Newsletter, *Hist. Rev.*, July 1893, p. 533.

[4] *A Declaration of the Lord General*, E, 692, 6. It was published on the 23rd.

manifested themselves.   Harrison declared for a nominated
assembly large enough to bear some resemblance to
a Parliament, and consisting if possible of seventy
members, following the number of the Jewish Sanhedrim.   Lambert, on the other hand, preferred
that power should be entrusted to a small Council,[1]
and, as far as inferences can be drawn from the very slight
evidence which has reached us, he seems to have wished that
this Council should ultimately share its powers with an elected
Parliament, to be held in restraint by the provisions of a written
constitution, entitled the *Instrument of Government*, after the
example of the *Agreement of the People*.[2]

At first it seemed likely that Lambert's opinion would
prevail.   For a few days after the expulsion every rumour
pointed to the establishment of a small Council, sometimes
coupling it with an intention never to assemble Parliament

Divergent
views on
the consti-
tution of
the new
Govern-
ment.

---

[1] *Ludlow*, i. 353.

[2] The reference to the *Instrument of Government* is given by Ludlow
(*ib.*), who says that soon after the dissolution Cromwell 'sent for Major
Salwey and Mr. John Carew, to whom he complained of the great weight
of affairs that by this undertaking was fallen upon him ; affirming that the
thoughts of the consequences thereof made him to tremble, and therefore
desired them to free him from the temptations that might be laid before
him ; and to that end to go immediately to the Chief Justice St. John,
Mr. Selden, and some others, and endeavour to persuade them to draw
up some instrument of government that might put the power out of his
hands.   To this it was answered by Major Salwey: " The way, sir, to
free you from this temptation is for you not to look upon yourself to be
under it, but to rest persuaded that the power of the nation is in the good
people of England, as formerly it was."'   Salwey did not serve under the
Protectorate, and Ludlow probably derived his information from him.
The only question, therefore, is whether their talk about an instrument of
government was antedated.   I do not think it was.   Lambert is indeed
only credited with proposing a small Council at this time ; but, considering
that the *Instrument of Government* when it did come into existence was
mainly his work, it is highly probable that Lambert now asked for what
was established at the end of 1653—a written constitution in which a
small Council would govern, whilst an elected Parliament was ultimately
to join it for legislative and other purposes.

again.[1] Yet, for all that, nothing was decided. To provide for current business, a body of seven military men and three civilians—the Decemvirate, as the Royalists styled it—was, on April 29, established as a Council of State,[2] and on the following day a proclamation announcing the fact was drawn up, and this proclamation it was proposed to issue in Cromwell's name, with the addition that persons of approved fidelity and honesty were 'to be called from the several parts of this Commonwealth to the supreme authority.' So far as this language went, it would appear that Cromwell had rallied to Harrison's principle of a large selected body. Yet several days passed without the publication of the proclamation, and on May 3 a Declaration was substituted for it,[3] which was a mere echo of the former Declaration of April 22, and can merely have been intended to occupy the public mind till the Army Council had come to a decision. At last, on May 6, Cromwell's proclamation, drawn up eight days before, was allowed to see the light.[4]

April 29. A Council of State established.

April 30. A proclamation drawn up.

In all probability the unusual delay was caused by Cromwell's anxiety to be able to announce that in accepting Harrison's principle he hoped to broaden it out in practice. No Sanhedrim of pious fanatics, but a gathering of patriotic—if Puritan—notabilities was the government which now shadowed itself in his mind. He even offered a seat to Fairfax, and if Fairfax had been there, room would surely have been found for others

Cromwell hopes to gather an assembly of notabilities.

An offer to Fairfax.

---

[1] Pauluzzi to Morosini, $\frac{\text{April 22}}{\text{May 2}}$, *Letter Book R.O.* "Whether or no," asks a friend of the late Parliament, "is the giving of the supreme power into the hands of five or six more such a thing as the government of a Commonwealth, when the Commonwealth is excluded from the liberty of making a choice of persons to govern?" *Ten queries* in MS., E., 693, 5.

[2] C. of St. Order Book, *Interr.* I, 69; Newsletter, May $\frac{6}{16}$, *Clarendon MSS.*, No. 1,144.

[3] *Another Declaration*, E, 693, 17.

[4] It was published in *The Faithful Post*, of May 6, E, 213, 3.

who, though they had more or less strongly disapproved of the attack on the late Parliament, would be ready to co-operate in the task of modelling the future government of the Common-wealth. Fairfax, however, begged to be excused, and the generous scheme could only be realised imperfectly, if at all.[1] The delay somewhat affected public feeling, and Cromwell was now charged with want of foresight in failing to take account of the inconveniences likely to follow from his act in breaking up the Parliament.[2] To no one, it seems, did the failure of Cromwell's hope give greater pleasure than to Harrison. "The Lord," he is reported to have written to a friend, "had now at last made the General instrumental to put the power into the hands of his people contrary to his intentions ; that it was the Lord's work, and no thanks to his Excellency."[3]

Public feeling affected by the delay.

Harrison's triumph.

Yet there were signs already that it would not be easy to bring Cromwell under the yoke of the bodies styled by a Royalist 'the fanatic gathered Churches,'[4] the con-gregations, that is to say, which met outside the regular parochial organisation. Already there was a division of opinion amongst the officers on the subject of religion.[5] We are not informed what was the nature of the dispute, but we know that Cromwell had been exhibiting a

Cromwell averse to fanaticism.

[1] After long discussions, 'così per lo stabilimento del numero come per la qualità de' soggetti, essendosi di più inteso che alcuno nominato a pressiedere in esso habbi civilmente e sotto il colore di qualche suo giunto impedimento o prettesto ricusato l'impiego, onde solamente ieri con una ampla dichiarazione datasi alle stampe con il titolo della sola auttorità del Cromuel . . . si è inteso stabilito un nuovo Consiglio del Stato.' The name of the person referred to is supplied by a newsletter of April 29. "Of this number the Lord Fairfax is one." *Hist. Rev.*, July 1893, p. 534.

[2] Bordeaux to Brienne, May $\frac{12}{22}$, *Arch. des Aff. Étrangères*, lxii. fol. 141.

[3] Newsletter, May 6, *Hist. Rev.*, July 1893, p. 529.

[4] *Ib.*

[5] Bordeaux to Brienne, May $\frac{5}{15}$, *Arch. des Aff. Étrangères*, lxii. fol. 133.

spirit of tolerance which can hardly have been to the taste of
He pro-
tects Pres-
byterians,
Cavaliers,
and Catho-
lics. many of his comrades. Not only had he sent a
guard to protect a Presbyterian minister who had
been turned out of his pulpit by an Independent
rival, but he had interfered to save Royalists and
even Catholics from their persecutors.[1] Cromwell was no
speculative theorist, and the advocacy of such must have
grated on his ears. John Spittlehouse, for instance,
Pamphlets
by Spittle-
house. a Fifth-Monarchist, who described himself as 'a
late member of the army,' published two pamphlets,
the one on April 24 and the other on May 19. In the first he
laid down the proposition that only those who had the interest
of the Commonwealth at heart ought to take part in the
government, and that these were almost confined to the
members of the gathered Churches and the army. As
members of the Churches were debarred from taking part as
such in temporal matters, it followed that the country ought
to be governed by a committee chosen by the officers.[2] In
his later pamphlet he revised his conclusion, holding now that
the government ought to be directly nominated by Cromwell
himself. Cromwell was appointed by God to rule England as
Moses had been appointed to rule Israel, and ought, as Moses
had chosen officers to settle the disputes of the Israelites, to
choose persons qualified to settle the disputes of Englishmen.
" If so," asks this triumphant logician, "where then will be
your privilege of electing men yourselves ? " [3] Another pamphleteer put the argument even more concisely, asserting it to
be 'of not less than Divine institution that men fearing God
should have the government.' [4]

---

[1] *The Faithful Post*, E, 211, 25 ; Bordeaux to Brienne, May $\frac{2}{12}$,
Arch. des Aff. Étrangères, lxii. fol. 125. " He is very kind to the old
malignant party, and some have found much more favour since the
late dissolution than in seven years' solicitation before." Newsletter,
May $\frac{6}{16}$, *Clarendon MSS.* ii. No. 1,135.
[2] *The Army Vindicated*, E, 693, 6.
[3] *A Warning-piece discharged*, E, 697, 11.
[4] *The Army no Usurpers*, E, 697, 13.

After the check inflicted by Fairfax's refusal to take part in the new government, Cromwell seems to have had no choice but to comply to some extent with the views thus set forth. Letters were despatched in the name of the General and the Council of the Army to the Congregational Churches in each county, asking them to send in the names of a definite number of persons whom they considered fit to be members of the new representative,[1] which, to use the language of the Venetian minister, was at the same time 'to be, and not to be, a Parliament.'[2] Until the return of the answers no forward step could be taken, and the uncertainty of the position bred distraction not only amongst the people but in the very counsels of the military leaders.

The Congregational Churches asked to send in names.

Delay breeds distraction.

In his heart Harrison remained distrustful of Cromwell. Unused to qualify his own enthusiasm by political considerations he could not understand that a man might himself be deeply religious and yet fear to place the government of the Commonwealth in the hands of excitable fanatics. "Harrison," it was said, no doubt with the exaggeration natural to a hostile witness, "sticks close to the gathered Churches, and . . . neglects no opportunity, either public or private, to preach unto them his revelations, as he calls them, whereof one lately was . . . that the Spirit told him that it was impossible to settle this government but in a monarchical way, and it was revealed unto him that there would speedily be a king again, but not one of the former race, nor such carnal persons as some eminent in present power, but a man after God's own heart, and a king anointed with the Spirit." It is unnecessary

Harrison distrusts Cromwell,

advocates a monarchy,

but neither in the hands of Charles or Cromwell.

---

[1] The letter can only be conjecturally described from the answers to it. It is called a private letter from Cromwell by the writer of a newsletter of May 13, *Clarendon MSS.* No. 1,153, but this must be a mistake. The first dated answer is that from Bedfordshire (*Milton State Papers*, 92), written on May 13, which would imply a date of May 6 or 7 for the letter itself.

[2] Pauluzzi to Morosini, May $\frac{13}{23}$, *Letter Book R.O.*

to follow the reporter in his argument that, as Harrison
often struck his breast to give emphasis to his fiery harangue,
he implied that he was himself the ruler whose advent he predicted. It is enough to note his desire that the place should
Feake's sermon. not be occupied by Cromwell. Feake, a wild Fifth-
Monarchy preacher, spoke out more plainly at
Christchurch in Newgate Street. " Although the General," he
declared, " had fought their battles with success, yet he was
not the man that the Lord had chosen to sit at the helm."[1]

The impression that the days of personal government were
returning was gaining ground, and there were some who fixed
Lambert's position. their eyes on Lambert. Lambert was now the ruling
spirit in the Council of State, and though his
following amongst the officers was less than that of Cromwell,
he was much looked up to as a Yorkshire man by those from
the northern counties, and was the idol of the common soldiers,
who admired his military skill, and who probably held him to
be a more comprehensible personage than Cromwell. In their
grievances about the non-payment of arrears they could count
upon him as an advocate, and they were not likely to mark his
poverty of ideas, his readiness to be drawn aside by personal
considerations, and his disinclination to commit himself to any
distinct line of action. ' Bottomless,' had been the epithet
which Cromwell had fixed on him some weeks before.[2]
Lambert, it was now said, was ' an unfathomed person, still
undeclared, and consequently most to be feared.' What he
disliked, however, was clearly known. He disapproved of
Harrison's rantings, and he disapproved of a proposal—we may
wish to think it the outcome of Cromwell's generosity—to admit
Vane to the new Representative. If that were done, he frankly
Hopes of the Royalists from him, told his associates, he would absent himself from their
councils.[3] Some of the Royalists, hopeless of re-
gaining their position without military assistance, were

[1] Newsletter, May $\frac{13}{23}$, *Clarendon MSS.* ii. No. 1,153.

[2] See p. 246.

[3] Newsletter, May $\frac{13}{23}$, *Clarendon MSS.* ii. No. 1,153. " Though,"
it is added, " Sir Henry doth most humbly sue for it." Can this be true ?

inclined to expect great things from Lambert. They remarked 'that he had not his hand immediately in the last King's blood; that he is not severely of any opinion in religion inconsistent with monarchy, neither is his interest made up of any such; that he is a gentleman born, and many of his kindred and friends formerly of that party; that he is a man learned and well qualified, of courage, conduct, good nature, and discretion.'[1]

With even less foundation other Royalists fixed their hopes on Cromwell. His evident desire to win them over to the Commonwealth by taking their complaints into favourable consideration seemed to them to be capable of no other explanation than that he was anxious to restore the exiled King. At last, a Welsh Royalist fanatic, a certain Rhys ap Evan, who, to suit English ears, styled himself Arise Evans, called on Cromwell to set King Charles on the throne that his own seed might live for ever.[2] Cromwell replied by committing Evans to prison. Yet he could not silence the rumour that he was fully purposed to restore the old line. Mazarin, it was even said, had proposed that Charles should buy his throne by marrying Cromwell's daughter, and by making his father-in-law a Duke and Lord Deputy of Ireland.[3]

and from Cromwell.

Not on such gauds as these was the heart of the great warrior set. " What," he had asked some months before, " if a man take upon him to be a king ? "[4] The thought cannot have been far distant from him now, and it certainly was not distant from those who yearned for a strong hand to beat down greed and faction, and who, wiser than Lambert's partisans, were aware that there was but one man in England capable of filling the throne of a new monarchy. It was taken for granted that Cromwell intended to rule, and

Will Cromwell make himself a king?

---

[1] Newsletter, May $\frac{13}{23}$, *Clarendon MSS.* ii. No. 1,153. Compare on Lambert's position, the later newsletter of May $\frac{20}{30}$, *ib.* No. 1,164.

[2] *Petition of Arise Evans*, MS., E, 697, 3.

[3] Newsletter, May $\frac{20}{30}$, *Clarendon MSS.* ii. No. 1,164.

[4] See p. 230.

the only question appeared to be whether he was to be styled
King or Protector. One day early in May his second and ablest

Henry
Cromwell
saluted as
Prince.

son, Colonel Henry Cromwell, having come over
from his command in Ireland to be married, was
strolling about Spring Gardens, when shouts of

Petitions
asking
Cromwell
to be Pro-
tector.

"Room for the Prince!" were raised amongst the
crowd. In Kent, Essex, and Wiltshire petitions were
being signed to ask Cromwell to assume the protectorate. Even in the City of London a similar
petition was in circulation.[1] On May 19 a gentleman stepped
into the Exchange and hung up a picture of Cromwell, with
three crowns, and the words ' It is I ' above, and underneath
the lines—

> " Ascend three thrones, great Captain and Divine :
> By the will of God, O Lion, for th' are thine.

May 19.
Verses set
up in the
Exchange.

> Come, priest of God, bring oil, bring robes and gold,
> Bring crowns and sceptres, it's now high time ; unfold
> Your cloistered bags, you state cheats, lest the rod
> Of steel and iron of the king of God
> Chastise you all in's wrath ; then kneel and pray
> To Oliver, the torch of Zion, star of day.
> Then shout, O merchants, cits and gentry sing,
> Let all men bare-head cry, God Save the King ! "[2]

The Lord Mayor, half frightened, took the picture down and
carried it to Cromwell, offering either to restore it to its place

Cromwell
and the
Lord Mayor.

or to treat it in any other way as he might please to
direct. Cromwell did but laugh at the poor man's
anxiety to please, telling him that such things were
but trifles, not fit to be considered in such serious times. The
world, which hoped to surprise Cromwell's secret, was left
unresolved. At last the gossips fancied that they had attained
their end. Cromwell was in the habit of walking in St. James's
Park with his friends, and either because of his position at

---

[1] Newsletters, May $\frac{13}{23}$, $\frac{20}{30}$, *Clarendon MSS.* ii. Nos. 1,153, 1,164.

[2] Verses, *MS.* E, 697, 16. They are given with slight variations
in the Clarendon Newsletter of May $\frac{20}{30}$, and in the *Tanner MSS.* lii.
fol. 13.

the head of the army or because they regarded him as at least temporarily at the head of the State, they had been accustomed to salute him by raising their hats when he turned round, according to the etiquette observed in the Court of the late King. One day, however, one of them forgetting to remove his hat, Cromwell reminded him that Buckingham, having kept his hat on before the King on a similar occasion, had it promptly knocked off by a raw but too zealous Scotchman who had appeared at Court for the first time.[1]

A scene in St. James's Park.

It is unlikely that Cromwell intended to do more than convey an impression that he meant to be treated in accordance with the claims of the dignified position he then held. He had already marked out his course, and he was not the man to change his line without reason. That that line was a mistaken one he afterwards acknowledged as fully as any of his opponents. Yet he never acknowledged that one cause of his failure was his inability to understand the strength of the conviction with which the English people clung to its parliamentary institutions. It is perhaps hardly strange that it was so. The later proceedings of the Long Parliament had left those institutions under a cloud, and, so far as we know, no voice was raised to warn Cromwell, as Monk was warned seven years later, that the nation would only be satisfied with the election of a free Parliament. Presbyterian ministers preached for the restoration of the old line, and one of their number asked God's forgiveness for the sin of rebellion, but not one of them either prayed or preached for a general election.[2]

Cromwell's course fixed for the present.

At last, on May 20, a petition which had been for some time hatching in the City under the influence of the old members, was presented to Cromwell. It was signed by six aldermen and thirty-one common councillors. After an exordium in which the services of the General and the army were extolled, the petitioners

May 20. A City petition for the restoration of the Parliament.

---

[1] Newsletter, May $\frac{20}{30}$, *Clarendon MSS.* ii. No. 1,164.   [2] *Ib.*

turned to the subject they had most at heart. "We therefore," they said, "humbly conceive ourselves bound . . . to represent to you . . . the sad condition of this nation, which seemeth as in one day to be deprived of its ancient liberty, to wit being governed by Representatives chosen by themselves, which in all ages since England hath been civilised the people have been so constantly addicted unto, as that notwithstanding the various changes of their kings and the exercise of their kingly power, even when they achieved it by conquest, there hath been ever found a necessity of governing this nation by Parliaments. Whereupon we cannot but hope and do believe it is the earnest desire and expectation of thousands well affected in this City that so ancient and so useful a privilege, the birthright of this nation, will be tenderly preserved in your counsels as it hath been resolutely maintained by your bloods." Had the petitioners stopped here, or had they added a request that some means might be taken for summoning an elective instead of a nominated Parliament, they might have asked what Cromwell might refuse to grant, but they would have asked nothing of which he could reasonably complain. As it was, they proceeded to ask that the old Parliament should again be placed in the seat of authority at Westminster, 'for the settlement of successive representatives.' No wonder Cromwell rated the petitioners soundly, or that he obtained an order from the Council directing the dismissal from the Committee at Haberdashers' Hall of the only three of them who drew pay from the State.[1]

On May 28, the replies from the Churches in the country having fully come in, the Council of the Army sat from day to day to select the persons to be nominated, and, if necessary, to substitute others for those on the lists. There was free discussion, and the lowest officers had as much opportunity to propose a name as the highest.[2] Only for three counties, Bedfordshire, Kent, and

May 28. Members' names discussed in the Army Council.

---

[1] *Petition with Council Order*, MS. E, 697, 18. Newsletter, $\frac{\text{May 27}}{\text{June 6}}$, *Clarendon MSS.* ii. No. 1,185.

[2] *The True State of the Case of the Commonwealth*, E, 728, 5.

Suffolk, have the original lists been preserved, and of the thirteen names contained in them four were replaced by others when the lists were finally made up.[1]   It is therefore evident that the Army Council exercised a real supervision, and we may perhaps conjecture that it is to this that men like Anthony Ashley Cooper owed their inclusion in the projected assembly.

Hesitation of Fairfax.   For some time Fairfax remained undecided whether he should sit or not.   As late as on June 20 his name is to be found in a printed list of the members, and it was only four or five days later that he left town, having finally made up his mind to abstain.[2]   It seems, too, that another attempt was made to attract Vane, who replied that though the reign of the saints was about to begin, he preferred to take his share of it in heaven.   Yet he came up to London, and it was for some time expected that he might be won over.   In the end, however, he was excluded, either on account of his own resolution, or because Lambert still barred the way.[3]

An overture to Vane.

By the beginning of June, however, the roll was made up. There were to be 129 representatives of England,[4] and to these were to be added five for Scotland and six for Ireland.   The five Scotchmen were taken from those least averse to the English Government; the six Irishmen, if so they may be styled, were four English officers who had fought in Ireland, Daniel Hutchinson, a Dublin

June 8. The writs issued.

---

[1] The people of Bedfordshire to Cromwell and the Army Council, May 13 ; the Churches in Suffolk to Cromwell, May 19 ; the Churches in Kent to Cromwell, May 25.   *Milton State Papers*, 92, 94, 95.   The people of Henley-on-Thames nominated one member who was not accepted (*ib.* 95), but for all we know the members who were accepted may have been nominated by other places in the county.

[2] Newsletters, June 10, 24, *Clarendon MSS.* ii. 1,213, 1,234 ; *Merc. Britannicus*, E, 701, 10.

[3] Newsletter, May 27, *Clarendon MSS.* ii. No. 1,185.

[4] It looks as if it was intended to have 130 members for England, one place being kept open for Fairfax, and that if he had accepted there would only have been five members for Ireland as originally proposed.

alderman,[1] and Vincent Gookin, the son of a typical English adventurer, who was himself one day to show that it was possible for one of English descent to be touched by the sorrows of Irishmen. For the first time in history a body was to meet in the name of the three peoples, but neither Scotland nor Ireland, any more than England, had been asked whether they wished to be so represented or not. In no real sense was there a Union at all.

Each of the 140 writs bore the character of the new Representative on its face. "Forasmuch," ran the summons, "as, upon the dissolution of the late Parliament, it became necessary that the peace, safety, and good government of this Commonwealth should be provided for; and in order thereunto, divers persons fearing God and of approved fidelity and honesty are, by myself, with the advice of my Counsel of Officers, nominated; to whom the great charge and trust of so weighty affairs is to be committed; and having good assurance of your love to and courage for God and the interest of His cause and of the good people of this Commonwealth: I, Oliver Cromwell, Captain General and Commander-in-Chief of all the armies and forces raised and to be raised within this Commonwealth, do hereby summon and require you

Character of the writ.

to be and appear at the Council Chamber at Whitehall upon the fourth day of July next ensuing the date hereof; then and there to take upon you the said trust; unto which you are hereby called and appointed to serve as a member for the County of   . And hereby you shall not fail."[2]

It was Cromwell's first attempt at a constructive policy.

---

[1] *Bethshemesh Clouded*, E, 722, 3.

[2] *Carlyle* after Letter clxxxviii. The writ there printed is dated the 6th and addressed in the original (*S. P. Dom.* xxvii. 37) to Praise-God Barebone. Probably this was a specimen writ, as Barebone was alphabetically first on the list. The writs prepared to be sent out were dated on the 8th. *S. P. Dom.* xxxvii. 37, 38. The name is there spelt as I have given it. Whether he called himself Barebone or Barbone is of no consequence.

Whether it was to fail or to succeed, it may at least be noted that it sprang not from his own brain but from that of Harrison.

Cromwell's first appearance as a constructive statesman.

Cromwell after some hesitation accepted it, and after modifying it so as to render it more palatable to the world, promulgated it as his own. It was at least the scheme with which he was in the greatest sympathy for the moment. With little reverence for the principle on which parliamentary institutions rest, he was keenly alive to the religious aspect of each question as it arose, and prepared to think that pious and honest men might drag the Commonwealth out of the slough into which it had sunk. He was hardly imaginative enough to perceive, till he was taught by bitter experience, that pious and honest men are not always wise, and that in any case the rule of men basing their claims to government on their selection by soldiers and religious enthusiasts is hardly likely to commend itself to the goodwill of a high-spirited nation.

There can be little doubt that Cromwell regarded his own unique position as purely temporary, and that he looked forward to a time when the nation should be once again under civilian government. He did not even attempt to curry favour with the reformers by anticipating that relief from legal and ecclesiastical grievances which, as he hoped, would be the earliest work of the new assembly. The Council of State, of which he was himself a member, and which was raised in number to thirteen in May, contented itself, as far as possible, with the transaction of current business. It was scarcely an exception that it ordered an investigation into the grievances of the prisoners under the custody of Sir John Lenthall,[1] or that it appointed a committee to report on a scheme for the better management of the Treasuries.[2] Nor did the Council assume too much upon itself by ordering the complete suppression of bear-baiting and bull-baiting at Southwark and elsewhere,

Cromwell intends to lay down his power.

Work of the Council of State.

---

[1] *Mod. Intelligencer*, E, 697, 4.
[2] C. of St. Order Book, May 14, *Interr.* I, p. 75.

appointing certain persons, of whom Colonel Pride was one, to see the order put in execution. Pride, it is said, in his zeal for public morals slew a bear with his own hand. The order was grounded not, as has been often repeated, on Puritan aversion to amusements giving 'pleasure to the spectators,' but upon Puritan disgust at the immorality which these exhibitions fostered.[1]

[1] C. of St. Order Book, May 5, *Interr.* I, 69, p. 27.

CHAPTER XXVII

THE NOMINATED PARLIAMENT

On July 4 the nominees of the officers and the Independent Churches assembled in the Council Chamber at Whitehall. With his officers on either hand, the source of the authority with which the members were about to be invested,[1] Cromwell expounded the causes which had led to the summons of a body so ill-suited to the constitutional practice of England. He was, however, in no exculpatory mood. With a heart swelling with enthusiasm, he based the action of himself and his officers not on any constitutional foundation, but on the new divine right—the divine right of victory. " We," he said, after a few introductory words, " have not thought it amiss a little to remind you of that series of providences wherein the Lord hath appeared, dispensing wonderful things to these nations from the beginning of our troubles to this very day." Success in the late war, he argued, had been owing to ' a poor and contemptible company of men,' and had been achieved simply by their owning a principle of godliness and religion. Nor was it only in war that God's presence had been manifested. In the political changes—the pulling down of one authority and the setting up another—His providence had been conspicuously seen. Then implying that those whom he addressed were placed

1653. July 4. Meeting of the nominees.

The opening of Cromwell's speech to them.

---

[1] I believe the usual statement that two, and only two, members absented themselves, to be founded on a mistake. Two on the list first made up by the officers were not on the final list. I take these to have been Fairfax and another.

where they were by God rather than by man, after a long invective against the misdeeds of the late Parliament, he launched forth into an exhortation to those whom God had chosen for His great work. It was one of the great 'issues' of all that had taken place that God's people should be called to the supreme authority. No such authority had ever before been entrusted to men on the ground that they owned God and were owned by Him.

Yet Cromwell could not but feel that the extraordinary course which he had adopted was too strongly opposed to the national habits to be permanently accepted. He had Cromwell on elected Parliaments. himself, before the dissolution of the Long Parliament, recommended the constitution of a small governing body merely as a temporary experiment,[1] and even under the gusts of strong emotion he could not entirely throw common sense aside. Some time, he added, and the sooner the better, the people would be fit to exercise the liberty of election, and what better way was there to make them fit than by exhibiting before their eyes a Government whose humble and godly conversation might win them to the love of godliness. "At least . . . convince them that, as men fearing God have fought them out of their bondage under the regal power, so men fearing God do now rule them in the fear of God, and take care to administer good unto them." With much quotation from the Psalms, Cromwell ended in a dithyrambic fervour, blessing the work which the chosen saints were to execute to the honour of God.[2] Harrison himself could not have addressed them in ecstasy more rapt.

Then followed the prosaic business of the day. After informing the members of the assembly that the Council of Cromwell resigns his dictatorship. State only held office during their pleasure, he caused an instrument to be read devolving on them the supreme authority till November 3, 1654, and directing them to choose, three months before their dissolution, another assembly to succeed them. This second assembly was

---

[1] See p. 257.　　　　[2] *Carlyle*, Speech I.

to sit for a twelvemonth only, and in that time to make provision for a further 'succession in government.'[1] It was only natural that Cromwell's right to devise the government of England should not pass unquestioned. Was one man, it was asked, to grant supreme power away under his hand and seal?[2]

His position and hopes. Cromwell himself could not even appreciate the objection. The spirit of the Fifth Monarchist was strong within him, as he rushed forward into the unknown future as impetuously as he had charged at Marston Moor or Naseby. Yet those who cared to remember how he had drawn rein on the battlefield, and had looked back to survey the course of the struggle behind him, might safely predict that the time would come, perhaps at no distant moment, when his practical sense would regain the mastery, and he would ask himself whether the work of those whom he now lauded as the instruments of divine providence had answered in reality to his glowing anticipations.

On the following day, July 5, the Assembly which had thus strangely entered on the possession of supremacy over the three

July 5. First acts of the Assembly. countries took up its quarters in the old House of Commons. Its first act, 'after seeking God by prayer,' was to elect a Speaker. Its choice fell on Francis Rous, the author of that prosaic metrical version of the Psalms which, after suffering considerable changes, has cast its spell over the Scottish Church through many generations.[3] Having thus constituted itself, the Assembly invited Cromwell, Lambert, Harrison, Desborough, and Tomlinson to take their

July 6. It assumes the name of Parliament. seats as members on its benches. On the 6th it resolved, though only by sixty-five to forty-six, to assume the august name of Parliament.[4] As the tellers of

---

[1] *The Faithful Post*, E, 215, 20.

[2] Newsletter, July 15, *Clarendon MSS.* ii. No. 1,277.

[3] See David Laing's note to *Baillie*, iii. 532, 549.

[4] Curiously enough it is said in *An Exact Relation* (E, 729, 6, p. 3) that ' the lowness and innocency of that title, having little of earthly glory or boasting in it, induced some to give their votes for that.' I suppose this is in contradistinction to some such title as ' the Governors of

the minority were both members of the Council of State, it is probable that it was the wish of that body, and perhaps even of Cromwell himself, to mark by a less familiar title the exceptional character of the assembly. The temper in which the House met was shown in a resolution passed on the 7th,

July 7.
All the
servants of
the House to
be godly. that no one should be employed in its service unless it were first satisfied of his real godliness, and by a call to the people of God to seek a blessing upon the counsels of Parliament. It then invited the nation to join on an appointed day in a 'service of prayer on behalf of those who had been entrusted with so great a burden of government.' The Long Parliament in like case would have issued an order. The nominated Parliament had too much respect for individual consciences to do more than issue a request.[1]

In constituting an executive government the new Parliament decided to establish a Council of State, consisting of

July 8-14.
A Council
of State
appointed. thirty-one members, to hold office only till November 3. To the thirteen who sat on the last Council were added eighteen, all of them—except Fleetwood, who was absent in Ireland—being members of the House.[2] There were several military members of the Council, but the civilian element again predominated. Cromwell being member of both Council and Parliament regained a position in the centre of affairs. In a Declaration issued on the 12th, the

July 12.
Issue of a
Declaration. House announced its assumption of the name of Parliament, and invited the prayers of the godly in

England' implying authority. This tract in defence of the proceedings of this Parliament is reprinted in the *Somers Tracts*, vi. 271. Its authorship was attributed to Praise God Barebone himself by Mr. Firth (*Ludlow*, i. 366, note). He now thinks it to be the work of Samuel Highland, the initials L. D. on the title-page being the last letters of the two names. Compare N. LL. for John Hall on the title-page of a tract attributed with hesitation to Milton by Professor Masson. See Mr. Firth's letter in the *Athenæum*, Feb. 6, 1897. The nickname of Barebone's Parliament was not, as far as I have been able to discover, given contemporaneously.

[1] *C.J.* vii. 281, 282.   [2] *Ib.* vii. 282–285.

support of its efforts to promote righteousness and curb oppression.[1] By this time the mace had been recovered from Colonel Worsley's house, in which it had remained since the dissolution in April.[2]

For some days the House busied itself with the appointment of committees, formed for various objects already marked out by public opinion as being ripe for consideration. One was to examine into the various treasuries, and to reduce them to a single office, as well as to report on the best way of calling to account persons who had received money from the Commonwealth, or, in other words, those who were suspected of malversation as members or officers of the late Parliament. Another was to look into the results of the obligation to take the Engagement. To a third and fourth were attributed the subjects of law reform, and of the poor ; whilst a fifth was to take into consideration the debt of the Commonwealth, and to 'receive accusations of bribery, public frauds, and breach of public trust.'[3]

Committees appointed.

Parliament next took into its own hands a subject of pre-eminent importance. On July 15, an attempt was made to sweep away tithe without further question by a proposal that no minister should receive his maintenance from tithe after November 3. The House, however, refused by sixty-eight to forty-three to put this drastic resolution to the vote, though it subsequently discussed the legal question whether incumbents and lay-impropriators had a property in tithe or not. After the question had been narrowed so as to include incumbents only, it was decided by a majority of fifty-six to forty-nine that it should be referred to a committee.[4] The division showed that there were already two parties in the House, one of a more reckless spirit than the other. It is significant that in both divisions Harrison was one of the tellers for the minority, whilst Cooper told on the winning side. Cooper's abilities had

*July 15.
Failure of an attempt to abolish tithe.*

Two parties at issue.

---

[1] *Declaration*, July 12, E, 1,062, No. 4.   [2] *C.J.* vii. 282, 284.
[3] *Ib.* vii. 283, 286.
[4] *Ib.* vii. 284–286. Compare *An Exact Relation*, p. 4, E, 729, 6.

already given him a leading place both in the Council and in Parliament, and his influence was certain to be exercised in moderating the demands of extreme theorists. Yet even the moderate party was prepared to advocate changes which, in any other assembly, would have been regarded as sweeping. They were ready, for instance, to put an end to the tithe system provided that lay-impropriators were compensated for the loss of their property, and that some other provision should be made for ministers before tithe ceased to be paid. To the idea of a clergy paid by the voluntary offerings of their congregations they were resolutely opposed.[1] There can be little doubt that in this Cooper and his party represented the mind of Cromwell.

The unpopularity of the tithe system, with all its hardships and inequalities, was hardly, if at all, greater than the unpopularity of the Court of Chancery. The delays of that Court were notorious and the rapacity of its officials beyond dispute.[2] So strong was the feeling against it that on August 5, after a single day's debate, the House voted its abolition without a division, referring it to the Committee of Law not only to bring in a Bill to carry out this resolution, and to report how pending suits might be disposed of, but also to consider in what manner the equitable jurisdiction of Chancery was to be exercised in the future.[3] The intention was good, but it can hardly be doubted that the House, to which not a single practising lawyer had been admitted, underestimated the difficulty of supplying the place of a system of law which had grown up in the course of centuries.

Unpopularity of Chancery.

Its abolition voted,

but provision to be made for the future.

---

[1] " Most of them seeming to vote them down as any conveniency can be had for the satisfying the impropriators, and finding some convenient maintenance for the ministry." *The Impartial Intelligencer,* E, 706, 2.

[2] "'Tis very fit the extorting examiners and griping six clerks should suffer ; for I think it was chiefly the excessiveness of their fees and the abuse of spinning out copies to so immoderate a length that rendered that Court so burdensome." Letter from Cambridge, Aug. 12, *Merc. Classicus,* E, 710, 2.

[3] *C.J.* vii. 296.

It was obviously far easier to replace the Ecclesiastical
Courts in their civil functions now that they had for some
years ceased to exist, and there were, therefore, none to cry
out for their continuance.   One of the last acts of the
Long Parliament had been to appoint commissioners
to grant probate of wills.[1]   The new Parliament
applied itself to the regulation of marriages.   On
August 24 it passed an Act declaring that only marriages solemnised before a Justice of the Peace would
be recognised by the State, thus putting an end to all difficulties arising from defective registration.   As the Act contained
no word prohibiting the parties from having recourse to such
religious ceremony as they thought fit, whether before or after
the official union, there was nothing in it to give offence to
any reasonable person who refused to regard marriage as a
purely civil institution.   To this Act were appended clauses
establishing parochial registers of births, marriages, and burial.
An attempt to foist upon it a clause providing for divorce in
cases of adultery was not even carried to a division.[2]

April 8.
A Commis-
sion for
granting
probate.

Aug. 24.
The Mar-
riage Act.

A governing assembly has matters to attend to outside its
legislative functions, and before the Marriage Act had been
passed the constitutional weakness of the position of
the self-styled Parliament was brought into relief.
Lilburne was once more in England, and it was
certain that wherever Lilburne could raise his voice, no institution resting on the power of the sword would escape unchallenged.

The Parlia-
ment and
Lilburne.

After a short residence at Amsterdam, Lilburne had removed
to Bruges, where he fell into the company of Hopton and other
Royalist exiles.   In his bitterness against the Government at home he made himself acceptable to these
men, and ventilated in conversation the idea of a
Royalist restoration on levelling principles, which he
had professed openly in 1649.[3]   He is reported to
have said that with 10,000*l.* he could easily settle Charles Stuart

Lilburne at
Bruges.

His inter-
course with
the Royalist
exiles.

<hr />

[1] *Scobell*, ii. 232.   [2] *Ib.* ii. 236 ; *C.J.* vii. 308.
[3] See vol. i. 162.

on the throne.   He appears to have been sanguine enough to
imagine that he could win the greater part of the army—to say
nothing of the people—to support him in this project.[1]   In a
collection of his own letters published in March, he
reviled Cromwell and the Long Parliament, and con-
gratulated the country on Blake's defeat off Dungeness.[2]   Yet
when news of the dissolution reached him he resolved, in forget-
fulness of the effect of his violent words, to petition Cromwell

He attacks
Cromwell.

---

[1] *Several Informations*, E, 705, 14.   No doubt the informants were
spies, and their evidence is to some extent tainted, but Lilburne's earlier
denials, as Godwin pointed out (*Hist. of the Commonwealth*, iii. 551,
note *d*), avoid direct contradiction of the main charge against him.   He
admitted, indeed, that he had talked with the Duke of Buckingham about
the best way for him to procure leave to return to England, and also said
that he 'was very familiar with the Lord Percy, the Lord Hopton, the
Lord Culpepper, the Bishop of Londonderry . . . and the Duke of
Buckingham, with all of whom, or the highest ranting Cavalier I met
with, upon all occasions of discourse whatsoever, I always maintained my
own principles that at first I engaged with in the Parliament's quarrel
against the late King, viz. unlimited regal prerogative and Parliament's
unknown unfathomable privileges, and with them, or any of the King's
party . . . I never . . . entered into the least contract, agreement, oath,
or confederacy to be his agent, or to advance his ends or interests, and
am as totally ignorant as a young child of the particulars of any present
design of his, and never in all my days held any counsels with them or any
of them for the managing of the King's designs against the interests of the
land of my nativity.'   *A Defensive Declaration*, p. 15, E, 702, 2.   Every
word of this would be literally true if, as was probably the case, Lilburne
had suggested a scheme which was rejected by the Royalists.   Later,
when the statements made by the spies were in print, he appears to have
practically told a direct falsehood.   He is charged, he says, with offering
to the Cavalier 'upon the procurement of 10,000*l.* to destroy the Lord
General, the Parliament, and Council of State, and that (as Captain Titus
informs) in half an hour.'   To this charge he replies 'that never any
words of this nature passed from my mouth or any such thoughts entered
into my heart, the Lord the Almighty God is my witness,' *Malice Detected*,
E, 705, 19.   It is true that Titus said nothing about 'half an hour,' but
this slight alteration of the words does not exonerate Lilburne.   It may be
accepted that Lilburne when engaged in a battle for his life did not scruple
at falsehood.

[2] *Lieut.-Col. Lilburne Revived*, E, 689, 32.

for leave to return to England. Receiving no answer, he

crossed the Channel, and on June 14 settled in lodgings in Moorfields. His first step was to petition Cromwell and the Council of State for leave to remain unmolested. He assured them of his in-

tention to live peaceably, and excused the wild language of his recent letters on the ground of his passionate temper.[1]

Lilburne did not long remain at large. On the 15th the Lord Mayor committed him to the custody of one of the

sheriffs. On the following day the Council of State ordered his transference to Newgate, and directed the Attorney-General to prosecute him. As

June 16.
and com-
mitted to
Newgate.
His prosecu-
tion ordered.

an Act of the late Parliament had declared him guilty of felony upon his mere return to England, there seemed little doubt that his enemies had now prevailed against him, and that he would be hanged out of hand.[2]

That Cromwell and the Council of State had taken this step in a moment of irritation is probable enough. The

apparition of the advocate of popular rights at the moment when a few nominees of the army were about to take the government of England on their shoulders must have been sufficiently annoying, and Cromwell was, more than most men then living, apt to underestimate the constitutional strength of Lilburne's position. He had soon to learn that there was a side of the question on

which he had failed to reckon. In a second petition which Lilburne drew up before leaving the sheriff's house in obedience to the Council's order, he denied the right of the late Parliament to sentence him to death by an *ex post facto* enactment for his part in presenting a petition which was condemned by no law, and that, too, without hearing him in his own defence. If this were to stand as a precedent, every

---

[1] *The Banished Man's Suit*, June 14, 669, p. 17, No. 16.

[2] *Several Proceedings*, E, 215, 3; C. of St. Order Book, *Interr.* I, 69, p. 323.

Englishman would be at the mercy of the Government of the day.[1] Lilburne's appeal was the more telling as Cromwell and those who acted with him had made a strong point against the late Parliament of its readiness to interfere in matters which ought to have been left to the law.

Cromwell replied that Lilburne should have a fair trial, and the 21st was fixed for the proceedings against him in the

Proceedings to be taken.

June 20. A third petition.

Upper Bench.[2] Fearing that the Court would make short work of his case, Lilburne, in a third petition, asked that action might be postponed till the new Supreme Authority had assembled, and had taken into consideration his demand for a judicial investigation into the charges brought against him in the dissolved

Proceedings suspended.

Parliament.[3] This request being at once granted, Lilburne employed the interval thus gained in circulating his petitions, and in protesting that he had not entered into any combination with Charles Stuart. These papers having been seized by the City authorities, he published a long tirade against his oppression by the Council of State.[4]

On July 13, Parliament having made no sign, Lilburne was brought for trial to the bar of the Old Bailey. When he found

July 13. Lilburne at the Old Bailey.

that the Court intended to put the simple issue to the jury whether he had returned to England or no, he exerted all his powers of delay, refusing to plead until his legal arguments had been met or admitted, in the

He petitions Parliament.

hope of obtaining a favourable answer from Parliament to a petition which he had presented on the morning of the commencement of his trial. From his judges he actually succeeded in wringing a copy of his indictment, an advantage which no prisoner at the bar had ever secured before, and when he had obtained it he found so many objections to

---

[1] *A Second Address*, 669, p. 17, No. 20.

[2] *The Faithful Scout*, E, 215, 2.

[3] *The Weekly Intelligencer*, E, 703, 1 ; Theodorus to Conway, June 23, *S. P. Dom.* xxvii. 134.

[4] *The Prisoner's most mournful Cry*, E, 703, 12 ; *Lieut.-Col. Lilburne's Plea at Law*, E, 703, 12.

urge against it that on the 16th, the last day of the session,
his trial was still unfinished, and was of necessity
adjourned.   The prisoner had with him the sympathies of the populace, and whenever he was pressed
hard he threatened to appeal to the people, a threat to which
the authorities replied by occupying the approaches of the
Court House with an armed force to place his judges at their
ease.[1]

July 16.
The case
adjourned.

In the meanwhile Lilburne's petition was being discussed
in Parliament.   On the 13th, the day on which it was presented,
the Council of State made a counter move, laying
before the House a number of depositions on his
offers to the Royalists,[2] which they circulated afterwards amongst the ranks of the army and the general
public.   It is possible that but for these disclosures the House
would have listened to Lilburne's request for the suspension of
his trial in order that the charge upon which he had been
banished might first be submitted to a judicial investigation.

July 13.
Lilburne
asks
Parliament
to suspend
his trial.

As it was, though several voices were raised in
his favour, Parliament finally decided to take no
action.[3]

July 14.
Parliament
refuses to
take action.

The time gained by the adjournment of the trial was used
by Lilburne's partisans to scatter appeals to the people in
his favour, and to urge Parliament to show mercy.[4]   On
July 30 a pamphlet, probably from Lilburne's
own pen,[5] asserted the right of the people to call to
account the officials charged with the administration
of the law.   On August 2 a petition in the name of
the young men and apprentices of London and
the neighbouring places drove the weapon home.   Telling
Parliament that it ' wanted the legal, formal election by the
people,' they pointed out that there was but one way in which
it could remove the blot—by doing justice to the oppressed.

July 30.
Lilburne
appeals to
the people.

Aug. 2.
A violent
petition.

---

[1] *The Trial of J. Lilburne*, E, 708, 3.   [2] *C.J.* vii. 284.

[3] *Ib.* vii. 285 ; *An Exact Relation*, p. 5, E, 729, 6.

[4] *The Weekly Intelligencer*, E, 706, 1.

[5] *O Yes!   O Yes!   O Yes!* E, 708, 7.

"When," they continued, "upon any respect you decline such works, you decline your own being ; and when you cease from doing of them, do you not cease also from being a Parliament ? "[1] The reply of Parliament was to commit to prison the six youths who tendered the petition, and to order that Lilburne himself should be restrained in close confinement.[2]

On August 10 the trial was resumed, but it made little or no progress till the 19th, when the prisoner was told plainly that, if he still refused to plead, he would be pressed to death in accordance with the law then existing.[3] On the 20th Lilburne, having put in a plea of ' Not guilty,' a jury was at last impanelled. Its duty according to the expressed opinion of the Court was simple enough. An Act of Parliament had declared that Lilburne would be a felon if he returned to England. All that was incumbent on the jurymen, therefore, was to take note of the fact of his return, and a verdict of guilty would of necessity follow. In defending himself against this direction of the Court, Lilburne asserted that he was not the Lieutenant-Colonel John Lilburne mentioned in the Act, apparently either on the ground that he had ceased to be a lieutenant-colonel when he left the army in 1645, or merely to throw the burden of proof on the prosecution. According to a hostile witness, he went further still, saying, " I call Jehovah to witness, and do here protest before God, angels, and men, I am not the person intended to be banished by the Act."[4] Whether,

Aug. 20. A jury impanelled.

Lilburne's defence.

---

[1] *Petition*, Aug. 2, 669, f. 17, No. 38.

[2] *C.J.* vii. 294.

[3] Newsletter, Aug. 23, *Clarendon MSS.* ii. No. 1,352.

[4] The statement appears in *Lilburne Tried and Cast*, p. 137 (E, 720, 2), an official narrative of the proceedings against Lilburne, combined with a sharp attack on his character. It was written, according to Thomason, by ' Cann the Sectary,' but it probably derived its quotations from Lilburne's speeches as presented in the notes in shorthand laid before Parliament on Aug. 27 (*C.J.* vii. 309). Shorthand was not in an advanced state in those days, and we cannot be quite certain of the verbal accuracy of the notes, but it is highly probable that they represent fairly what Lilburne said, and that, believing as he did that he was being unfairly

however, Lilburne told a positive lie or merely prevaricated is
of little general interest.   There is no doubt that he asserted
that the jury were judges of law as well as of the fact.   His
most telling arguments were probably those with a more
personal flavour.   If Cromwell, he reasoned, had turned out
the late Parliament justly, its unjust actions ought not to be
maintained ; if unjustly, Cromwell ought to be punished.[1] He
asked, too, whether ' if I die on the Monday, the Parliament
on Tuesday may not pass such a sentence against every one of
you twelve, and upon your wives and children ; and then upon
the rest of this city ; and then upon the whole of the county
of Middlesex ; and then upon Hertfordshire ; and so by
degrees there be no people to inhabit England but themselves.'[2]
He concluded by a warm appeal to the jury to be merciful to
him as they sought for mercy themselves.[3] The jury listened

The
verdict.
    to his pleading, and after a prolonged absence
returned a verdict of ' Not guilty of any crime worthy
of death.'[4]

So far as the law was concerned the jury had plainly over-
stepped their functions.   It was not their part to be judges of

Are the
jury judges
of the law?
    the law, or in any way to go behind an Act of Parlia-
ment.   Yet modern jurists who condemn the verdict,
fail to take into account the special circumstances of
the case.   In the first place, the Act of Parliament on which
the proceedings were taken emanated from a body to which, as
being a single House, the usage of centuries denied the name
of Parliament.   In the second place—and this is of far greater
importance—the circumstances under which the Act was passed
were such as to raise grave suspicions against its justice.

driven to the gallows, he was quite ready to lie openly. At the same
time, it must be acknowledged that the lie was one that could have
deceived nobody.

[1] Pauluzzi to Morosini, Aug. $\frac{20}{30}$, *Letter Book R.O.*
[2] *Lilburne Tried and Cast*, p. 136, E, 720, 2.
[3] Newsletter, Aug. 26, *Clarendon MSS.* ii. 1,352.
[4] *The Trial of . . . John Lilburne . . . the 19th and 20th of
August*, E, 711, 9.

Lilburne's violent attack on an influential member upon which
that Act was grounded could scarcely excuse the action of the
House in sentencing him to banishment, on pain of death in
the case of his return, without hearing him in his own defence.
It is possible—perhaps even probable—that Lilburne was
entirely in the wrong in his charge against Hazlerigg. It was
none the less a monstrous proceeding to expose a man to the
gallows for a breach of privilege, without any judicial proceedings whatever to determine whether he had committed a crime
or not.[1] The fact is that a legal maxim, such as 'juries are
not judges of the law,' is simply accepted because more
injustice is likely to be done if they assumed the power of
interpreting the law than if they did not. No such case as that
of Lilburne could possibly arise now, because no Parliament
would now dream of passing such an Act as was passed in
Lilburne's case. Against such proceedings the conscience of
all disinterested men protests, and it was to this conscience
that the jury gave voice in the verdict they delivered.

That verdict was received with loud acclamations by three
or four thousand spectators. It was of vastly more importance
to the Government that the very soldiers who had
been placed to guard the Court joined in the shouts,
beating their drums and sounding their trumpets in
spite of the orders of their officers, as they passed
along the streets returning to their quarters.[2] As might have
been expected, the Government made up its mind not
to set the prisoner at liberty in such a turmoil, and
Lilburne, in spite of his acquittal, was retained in
durance. On the 23rd the jurymen were summoned
before the Council and examined as to their motives.
Some refused to answer; others replied that they did not
believe the prisoner at the bar to be the person named in the
Act; others, again, that they conceived themselves to be

[marginal notes: Loud applause from the spectators shared by the soldiers. — Lilburne retained in custody. — Aug. 23. The jury questioned.]

---

[1] The Act of Parliament and the proceedings on which it was founded
are in E, 1,061, Nos. 61, 62.

[2] Newsletter, Aug. 26, *Clarendon MSS.* ii. No. 1,352.

judges of law as well as of fact.[1] The Council was too prudent
to meddle with them further, but Parliament refused to have
the same consideration for Lilburne. The nominees of the
Lord General were hardly robust enough to face a constitutional agitation, headed by the most aggressive politician of

Aug. 27.
Lilburne to
be secured.
the day, and they directed the Council to secure
Lilburne, 'for the peace of the nation,' upon which
he was transferred from Newgate to the Tower.[2]
Some weeks later, on November 21, Lilburne applied for a
habeas corpus, but the Upper Bench refused to interfere, and
on the 26th Parliament decided that his imprisonment should
continue in spite of his demand.[3] If arbitrary acts are to be
done at all, it is better that they should avow themselves for
what they really are. Lilburne had rendered at least one
service to posterity. Never again was an Englishman tried for
his life on a charge which eventually resolved itself into a
breach of privilege.

It was but natural that the proceedings against Lilburne
should have drawn Cromwell and the Parliament together.

Cromwell
and Parlia-
ment.
The nominees by their position, and Cromwell by
his temperament, found themselves ranged in line
against the man whose whole life had been a protest
on behalf of democratic government. Yet Cromwell could
hardly fail to observe how provocative of opposition was an
assembly which neither derived its powers from the nation
itself, nor made good that defect by representing its tendencies.
The first weeks of its sittings were marked by an evident

July.
Recru-
descence
of Royalist
feeling.
recrudescence of Royalist feeling. Before the end of
July, we hear that 'conventicles for Common
Prayer' were on the increase, and that the prospects
of a Restoration were freely discussed.[4] Presbyterian ministers, too, assured their admiring congregations that

---

[1] *Lilburne Tried and Cast*, p. 157, E, 720, 2.

[2] *C.J.* vii. 309 ; C. of St. to the Lieutenant of the Tower, Aug. 27,
Interr. I, 70, p. 280.

[3] *The Weekly Intelligencer*, E, 722, 6 ; *C.J.* vii. 358.

[4] Newsletter, July 22, *Clarendon MSS.* ii. No. 1,294.

England would never be happy without a king.[1] In Westmin-
Aug. 25.
A scene in
Westminster
Abbey. ster Abbey, a minister having prayed that Parliament
might be guided to the settlement of a lasting peace,
a young man amongst the audience cried out that
this would never be till God restored King Charles.[2]

In such an atmosphere Royalist agents were likely to be
active, and in the second week of August, Colonel Robert
Royalist
agents
arrested. Phelips,[3] the second son of the Sir Robert Phelips
who had been the spokesman of the later Parlia-
ments of James and the earlier Parliaments of
Charles, was arrested on a charge of being concerned in a plot
for the surprisal of Portsmouth, whilst another Royalist, Major
Fry, was implicated in a plot for the surprisal of Poole.[4] On
Aug. 10.
Proposed
High Court
of Justice. August 10, in consequence of the detection of these
designs the Council of State proposed the appoint-
ment of a new High Court of Justice to proceed
against Royalist plotters without the intervention of a jury.
Parliament at once directed the Council to draft the necessary
Act, but though a committee was appointed for the purpose,
its report was long delayed. If, as there is some reason to
suppose, the opposition in the Council came from Harrison
and his followers,[5] we can imagine that Cromwell would be
embarrassed by their opposition to what he may well have
regarded as a practical measure for the maintenance of order.
He had, indeed, no sympathy with those extravagances which
did much to encourage Royalism. He cannot, for instance,
Aug. 15.
Atheism
openly pro-
claimed. have been otherwise than disgusted at hearing that
a man had preached flat atheism in Westminster
Hall, uninterrupted by the soldiers of the guard.[6]

---

[1] Pauluzzi to Morosini, Aug. $\frac{7}{17}$, Sept. $\frac{2}{12}$, *Letter Book R.O.*

[2] Newsletter, Aug. 25, *Clarendon MSS.* ii. No. 1,352.

[3] For an account of him see Ludlow's *Memoirs* (ed. Firth), i. 54, note 2.

[4] Account of the examination of Phelips, Aug. 12 ; Newsletter, Sept. 9, *Clarendon MSS.* ii. Nos. 1,340, 1,383.

[5] It will be seen that this party was in opposition to the Act when it was finally passed on Nov. 21.

[6] Newsletter, Aug. 19, *Clarendon MSS.* ii. No. 1,352.

It is at this time that we first hear of Cromwell's dissatisfaction with the Parliament of his creation.[1]   He may have been

Cromwell
begins to be
dissatisfied
with
Parliament.
the more irritated because, whatever unpopularity was aroused by it, was reflected on himself as he was believed to command the movements of the puppets assembled by his orders.   At Westminster the Committees resounded with strong language on the duty of

A voluntary
system
advocated
for the
Church.
abolishing tithes, and of placing the support of the clergy on a voluntary basis ; whilst the preachers at Blackfriars condemned unceasingly those who upheld the connection between Church and State.[2]   Nor was it only the existing ecclesiastical system that was threatened. As if the attack on Chancery had not been enough to exasperate

Aug. 19.
Proposed
codification
of the law.
the lawyers, Parliament proceeded on August 19 to appoint, with a light heart, a committee to codify the law, though not a single lawyer held a seat in the

House.[3]
Cromwell, indeed, was no friend of legal abuses, but

Cromwell
gives his
opinion.
such an upturning of the whole existing system by incompetent hands was hardly likely to secure his approval.   "I am more troubled now," he said, in

Sept.
He draws
near to
Lambert.
confidence to a friend, "with the fool than with the knave."[4]   By the middle of September it was observed that Cromwell was on terms of intimacy with Lambert,

[1] Pauluzzi to Morosini, Aug. $\frac{20}{30}$, *Letter Book R.O.*

[2] *A True State of the Case*, pp. 14–19, E, 728, 5 ; Newsletter, Sept. 2, *Clarendon MSS.* ii. No. 1,377.

[3] *C.J.* vii. 304, "To consider of a new body of law," was the phrase used.   That codification was intended is evident from the language of An Exact Relation (*Somers Tracts*, vi. 276), where it is said that the word ' body' was introduced by the clerk, the intention of the supporters of the Committee being to vote for a ' new model of law.'   The object, it is further said (p. 277), was to make the laws ' easy, plain and short,' and to get rid of the uncertainty caused by contrary precedents in law cases. Later on (p. 278) we hear that, when the Committee got to work, they began with ' criminals,' considering ' treason, theft.'   "By which means the great volumes of law would come to be reduced into the bigness of a pocket book . . . a thing of so great worth and benefit as England is not yet worthy of, nor likely in a short time to be so blessed as to enjoy."

[4] Newsletter, Sept. 2, *Clarendon MSS.* ii. No. 1,377.

who possessed more common sense than any other general officer.[1]   Harrison's influence with him was already at an end.

It little mattered to those who had rallied to the standard which Lilburne had set up whether Cromwell sided with Lambert or with Harrison.   To them he was still the military despot ruling under the name of his humble instruments.   On the night of September 14 they gave vent to their feelings by scattering in the streets a printed broadside, accusing Oliver Cromwell of high treason to 'his lords the people of England.'   He would not, it was argued, have committed treason if he had merely broken up a Parliament which was attempting to perpetuate itself.   He was a traitor because, after the forcible dissolution, he omitted to entreat 'the lords the people of England,' to elect representatives according to their indubitable rights, and to stand by them with his army 'as servants, as in duty he and they . . . ought to have done.'   In consequence of this traitorous neglect of duty all the people of England were invited to convene, on October 16, in their several counties, in order to elect a true Parliament by manhood suffrage.[2]   Ineffectual as the threat necessarily was, it served to clear the political air.   There was no talk here, as in the address of the aldermen,[3] of resuscitating the dissolved Parliament.   A new representative body elected by the people without restraint was appealed to as the only legitimate source of authority.   It was just because neither the Commonwealth nor any government in the power of Cromwell to set up could ever obtain this sanction that they were no more than temporary makeshifts against the blasts of anarchy.

Practically, the most serious part of this manifesto was that it concluded with an appeal to the soldiers.   It was beyond doubt that many of them were touched with Lilburnian principles.   Yet the authority of their officers, coupled with the deadness of the majority of the rank and

Marginal notes: Sept. 14. A Lilburnian attack on Cromwell.

An appeal to the soldiers.

[1] Newsletter, Sept. 16, *Clarendon MSS*. ii. No. 1,390.
[2] *A Charge of High Treason*, 669, f. 17, No. 52.   Thomason dates it Aug. 14, a mistake for Sept. 14, as is shown by contemporary notices.
[3] See p. 281.

file of the army to political arguments, held them in constraint. Those who shared Lilburne's views were cowed by the prompt action of the Lord General. Lieutenant-Colonel Joyce—who, as a cornet, had carried off the King from Holmby House—was cashiered for saying that he wished that the pistol aimed at Cromwell on Triploe Heath had been actually discharged.[1]

Joyce cashiered.

It was an important element in the situation that the popular feeling in favour of Lilburne's plea for government by an elected Parliament was enlisted against the fanatics. On October 16, the day proposed for the unauthorised election, Edmund Chillenden, a Fifth-Monarchy man,[2] was preaching at St. Paul's in a chapel in the north-east

Popular feeling against the fanatics.

[1] Newsletter, Sept. 16, *Clarendon MSS.* ii. No. 1,390.

[2] Towards the end of the Long Parliament he and his congregation presented a petition to the Propagation Committee, asking that the State might cease to intervene in the appointment of ministers, that tithes might be abolished, &c. In this he is described as a captain. (Grey's *Examination of the 4th vol. of Neal's Hist. of the Puritans*, App., p. 149.) In December 1653 he published *Nathan's Parable*, in which he assumes no such title, from which it may be inferred that he had by that time been cashiered or allowed to retire. In his despatch of Nov. $\frac{17}{27}$ Bordeaux speaks of a lieutenant-colonel and a captain as having been cashiered. The first is certainly Joyce, and the second most probably Chillenden. The offence of the latter is not known, but the following extract from his letter to Cromwell, dated Nov. 30 (*Nathan's Parable*, App.), is worth quoting. " I do think it very meet to vindicate Colonel Goffe, Colonel Cooper, Lieut.-Col. Mason, Lieut.-Col. Worsley, Major Packer, which were appointed by your Excellency to look into my cause, that they did faithfully and honestly, with a great deal of love and tenderness, endeavour to find out the truth, especially Col. Goffe and Lieut.-Col. Mason, that in my heart I did not look to them as acting against me as my very enemies ; especially Lieut.-Col. Mason was so busy and restless that truth might be found out ; and for that I do pray Colonel Goffe and Lieut.-Col. Mason in particular, forgiveness. And now, my lord, I cannot conclude without an acknowledgment of the many signal favours I have received from your Excellency, and how tenderly your Excellency did deal with me about this business ; so that I may say of your Excellency as is written of Joseph, Mat. i. 19, that your Excellency being just and full of pity, you were not minded to make me a public example, but to put me off privily,

end of the cathedral which had been assigned to him and his

Chillenden attacked by a mob. congregation, when he was assailed by a mob of apprentices, who were only driven off by the appearance of the Lord Mayor and Sheriffs.[1] The subversive doctrines preached in Parliament and in the pulpit must have appeared to Cromwell to be heading straight for anarchy, whilst the methods of those by whom they were resisted were equally anarchical.

The distrust of Parliament entertained by the officers on political grounds was, by this time, deepened by a conviction Ill-feeling between Parliament and army. that the enthusiasts at Westminster were regardless of the legitimate requirements of the army. During the months of tension which had preceded the dissolution of the Long Parliament, there had been no point on which the military party had insisted more strongly than on the strict performance by Parliament of the conditions on which garrisons had surrendered at the close of the Civil War. Amongst those Case of Sir John Stawell. concerned was Sir John Stawell, whose case was comprised in the amnesty granted by the articles of Exeter.[2] In consequence, however, of a charge of cruelty in connection with his governorship of Taunton at an earlier date, he had been brought to trial and punished with the confiscation of his estate. After the dissolution Cromwell had set him at liberty, and had supported him in pleading his case before certain commissioners appointed by the late Parliament to redress the grievances of persons complaining of the Aug. 15. violation of articles of surrender.[3] On August 15, these commissioners reported in his favour. By this Sept. 15. time, however, his estates had been sold, and, on September 15, Parliament, on a petition from the purchasers, confirmed their title.[4] Though it was afterwards alleged that some

casting also in your thoughts how to do me good, that I might not be utterly ruined."

[1] *The Weekly Intelligencer*, E, 715, 1 ; Pauluzzi to Morosini, Oct. $\frac{20}{30}$, *Letter Book R.O.*   [2] *Great Civil War*, iii. 91.

[3] Newsletters, June 3, July 8, *Clarendon MSS.* ii. Nos. 1,213, 1,271.

[4] *C.J.* vii. 319.

of those who, on this occasion, voted in the majority wished that Stawell should be compensated for his loss, nothing was done to carry their purpose into effect. No heavier blow could be struck against Cromwell and his brother officers than this resolution to set at naught their plighted word.[1]

[1] Stawell's petition is printed in *Somers Tracts*, vi. 32. A full account of the case is to be found in several folio pamphlets bound together in a volume of the Thomason Tracts marked E, 1,072. Compare *A True Narrative of . . . the Dissolution*, E, 724, 11; *An Answer to . . . a True Narrative*, E, 725, 20; An Exact Relation, *Somers Tracts*, vi. 266; *A True State of the Case of the Commonwealth*, E, 72S, 5.

CHAPTER XXVIII

THE INSTRUMENT OF GOVERNMENT

INFLUENTIAL as the fanatics were in the nominated Parliament, they did not constitute a majority in a full House, and the House was far more likely to be full when a new Council of State had to be chosen than when important legislation was in hand. It was arranged that, on November 1, sixteen members of the outgoing Council should be re-elected for the ensuing six months, and that to these should be added fifteen who had hitherto stood outside the Council. When the votes were counted it was found that Cromwell was unanimously elected by the 113 voters present. The next seven, with votes ranging from 110 to 62, were all of them afterwards members of the first Council of the Protectorate, whilst Harrison, who stood thirteenth on the list, received only 58 votes. The Council as finally appointed gave to Cromwell a working majority in favour of peace with the Dutch, and of a more conservative policy in Church and State. Yet there was no such working majority in the House. Like the opponents of the Bishops in the first months of the Long Parliament—according to Falkland's jest—the Moderate party amongst the nominees could not endure the irksome duty of constant attendance on the debates. Before the day of the election was over the numbers present dropped from 113 to 95. During the next ten days the highest number present at a division was 81. It thus came about that the two

1653.
Nov. 1.
A new
Council of
State.

A Cromwellian majority on the Council.

A balance of parties in the House.

x 2

parties were pretty equally balanced when an actual vote was taken.[1]

[1] Since this chapter was completed I have met with the following printed list of members (669, f. 19, No. 3), in which the Moderates are marked with a (*) and their opponents with a (†). The publication is assigned by Thomason to June 22 [1654].

" A Catalogue of the names of the members of the last Parliament, whereof those marked with a star were for the Godly Learned Ministry and Universities.

Berks

* Samuel Dunch.
† Vincent Goddard.
* Thomas Wood.

Bedford

† Nathanael Taylor.
† Edward Cater.

Buckingham

* George Fleetwood.
* George Baldwin.

Cambridge

* John Sadler.
† Thomas French.
* Robert Castle.
* Samuel Warner.

Chester

* Robert Duckenfield.
† Henry Birkenhead.

Four Northern Counties

* Charles Howard.
* Robert Fenwick.
* Henry Dawson.
* Henry Ogle.

Cornwall

† Robert Bennet.
† Francis Langdon.
* Anthony Rous.
† John Bawden.

Derby

* Jervas Bennet.
* Nathanael Barton.

Devon

* George Monk (one of the generals at sea).
† John Carew.
* Thomas Sanders.
* Christopher Martin.
* James Erisey.
* Francis Rous.
† Richard Sweet.

Dorset

* William Sydenham.
* John Bingham.

Essex

* Joachim Matthews.
† Henry Barington.
* John Brewster.
† Christopher East.
* Dudley Templer.

Gloucester

† John Crofts.
* William Neast.
† Robert Holmes.

Suffolk

† Jacob Caley.
* Francis Brewster.
† Robert Dunkon.

There was, indeed, some progress made in legislation, to which little or no exception was taken. Amongst the Acts passed

* John Clark.
† Edward Plumstead.

Somerset

* Robert Blake (one of the generals at sea).
† John Pyne.
† Dennis Hollister.
* Henry Henley.

Surrey

† Samuel Highland.
† Lawrence March.

Sussex

† Anthony Stapley.
† William Spence.
† Nathanael Studeley.

Warwick

* John St. Nicholas.
* Richard Lucy.

Wilts

* Sir Anthony Ashley Cooper.
† Nicholas Green.
† Thomas Eyre.

Worcester

* Richard Salway.
† John James.

York

* George, Lord Eure.
* Walter Strickland.
* Francis Lassels [Lascelles].
† John Anlaby.
* Thomas Dickenson.
† Thomas St. Nicholas.
† Roger Coates.
* Edward Gill.

London

* Robert Tichbourne.
† John Ireton.

† Samuel Moyer.
* John Langley.
* John Stone.
* Henry Barton.
† Praise-God Barbone.

Wales

† Bushy Mansel.
* James Philips.
† John Williams.
† Hugh Courtney.
† Richard Price.
† John Brown.

Scotland

† Sir James Hope.
* Alexander Bredy [Brodie].
† John Swinton.
* William Lockart [Lockhart].
† Alexander Jeffries [Jeffray].

Southampton

* Richard Norton.
* Richard Major [Mayor].
* John Hildesley.

Hertford

* Henry Lawrence.
† William Reeve.

Hereford

† Wroth Rogers.
† John Herring.

Huntingdon

* Edward Montague.
* Stephen Phesaunt.

Kent

* Lord Viscount Lisle.
† Thomas Blount.
† William Kenrick.
* William Cullen.
† Andrew Broughton.

without resistance was one for the relief of creditors and poor
prisoners,[1] another for the safe custody of idiots and
lunatics,[2] and a third repealing the iniquitous clause by
which persons refusing to take the Engagement were
denied the benefit of courts of justice, although the Act by

Non-contentious legislation.

Lancaster
† William West.
† John Sawrey.
* Robert Cunliff.

Leicester
† Henry Danvers.
* Edward Smith.
* John Pratt.

Lincoln
* Sir William Brownlow.
† Richard Cust.
* Barnaby Bowtel.
* Humphrey Walcot.
* William Thompson.

Middlesex
* Sir William Roberts.
* Augustine Wingfield.
† Arthur Squib.

Monmouth
* Philip Jones.

Northampton
* Sir Gilbert Pickering.
* Thomas Brook.

Norfolk
† Robert Jermy.
* Tobias Freere.
* Ralph Wolmer.
* Henry King.
† William Burton.

Nottingham
* John Oddingfels.
* Edward Clud.

Oxon
* Sir Charles Worsley [Wolseley].
† William Draper.
* Dr. Jonathan Goddard.

Rutland
* Edward Horsman.

Salop
† William Bottrel.
† Thomas Baker.

Stafford
† George Bellot.
† John Chetwood.

Ireland
* Sir Robert King.
* Col. John Newson.
* Col. Henry Cromwell.
* Col. John Clark.
* David Hutchinson.
* Vincent Gookin.

[*Co-opted Members*]
* Lord General.
* Major-General Lambert.
† Major-General Harrison.
* Major-General Desborough.
* Colonel Matthew Tomlinson."

There were therefore 84 Moderates and 60 of the Advanced party. A
note of Thomason's incorrectly makes the latter 61.

[1] *Scobell*, ii. 259.　　　　[2] *Act*, 669, f. 17, No. 58.

which the Engagement was imposed was left unrepealed.[1]
Public attention, however, as is usually the case, was directed
specially to contentious legislation, and amongst this class was
pre-eminently to be reckoned the proposals relating to the
reform or abolition of Chancery and tithes.

On October 15 the struggle over Chancery, laid asleep in
August,[2] was revived by a motion that all suits in that Court

Oct. 15.
Conflict of
opinion on
the abolition
of Chancery.

should be suspended for a month to clear the way for
new legislation. The motion was, indeed, carried
by a small majority, but a Bill founded on it was rejected on the 17th, though only by the casting vote

Oct. 17.

of the Speaker. On the 22nd a Bill appointing com-

Oct. 22.

missioners to hear causes up to a certain date was
rejected by the Moderates on the ground that it made no pro-

Oct. 29.

vision for the future, and on the 29th another Bill
was rejected by the Advanced party on the opposite
ground that it threatened to perpetuate existing abuses. At

Nov. 3.

last, a third Bill was produced in which provision
was made—to use the language of an enthusiastic
supporter—' for the taking down the Court, and for the despatch
of the causes depending, and providing for the future in a sum-
mary way, so as any ordinary cause might be determined and
ended for twenty or forty shillings, and in a very short
time, and much strife and going to law prevented.' Yet,
though Parliament continued sitting for more than five weeks
after this marvellous Bill was read a second time, it never
emerged from the Committee of Law to which it was immediately referred.[3]

Whatever might be the fate of Chancery, the Assessment
Act must be renewed if the military and naval services were to

Nov. 4-24.
The
Assess-
ment Bill.

be preserved from an entire collapse. Accordingly,
a Bill renewing the monthly assessment of 120,000*l.*
for another half-year was brought in on November 4.
It at once met with serious opposition, and before it was brought

---

[1] *Act*, E, 1,062, 23 ; see vol. i. 193.   [2] See p. 291.

[3] *C.J.* vii. 335, 338, 340, 346. An Exact Relation, *Somers Tracts*,
vi. 276.

into its final shape alterations were made in the sums imposed on various counties and towns, the quota of the City of
London especially being raised from 6,000*l.* to 8,000*l.* As far

Nov. 24
Passing of
the Act.

as it is possible to understand what passed in the final
debate, it seems that the opposition of those who objected to the additional burden imposed on their
constituencies was re-enforced by the outcries of those who,
on general grounds, thought that too much money was being
spent upon soldiers and sailors.[1] Why, it was asked, should not
the county assessment be abandoned, and each individual holder
of real or personal property be assessed at the same percentage
of each pound-value of his holding? It was even suggested

---

[1] In An Exact Relation (*Somers Tracts*, vi. 273) it is said that 'there
being a desire, if possible, it might have been to have abated something
of that sum, and that it might be laid more equally; many votes passed,
and very sharp debates by reason of the great inequality that was evident
in the laying of the tax, some countries bearing beyond their proportion,
and some much less; which made the burthen more grievous than otherwise it would be; when after many days spent in the modelling the Bill,
and it came to be passed, some gentlemen gave their reasons why they
could not give their Yea to pass it for a law, for the unrighteousness that
was in it—and something else—which had been laid forth in the debate.
The great inequality betwixt county and county, city and city, hundred
and hundred, and so of particular estates, some paying but two or three
shillings in the pound, and others four or five; yea some ten or twelve
shillings for their real estate, besides what they paid for their personal; in
which, some of London passionately complained of their being over-rated,
they paying eight thousand pounds a month, the fifteenth part of the
whole assessment of the Commonwealth, when as they with great confidence affirmed that they were not the fortieth part of the Commonwealth
in value as their case now was.' A comparison between this Act (E, 1,062,
No. 32) and the last Assessment Act of the Long Parliament (E, 1,061,
No. 81) shows that the two agreed on assessing each county at a certain
sum, and dividing the county assessment by a pound-rate—*i.e.* charging
an equal fraction of the whole on so much of each estate as was valued at
one pound. They differ in the sums assessed on each county; the increase on London being as stated above from 6,000*l.* to 8,000*l.* I suspect
that what was asked was that the assessment on counties should be dis-
continued, and a definite rate assessed on each pound-value held by every
individual owner all over the country.

that the officers who had enriched themselves by the purchase of forfeited estates at low values should come to the help of the suffering Commonwealth, and serve without pay for a year.[1] So strong was the opposition that it was believed in the House that if a division had been taken the Bill would have been rejected. Wiser counsels, however, prevailed, and in the end its opponents allowed it to pass, in the hope that there would be time enough in the next six months to contrive some more

Dec. 1. The Excise to be only temporary. equitable method of levying the tax.[2] A few days' discussion on the Excise convinced the members that that impost was an oppressive one, and the Committee ordered to draw up the Bill authorising it was instructed to treat it as merely a temporary measure.[3]

---

[1] " The Church-party urged " (*i.e.* on the last day of the sitting of the Parliament) "that the dissenters had dealt disingenuously with the army in moving that the officers should be treated with to lay down their pay, and likewise to endeavour to the casting out the Bill of Assessment. To which they answer that, as to what was urged as disingenuity to them, is endeavouring to retrench some of the officers' pay : it was moved indeed in order to the abatement of the tax that, in respect of their great estates already gotten, and the little pains and hazard they were now at in this time of peace, and the sore and heavy burden that was upon the people, that the chief officers would for one year in this time of strait serve the Commonwealth freely, as they had called the Parliament to do: and concerning the motion of casting out the Bill of Assessment [it] was upon this ground that it was an unequal and oppressive way of levy, which yet, lest then the emergent affairs of the nation should suffer, it was waived, hoping ere another assessment should be laid, it might be done by a ground rate in some other more equal way of assess ; instance being given of some towns and counties in the Commonwealth paying 12s. and 13s. in the pound, and others but two or three." *Great Britain's Post*, E, 222, 28.

[2] " The Act ingrossed, and the question being put, the Noes as to the making it a law that very day, had they been prosecuted to the poll had hazarded the passing of it ; it having been earnestly pressed, that it might be amended at the table or recommitted to be amended against the next day." An Exact Relation, *Somers Tracts*, vi. 274.

[3] *C.J.* vii. 381. The author of An Exact Relation, *Somers Tracts*, vi. 272, seems to go too far in saying it was 'by general consent waived and laid aside.'

Fierce as had been the contest on financial questions; the contest on Church questions was still fiercer. Cromwell, in-

Oct.
Cromwell tries to promote harmony amongst the clergy.

deed, had been doing his best, not unsuccessfully, to put an end to heart-burnings amongst the clergy. For some time he had taken part in conferences with the leading ministers, Presbyterians, Baptists, or Inde-pendents, attempting to induce them to live har-moniously in spite of differences on points of order.[1] The real

The Fifth-Monarchy preachers.

danger came from the Fifth-Monarchy preachers, whose lectures at Blackfriars drew crowded audiences. These enthusiasts called for nothing less than an en-tire abolition of the existing law, and a substitution for it of a simple code based on the law of Moses.[2] As for the Church,

---

[1] *Verbael*, 177 ; *The Faithful Scout*, E, 222, 2.

[2] The statement of Cromwell, in his speech at the opening of the first Protectorate Parliament (*Carlyle*, Speech II.), that these men perhaps wished 'to bring in the Judaical law' has been controverted. It is, however, fully borne out by a passage from a pamphlet published on November 7 by John Rogers, one of the preachers : "Therefore look to it now, whiles you have a time to do it, and let me add this to urge you that this Monarchy of Christ will deliver us from slavery and tyranny, and set up the laws of God in the stead of men's : see Isa. xii. 21, 22, ' The Lord is well pleased for his righteousness sake, He will magnify the law and make it honour-able,' but (as yet in the Fourth Monarchy) this is a people robbed and spoiled ; as the Jews were by the Romans, so we by the Normans robbed of all our rights, which we hope to be restored into . . . My work and word is to say ' Restore,' which if you that are in power refuse to do it, yet deliverance shall come ; but woe be to you, as to the tail of the Fourth Monarchy, which is not as yet out of rule, for God hath tried and trusted you with the honour which else others shall take from you within few years. . . . The law of God (which is now slighted as imperfect, whiles men set up their own notions and forms in the stead, and prefer Gratian's, or a Justinian's law, and to make themselves as heathens without the law of God amongst them), this law lies in Deut. vi. 1. These are the Command-ments (*i.e.* the ten in two tables given Moses on Mount Sinai, Exod. xx.), the Statutes (*i.e.* the several cases depending on and arising out of each command). . . . Now this Law, Statute-book and Judgment-seat of God must be set up (and not man's) in this Fifth Monarchy. . . . Wherefore if you be the men whom the Lord will own and honour in this work ; up then ! and about it ! for the Body of laws lies ready before you in the

they sought to abolish the whole system of patronage and tithes and place the ministry upon an entirely voluntary basis. The Fifth Monarchy of Christ, they held, was soon to be established on the earth, and it was the duty of those now in power to anticipate its laws so far as possible, though still living amongst the dregs of that Fourth Roman Monarchy which was opposed to the triumph of the Saints. Office and authority were to be given to the Saints alone,[1] and all institutions derived from William the Conqueror—the Little Horn concerning whom Daniel had prophesied—were to be swept away without hesitation.[2] In their declamation against tithes and in their desire for a simplification of the lives of Christians, there is much to remind us of Fox's teaching, but they had nothing of the sobriety and submissiveness of the founder of the Society of Friends. It was no voluntary company inspired by noble ideals that they hoped to organise. Their aim was to grasp the sword and to compel their countrymen to adapt themselves to the government of the Saints. To oppose their whims was to be the servants of Antichrist himself.

At the meetings at Blackfriars the leading part was played by Christopher Feake. On November 16 an astonished listener

Nov. 16.
Christopher Feake.

heard either this preacher or one of his associates condemn the Reformed Churches as outworks of Babylon, and follow up his blow by predicting the downfall of ' Parliament, army, Council of State, and all now in power,' and the substitution of another authority for theirs.

A call for constitutional reform.

The reporter of these wild words told Cromwell that the preachers called on him to fix the nation's interest and his own 'upon some solid fundamentals in reference to the State, both of religion and policy.'[3] The notion that the whole government was out of joint, and that the

---

word of God. O that you might be used of God for Christ in this work of magnifying His Law in this Commonwealth of England ! " *Sagrir*, pp. 138–140, E, 716, 1.

[1] *Sagrir*, p. 136.

[2] *Ib.* pp. 125–129.

[3] Letter of Intelligence, Nov. 16, *Thurloe*, i. 591.

nominated Parliament was as little able as its predecessor, the

Earlier proposals for limiting the powers of Parliament. Long Parliament, to provide for the necessities of the time, was shared by many others. The idea of securing a bulwark against heady and intemperate legislation by subjecting the action of Parliament to a written constitution had been sketched out in *The Heads of the Proposals*, and had subsequently been reduced to a system in the various editions of *The Agreement of the People*. The last-named document, as presented by the officers, having been framed in the bitterness of the struggle against the absolute monarchy of Charles I., had looked for a remedy partly in the reservation of certain important subjects from parliamentary legislation, and partly in shortening the duration of Parliaments and the length of their sessions. It is true that in the subsequent Lilburnian draft the sessions were to last all the year through, but when the year came to an end there was to be a general election by manhood suffrage, in order that Parliament might be held in check by constant references to the popular will.

A different idea had for some time been growing up in the army. In 1648, those who framed *The Agreement of the People*

Idea of strengthening the executive. had been mainly concerned with imposing checks on the executive authority. In 1653 the same men were alarmed at the prospect of parliamentary tyranny, and, distrusting the popular will as they did, they sought for a check on the despotism of a single House, partly, indeed, by shortening the terms during which Parliament was to be operative, and by reserving certain questions from its consideration by means of a written constitution ; but still more by increasing the powers of the executive Government.

Some proposal of this kind had been made to Cromwell shortly after the dissolution of the Long Parliament,[1] but it had not at that time been taken into serious consideration. About the middle of October it was, however, revived by the officers,[2]

---

[1] See p. 272.

[2] Ludlow (*Memoirs*, i. 369) says that after the abdication of the nominees, Lambert declared that the Instrument had been 'under consideration for two months past.'

but for a time it made little way, perhaps because Cromwell was averse to any forcible interruption of the Parliament which he had called into being. Cromwell's dislike of violent measures, whenever it was possible for him to avoid them, was no doubt strengthened by the result of the election of November 1,[1] showing that the Moderate party was able to gain the upper hand in Parliament if only its members would give themselves the trouble of more constant attendance. During the early part of November he seems to have maintained a position of expectancy, taking care not to commit himself to either of the extreme parties respectively represented on the Officers' Council by Lambert and Harrison.[2]

Before the end of the month an effort was made by the Moderate party to strengthen the executive without having

Nov. 21.
Creation of a new High Court of Justice.

recourse to constitutional change. With Lilburne's acquittal before their eyes, they deemed it hopeless to obtain a fair verdict from a jury in a political trial, and they accordingly resolved to push on the scheme of erecting a new High Court of Justice, which had for some time lain asleep in the committee to which it had been referred.[3] A Bill to that effect was accordingly brought in on November 21 on the pretext of danger from a Royalist conspiracy, the leaders of the Moderate party protesting that if it were delayed by a single day ' they knew not but by that time they might have their throats cut.' The true reason for their haste was that the Bill was resisted by their opponents, who probably suspected that the weapon might be employed against others than Royalists. Many of the opposing members being, however, absent at the preachings at Blackfriars,[4] the Bill was

[1] See p. 307.

[2] This I gather from the language of Bordeaux about the relations of Lambert and Harrison to one another and to Cromwell ; Bordeaux to Brienne, Nov. $\frac{17}{27}$, R.O. Transcripts.

[3] See p. 301.

[4] The author of An Exact Relation (Somers Tracts, vi. 273) plainly connects the hurrying on of the Bill with the Moderate party. That it was understood that the Act would be used against other than Royalists appears from Pauluzzi's language : " Alle voci de' diversi particolari e di

read three times before they returned and passed into law in a single morning.[1]

There can be little doubt that this Act wrung from Parliament by a trick had Cromwell's approval. At all events within three days after its passing Harrison retired into the country, and it was generally understood that his withdrawal was the result of Cromwell's dissatisfaction with his conduct, a dissatisfaction which must have been the keener if there was any truth in the rumour that the more active spirits in Parliament had formed a design of substituting Harrison for Cromwell in command of the army.[2] Lambert, who had been absent from town in consequence of ill-health, now returned to preside over a meeting which all officers within travelling distance had been invited to attend.[3]

Cromwell dissatisfied with Harrison.

Lambert presides over a meeting of officers.

qualche ministro predicante di nominazione et acclamazione di un Rè in questo Regno vi ha rimediato l' auttorità del Parlamento medesimo con atto rigoroso proibente a chi che sia, di parlare a questo fine per l'avvenire; et ognuno che rappresentasse il Governo presente tirannico ingiusto et illegitimo, e ne fosse accusato, s' intende colpevole di alto tradimento di stato, et in conseguenza giudicato e condannato alla morte senz' altra formazione di processo." Pauluzzi to Morosini, *Letter Book R.O.* The French ambassador writes even more clearly:—"Il s'est desjà estably une Chambre de Justice à desseing de contenir les mal intentionnez et une espèce de Predicateurs qui declament hautement contre ce Regime; dont mesmes quelques uns sont officiers de l'armée." Bordeaux to Brienne, $\frac{\text{Nov. 26}}{\text{Dec. 6}}$, *R.O. Transcripts.*

[1] *C.J.* vii. 353; *Act*, E, 1,072, No. 26.

[2] Despatch of the Nuncio at Brussels, Dec. $\frac{3}{13}$, *Vatican MSS. Nunziatura di Fiandra.*

[3] Bordeaux to Brienne, Nov. $\frac{17}{27}$, *R. O. Transcripts*, Newsletter No. 24, *Clarendon MSS.* ii. No. 1,547. On Nov. 26 Bordeaux writes that Lambert had arrived 'pour changer le Parlement, reduire l'authorité en un conseil de peu de personnes et abattre les Anabaptistes. L'on me vient de donner advis que leur chef Harrison est sorty de la ville, n'y voyant pas son party assez fort.' Bordeaux to Brienne, $\frac{\text{Nov. 26}}{\text{Dec. 6}}$, *R.O. Transcripts.* According to the Newsletter quoted above from the *Clarendon MSS.* a petition had already been presented to Parliament 'desiring them to constitute the General Lord Protector of this Common-

At this meeting the existing situation was fully discussed, and with Lambert in the chair the conversation naturally turned on that new constitutional settlement which he and his immediate allies had for some time had upon the anvil, and which was in its main lines identical with the one ultimately adopted. Nor is there much reason to doubt that the chief obstacle to its immediate adoption lay with Cromwell. He seems to have been informed of what was passing at an early stage of the proceedings, and though, as may safely be conjectured, he sympathised with Lambert in his wish to render the existing Parliament innocuous, he appears to have set himself against a second military expulsion, and to have shrunk from accepting the title of King which it was now proposed to revive in his favour. There are reasons for thinking that Cromwell's final refusal was given on December 1, and that on that day Lambert, disappointed of his object, again withdrew into the country, whilst Harrison returned triumphantly to his post in Parliament and Council.[1]

---

wealth, but the House seemed not to resent it. 'Tis said his Excellency intends some alteration of the members of the House.'

[1] The whole of this rests on scanty indications, but such as they are they appear to me to justify my statements as fitting in with all the evidence that has reached us. Cromwell's own account of his relations with the framers of the Instrument is given in his speech of Sept. 12, 1654 (*Carlyle*, Speech III.): "The gentlemen that undertook to frame this Government did consult divers days together . . . how to frame somewhat that might give us settlement. They did consult; and that I was not privy to their counsels they know it. When they had finished their model in some measure, or made a good preparation of it they became communicative. They told me that except I would undertake the Government they thought things would hardly come to a composure or settlement, but blood and confusion would break in upon us. I refused it again and again; not complimentingly, as they know, and as God knows." When, it must be asked, did Cromwell refuse to take the Government on himself ' again and again '? Probably most readers have supposed it to have taken place during the interval between Monday, Dec. 12, when Parliament abdicated, and Friday, Dec. 16, when Cromwell assumed the Protectorate. There is, however, an intercepted letter from an apparently well-informed Royalist, written on Wednesday,

That, during the progress of these negotiations, Cromwell's mind was set rather upon conciliation than upon a breach with the existing Parliament may be gathered from information which has reached us of his overtures to the Blackfriars preachers, by whom the alienation of the officers and the establishment of the High Court of Justice were not unnaturally attributed to Cromwell's machinations.   On November 28 they poured forth

Dec. 14 (*Thurloe*, i. 362), in which the writer says ' that Thursday last, being the next day after our late Parliament was broken up '—Thursday is an obvious mistake for Tuesday—Lambert in the Council Chamber at Whitehall produced the deed of abdication before the officers and proposed a scheme in its main features resembling this Instrument in its final shape, but giving Cromwell the title of Lord Governor and not that of Protector.   This was discussed on the following day, Dec. 14, by Cromwell and the officers.   On the other hand, we know from his speech to the Hundred Officers in 1657 (Burton's *Diary*, i. 382) that Cromwell then declared that ' the Instrument by which the Government now stands was presented to his Highness with the title (King) in it,' and from this it seems to follow that as this account cannot apply to the presentation on Dec. 13, in which the title was ' Governor,' the instrument must have been privately presented with the title of ' King ' at an earlier date.   Various subsidiary arguments tend to the same conclusion : (1) A discussion of the Instrument on the last days of November and on Dec. 1 leaves room for Cromwell's repeated rejections of the power conferred by the Instrument, which is not the case if we have only to do with an offer made on Dec. 13 and accepted, at latest, on the next day.   (2) The title ' Governor ' is an intermediate one between ' King ' and ' Protector,' the latter being the old English equivalent for the modern ' Regent ' and therefore implying a temporary, not a permanent office.   The statement of the intercepted letter on the employment of this title on Dec. 13 is confirmed by Bordeaux's despatch of Dec. $\frac{15}{25}$, when it is stated that the General ' soubz le tiltre de Gouverneur aura l'auctorité entière.'   (3) In the Record Office (*S. P. Dom.* xlii. 5) is a collection of specimens of the style used by the late King in issuing warrants.   This is dated Dec. 1, and therefore appears to show that the discussion on Cromwell's acceptance of the kingship came to a point on that day.   Lambert's departure and Harrison's return are mentioned in Bordeaux's despatch of Dec. $\frac{1}{11}$. Taken in connection with the evidence of the warrants, we may, I think, assume that Lambert left on the day on which the despatch was written. Harrison may have returned earlier when he discovered how matters were going.

the vials of their wrath on his head, appropriating to him the

Nov. 28.
Cromwell
abused by
the Black-
friars
preachers.

Scriptural epithets of 'The Old Dragon' and 'The Man of Sin.' This abuse only served to rouse its object to one more attempt to conciliate these irreconcilables. Summoning the preachers before the

Nov. 29.
He attempts
to conciliate
them,

Council, Cromwell prayed them to remember that their violent language put heart into the enemies of the Commonwealth. Feake, after expressing a wish that the General's words and his own answer might be recorded in heaven, proceeded to throw the blame of the quarrel upon Cromwell's 'tampering with the King,'[1] and 'assuming exorbitant power.' "I did not expect," was Cromwell's reply, "when I heard you begin with a record in heaven that you would have told such a lie on earth." The position ultimately taken by the preachers was, that they could not refuse to utter words with which they were inspired by the Holy Spirit. After this there was nothing left for Cromwell to do but to dismiss

and sends
ministers to
plead with
them.

them with an admonition. Yet, in spite of their uncompromising resistance, Cromwell afterwards sent to them his chaplain Sterry and other ministers to plead the cause of the civil government in the vain hope that they might be induced to promote the Kingdom of Christ by less turbulent methods.[2]

Cromwell's rejection of the place allotted to him under the Instrument was followed—probably at his own suggestion—by

Attempt to
win over
Parliament.

another effort to win over Parliament to the paths of moderation. A short time before, on November 17,

Nov. 17.
Resolution
to abolish
patronage.

the House, by a majority of fifty-eight to forty-one, had resolved to abolish patronage, and had subsequently ordered that a Bill to this effect should be

Dec. 1.
A Bill
ordered to be
brought in.

brought in on December 6.[3] The arguments which influenced the majority were not far to seek. Was

Arguments
for it.

it fitting that any man should claim the right of presenting to a cure of souls, thus letting in 'such

---

[1] Referring to his efforts to retain Charles I. on the throne.

[2] Bordeaux to Brienne, Dec. $\frac{1}{11}$, *R.O. Transcripts*; An Intercepted Letter, Dec. 2, *Thurloe*, i. 621.   [3] *C.J.* vii. 351, 361.

a one as will comply and serve his interest and wink at his vicious courses and not vex and disquiet his greatness by telling him his faults?' Was it fitting that the same man should be entitled to sell the advowson to some other person who was breeding up a son at a university to enjoy the parish provided him by his father: 'the glebe, the tithes and oblations, together with the care and cure of souls, and right of officiating to God and man there—for this his father bought and purchased for him, and who shall take it from him?' Was it not, too, a curious kind of property which was only to be turned into money by the patron when the incumbent was living? The moment the incumbent died this property dwindled 'to a shadow, unless it be sure to put in one that, being beholden to him, shall be sure to serve him, and so forbear his lusts; or else marry his kinswoman, or his wife's gentlewoman or chambermaid, in consideration of being presented to be settled there.'[1]

Such arguments do not imply abnormal fanaticism, and it is fairly certain that the votes of the Fifth Monarchists were on General con- this occasion strengthened by those of men eager to sternation. right the wrongs of the world in a somewhat inconsiderate fashion. The opponents of the scheme, led by their conservative instincts to set themselves against so sweeping a change, were further irritated by the wild language in which a handful of excitable persons characterised as antichristian everything they disliked. Nor had the assailants of tithes learnt the wisdom of concentrating their attack upon a single point. It seemed as if no institution was to be spared. With patronage and tithes the Court of Chancery and the very framework of the law of England were marked for destruction.[2]

---

[1] An Exact Relation, *Somers Tracts*, vi. 279.

[2] There was also alarm lest the Universities might be destroyed on the ground of the doctrine of William Dell, Master of Caius, that University teaching was useless to produce spiritual ministers of religion. Dell, however, distinctly held that universities might be useful to the Commonwealth, standing 'upon a human and civil account as schools of good learning for the instructing and educating youth in the knowledge of the tongues

In each particular, indeed, the assailants were able to make out a case against the institution as it stood. It was the far-reaching character of the changes demanded, together with the number of institutions attacked, which presaged a universal deluge. The conservative spirit was aroused in the nation, and those members of Parliament who shared in the general alarm knew that they would find support outside the walls of the House.

It was not, however, on the proposed Patronage Bill that the parliamentary battle was fought. On December 2, the day

Dec 2. Report of the Committee on Tithes.

after that on which the order for its introduction had been made, the Committee on Tithes brought in a report calculated to exhibit the Moderate party in the character[1] of practical reformers. They might thus hope to gain votes which would probably be alienated were a division taken on a mere negative to a Bill for the abolition of patronage. If Cromwell asked the Moderates to make yet another parliamentary effort to win a majority to their side, the attempt to give effect to his wishes could not possibly have been made with more favourable prospects.

This report, on which the future relations of Parliament with the army turned, was modelled, with some changes of

Scheme for the establishment of Ejectors.

detail, upon Owen's scheme for the establishment of Ejectors.[2] It was now recommended that England should be divided into circuits, each of which was to be visited by commissioners appointed by the State who were to co-operate with local commissioners in ejecting scandalous and ignorant ministers, and in settling in their places others better qualified, as well as in making direct appointments to livings left vacant from any cause. The

and of the liberal arts and sciences.' *The Stumbling Stone*, p. 27, E, 692, 1. See Godwin's *Hist. of the Commonwealth*, iv. 88. Yet Pauluzzi had heard of a design of the Parliament to destroy the two Universities. Pauluzzi to Morosini, Dec. $\frac{15}{25}$, *Letter Book R.O.* The charge which was brought against this Parliament of wishing to substitute the Mosaic law for the law of England was probably entertained by some of the fanatics, but never expressed by the House. See p. 314, note 2.

   [1] *C.J.* vii. 361.   [2] See p. 99.

maintenance of all settled ministers was to be guaranteed by
Parliament. As for tithes, any one who scrupled their payment might be summoned before the neighbouring justices of
the peace, who, after due examination, were to 'apportion the
value of the said tithes to be paid either in money or land,'
thus getting rid of the grievances connected with payment in
kind. If, however, the owners of titheable property still
refused to pay the composition fixed on them by the justices,
the tithe might be recovered from them in kind. Finally it was
recommended that the legal property in tithes should not be
questioned.[1]

As other business intervened, it was not till the 6th that
this scheme was taken into consideration—a scheme which at
least attempted to provide a remedy for special
abuses without irritating those who feared that the
establishment of the voluntary system was tantamount
to the establishment—at least in many parts of the country—
of spiritual desolation. For five whole sittings the discussion
continued, and it was not till Saturday, December 10,
that the first clause of the report providing for the
ejection of ministers was rejected by fifty-six votes
to fifty-four.[2] The majority of two was sufficient to decide the
fate of the whole measure, though it was much less than that
which had carried the resolution for the abolition of patronage,
and it would doubtless have been converted into a minority
but for the votes of some who, without rejecting the general
principle of the report, refused to acknowledge that it had provided the best way [3] of ejecting unsatisfactory members. Such
refinement finds no place in the world of action, and every
one of those who voted in the majority was set down by
those on the other side as aiming at the destruction of
the clergy by depriving all ministers, the worthy as well as

*Dec. 6–10.
Debate on
the report.*

*Dec. 10.
Rejection
of the first
clause.*

---

[1] *C.J.* vii. 361.   [2] *Ib.* vii. 363.

[3] The author of An Exact Relation (*Somers Tracts*, vi. 281) tells us
(p. 22) that it was moved to omit the word 'best' from the clause. If
this had been carried, the House would have adopted the report as a way
of ejecting, &c., but not as the best way of attaining those ends.

the unworthy, of ascertained maintenance in any shape whatever.[1]

The vote of December 10 must have been as obnoxious to Cromwell as to the parliamentary and military adherents of *The Instrument of Government.* It was therefore open to Lambert and the officers, if they had been so minded, to take up the negotiation dropped on the 1st, and to urge Cromwell to interfere forcibly with a Parliament which had failed to fulfil the expectations of those who had summoned it. They better knew the man with whom they had to deal. They were well aware of the length of provocation which had been needed to bring Cromwell to act in the dissolution of the Long Parliament, and of the reluctance with which he had met their recent invitation to take a similar course with the nominated Parliament. They were aware, too, that his approval of the new constitution would be more easily won if they could present the dissolution of Parliament to him as an accomplished fact, especially if it could be made to look as an act proceeding from the Parliament itself,[2] in which there was a majority of members on their side, if only such could be induced to give constant attendance in the House.

Resolutions of the defeated party.

Cromwell to be kept in the dark.

The following day, Puritan Sabbath though it was, was accordingly given up to consultations tending to promote this desirable consummation. Before the end of the day it was ascertained that it would be possible to detach some of the less convinced of the majority, and thus to secure on the following morning what would ostensibly be

Dec. 11. Sunday consultations.

---

[1] *An Answer to a Paper entitled A True Narrative*, E, 725, 20. One member is said to have declared that ' he spake not, but the Lord is true.'

[2] Cromwell's own statement of his ignorance may be taken as decisive, especially as it was made in the presence of those who knew the truth. "I can say it, in the presence of divers persons here who know whether I lie or not, that I did not know one tittle of that resignation till they all came and brought it and delivered it into my hands." *Carlyle*, Speech III.

a purely parliamentary abdication [1] with which the Lord General would have no official right to interfere. As the goodwill of the Speaker, Francis Rouse, had been secured, the intrigue was the more likely to prove successful.

Accordingly, on the morning of Monday, the 12th, those who were in the secret flocked early to the House to secure a majority, whilst their opponents, in ignorance of the course intended to be taken, made no haste to appear in force.[2] As soon as the Speaker had taken the Chair, Sir Charles Wolseley, a member of the Council of State, reproached his opponents with attempting to rob the officers of their pay, to destroy Chancery, and to substitute a totally new legal system of their own invention for the old common and statute law of England, and, lastly, with aiming a blow at property itself by their attack on patronage. For his part, he declared, he would no longer be responsible for such proceedings, and he therefore moved 'that the sitting of this Parliament any longer as now constituted will not be for the good of the Commonwealth, and that therefore it is requisite to deliver up unto the Lord General Cromwell the powers they have received from him.'[3] The motion was seconded by another member of the Council of State, Colonel Sydenham, and supported by other speakers.[4] Their arguments were not allowed to pass unchallenged, but after one member had defended the cause of Saturday's majority, others who essayed to follow him on the same side were bluntly told that 'it was not now a time to debate.'[5]

Dec. 12. An early sitting.

A motion that Parliament resign its powers.

---

[1] An Exact Relation, *Somers Tracts*, vi. p. 282.

[2] 'Rising early, and coming betimes to put in practice their design.' An Exact Relation, *Somers Tracts*, vi. p. 282.

[3] *C.J.* vii. 363 ; *A True State of the Case of the Commonwealth*, p. 22, E, 728, 5.

[4] Ludlow (*Memoirs*, ed. Firth, i. 366) gives the names of the speakers as 'Colonel Sydenham, Sir Charles Wolseley, and others.' The Dutch Commissioner, writing at the time, gives Wolseley's name only as the mover of the resolution, *Verbael*, 255.

[5] *A True Narrative*, p. 2, E, 724, 11.

There was danger, as the minutes passed on, lest the motion should be lost when the House was fuller.

There is little doubt that the Speaker had been instructed what to do on the approach of such a contingency.[1] Instead of putting the question in due form, he rose hastily from the Chair, and, followed by some forty members, made his way to Whitehall. According to parliamentary custom it was a most irregular proceeding, if, indeed, anything can be called irregular in a body so strangely formed as that which now decked itself in the mantle of Parliament.

The Speaker leaves the House.

A minority, variously reckoned from twenty-seven to thirty-five, remained behind, comforting themselves with the assurance that they had been 'called of God to that place and that they apprehended their said call was chiefly for the promoting the interest of Jesus Christ.' They were beginning to draw up a protest, but had not proceeded far when Colonel Goffee and Lieutenant-Colonel White entered and requested them to withdraw. "We are here," answered one of them, "by a call from the General, and will not come out by your desire unless you have a command from him."[2] It was precisely what the two colonels could not show, and they had nothing for it but to call in the soldiers standing at the door and to drive the faithful remnant from the House.[3]

A minority holds out,

and is expelled by soldiers.

---

[1] *A True Narrative*, p. 2, E, 724, 11.

[2] Mansell to Prichard, *Thurloe*, i. 637.

[3] Godwin (*Hist. of the Commonwealth*, iii. 590) argues it to be incredible that soldiers would have been marched in without the privity of the General. The expelled members, however, had neither speaker nor mace. Technically therefore they were no Parliament, and the colonels may have felt justified in expelling them without an order from the General. There can be little doubt, however, that they acted by Lambert's directions, and Lambert was looking forward to have all irregularities covered by Cromwell's acceptance of the Instrument. Some support of Cromwell's statement that he did not know what was going on may be derived from the failure of the colonels to answer the question put to them. If they had really had Cromwell's orders, they would naturally have replied in the affirmative to the implied question

So rapidly did the expulsion take place that all was over before the majority reached Whitehall.[1] When they arrived at their destination copies of Wolseley's motion were circulated amongst them and hastily subscribed. Then they were received by Cromwell. He appeared to be surprised and told them that it was a heavy burden that they were laying on his shoulders. He did not, however, refuse to accept their resignation, adding that he would use the authority they had restored to him to protect honest people.[2] During the next few days additional signatures were affixed to the deed of abdication, and finally the numbers of those assenting fell little short of eighty, thus securing the adhesion of a clear majority of the members.[3] Undecided spirits were prompt to desert a fallen cause.

Abdication of the majority.

A discussion which followed between Cromwell and the officers led to the consent of the former to accept the new con-

whether they had a command from the General. This view of the case is plainly indicated in a Cromwellian pamphlet, *An Answer to a Paper entitled A True Narrative*, p. 5 (E, 725, 20): " What happened to those few members that remained in the House I know not, but am conscious of no force . . . either intended or offered to the Parliament, whilst a House was sitting." Of course, we must not stretch the argument for Cromwell's ignorance too far. He may very well have suspected that something was going on, and have taken good care not to push his inquiries into the matter.

[1] An Exact Relation, *Somers Tracts*, vi. 283.

[2] " Il a paru d'abord surpris, et leur a tesmoigné que c'estoit un fardeau très pesant. Néantmoins il ne l'a pas refusé et a promis de s'en servir pour la defense des gens de bien." Bordeaux to Brienne, Dec. $\frac{12}{22}$, *R.O. Transcripts*. This has to do only with the resumption of the dictatorial authority which Cromwell had renounced at the opening of the nominated Parliament. It had nothing to do with the Instrument of Government.

[3] An Exact Relation, *Somers Tracts*, vi. 283, where adhesions are said to have been given in ' three or four days after.' *An Answer to a Paper entitled A True Narrative*, p. 5 (E, 725, 20), says that ' near eighty members voluntarily subscribed a resignation' apparently on the 12th. It seems more probable, however, that some of the signatures were given later. There were eighty-four Moderates in all (see list at p. 308, note 1), but Cromwell himself, and probably his chief officers, would not sign.

stitution on the definite understanding, if it had not been
earlier arrived at, that the title of 'king' was to be no
more heard of, and that he might still be allowed
to object to details. The argument which weighed
most with Cromwell in bringing him to withdraw his
former opposition was that, as by the abdication of the nominees
he was once more in possession of an absolute dictatorship, the
question was no longer whether power which he did not possess
should be conferred on him, but whether power which he did
possess should be constitutionally restricted.[1] If Cromwell
could be credited with any fixed constitutional principles at all,
it would be worth noting that he placed the basis of the new
government, not on the Instrument, but upon the generalship
which he held already. In other words, the experiment he was
about to try was one in which a military despotism in actual
existence consented to impose limitations on itself. This vice
of origin the new government was never able to shake off.[2]

Cromwell agrees to the general principle of the Instrument.

On the strength of this agreement, Lambert, accompanied
by a considerable number of officers, appeared in the Council

---

[1] That there was, as might be expected, a meeting between Cromwell
and the officers on the 12th appears from the statement in *Several Proceedings* (E, 222, 24). As the Instrument was formally presented to
Cromwell on the 13th, this meeting must have been the occasion referred
to by Cromwell on Sept. 12, 1654 : "My power, again by this resignation,
was as boundless and unlimited as before ; all things being subjected to
arbitrariness, and a person having power over the three nations bound-
lessly and unlimitedly. . . . I confess after many arguments, and after
the letting of me know that I did not receive anything that put me into
a higher capacity than I was in before, but that it hindered me and
bound my hands to act nothing to the prejudice of the nations without
consent of a Council until the Parliament, and then limited by the
Parliament, as the Act of Government expresseth, I did accept it." *His
Highness the Lord Protector's Speech*, E, 812, 11*. Carlyle's version is
so inaccurate, though only verbally, that I prefer quoting from the
original pamphlet.

[2] For the same reason perhaps the Instrument was produced by
officers without civilian assistance. It was the military power as well as
the General that was limiting itself.

Chamber on the morning of the 13th.[1] After dismissing the civilians who had crowded in to witness the historic scene, Lambert produced the deed by which the late Parliament had resigned its powers to Cromwell He then obtained the consent of the officers present to the constitutional scheme which had been under discussion a fortnight before.[2] During the 14th and 15th there were fresh discussions, in the presence of Cromwell himself, which resulted in certain modifications in detail, after which the final redaction was accepted by Cromwell without further difficulty.[3]

Dec. 13.
The Instrument of Government produced.

Dec. 14, 15.
The Instrument adopted with amendments.

The idea of a written constitution was almost coeval with the Revolution itself. As soon as King and Parliament had come to regard one another as contentious powers, it was to be expected that efforts at accommodation should take the shape of attempts to define the limits

Precursors of the Instrument.

---

[1] On the date, see p. 319, note 1.

[2] In *The Protector, so-called, in Part Unveiled* (E, 857, 1), published in 1655, we are told that though all the officers were 'sent for upon a pretence of being taken into consultation, yet when they came thither they did little else but walk to and fro in the rooms without, whilst the business was carried on by a few within.' This is probably an exaggeration; but what truth there is in it may be assigned with most probability to these two days when delicate negotiations, which would hardly prosper in the hands of a large number, were being carried on with Cromwell.

[3] An intercepted letter, Dec. 14, *Thurloe*, i. 622. The points given in this letter which do not appear in the Instrument as finally adopted are: (1) The title of 'Lord Governor' for the Chief of the State, on which see p. 320, note; (2) The assignation to the 'Lord Governor' of the right of dismissing two members of the Council once in two years; (3) The dividing of the 400 members of Parliament into 280 for England and sixty apiece for Scotland and Ireland. The two latter countries had under the final Instrument to content themselves with thirty apiece. One trace of haste appears in the Instrument as actually promulgated. According to Art. ix. members of Parliament are to be elected within England, Wales, the Isles of Jersey, Guernsey, and the town of Berwick-on-Tweed. Art. x. assigns no members to Jersey or Guernsey, and none were ever chosen by them. The most probable explanation is that the secretary appointed to draw his pen through words intended to be struck out omitted in this instance to do so.

of their respective authority, and it was also to be expected that Parliament should thereby seek to gain that control over the executive which, but for the exceptional remedy of impeachment, it had hitherto failed to secure. As early as in 1642 the *Nineteen Propositions* emanating from Pym himself asked that the King should only act by the advice of the majority of the Council, that the number of councillors should be limited, and that none of their places, if vacant, should be filled except with the assent of the majority, to be confirmed or repudiated by Parliament when it next sat, whilst the great officers of the realm were to be appointed under the same conditions. These proposals were maintained in the propositions made at Uxbridge and Newcastle, and to a certain extent in the *Heads of the Proposals*. *The Agreement of the People* took an entirely new ground. It recognised Parliament as supreme, and gave to it not only the appointment of the Council of State, but also power to issue instructions for its guidance. Parliament having thus stepped into the place of the King, an attempt was made to limit its absolutism by setting up reservations within which it was not allowed to legislate.

Since *The Agreement of the People* had been presented to Parliament in January 1649, the governmental problem had been shown by experience to be far more complicated than it then appeared to be. It was not enough to restrict a single House with sovereign powers from meddling with certain important subjects, as scarcely a point could arise on which it might not refuse legal redress to the persons injured, or might not assume administrative or judicial functions without any possibility of checking it. The framers of *The Instrument of Government*, therefore, abandoned the absolute supremacy of Parliament as set forth in *The Agreement of the People*, and even the parliamentary control as set forth in the *Nineteen Propositions*, in order to recur to the practice of the Elizabethan monarchy amended in accordance with the needs of the time.

It was in the clauses relating to legislation that the alterations were most conspicuous. The first article bore that the

The constitutional problem.

supreme legislative authority should be and reside in one

Legislation.

person—the Lord Protector of the Commonwealth of England, Scotland, and Ireland, and the people assembled in Parliament. Subsequent articles declared that

Cromwell to be Protector.

the first Protector should be Oliver Cromwell, and that his office should be elective and not hereditary.

It appeared, however, that the part to be taken by the Protector in legislation was merely indirect.[1] Bills passed by Parliament were to be presented to him, twenty days being allowed him to formulate any objections he might entertain. If within this period he failed to satisfy Parliament that his objections were well-founded, the Bills would become law in the teeth of his opposition, unless they contained anything

He has no negative voice.

contrary to the Instrument. The negative voice which had been denounced by the army when it was exercised by the King was not allowed to the Protector. Yet, as the Instrument failed to nominate any

Opening for friction.

body of men to decide whether any given enactment was contrary to the Instrument or not, plenty of room was left for friction.

The proposed constitution of Parliament made that assembly more representative of the nation than any former

Constitution of Parliament.

House of Commons. The English members were to number 400, chosen by constituencies remodelled after the plan which the authors of the Reform Bill

The franchise.

of the Long Parliament had borrowed from those of *The Agreement of the People.* As regards the franchise, however, though the new system was more liberal than the old, so far as the great majority of the boroughs were concerned, it was less liberal than *The Agreement of the People* in conferring the right of voting on the holders of real or personal property to the value of 200*l.*, instead of upon those who were rated—even to the smallest amount—to the relief of

[1] Can it be that the clause about legislation being in the Protector and Parliament is a remnant of a draft conferring the title of King with the negative voice in the old fashion?

the poor.[1]   The only permanent exclusions were Roman

Qualifica- Catholics and persons who had abetted the Irish re-
tions.   bellion ; but for the first three Parliaments all who
had taken part in any war against the Parliament by action or
advice were to be debarred from electing or being elected, so
that Presbyterian supporters of Hamilton and Charles II., as
well as Royalist supporters of Charles I., were temporarily shut
out. Parliament thus constituted was to meet for the first
time on September 3, 1654, and to sit for five months. A

Parlia-   fresh Parliament was to be elected every three years,
ments to be and provision was made, as in the Triennial Act of
triennial.
             1641, for its automatic election, if the Protector
neglected to summon one. In the intervals between the
triennial Parliaments, a special Parliament might be summoned
if the Government thought it advisable, and must necessarily
be summoned if war broke out.

Administration, however, is more important than legislation,
and over the administration Parliament had no direct, and very

They have   little indirect, control. It was mainly on the
no direct   Council that the framers of the Instrument relied as
control over
administra-   a check on the arbitrary tendencies of the Protector.
tion.   That Council was to be an independent body,

The inde-   neither, as under the monarchy, the tool of the
pendence of   Crown, nor, as under the last two Parliaments, the
the Council.
The mode   tool of Parliament. It was to consist of not less than
of its nomi- thirteen, and not more than twenty-one members, of
nation.
which latter number fifteen were named in the Instrument
itself, whilst power was reserved to the Protector and Council
to fill up the remaining six places at any time before the meeting of the first Parliament. The councillors thus selected were
irremovable, except during the sessions of Parliament, when a
special Court was to be nominated, half the members of which
were to be named by Parliament, for the trial of any councillor
charged with corruption or miscarriage. If the accusation was
brought when Parliament was not in session, power was given

[1] In this *The Agreement of the People* anticipated the practice of the
present day.

to the Council, with the consent of the Protector, to suspend the incriminated person from his functions till Parliament should meet. In the case of vacancies created by death or removal, Parliament was to present six names, of which the Council would lay two before the Protector, who was to select one of them as that of the new councillor. This presentation of names occurring at rare intervals was the only hold—if hold it can be called—which Parliament possessed on the executive.

To the advice of the Council thus constituted the Protector was bound in almost every case. Writs, commissions, grants, and similar official documents, indeed, ran in his name, and from him all honours and magistracies were derived, and he had the power of pardoning all offences except murder and treason. On the other hand, in the appointment to the highest offices : those of Chancellor, Keeper or Commissioner of the Great Seal, of Treasurer, Admiral, Chief Governor of Ireland or Scotland, or of either of the Chief Justices, he was bound to secure the approbation of Parliament, or if Parliament were not sitting, of the Council, its acceptance of his selection being afterwards approved by Parliament. For acts of government, for everything connected with the foreign relations of the country, including the conclusion of peace and the declaration of war, and for the issue of writs to summon special Parliaments, the Protector was dependent on the Council alone. With the advice of the Council he was allowed to issue ordinances with validity till his first Parliament met to decide on them, and to levy taxes during the same interval of time. In the event of his death the Council was to elect his successor.

Hold of the Council on the Protector.

The financial arrangements intended to be permanent were subject to somewhat remarkable provisions. ' No tax, charge, or imposition ' was to be ' laid upon the people but by common consent in Parliament only,' though the Protector and Council might provide for the necessities of the country up to the date of the meeting of the first Parliament. It was doubtless a result of the composite

Financial arrangements.

authorship of the Instrument that another article, without taking note of this sweeping generalisation, provided that a constant yearly revenue sufficient to meet the expenses of an army of 30,000 men, and of a navy capable of guarding the seas, together with 200,000*l.* for civil expenses, should be raised out of the customs 'and such other ways and means as shall be agreed upon by the Protector and Council.' The only part assigned to Parliament in this matter was that, if the Protector thought fit to diminish the forces of the country, he should not dispose of the money thereby saved without the consent of Parliament, if it was in session, or of the Council, if it was not. After the first meeting Parliament would, however, have complete control over 'the raising of money for defraying the charge of the present extraordinary forces, both at sea and land, in respect of the present wars.'

The intention of these somewhat complicated arrangements was evidently to return to the ideas of the earlier sovereigns. Intention of the framers of the scheme. The Protector—like the King—was expected 'to live of his own,' though 'his own' now included an army of 30,000 men in time of peace. It was only in time of war, or of extraordinary expenditure for any other cause, that the deterrent voice of Parliament could be raised with effect.

The power of the purse being thus limited, the power of the sword was left in studied vagueness, which left little room for the exercise of authority by Parliament. The power of the sword. The Protector was during the session—that is to say, for five months in three years—to 'dispose and order the militia and forces, both by sea and land, for the peace and good of the three nations by consent of Parliament,' a clause the meaning of which is uncertain, but which might be interpreted to mean merely that during these months ships and men were not to be employed against an enemy or against rebels unless Parliament acknowledged them to be enemies or rebels. During the remainder of the three years the Protector was bound to have the consent of the Council in disposing and ordering the militia, but, as nothing was said of the standing forces, it may be gathered that they would be under his own personal control.[1]

To the strictly constitutional articles were added others answering to the reservations in *The Agreement of the People.*

Article on religion. As regards religion the lines of the earlier document were followed in the main, it being stipulated that there should be a public profession of Christianity with full protection for those congregations which felt themselves unable to comply with the established forms, provided that they did not abuse this liberty 'to the civil injury of others, and to the actual disturbance of the public peace on their parts.' In the Instrument, however, it was distinctly added that this liberty was not to be extended to popery or prelacy, whereas the Agreement had been content to guard against the interpretation 'that this liberty shall necessarily extend to Popery or Prelacy.' The only other difference of importance concerned the maintenance of the ministry. The Agreement emanating from a merely petitioning body had been content to ask that the clergy should be provided for 'out of a public treasury, and, as we desire, not by tithes'; whereas the Instrument, being the work of men assuming constituent powers, and having recent controversies in view, decreed 'that as soon as may be a provision less subject to scruple and contention, and more certain than the present, be made for the encouragement and maintenance of able and painful teachers, ... and until such provision be made the present maintenance shall not be taken away or impeached.'

Then followed articles confirming the sale of forfeited lands, the securities given for the debts of the Commonwealth, and the articles made upon Royalist surrenders in time of war. Finally, the Protector was to take an oath to observe the Instrument and to execute justice according to law for the good of the Commonwealth, whilst

The remaining articles.

---

[1] Unless indeed the words attributing the control of 'the forces' to the Protector and Council were accidentally omitted. Everything seems possible in a document so hastily constructed.

each councillor was to swear to be faithful to the trust committed to him.[1]

It cannot escape remark that this constitution contained no provision for its own amendment; but there is no reason to suppose that its authors contemplated the event of its requiring modification. Like other constitution-mongers they sought not the abstract best, but the best to form a bulwark against certain concrete dangers of which they had had bitter experience. Alarmed at the despotic action of a single House, and not venturing to call in the nation to control the vagaries of its nominal representatives, these men, falling back on the main lines of the Elizabethan constitution, sought to establish an executive authority independent of parliamentary exigencies, and secure, at least in time of peace, against financial ruin. Nevertheless, being the same men who a few years back had combated royalty, they did their best to avoid the dangers attending the old system; whilst, by assigning to Parliament unrestricted legislative functions, and more especially by subjecting the actions of the Protector to the control of the Council, they hoped to avoid the reproach of having substituted the arbitrary government of one man for the arbitrary government of an assembly.

No provision for amending the Instrument.

Aims of the founders of the Protectorate.

That the restriction on the action of the Protector by his obligation to consult the Council was intended to be a real one there is every reason to believe. The notion which prevailed at the time, and which has continued to prevail in modern days, that Cromwell was a self-willed autocrat imposing his commands on a body composed of his subservient creatures, is consistent neither with the indications which exist in the correspondence of that day, nor with his own character. From time to time we hear of parties in the Council and of Cromwell's reluctance to act in defiance

Cromwell not an autocrat.

---

[1] *Constitutional Documents*, 314. I have retained the title by which this constitution is usually known, *The Instrument of Government*, though it was usually styled at the time ' *The Government*,' thereby causing some confusion.

of strong resistance, whilst, unless he had totally changed his

His relations with the Council. nature since he sat in the chair of the Army Council in 1647, we should expect to find him proceeding, at least for a time, tentatively rather than authoritatively, prone to accept suggestions from others, and to lead them by the force of argument and still more by the impressiveness of facts to the acceptance of his own dominant ideas. On the other hand, we should expect that this general habit of seeking to carry the Council with him, and even of yielding to its demands as long as his own mind was not positively made up, would be by no means incompatible—if strong occasion arose—with gusts of passionate resolution sweeping away all constitutional barriers before the insistency of his will.

Real as the control of the Council for the most part was, it would be found impossible to carry home the fact to the minds

Secrecy of debates in the Council. either of contemporaries or of posterity. The Council, having to deal with executive affairs often of the utmost delicacy, must sit with closed doors, and could no more allow the public to witness its debates than a modern cabinet or the Privy Council of a Tudor or Stuart Sovereign.

Fosters the idea that Cromwell is an absolute monarch. To the world at large the Council spoke with a single voice, and that voice Cromwell's. What wonder if the world came to the conclusion that Cromwell had established an absolute monarchy, in which no will was regarded but his own? Yet it was this very idea of an absolute monarchy against which the nation had unanimously struggled in 1640, and nothing that had since occurred was likely to lessen its repugnance to it.

If the Instrument itself contained pitfalls hazardous to the success of Cromwell's experiment, there was another, outside

Difficulty of combating the impression that his government will be military. any possible constitutional document, which he could hardly succeed in escaping. England was averse to a military even more than to an absolute government, and however much Cromwell might desire it, it would be hard indeed for him to divest himself of the military title to which he owed his position.

His own selection as Protector, the very Instrument of Govern-

ment itself, had arisen from the Council of the Officers, which
had again and again intervened to change the course of political
events.   No doubt the army, which gave strength to the officers'
demands, was as no other army has ever been, sedulous for the
liberty of its fellow countrymen, and not desirous to intrude—
unless in cases held to be of absolute necessity—upon the
political government of the country.   The fact remained that
soldiers and not civilians had taken upon themselves to judge
when that absolute necessity had arisen, and that soldiers, and
not civilians, had now decided under what institutions the
country should be governed for the future.

Whatever the future might reveal as to the fortunes of the
Protectorate, there can be no doubt that the crisis out of which
The Instru- the new government sprang was a landmark in
ment of English history.   From the day of the opening of
Govern-
ment a the Long Parliament every change had placed the
landmark Government in the hands of men more exclusively
in English
history. Puritan than their predecessors.   Advocates of a
modified Episcopacy had given place to Presbyterians, Presbyterians to Independents, Independents to Fifth Monarchists
and assailants of Established Churches.   Now, for the first
time, the tide began to run in a contrary direction.
Turning of
the tide in As long as Cromwell was at the head of affairs
respect to there could, indeed, be no question of substituting
Puritan-
ism, any other form of religion for the directest Puritanism.   For all that, the events which called Cromwell to power
made it certain that even under him Puritan zeal would be
modified by political and mundane considerations.   In course
of time the question might be asked whether Puritanism was
to be permitted to dictate its laws to statesmen and men of the
world.

Nor could this change in the position of Puritanism fail to
affect the political as well as the ecclesiastical situation.   To
and in re- give predominance to Puritanism—still more to give
spect to it to extreme Puritanism—it had been necessary to
constitu-
tionalism. set aside the doctrine of the supremacy of Parliament as the representative of the nation, with which the

revolution had started. To sustain Puritanism Parliament had to be purified, first, by the expulsion of the Royalists, secondly, by the expulsion of the eleven members, and, thirdly, by Pride's Purge. Finally, a so-called Parliament had been summoned, not a single member of which sat in virtue of election by any constituency whatever. *The Instrument of Government* did not, indeed, frankly adopt the system of sovereign elective Parliaments, but it did establish elective Parliaments, though with certain considerable restrictions on their powers. The theory on which the claims of the nominated Parliament were based—that right-minded and religious persons ought, at least in critical times, to assume the powers of government even in defiance of the national will, was not, indeed, wholly abandoned—the mode in which the Protector and his first Council were appointed testify to the contrary—but it was intended to drop gradually out of sight. The time was expected to come, and that, too, after no long interval, when even Royalists would be admitted to vote at elections and to take their seats in Parliament. Nor was the executive to remain for ever outside the influence of Parliament. Slowly enough, it is true, but still in some limited measure, Parliament would impress its ideas upon the Council and on the Protectorate itself.

To the nominated Parliament, therefore, belongs a noteworthy place in the historical development of England. Its mere existence, irrespective of the good or evil it may have essayed to do, exhibits the high-water mark of Puritanism in Church and State, of a Puritanism which, on the one hand, rejected all mundane influences and rights over the individual conscience, and upheld in opposition to the State a purely voluntary ecclesiastical system ; and which, on the other hand, strove to use the absolute powers which it had under the most unlikely circumstances acquired to force this system—or rather, absence of system—on a nation which had never demanded it, and was never likely to demand it within any reasonable limits of time. The establishment of the Protectorate was

The nominated Parliament the high-water mark of Puritanism.

an effort to stem the tide after it had begun to ebb, to secure the gains of the Puritan Revolution whilst curbing its excesses. It was for the future to reveal whether thi., effort would be successful, or whether, as was only too probable, the reaction would be strengthened till it swept away the men who were now attempting to guide it into constitutional channels. Cromwell and his associates had determined for all time what should not be. They had now before them a harder, probably an insuperable, task in determining what should take the place of the constitutional edifice they had destroyed.

THE END OF THE SECOND VOLUME